BK 746.4   S429C
COMPLETE BOOK OF STUFFEDWORK
                              /SCOTT, TON
    1978   14.95 FV

3000 498519 30017
St. Louis Community College

```
746.4 S429c                    FV
SCOTT
THE COMPLETE BOOK OF STUFFED-
WORK
                    14.95
```

WITHDRAWN

St. Louis Community
College

Library

5801 Wilson Avenue
St. Louis, Missouri 63110

PRINTED IN U.S.A.   23-263-002

The Complete Book of Stuffedwork

Toni Scott

Houghton Mifflin Company
Boston   1978

The models that illustrate the text were photographed by Doug Long. He also photographed the pieces, in the gallery sections between chapters, by Ostrowe, Teller, Trilling, Lippman/Strauss and Datz.

Pieces not otherwise attributed were designed and made by the author.

Copyright © 1978 by Toni Scott

All rights reserved. No part of this work may be reproduced or transmitted in any form by any means, electronic or mechanical, including photocopying and recording, or by any information storage or retrieval system, without permission in writing from the publisher.

Library of Congress Cataloging in Publication Data

Scott, Toni.
   The complete book of stuffedwork.
    1. Needlework. I. Title. II. Title: Stuffedwork.
TT715.S25   746.4   77-25500
ISBN 0-395-25775-1

Printed in the United States of America

M 10 9 8 7 6 5 4 3 2 1

For Susanna

Contents

INTRODUCTION 9

PART I
STUFFED SURFACES

CHAPTER ONE   TRAPUNTO 13
Cord Quilting 14
Stuffed Quilting 16
Layered Trapunto 20
Negative Spaces 25

CHAPTER TWO   STUFFED APPLIQUÉ 35
Basic Appliqué 36
Continuous Appliqué 40
Stuffed Appliqué 42

CHAPTER THREE   NEW TECHNIQUES 55
Stuffed Pleats 55
Stuffed Circles 59
Stuffed Smocking 61
One-piece Smocked Forms 62
Stuffed Tubing 65
Stuffed Patchwork 66

PART II
STUFFED FORMS

CHAPTER FOUR   FLAT FORMS 85
Stuffing 85
Knife-Edged Pillows 85
Drawn Forms 86
Patternmaking 86
Muslin Tryouts 86
Pattern Adjustments 88
Pattern Marks and Labels 90
Decoration 94

CHAPTER FIVE   GEOMETRIC FORMS 101
Three-Dimensional Pillows 101
Geometric Forms 104
Balls 105
Pattern Draping 110

CHAPTER SIX   BODIES 121
Seams 121
Doll Bodies 126
Doll Heads 132
Animals 136

CHAPTER SEVEN   BUILDING AND MOLDING 159
Building Demonstration 159
Molding Demonstration 166

CHAPTER EIGHT   CONSTRUCTION 183

Introduction

SOFAS AND SAUSAGES come to mind, but the word "stuffedwork" is used here to name the craft of sewing and stuffing fabric skins. The skin may be closed by intermittent stitching to make a quilted surface or it may expand completely to make a stuffed form.

I have used the word "skin" to help clarify the difference in structure between the stuffed quilting that is part of our subject and the more familiar technique of wadded quilting. The stitching in wadded quilting, most often seen in bed quilts, is sewn through a *sandwich* of three layers: a fabric top, a batting (filling), and a fabric backing. The design is therefore *impressed* by the stitching. On the other hand, the stitching in stuffed quilting, also known as trapunto, is sewn through a *skin* of only two layers — a top and a backing fabric. Afterward the stuffing is inserted from the back through cut slits or spread threads. The design is thus *raised* by the stuffing.

I have found it convenient to use the term "stuffedwork" to discuss all sewn work, whether surfaces or forms, that is raised by stuffing rather than impressed by stitching.

Trapunto, in its more restrained, traditional "cord-in-narrow-channels" version, has a long history in the making of clothing and needlework. We have expanded these techniques to include stuffed appliqué procedures, stuffed pleats, and stuffed smocking. By altering the shape of the top layer, we have also developed stuffed patchwork that can function like a kind of fabric masonry to make firm constructions like the bowl in Plate 5. These new manipulations and the lighter, loftier synthetic stuffing now commonly available, make contemporary trapunto as punchy as neon yet softer than ever.

When it comes to the skins that open up into forms, fabric can be cut and seamed to produce anything from a classic cube to a particular animal. The stuffing fills the space provided by the skin and demonstrates the shape that is already inherent in the cutting pattern, for it is the cutting, not the stuffing, that determines the shape of the piece.

How we arrive at these patterns is not easy to explain. But I have described and demonstrated several methods of patternmaking: simple *computation*, *drawing* and the related methods of alteration and adjustment, *draping* over a form and, finally, more complex *drafted* patterns derived from a drawn profile. Multiple views of flat and of three-dimensional forms face their pattern pieces, so that you can study them and see how the pattern has been extracted from the form and how the planes have been provided for. The step-by-step diagrams in Chapter 8 further clarify the construction.

Two improvisational methods are also demonstrated. In *building*, a finished doll is taken in, let out, and built up by slashing, stitching, and patching. In *molding*, a stuffed form is pinched and pulled and drawn together with strong thread.

All forms are not fully stuffed. Some are meant to shift, like beanbags and loose floor furniture. Here stuffing must consist of many small independent pellets — beans, rice, sand, birdseed, or tiny balls of synthetic foam.

Sometimes the stuffing is more significant than the form: the balsam needles in a pillow, the dried flowers in a sachet, the herbs in a potpourri. The mystery of what's inside the bumps and bulges of a Christmas stocking is more important than the form itself. The gift wrapping must go before a present is fully received. The amulets containing words from the Koran, hung on the war shirt from Ghana on page 95, have significance far beyond the diverting decoration their forms provide.

Stuffedwork in the hands of artists has been called "soft sculpture" and has utterly transformed the rigid, rectangular disposition of painting. Its very softness points out paradox — the absurdity, for instance, of Claes Oldenberg's soft scissors, the majesty of his giant hamburger and the vulnerability of his soft cars. Soft art is inescapably human.

Figures by Bill King, Lenore Davis, and Susan Morrison impeccably reflect human gesture. Other artists sound overtones of primitive magic and ritual. Still others revel in sensuous surfaces — the voluptuous reliefs of Norma Minkowitz and Kathryn Lipke or the dazzling batiks of Morag Benepe.

As you will see from the "galleries" at the end of each chapter, other crafts are often incorporated with the sewing — painting, dyeing, stitchery, photography, even ceramics. All contribute to the pleasure of seeing. In utilitarian pieces, the pleasure is not only in the seeing but in the soothing that is customarily provided by such familiar furnishings as cushions and comforters.

The new wide-ranging pursuit of the many forms of stuffedwork has led me to feel that it is now useful to begin to categorize the cutting and sewing procedures that make up its vocabulary. This book is the result of the effort, and I hope it will be serviceable in the same way as a book that compiles the basic embroidery stitches, for example. Some of my own techniques appear here for the first time, other methods are firmly rooted in past practices. Anyone who works creatively will find his or her own ways to work, but such discoveries usually come from delving into as well as deviating from basic procedures.

I am enormously grateful to the artists who have allowed us to include their work. I hope *Stuffedwork* will be helpful to some of the many other people who are working to make their own contribution to this emerging, expressive, thoroughly modern craft.

Part I
STUFFED SURFACES

Chapter One
Trapunto

THE IMPULSE to add warmth, softness, and relief to textiles by stitching them together in layers seems to have begun more than 3000 years ago. Egyptian garments, along with the quilted armour of the Middle Ages, appear to employ the method we know as *wadded quilting*. Wadded quilting is not part of what I have classified as stuffedwork. It is the stitching together of a top, a padding and a backing, in the course of which the impressed stitches render the design below the top surface of the fabric.

On the other hand, *stuffed quilting*, also referred to as *trapunto* and certainly in the domain of stuffedwork, pushes the surface upward, within the pockets and channels provided by the initial stitching of a top to a backing. The famous fourteenth-century Sicilian quilt that depicts the life of Tristram, where important features of the design are raised with stuffing, is a ravishing example.

By the eighteenth century, the use of cord inserted into stitched channels had transformed smooth linen into the elaborate sculptured reliefs that embellished waistcoats and caps, cuffs and quilts. Often the quilting was enhanced with pulled stitches and French knots, making a lively white contrast of open grids, smooth cording, and crunchy embroidery. Furthermore, from the point of view of the construction of the garment, trapunto provided firm body in parts normally interfaced or otherwise reinforced.

American nineteenth-century white quilts included superb examples of stuffed quilting, where the design was raised by separate insertions of stuffing in each stitched area, between the top and the backing. The spaces between the stuffed design were filled with very close lines of wadded quilting, further dramatizing the high, smooth relief of the stuffed portions.

In the twentieth century, we see surfaces softer and fatter than ever before. Comforters and upholstery, ski jackets and sleeping bags are light but lofty, with fillings of down or foam or synthetic stuffing. Stuffed surfaces have stirred interest beyond their domestic and fashionable applications. Artists are exploring their potentials for aesthetic expression. At the same time both wadded and stuffed quilting endow the "remade fabric" with body, stability, shaping, and finishing that are needed by pieces that hang or are in other ways displayed as art objects. Furthermore, such pieces can be rolled, wrapped, shipped, stored, and cleaned easily.

CORD QUILTING

DESIGN

The designs for cord quilting consist of arrangements of double parallel lines. Sometimes the quilting is solid; sometimes there are flat spaces within the design. In the latter case, the distribution of the cording should be well balanced so that the outer edges of the fabric, after stuffing, retain their original shape, even though their dimensions will have shrunk somewhat.

Before developing the whole design, it is a good idea to draw a small sample of the double line on a scrap of fabric. Stitch it to a backing fabric, and fill the channels to see what cord or yarn fills well. The channel should not be filled so tightly that the fabric is pulled out of shape, but it should be sufficiently filled so that it will be firmly raised. A slight adjustment in the width of the channel might be more convenient than finding a substitute cord. Several lengths of yarn can be run through the channels, but hard cord so used may leave undesirable ridges.

In contemporary work, the wrong side of the work is sometimes used as the right side. The nubs of filler are exaggerated for their decorative effect. In this *reverse* cord quilting the yarn would enter and exit from the top layer, which would be uppermost in the frame. Such work would combine well with other embroidery stitches.

MATERIALS

Fabric: The top is fine linen or cotton (silk can be used but does not wear as well). The back is linen scrim or loosely woven muslin. A lining is usually advisable, and the fabric from which it is made should be a weight similar to or lighter than the top.

Filling: Cotton piping cord or candlewick should first be shrunk and well dried. It must fill the channels comfortably (see Design, above) and must pass through the eye of a blunt tapestry or yarn needle.

It is possible to use rug wool, bulky knitting wool, or soft yarn rather than firm cord, but they will tend to flatten after many washings.

Cable or other large piping cords can be used by sewing through one end of the cord. This thread, in a blunt needle, is then drawn through the channel, drawing the cord behind.

Thread: The thread may be in a color matching or contrasting with the fabric. Ordinary cotton sewing thread is usually used, but silk button twist or a thin embroidery thread will make more emphatic lines.

Frame: It is helpful, for hand stitching, if fabrics are held in a quilting or embroidery frame.

TRANSFER

After the preshrunk fabric has been well pressed, the design is traced to the right side of the top fabric.

Traditionally the design, drawn on paper, was pricked with a needle. Then pounce, a powder available at some chemists, was rubbed through the pricking to the fabric. Drawing with a hard pencil or sharp chalk, or tracing with a wheel through dressmaker's carbon are alternate methods now generally used.

The design must be placed on the fabric in such a position that there is ample surrounding fabric for seams, hems, and finishing. If the fabric is still too small to engage the embroidery hoop, temporary muslin strips can be basted to the edges.

PREPARATION

The top fabric is pinned over the back fabric, wrong sides together and with edges matching. Large pieces are basted together from the center outward, horizontally, vertically, and diagonally across the fabrics. The basting is removed after stitching and before filling. For small pieces, basting around the design is enough.

The fabric is placed in a double-ring frame or attached to an embroidery frame, right side up.

STITCHING

A backstitch (Fig. 1) is traditionally used to cover the drawn lines, but a running stitch (Fig. 2) also makes a good, though softer, effect and is more quickly executed. Small, even stitches should cover all the drawn lines (Fig. 3).

FILLING

A blunt needle threaded with yarn is inserted in the back fabric, so that it enters the channel but does not puncture the front. The needle slides through the channel for about an inch and emerges through the back (Fig. 4).

The needle is reinserted into the exit hole and slides forward again, leaving a small nub of yarn at each exit to prevent puckering (especially af-

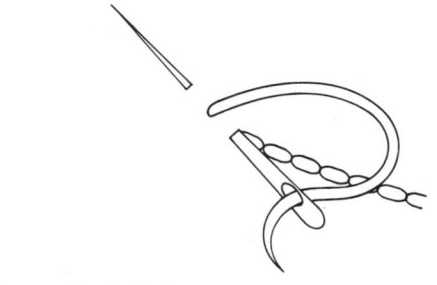

Fig. 1 Backstitch

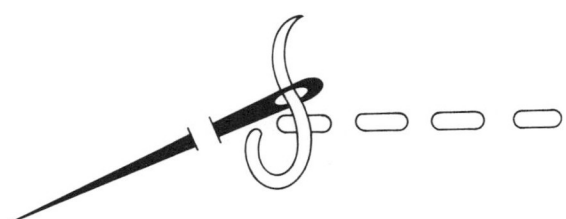

Fig. 2 Running Stitch

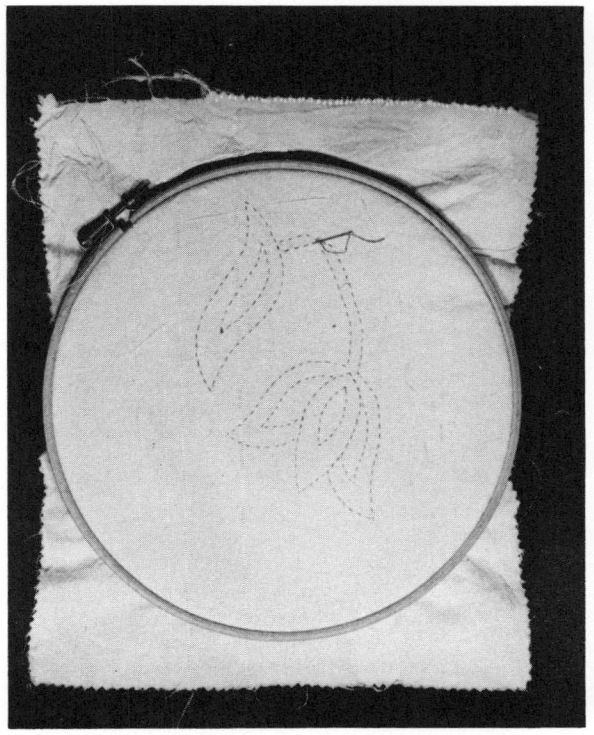

Fig. 3 Front

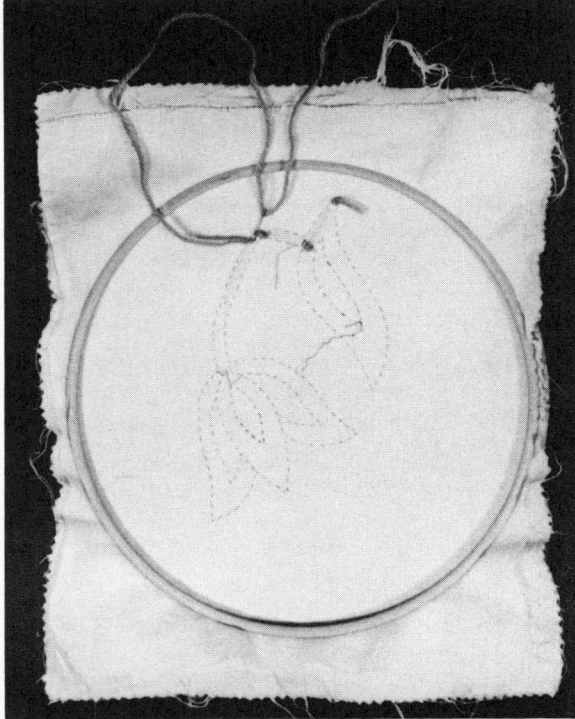

Fig. 4 Back

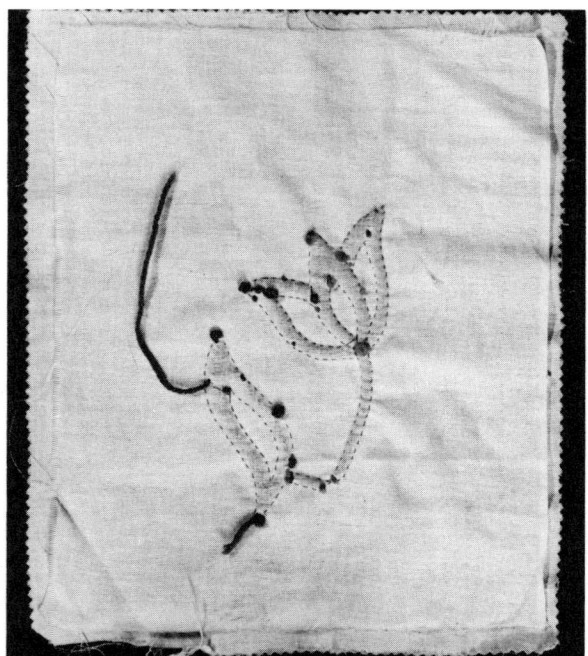

Fig. 5 Back

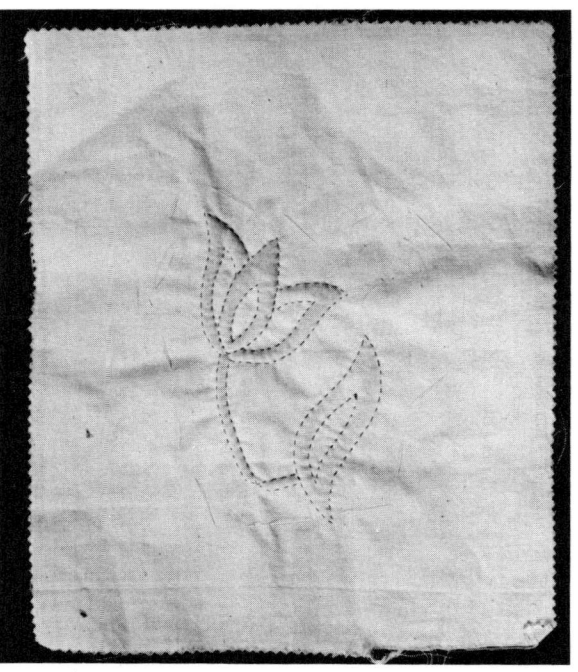

Fig. 6 Front

ter laundering). Additional lengths of yarn may have to be run through the channels in order to fill them well (Figs. 5 and 6).

STUFFED QUILTING

DESIGN

Since loose stuffing — the sort that looks like cotton candy — is the filler, the designs for stuffed quilting are not restricted to channels, as they were in cord quilting. Any shape will do, but since stuffing tends to retreat from sharp corners, designs with rounded corners and slow curves are best. Also, since the surface interest depends largely on highlights and shadows, large areas unbroken by stitching are not appropriate. The surface will be a little smaller after it is stuffed.

As in cord quilting, the fabric can be raised all over, when it appears more like a deep wadded quilting, or the raised designs can be separated by unraised areas. Stuffed quilting is often combined with cord quilting in the same design, as in the pincushion on Plate 2A, page 24. If the fabrics are transparent the work is sometimes called *shadow* quilting and it has a dreamlike quality. Usually the stuffing is white, with a light top fabric and a dark bottom fabric. The dark ground, which shows through near the stitching, exaggerates the shadows in the quilting. The stuffing can also be colored yarn or dyed fiber, but the color seen through the top will be only a tint of the real stuffing color.

MATERIALS

Fabric: For the top, nearly any soft, smooth fabric can be used; the back is linen scrim or loosely woven muslin. For the shadow quilting just described, the top is sheer light fabric and the back is dark (Figs. 7 and 8).

Knitted fabrics such as jersey and velour can be stuffed higher than woven fabrics, so a knit fabric might be used over a woven back, as in the bracelet in Plate 2B, page 24 (see also Figs. 9 and 10).

Filling: Cotton or synthetic stuffing is the most adaptable filling. Yarn can also be used for small areas. For shadow quilting, yarn of strong color will appear much paler. Shredded fabric and stockings are sometimes employed.

Trapunto 17

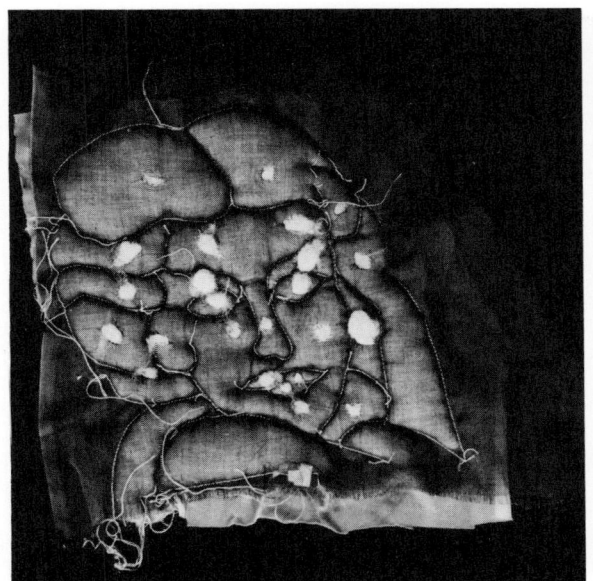

Fig. 7 Back

Fig. 8 Front

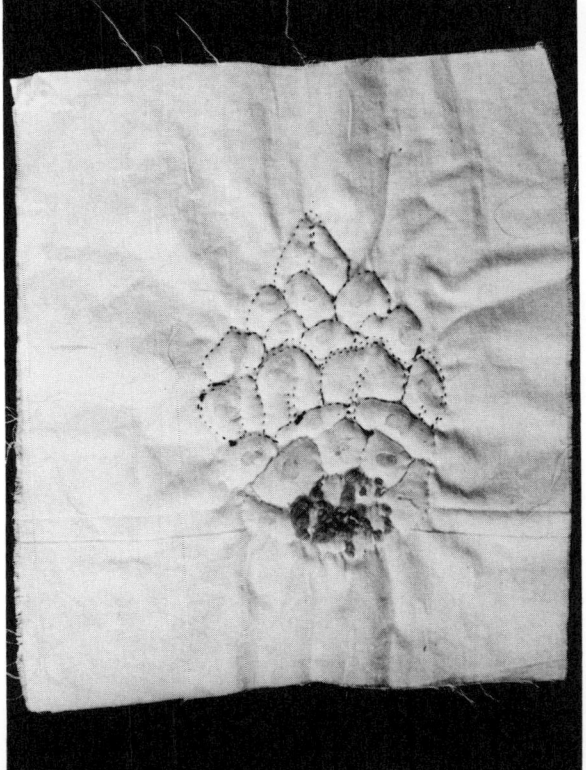

Fig. 9 Back

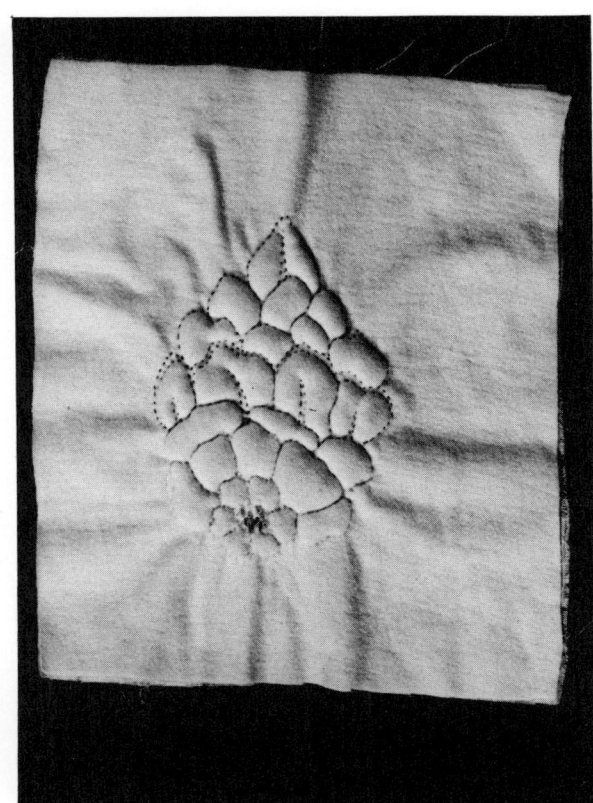

Fig. 10 Front

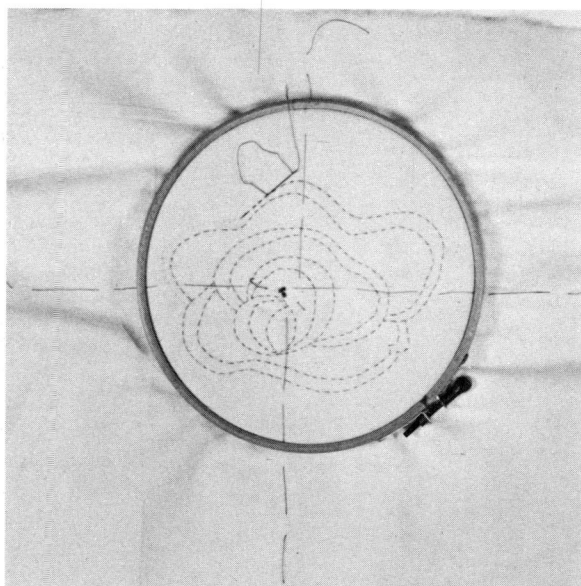

Fig. 11 Front

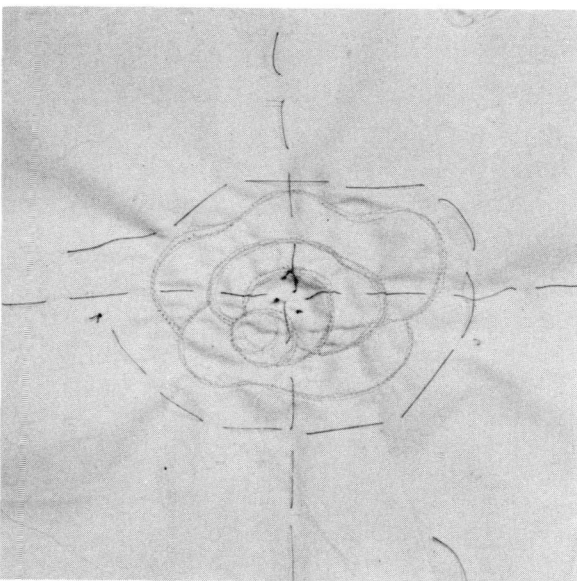

Fig. 12 Front

Thread: The thread is the same as for cord quilting.

Frame: When the shapes to be filled are small, a quilting or embroidery frame is very helpful to prevent overstuffing and distortion of the fabric.

With much contemporary work, however, the design is in a bolder scale, with large "pockets" to be stuffed. Stitching and stuffing may be carried out without a frame, but the tendency toward overstuffing and distortion must be kept in mind.

TRANSFER

The design can be marked either on the right or the wrong side, but remember that the design will be reversed if the back is marked with the tracing right side up. Otherwise, the transfer directions under cord quilting will apply. Where sheer fabrics are used, it is possible to place them over the drawn design and trace directly to the fabric.

PREPARATION

With the top over the back, right sides out and edges matching, long basting stitches are sewn from the center outward, horizontally, vertically, and diagonally across the fabrics. Then the work is ready to place in a frame.

STITCHING

Backstitch or running stitch is worked by hand over the drawn lines (Fig. 11). Machine stitch can also be used, usually without a frame, sewing over the design several times to vary the width and darkness of the lines (Fig. 12).

FILLING

With the back facing upward, each design area is filled with stuffing after the basting is removed. For the small spaces customary in traditional work, two threads were spread apart to make an opening. With a slender knitting needle or similar tool, the stuffing was pushed inside to fill the space up to the stitching, and the threads were stroked back together.

Trapunto 19

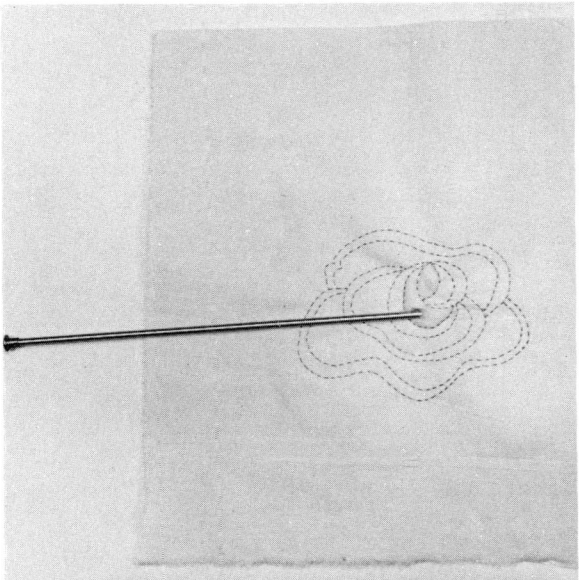

Fig. 13 Back

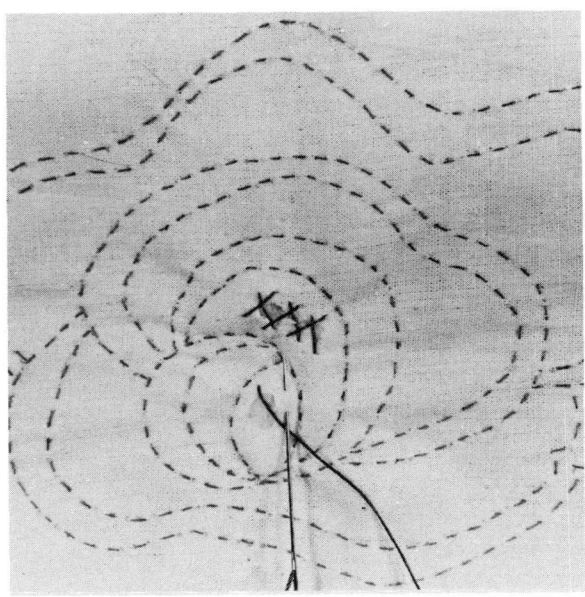

Fig. 14 Back

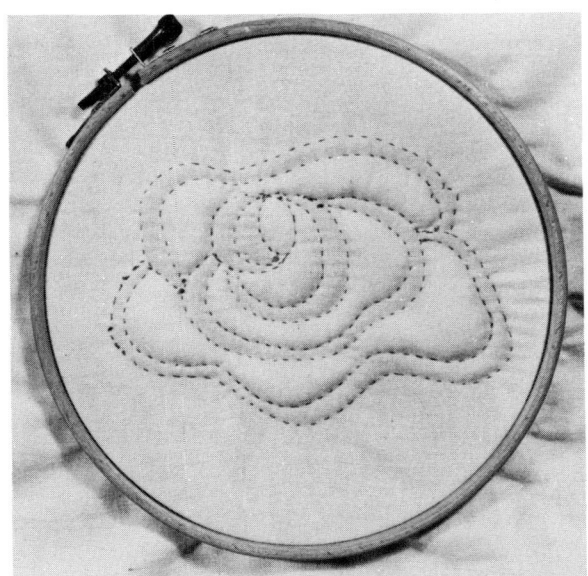

Fig. 15 Front

Fig. 16 Front

In contemporary work a small slit is usually cut in the back fabric. (Cutting on the bias grain minimizes fraying.) The space is stuffed (Fig. 13), and a few stitches are taken across the slit to close it (Fig. 14). On a larger work, bits of iron-on tape can be pressed over the slits instead.

Small areas can be filled with yarn in a blunt needle, which eliminates the need for slitting (Figs. 15 and 16).

LINING

The work is usually lined with a material similar to or of lighter weight than the top.

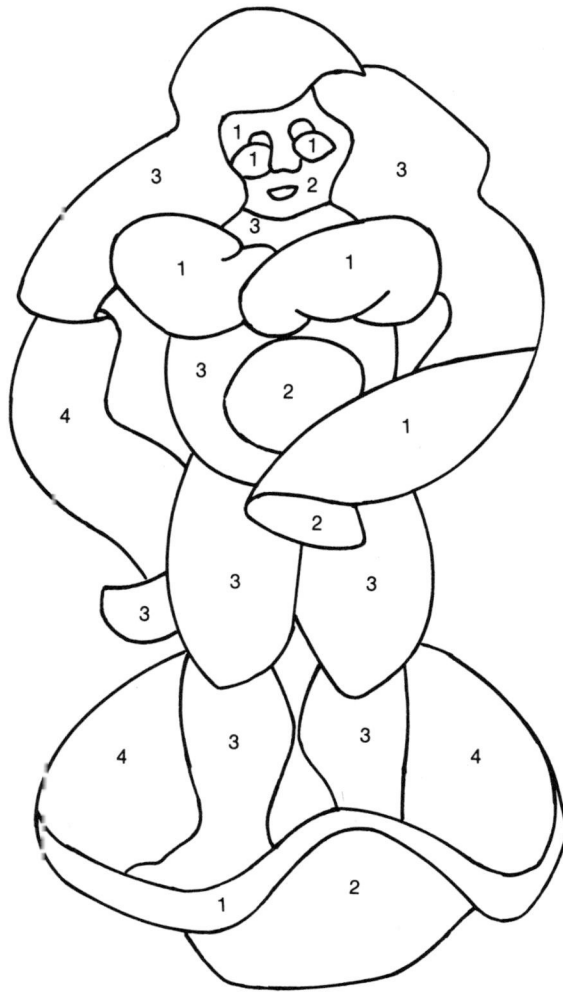

Fig. 17

LAYERED TRAPUNTO

Stuffed quilting can also be worked in layers to produce relief in graduated heights. The layered trapunto in Plate 2C, page 24, is demonstrated by steps to suggest how you might stuff a drawing of your own.

DEMONSTRATION

1. Decide which of the areas should project farthest from the surface and, on the drawing, number the layers, starting with the highest, which will be number 1 (Fig. 17).
2. Trace the design to the right side of the fabric. Piece the fabric, if you need to, to reach the sides of a hoop. The hoop may have to be abandoned as the stuffing proceeds.
3. Cut a muslin patch big enough to extend beyond the stitching lines of the number 1 area. Pin the patch against the wrong side of the fabric under the design lines. From the right side, work a running or backstitch over the design lines, making a pocket to carry the stuffing.

    From the wrong side, stuff the pocket before completing the stitching (Fig. 18). From the right side complete the stitching to close the pocket (Fig. 19). Stuff the shell rim with yarn in a needle.
4. Each patch for a higher numbered area should cover any previous patches within its outlines. Eyebrows and cheeks, for instance, are included in the face patch. Thus, when this pocket is filled, the whole face will rise, with cheeks and eyebrows still projecting the farthest.

    Stuff the belly and tip of the hair over another patch. Stuff the front shell over a patch (Figs. 20 and 21).
5. As stuffing proceeds, the patches become larger (Figs. 22 and 23).
6. From the side you can see the several depths of stuffing (Fig. 24).
7. Cut out the figure with a seam allowance and apply it to another surface. Or leave the figure as part of its present surface, smoothing the negative space with wadded quilting (Plate 2).

Trapunto 21

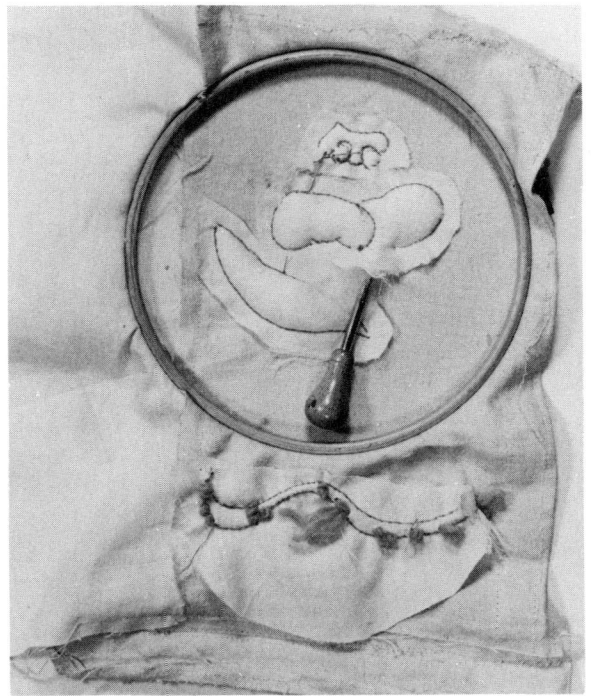

Fig. 18 Back

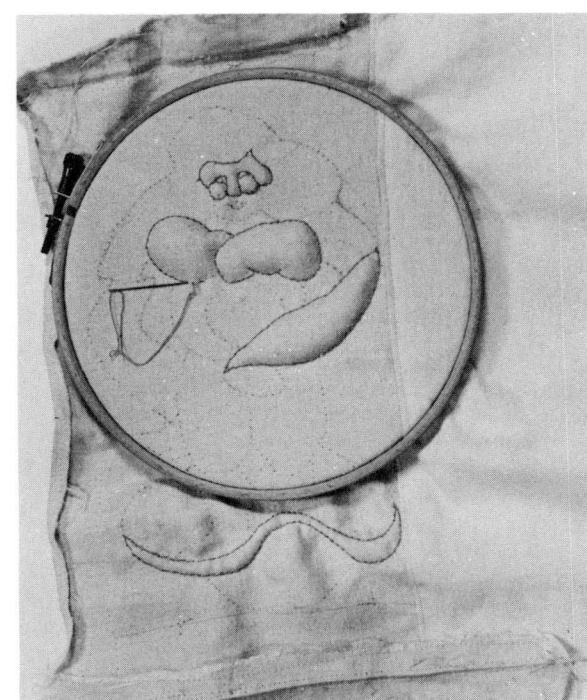

Fig. 19 Front

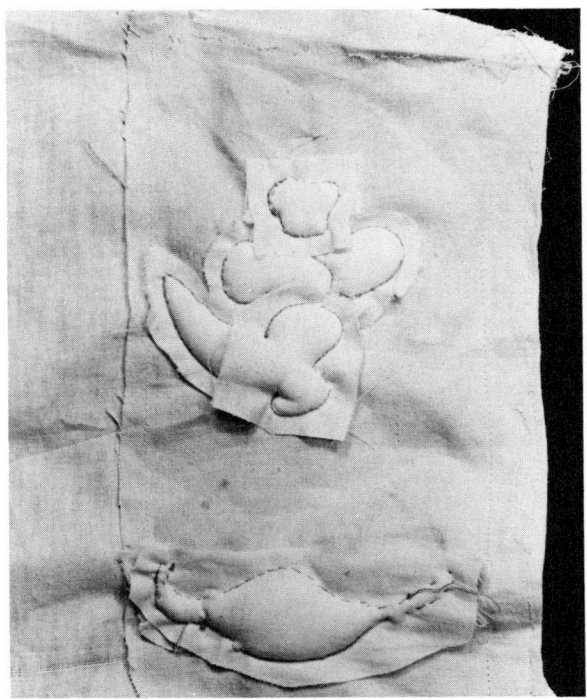

Fig. 20 Back

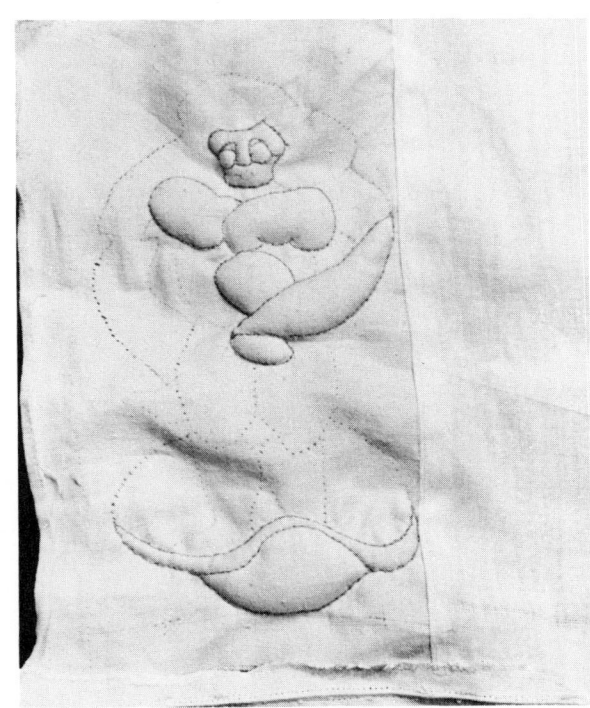

Fig. 21 Front

22 The Complete Book of Stuffedwork

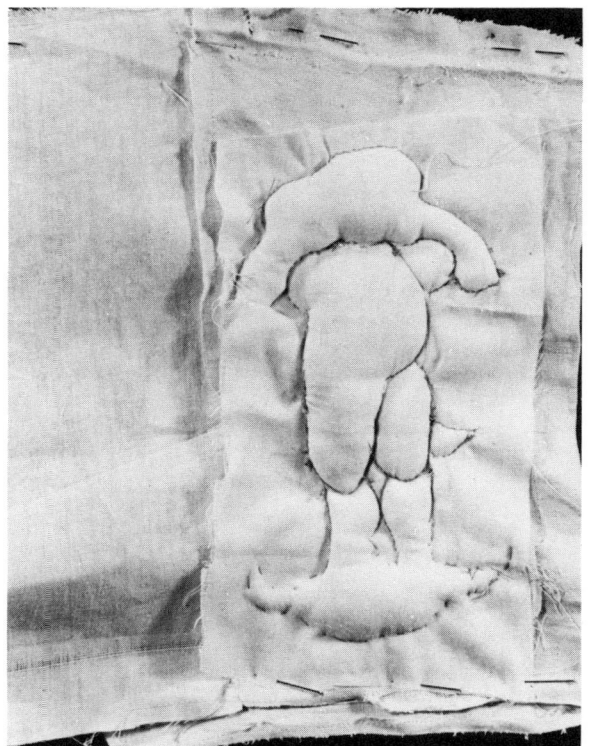

Fig. 22 Back

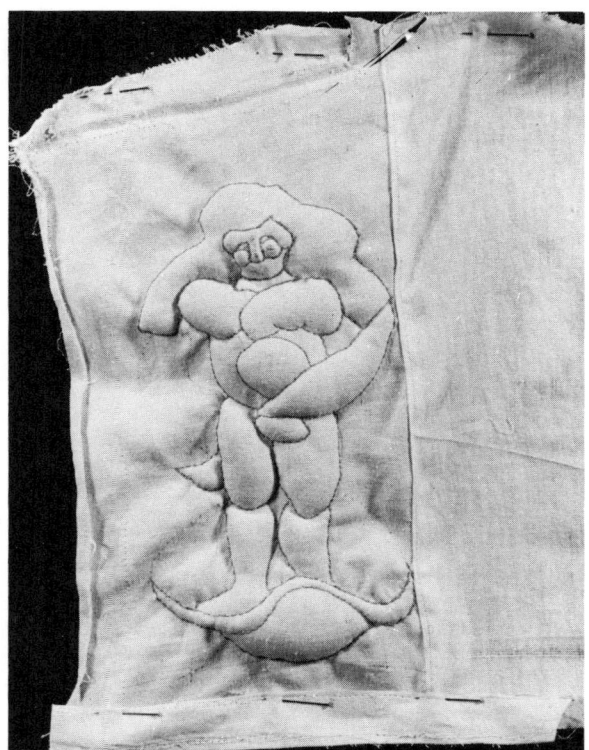

Fig. 23 Front

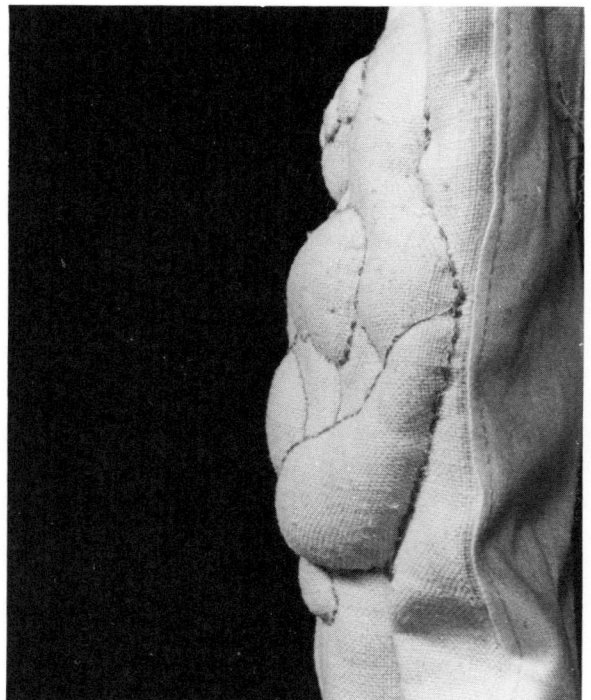

Fig. 24 Side

Plate 1 QUILTING AND TRAPUNTO

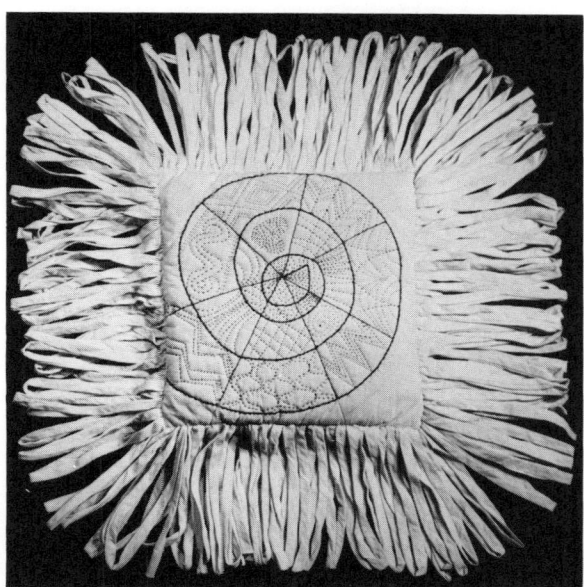

A. Muslin pillow of wadded quilting featuring a sampler of stitching patterns. Self-fringe is bias tubing.

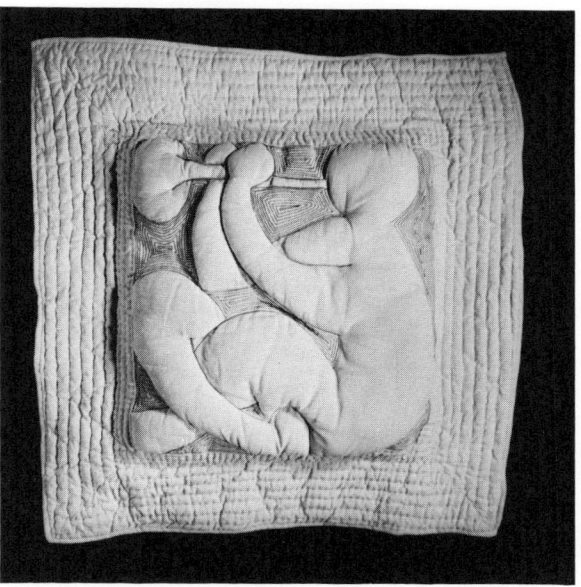

B. Muslin trapunto pillow featuring concentric rows of machine stitching around a stuffed figure; hand-quilted border.

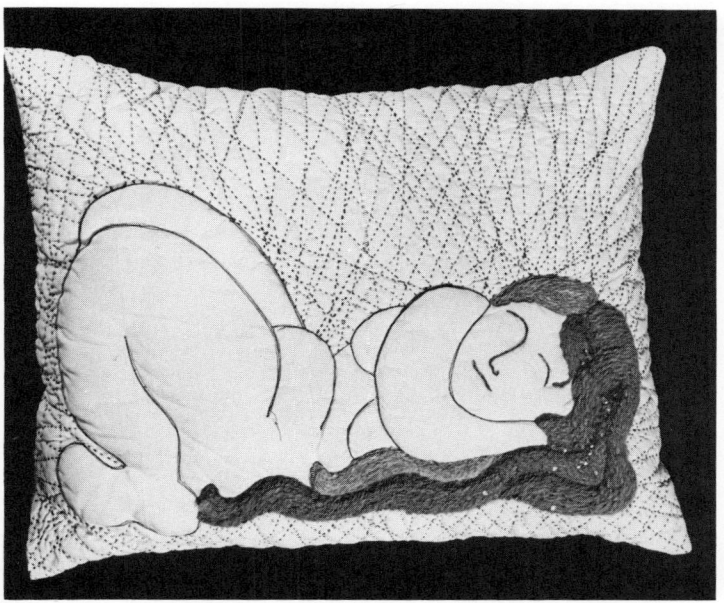

C. Muslin trapunto pillow with hand-quilting around a stuffed figure. Yarn is couched over the stuffed hair. The figure is machine stitched.

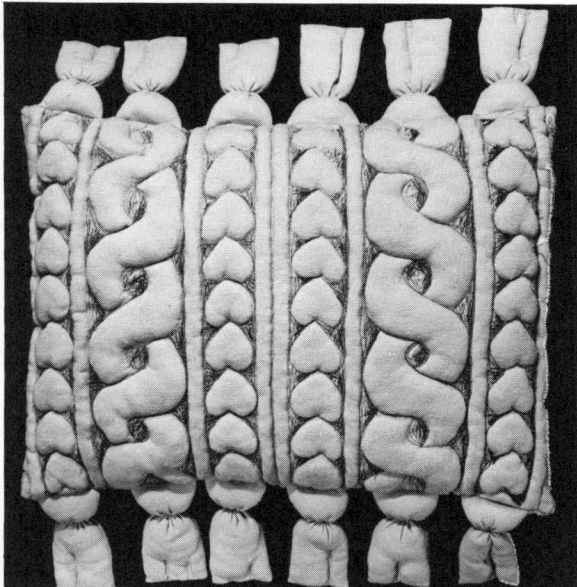

D. Trapunto pillow with machine-stitched "Irish sweater" quilting design. The pillow front and self-tassels are made of putty-colored knit fabric.

Plate 2 TRAPUNTO

A. Satin pincushion with cord and stuffed quilting

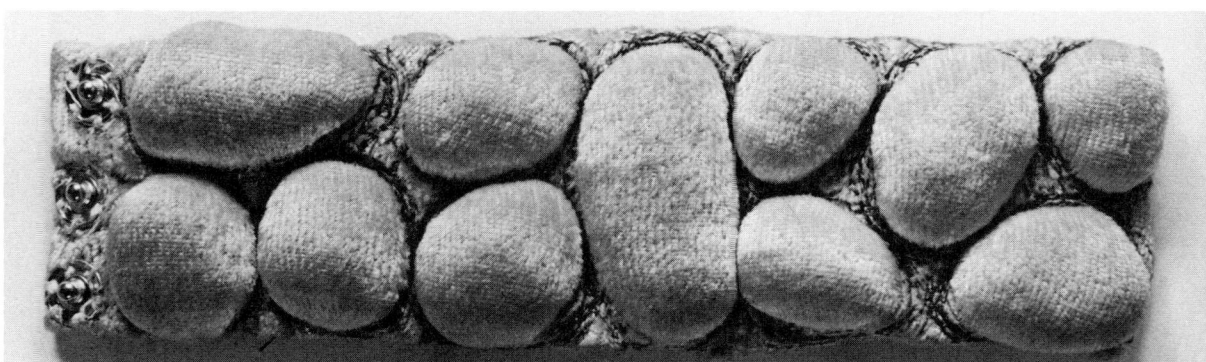

B. Trapunto bracelet of gold knit velour with stuffed machine-stitched design

C. Linen picture. The figure is rendered in layered trapunto, then the whole piece hand-quilted over batting and matted with corduroy strips. The piece is inserted over cardboard into a standard picture frame with the glass removed.

NEGATIVE SPACES

Where the stuffed areas are interrupted, there is an opportunity to add color by stitching in contrast color. *Handstitching,* in repeated or random lines, is most effective done as wadded quilting, through an underlying batting and an additional backing (Fig. 25). It smooths the puckers into the overall dimples that characterize quilting. It also provides a smoother modulation from the stuffed quilting that can tend to make the background look flimsy. A mixture in the same design of three weights, from wadded to corded to stuffed quilting, provides richness and contrast.

The stuffed quilting is completed before the wadded quilting is begun. One of the stitched sections in the fringed pillow, Plate 1A, page 23, may suggest a stitching pattern. The quilting design can be marked on the right side of the top with a hard pencil or dressmaker's chalk.

The back fabric is smoothed, right side down, under the batting; then the stuffed top is placed right side up over the batting. After basting from the center outward through the three layers, the work is placed in a frame if possible. Starting from the center, a running or backstitch is sewn over the drawn quilting lines. The frame and basting are removed when the quilting is finished.

Machine stitching through the two layers (top and back) also makes a very effective background (Fig. 26). Stitching freely backward and forward, as demonstrated in the "cable stitch" pillow on Plate 1D and Figure 26, gives an opportunity to darken some areas, perhaps with more than one thread color. This is worked before the stuffing begins, at random, like machine darning or in concentric rows around the design as shown in the Pan pillow on Plate 1B. Zigzag and machine embroidery stitches can be used as well.

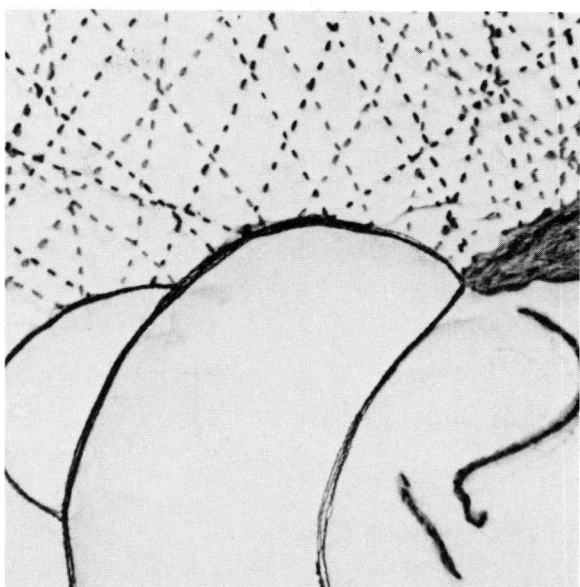

Fig. 25

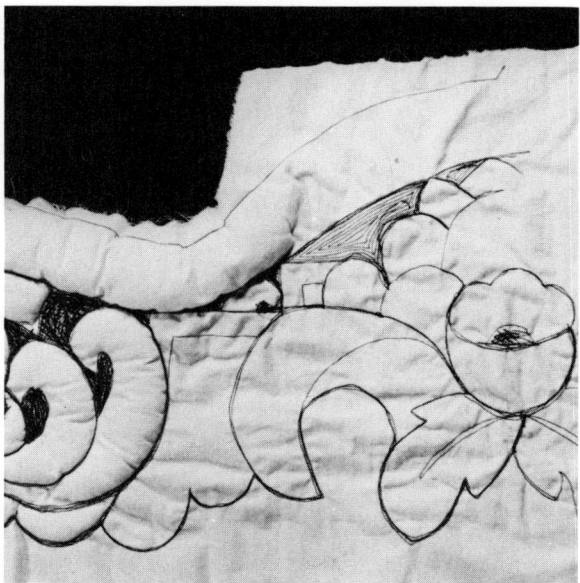

Fig. 26

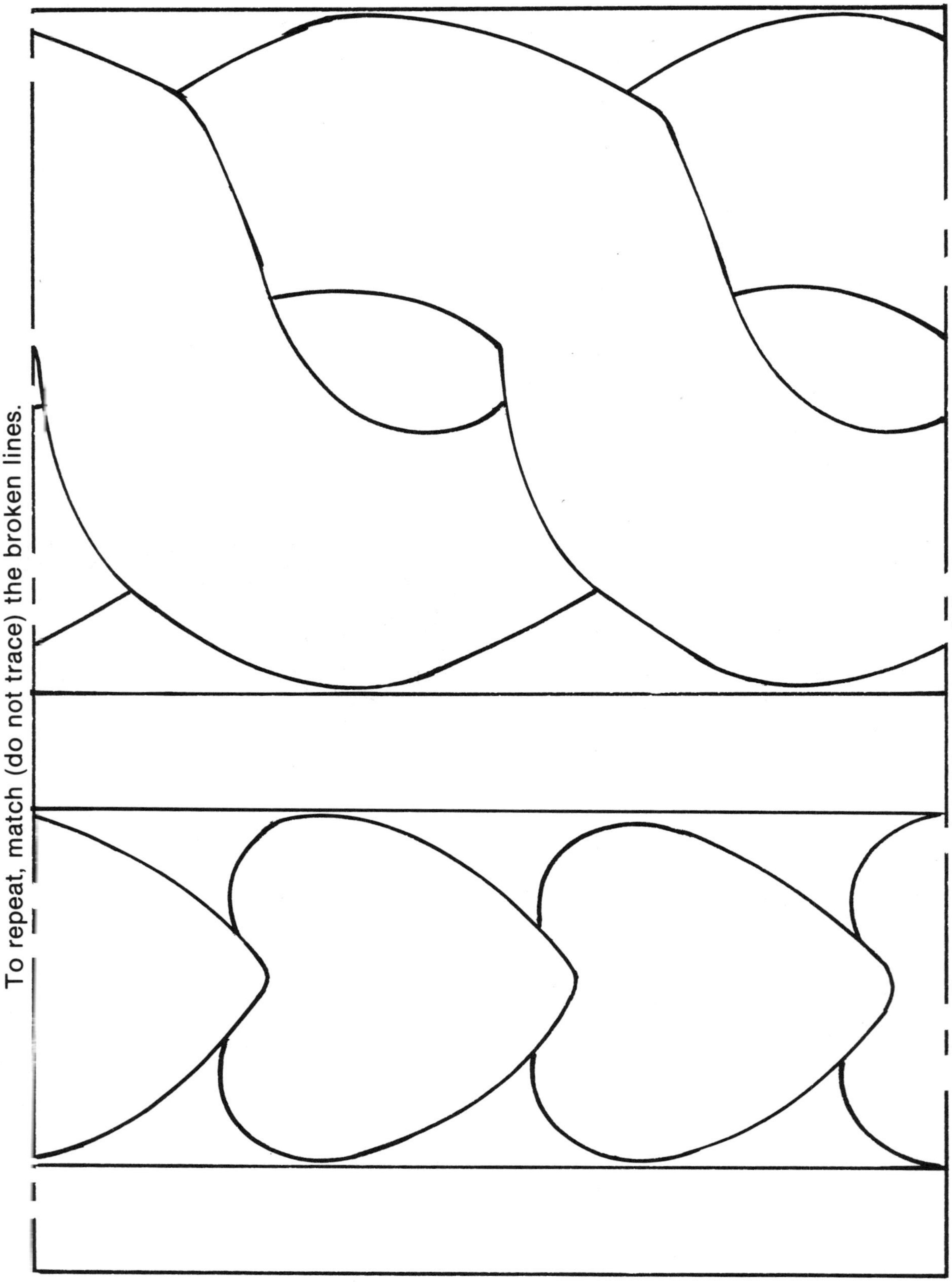

26   The Complete Book of Stuffedwork

Fig. 27   Quilting pattern for pillow, Plate I view D.

Trapunto 27

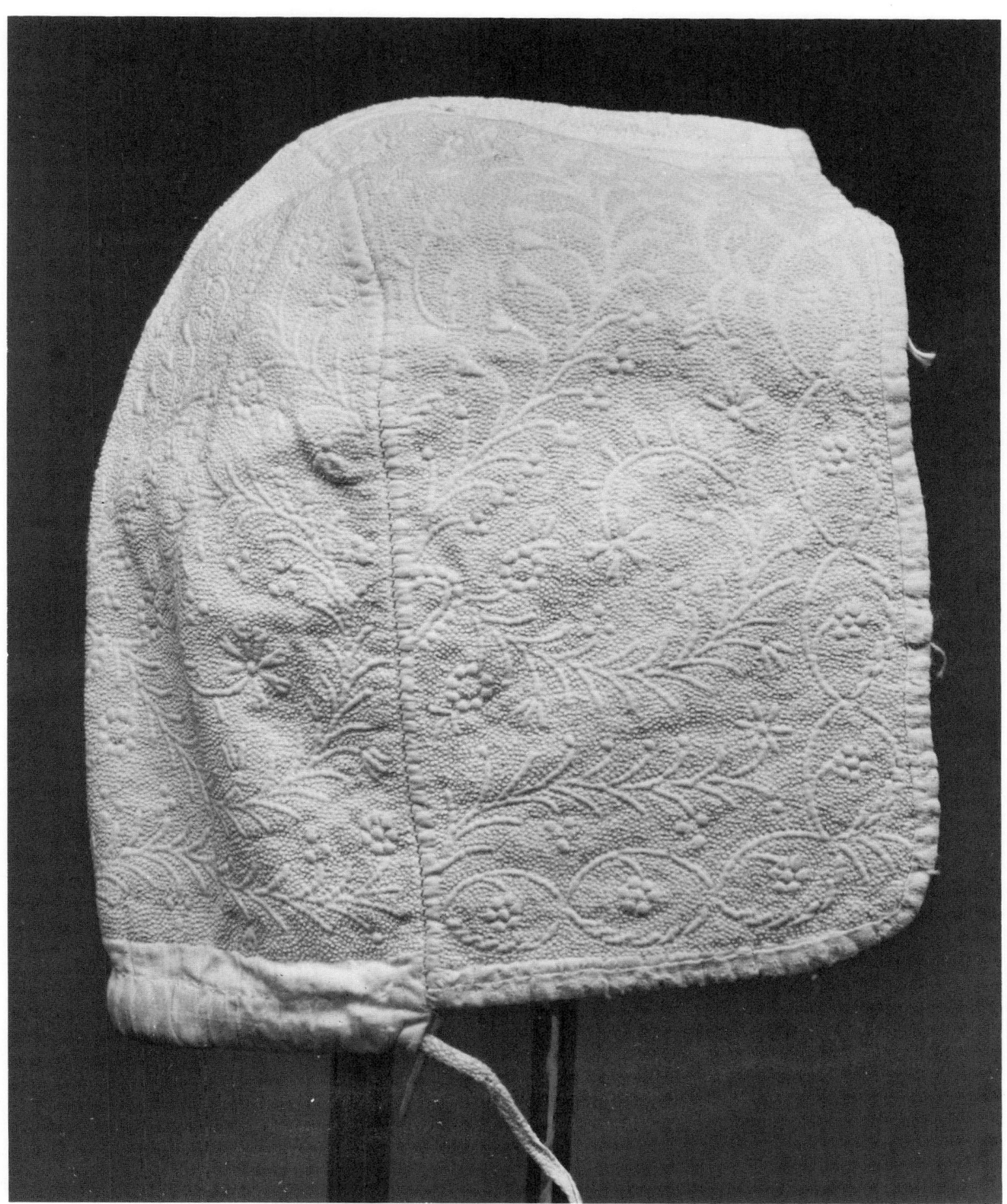

Eighteenth Century, French *Baby's Cap*.
White linen, quilted. The Metropolitan Museum of
Art, gift of Mrs. Robert Woods Bliss, 1943.

28 The Complete Book of Stuffedwork

New England, ca. 1825 *Stuffedwork Crib Quilt* (33" square). Cotton fabric and stuffing. Bowl and stems in cord quilting, fruit and leaves in stuffed quilting, background in wadded quilting. Courtesy America Hurrah Antiques, New York.

Trapunto 29

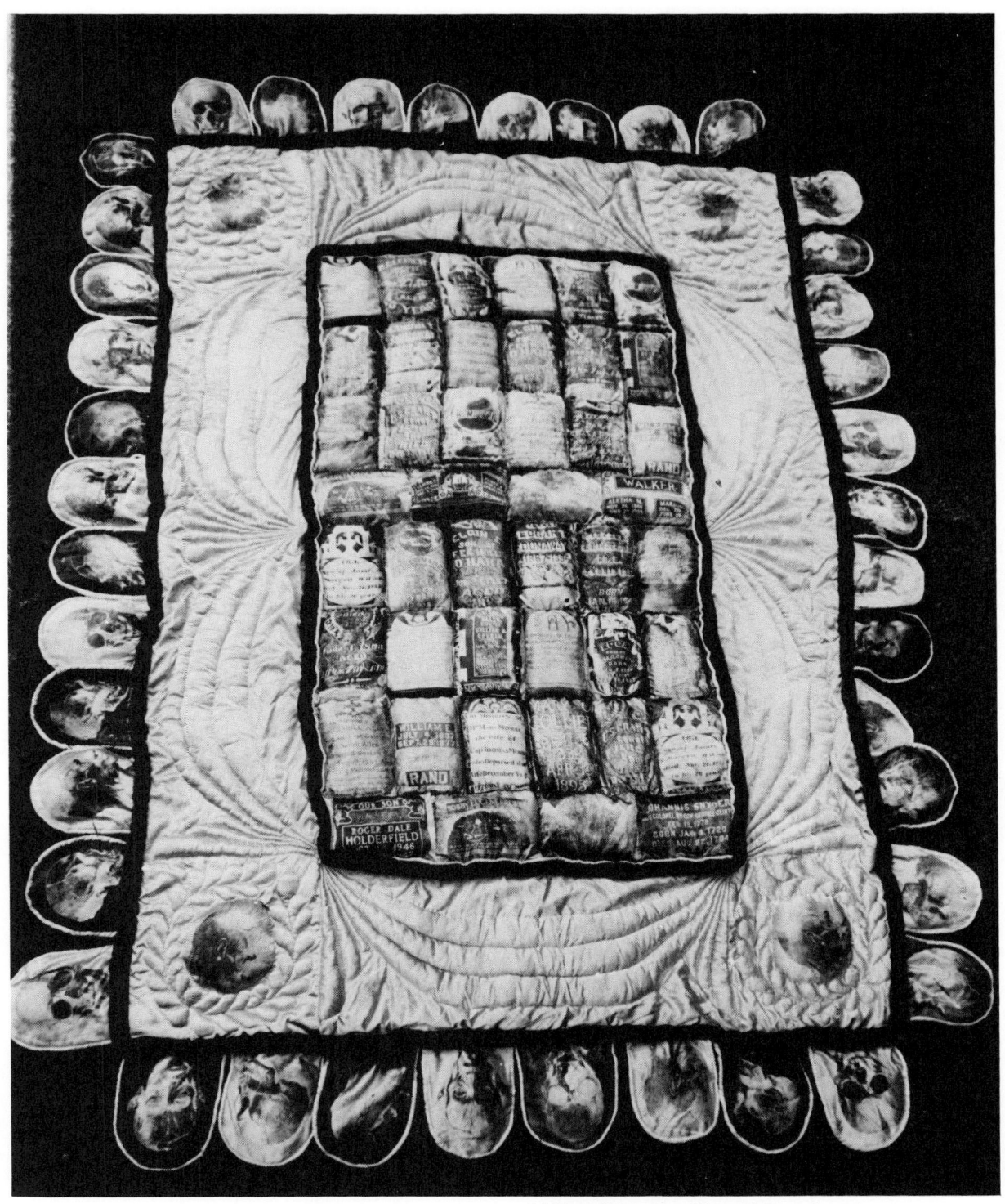

M. Joan Lintault *Shroud II — American Graveyard*. Photosensitive satin, pieced and stuffed.

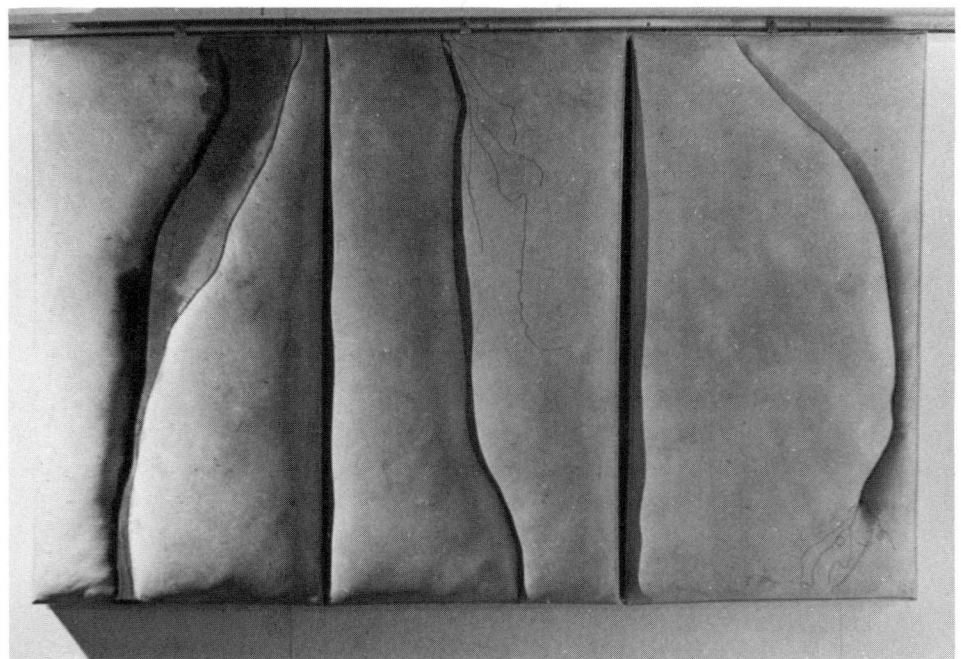

Maxine McClendon *Cuilapam* (Oaxaca, Mexico) (48" x 76"), 1974. Wet on wet watercolor techniques with thinned acrylic on canvas. The painting is stitched to canvas backing with black thread, then stapled to a wooden support. It is stuffed through slits in front and back. Front slits are sutured with black threads, some of which are left hanging.

Madge Huntington *Rolling Fields* (47" x 36"). Linen, silk, silk chiffon; machine appliqué and trapunto.

Trapunto 31

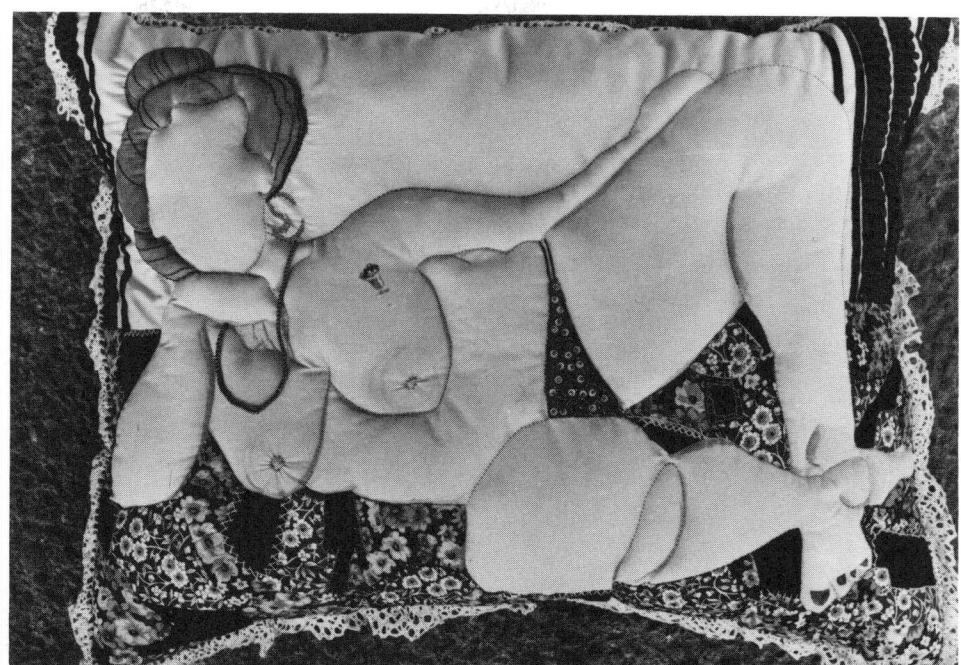

Cynthia Springer *Hot Fudge Sundae*. Pillow, appliqué and trapunto.

Anne Raymo *Shroud* (53″ x 60″), 1970. Fabric collage. Courtesy Terry Dintenfass, Inc., New York.

Lenore Davis *Mermaid Parade Float* (23″ x 20″ x 5″). Direct dyed cotton velveteen, squeeze bottle, dry brush, brush and wash techniques. Trapunto quilting; machine stitching using darning attachment; polyester stuffing. Pine base and wheels.

Chapter Two
Stuffed Appliqué

CORDED AND STUFFED quilting are one-color mediums, except where stitching can introduce additional color. *Stuffed appliqué,* however, offers the opportunity for unlimited changes of color and fabric.

A stuffed embroidery technique known as *stumpwork,* popular in Stuart England, was a version of stuffed appliqué. Figures made of wadding or carved wood were covered with embroidery. The forms stood out in very high relief (see the photograph on page 50).

When appliquéd quilts became so popular in the nineteenth century, some of the motifs (notably grapes and cherries) were padded to raise them above the quilting.

Today, with the general ownership of zigzag-stitch sewing machines, large appliquéd banners and wall hangings have become practical and popular. Stuffed and unstuffed patches are used, along with quilting techniques, to provide varying depths of relief.

The careful handstitched and rather modestly raised patches on old quilts have stood the test of time and many washings. Much of the decorative work that is now rapidly done by sewing-machine zigzag stitch will not survive because the raw edges of the patches will eventually fray and become detached from the stitching. For enduring work, raw edges of woven fabrics must be turned under, whether the stitching is by hand — usually slipstitching (Fig. 28) — or by machine. Unwoven fabrics, however, like knits, felt, vinyls, and some interfacings will not fray and can be more safely stitched at raw edges.

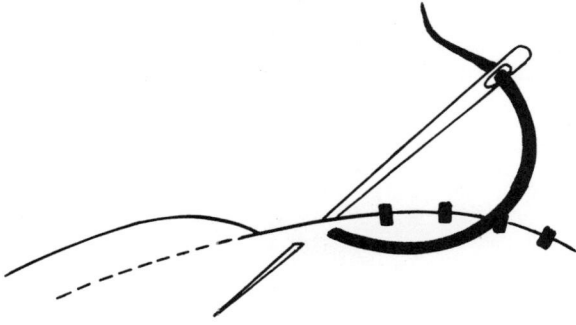

Fig. 28 Slipstitch

BASIC APPLIQUÉ

DESIGN

Here again, patches cut in shapes employing smooth lines and wide angles are the easiest to apply and to fill. The stuffing can be inserted while the patch is being stitched. Then the underlying fabric, which is at the same time the background, does not need to be slit. Some patches, of course, may be left unstuffed for contrast and the negative areas are often quilted, as described in Chapter 1, Stuffed Quilting.

Well-designed appliqué is accomplished with no more pieces than necessary. Such economy is accomplished by overlapping and by stitching on the patch as well as around it. Much of the detail can be executed by stitching or embroidery. Filling in small negative spaces with stitching in background color can eliminate additional appliqué pieces.

MATERIALS

Use soft, smooth fabrics in a lighter weight than the background fabric; avoid fabrics that shift or fray easily. Crisp fabrics like cotton broadcloth, calico, or fine linen turn under easily and are simplest to apply.

The patches are stuffed with cotton or synthetic stuffing, soft yarn, or nylon clippings. Sometimes a flat padding like felt or batting, cut a little smaller than the appliqué, is placed under the patch.

TRANSFER

The appliqué design does not generally need to be transferred to the background fabric. Two or three short guidemarks for placement are all that is needed — perhaps the center and a baseline, or a characteristic outline to indicate placement.

HAND APPLICATION (Fig. 29)

a. Draw or trace the patch outline on a piece of fabric large enough to provide seam allowance (⅛ inch to ¼ inch) beyond the drawn lines.

   Staystitch by hand or machine along the drawn line. (Staystitching is a regular running stitch used to define a seamline, prevent stretching, and facilitate turning.) Staystitching not only makes it much easier to turn under curved edges, but also provides reinforcement at the end of the clips and notches that must be cut in the seam allowance.

b. Cut out the patch ⅛ inch to ¼ inch outside the staystitched lines.

   Clip inside curves to but not through the staystitching. Notch the outside curves. Clipping the inside curves and corners is always necessary because the edge will not turn under without it. But notching outside curves can often be omitted in thin materials since it serves only to eliminate bulk.

c. Pin the patch to position on the background fabric. Place the pins so that the patch does

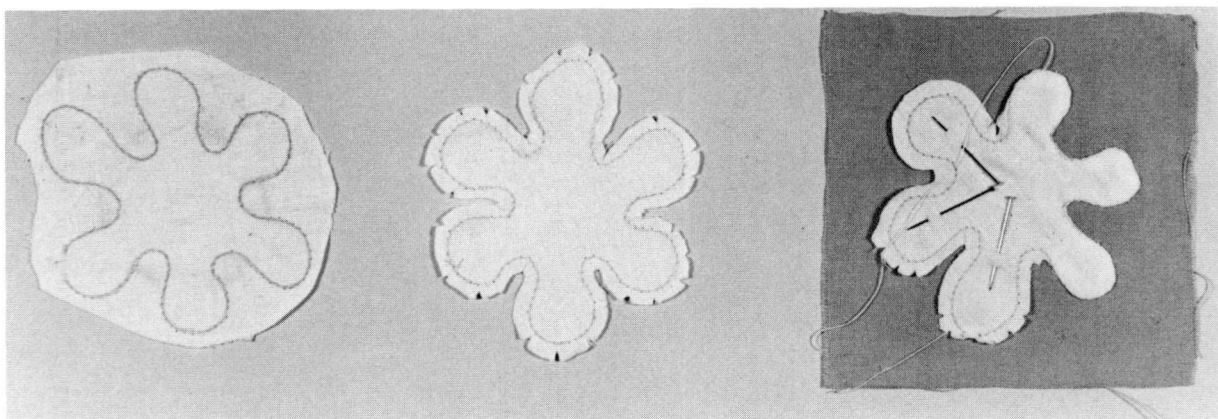

Fig. 29   a   b   c

Fig. 30 a   b   c

not shift but in such a way that they don't interfere with turning under the edges.

Turn under the edges along the staystitching. Crisp fabrics can be creased at the fold with the thumbnail. Other fabrics can be rolled under with the needle as you sew. The staystitching usually disappears just under the turn. Slipstitch (Fig. 28). If some of the staystitches are still visible, they can be drawn out later.

INSIDE CORNERS (Fig. 30)

a. In a form like the X, it is easier and stronger to cross two straight strips than to apply one piece that has four inside corners. Since inside corners have to be clipped right to the folded-under edge, they create weak spots that eventually tend to fray.

b. Straight edges do not need preliminary staystitching.

c. Trim the seam allowance at the corners. Pin and slipstitch one strip, turning under one edge at a time. Apply the second strip the same way.

CONNECTING COLORS (Fig. 31)

a. Reduce the patches to a minimum number. Usually neighboring patches can be connected at hidden layers.

b. To extract patterns from this design, for example, make a tracing for each color. Notice that the white stripes can be cut as one. Thus five stripes can be only two patches.

c. Apply the underlying, larger patch. Apply the uppermost, smaller patch, sewing through all layers.

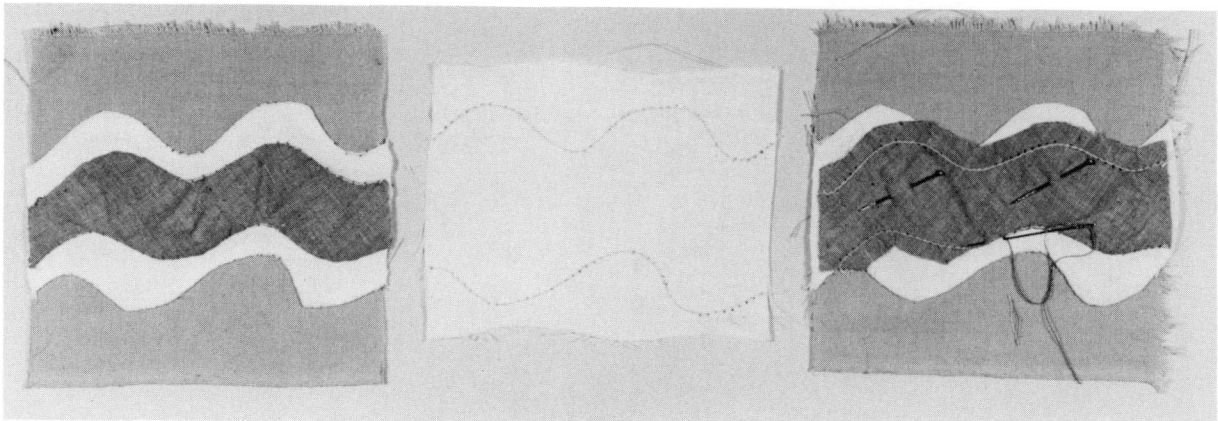

Fig. 31 a   b   c

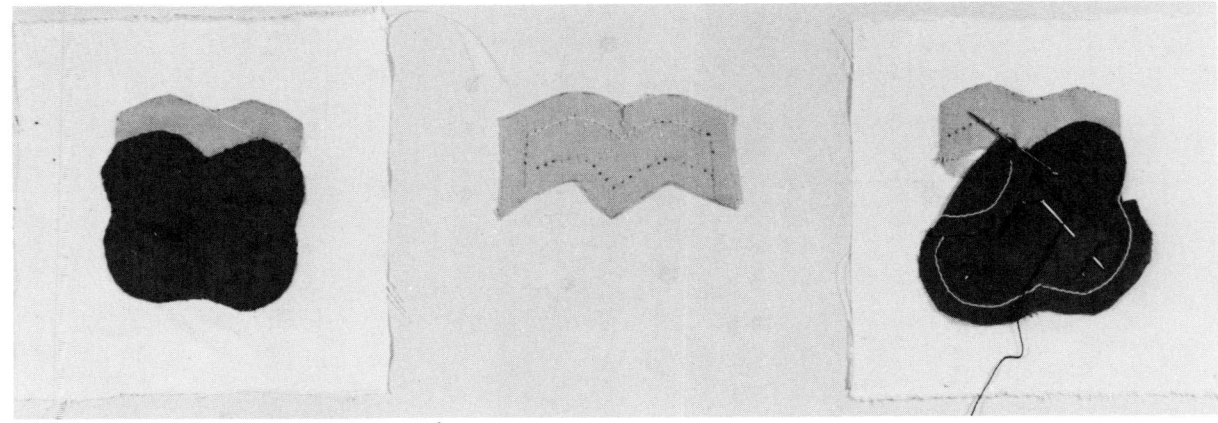

Fig. 32 a   b   c

Fig. 33 a   b   c

LAYERS (Fig. 32)

a. Think of appliqué in terms of layers. Where two patches meet, one edge can be slid under the other. Draw this bottom appliqué as it appears. The overlapped edge does not need to be staystitched.

b. Cut out the patch ⅛ inch to ¼ inch outside the drawn lines. Clip to the inside corners. Overlapped edges do not need to be clipped since they will not be turned under.

   Apply the bottom patch, turning in the visible edges. Baste the raw edge.

c. Apply the top patch, overlapping the first.

REVERSE APPLIQUÉ (Fig. 33)

a. Reverse appliqué, in all or part of the design, is a useful alternative to direct appliqué in some situations.

   To make an open square at the center of this patch, mark a cross and cut along the drawn lines.

b. Rolling under each corner of the cross with the needle, slipstitch the four sides of a square, to reveal the background fabric.

c. Directly apply the outer edges in the usual way.

Stuffed Appliqué 39

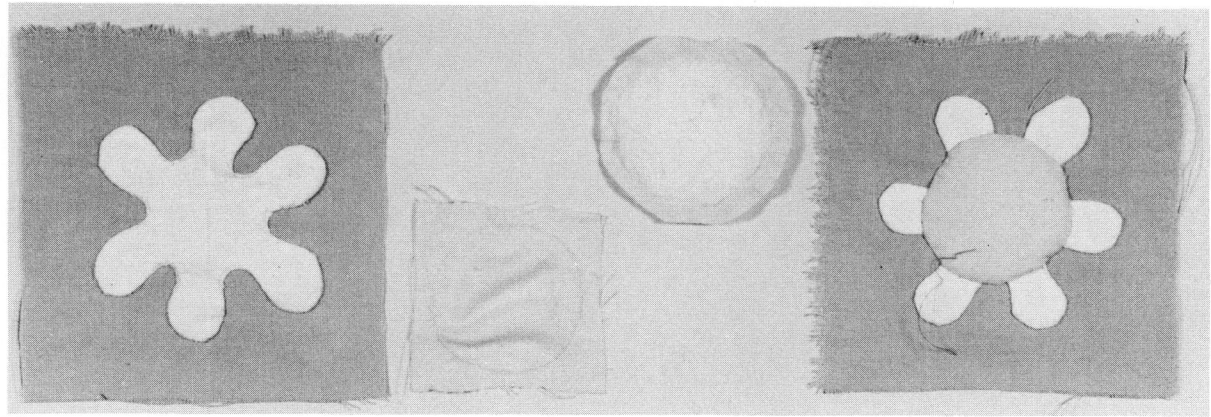

Fig. 34　a　　　　　　　　b　　　　　　　　c

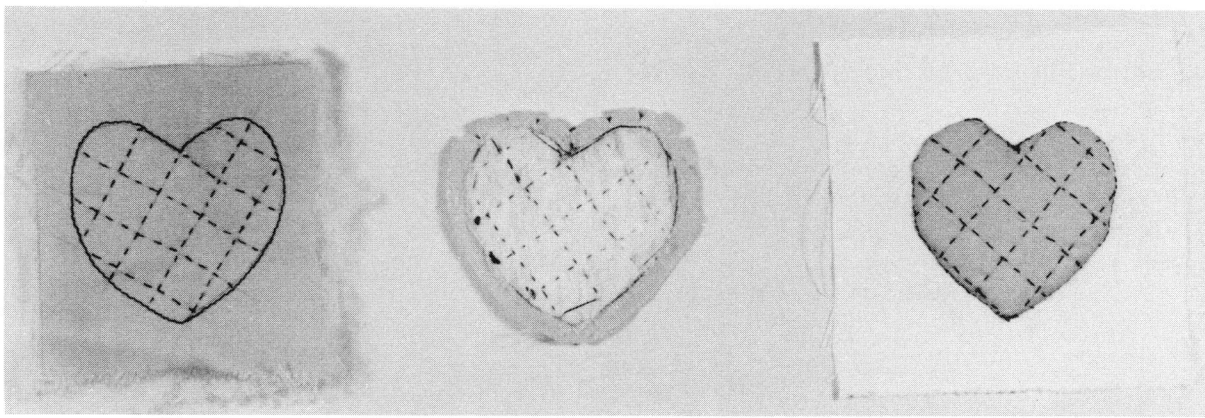

Fig. 35　a　　　　　　　　b　　　　　　　　c

PADDING (Fig. 34)

a. Patches can be lightly padded before they are sewn down. To cover this flower with a padded center, for example, draw, staystitch, and cut the patch as usual.
b. Cut a piece of quilt batting the finished size of the patch, without a seam allowance.
   Baste the batting to the wrong side of the patch.
c. Apply the padded patch.

QUILTED APPLIQUÉ (Fig. 35)

a. Any patch can itself be quilted, appliquéd or embroidered. This embellishment — quilting, in this instance — should be worked before cutting out the patch, in order to allow for enough fabric to fit an embroidery hoop.
b. Cut seam allowances outside the staystitching. Trim the batting (and backing if used) to the staystitching.
c. Apply in the usual way. A very small amount of stuffing may also be inserted under the patch before stitching is finished.

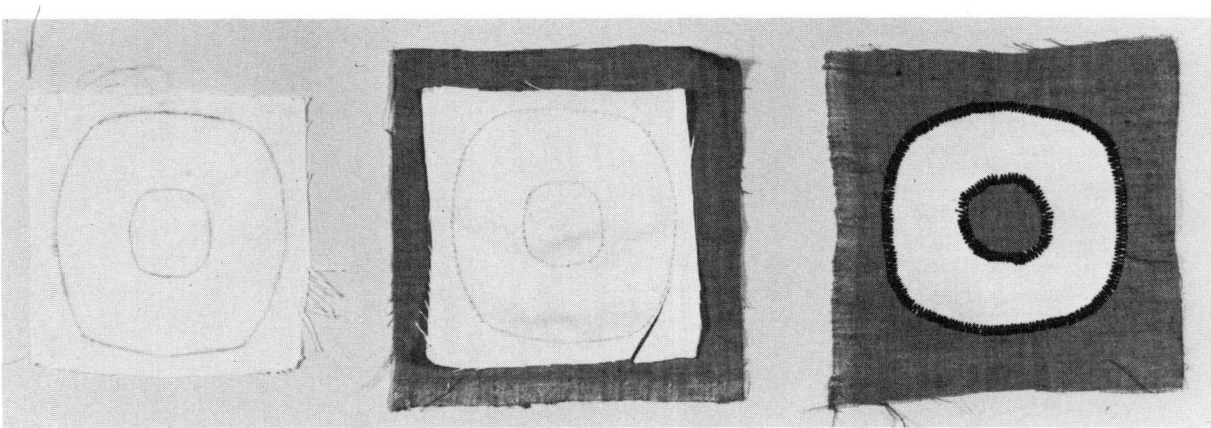

Fig. 36 a b c

MACHINE APPLICATION (Fig. 36)

a. Center and draw the design on a block of appliqué fabric.
b. Place the appliqué block over the background fabric. Stitch them together over the drawn lines with a machine straight stitch. Trim away excess appliqué fabric close to the stitched lines.
c. Outline the appliqué with machine satin stitch, covering the raw edges and the straight stitching.

CONTINUOUS APPLIQUÉ — STUFFED PRESSEDWORK

The technique of pressedwork comes from patchwork, where it is used to construct crazy quilts and log cabin designs. It is perfectly adapted to stuffedwork, as well, because the muslin block on which it is worked will remain flat and stable while, over it, scraps of fabric are lapped and stuffed and shaped in a free and improvisatory way. It is a rare opportunity for spontaneity along with stability. It should be executed over blocks, strips, or other units of foundation fabric. These are later seamed together to make a large piece that does not need further quilting since it has already been stuffed.

The patches make patterns of relief as well as of color and value. Therefore, after choosing the fabrics, it is helpful to improvise part of one block to see how the fabric naturally shapes itself in terms of block size and height. Rough thumbnail sketches of the adjoining blocks will help to establish variety and repetition in the placement of shapes and dark and light values. All the foundation blocks can be put on a bulletin board where scraps of fabric can be pinned in place, to try out alternatives, before sewing and stuffing.

DEMONSTRATION

1. Cut matching muslin squares or strips for the foundation blocks. Those shown (Fig. 37) are 8-inch cut size and 7-inch finished size (½-inch seams are allowed).

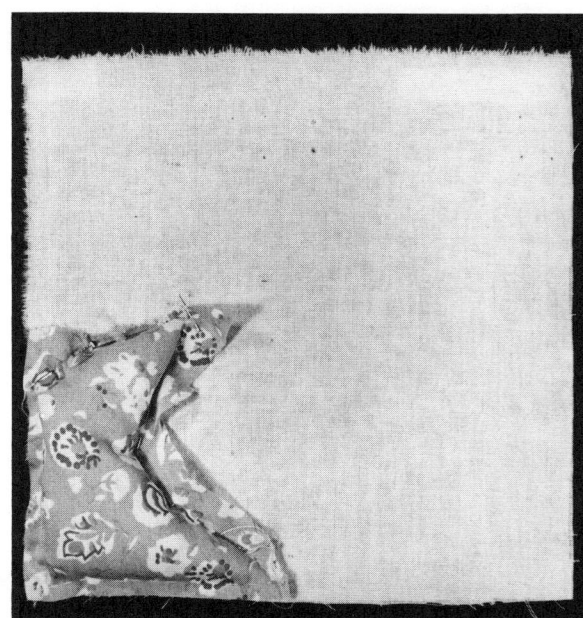

Fig. 37

2. At the corner of a foundation block, pin a patch, right sides up. Sew along the seamlines at the corner edges of the block. Insert stuffing into the corner, pushing up and clipping the loose edge of the patch as needed. Pin and baste at the desired seamline.

   Since this is an improvisatory technique, your seamlines need not follow the cut edge of the patch. Place the seam where it "wants to go," allowing the stuffing to form appealing contours and the fabric to round smoothly over it, pushing the patch back as far as necessary to reach a height that will nevertheless keep the foundation fabric flat.
3. Place a second patch over the first, right sides together; pin and stitch it at the seamline of the first patch (Fig. 38). Turn the patch right side up over some stuffing, as you did for the first, and baste the other edges. Continue across the block, in the same way.
4. Where you can, cover the ends of several short patches with one long patch (Fig. 39).
5. Edges that reach the outlines of the foundation block are not turned under. Those that end within the block must either be covered by another patch or turned under and slipstitched over another raw edge. This is frequently necessary with the third edge of any patch and is especially useful for curved edges (Fig. 40).

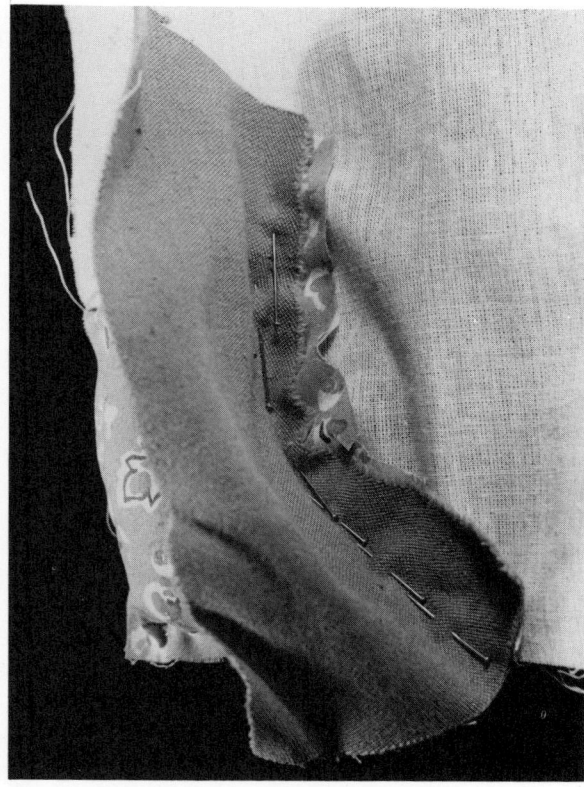

Fig. 38

Fig. 39

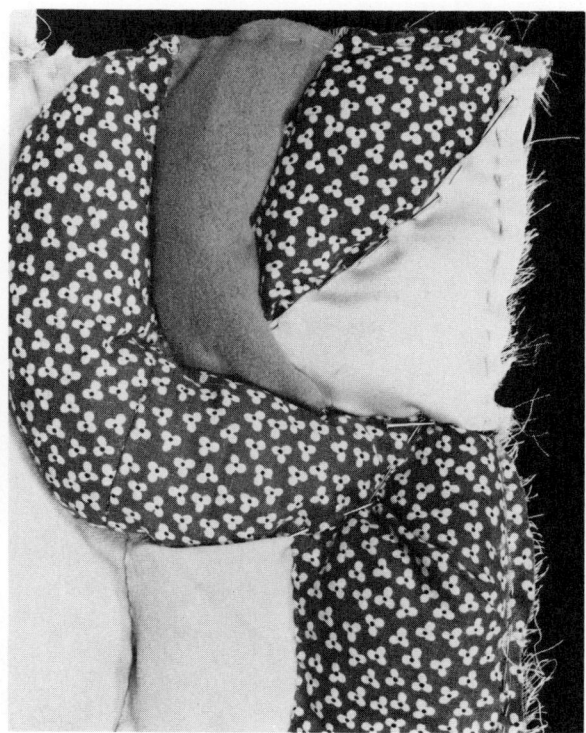

Fig. 40

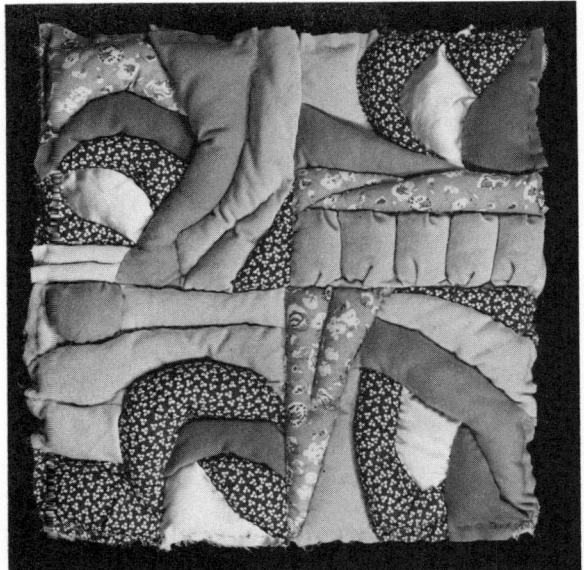

Fig. 41

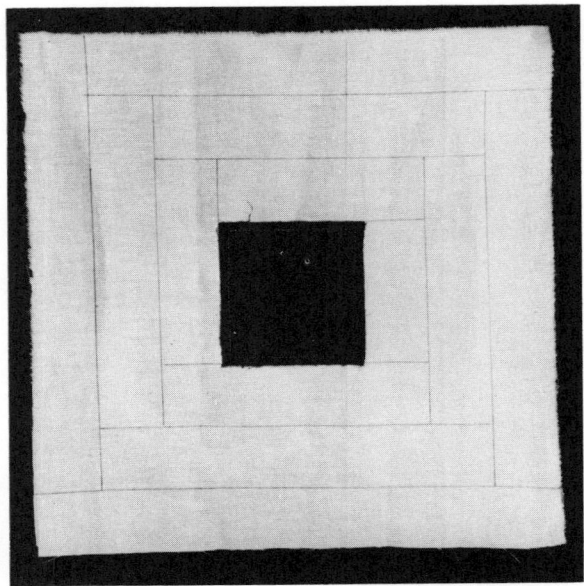

Fig. 42

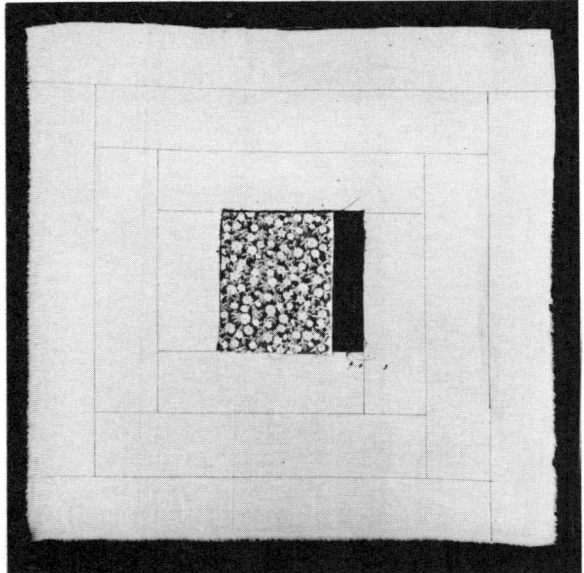

Fig. 43

6. Continue across the patch until it is filled. Turn the patch wrong side up and trim excess patch ends flush with the foundation fabric. Stitch a scant ½ inch from the edges of the block through all layers.
7. Seam the finished blocks or strips, right sides together, to make a continuous surface (Fig. 41).

Note: The first patch could also be placed at the center, as in this stuffed log cabin pillow, Plate 3B. Since it is a controlled design, the placement of the patches has been drawn on the foundation block (Fig. 42). The patches around the flat center are cut wider than the drawn spaces (Fig. 43) and are pleated at each end to take up the extra fabric which, in turn, allows the patch to rise and accommodate the stuffing (Fig. 44). Additional patches are applied one at a time in the same direction around the center until the foundation block is covered (Fig. 45).

STUFFED APPLIQUÉ

In Basic Appliqué, we illustrated padding and very light stuffing. More stuffing would have caused distortion in the background fabric. In order to make really "fat" appliqués, the patch

Stuffed Appliqué 43

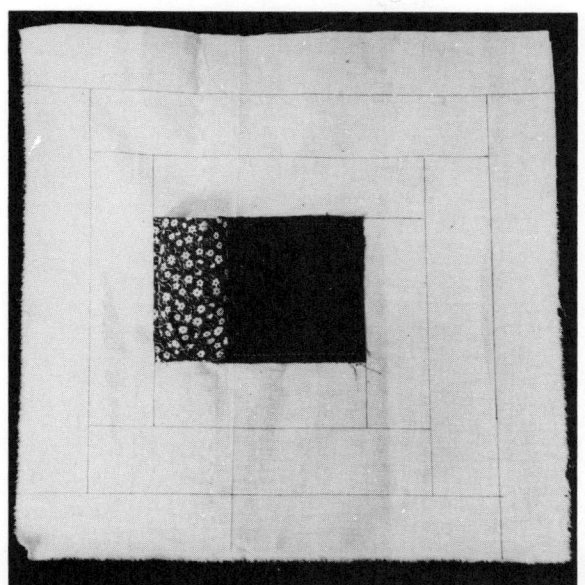
Fig. 44

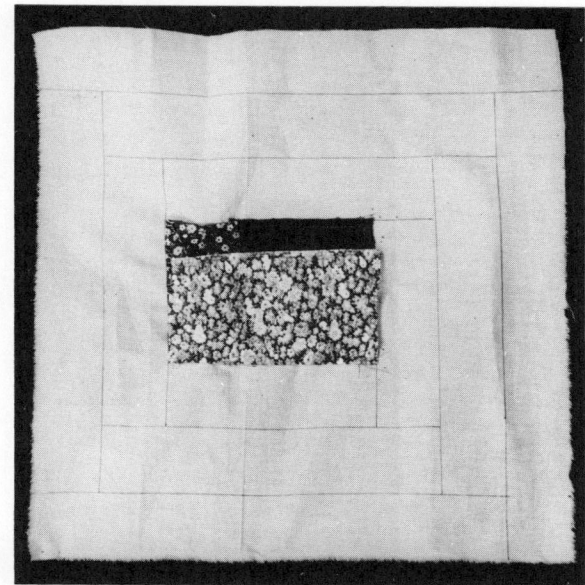
Fig. 45

must be cut larger than the space it will occupy. Gathering stitches are run around one or more of the patched edges. When the stitches are drawn up, the edges reduce to the original size and, at the same time, allow the patch to rise over the stuffing without distorting the background or foundation fabric.

In Continuous Appliqué, we illustrated fairly high stuffing achieved with an improvised design. Stuffed appliqué, as we shall see, shares these possibilities while it can also execute a controlled design that has been drawn on the foundation fabric.

TRANSFER

Draw the design directly on the background or underlying fabric. From the drawing, extract the separate patch patterns by tracing each section. Add about ¾ inch outside each drawn edge to mark the cutting lines. Part of the ¾ inch will be seam allowance; the rest will provide extra height in the patch to contain the stuffing.

FINISH LINES

When several patches stop at a single line, apply them first, so that all those raw edges can be covered with a single patch. In the following design (Fig. 46), there is a loop around the center oval that can cover the ends of many smaller pieces. Consequently, work toward that loop, first applying the center oval and then, from the outside inward, the remaining patches.

Fig. 46

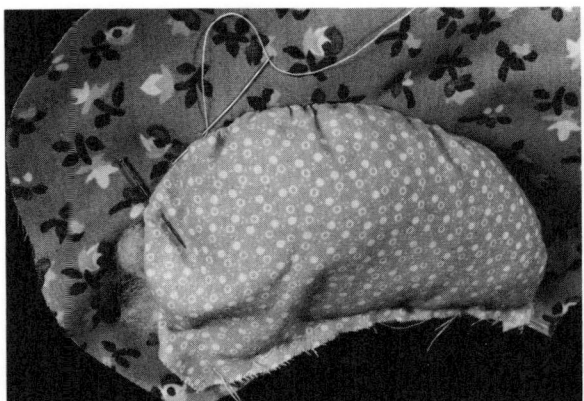

Fig. 47

GATHERED PATCHES

Ungathered edges of the patch are basted to position. Gathered edges are drawn up and turned under, then pinned to the drawn position on the underlying muslin (or intervening patch). The patch is slipstitched to position and stuffed before the sewing is completed (Fig. 47).

COMPOUND PATCHES

Some patches are themselves appliquéd. The center oval in Fig. 46, for example, will be crossed by two strips of stuffed fabric (Figs. 48–50). The large light inside petal is stuffed and applied to its neighbor that also underlies it (Fig. 51). This makes for additional height on the smaller patch.

If you plan to have compound patches, remember, when extracting the patterns, to have the bottom patch extend all the way under the top patch.

The top patches of all the compound patches should be applied and stuffed first.

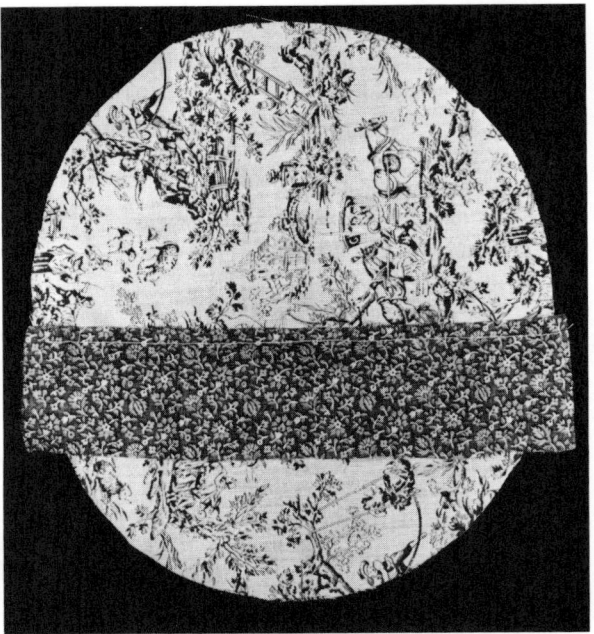

Fig. 48

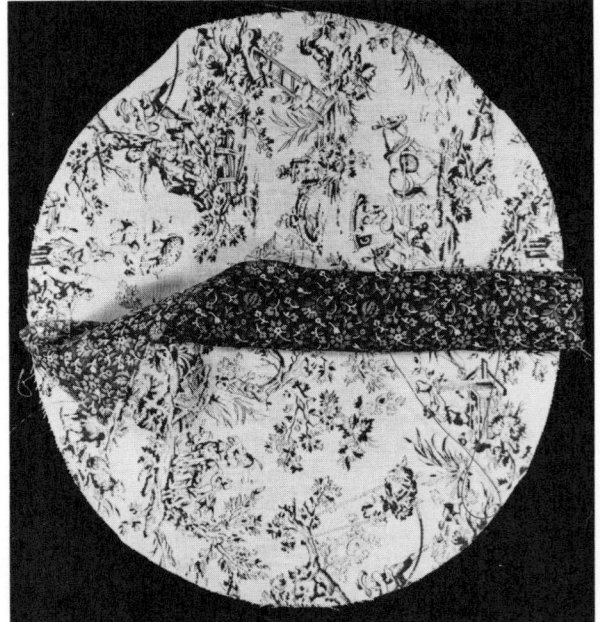

Fig. 49

Stuffed Appliqué 45

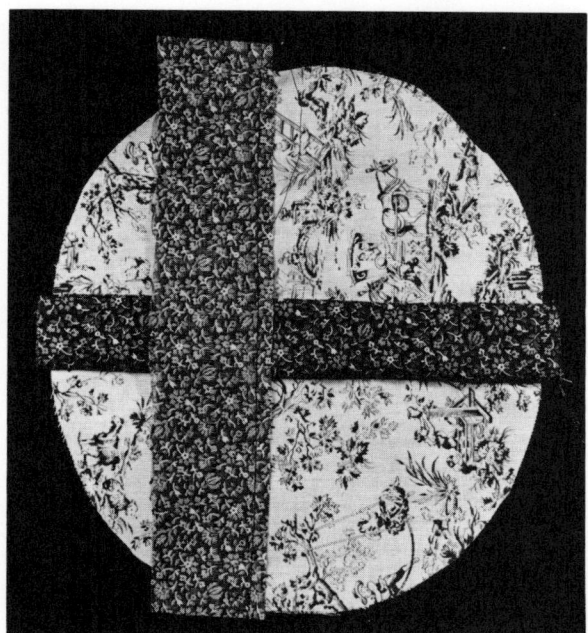

Fig. 50

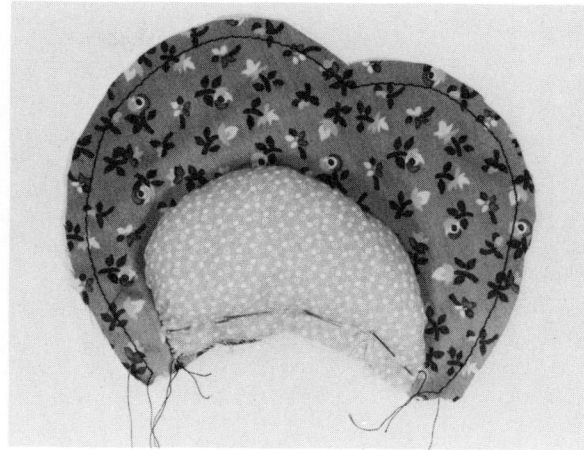

Fig. 51

Fig. 52

OUTSIDE EDGES

If the design has been worked on a background fabric that is itself part of the design, the outside appliqué edges will be turned under. If, however, the design is a pillow top, for instance, the outside edges will be seamed to a pillow back. Therefore, do not turn them under, but leave them raw, outside the design, to become part of the seam allowance.

DEMONSTRATION

1. For the pillow on Plate 3, A and D, trace the design (Fig. 46) to a piece of muslin about 23-inch square.
2. Prepare the compound oval: apply one strip to the oval, seaming at one edge with right sides together (Fig. 48). Turn the patch right side up, turn under the long free edge and slipstitch, leaving some height for stuffing (Fig. 49). Repeat with the other strip, crossing over the first one (Fig. 50). Stuff strips and sew across open ends at the seamline.
3. Prepare the compound petals: sew a gathering row around the top and sides of the top patch. Place the top patch over the bottom patch, matching the lower edges. Pin and baste the lower edges. Draw up the gathering row until the edge matches the design line on the bottom patch. Insert stuffing and pin the gathered edge in place so that the lower patch remains flat. Slipstitch, finishing the stuffing before completing the slipstitching (Fig. 51). Assemble the other compound petals (Fig. 52) in the same way, starting with the center patch.

Plate 3   STUFFED APPLIQUÉ

A. Stuffed appliqué pillow, side view

B. Stuffed pressedwork pillow, log-cabin design

C. Quilted purse with stuffed appliqué

D. Stuffed appliqué pillow, top view

4. Apply the center oval: sew a gathering row around the oval and pin it to the muslin, drawing up the gathering row until it matches the drawn oval. Sew the patch to the muslin on the seamline, stuffing the patch before you finish sewing.
5. Outside patches: apply patch number 1. Stitch the patch, ½ inch from the edge, to the outside drawn line on the muslin. Roll the patch over some stuffing. Pin and seam the inside and the ends over the drawn line on the muslin. Remove the pins (Fig. 53).
6. Inside patches: gather the outside edge of patch number 2, ¼ inch from the edge. Pull up the gathering row so that the patch cups, rising about ½ inch from the gathering. Turn in the edge at the gathering and pin the fold over patch number 1, having the side edges extend outside the drawn side lines. Slipstitch the gathered edge in place. Fold the patch over some stuffing and sew the two inside seamlines. Complete all the numbers 1 and 2 patches in this way.
7. Sew the number 3 patches in the same way as patch number 1. Where the patches meet the number 1 patches, clip them to the seamline. Sew a hand gathering row along the seamline beyond the clip. Draw it up slightly, turn under the seamline, pin, and slipstitch it to patch number 2. Stuff. Sew the inside edge of the patch, clipping it to the seamline where necessary (Fig. 54). Sew all the number 4 and number 5 patches in the same way (Fig. 55).
8. Apply and stuff the compound patches (Fig. 56) to complete the petals.
9. Apply stuffed tubing: cut a bias strip 24 inches × 3 inches (see Fig. 90, page 65, to cut bias). Fold it in half lengthwise, right sides together. Stitch ¼ inch from the long edges, leaving 2-inch openings at four places for stuffing. Turn it right side out. Turn under one end ¼ inch and slipstitch it over the other end to make a loop.

Stuff the tubing very softly and slipstitch the openings. Arrange it around the center oval. Turn the piece over and baste from the back through the bottom side of the loop, except for 2 inches at each end to insert the trim.

Fig. 53

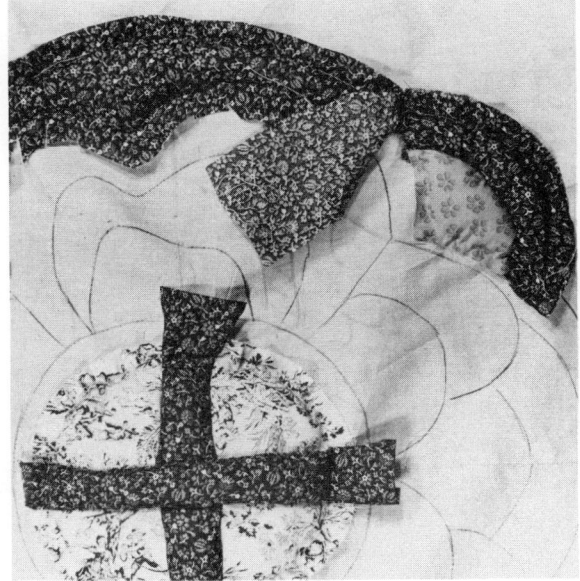

Fig. 54

48   The Complete Book of Stuffedwork

Fig. 55

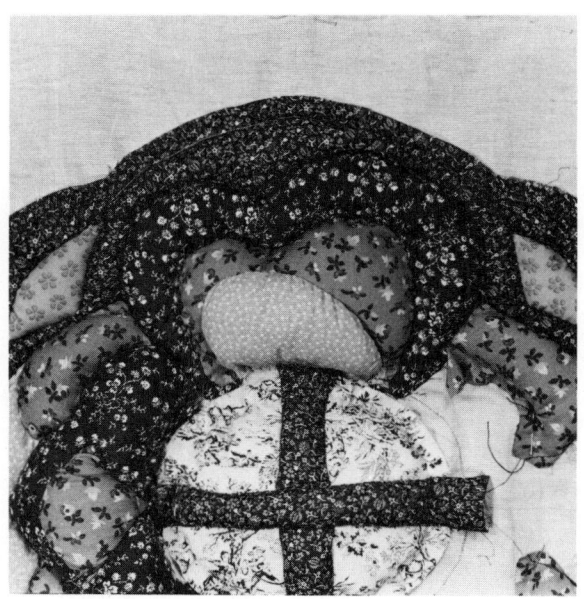

Fig. 56

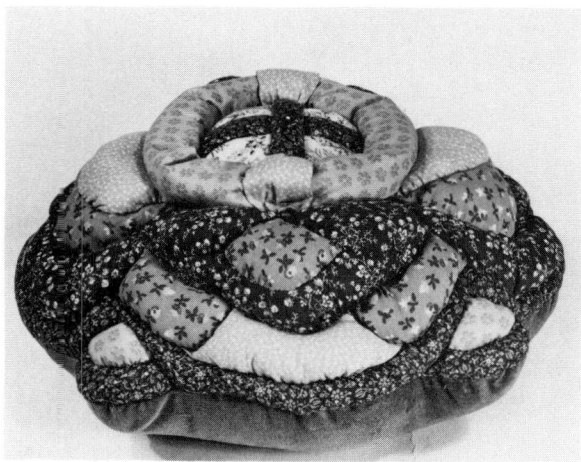

Fig. 57

Cut two 4½-inch squares. Fold them in half right sides together and stitch ¼ inch from the long edges. Turn them right side out and stuff very slightly. Tuck one under each end of the center loop and whip the ends together. Gather up the inside edges (Fig. 57).

10. Cut a matching pillow back. Stitch along the seamlines and clip inside corners to the stitching. Fold under ½-inch seams and slipstitch to the stitching line on the front, leaving about 5 inches open for stuffing.

Stuff firmly. Slipstitch the opening (Fig. 57).

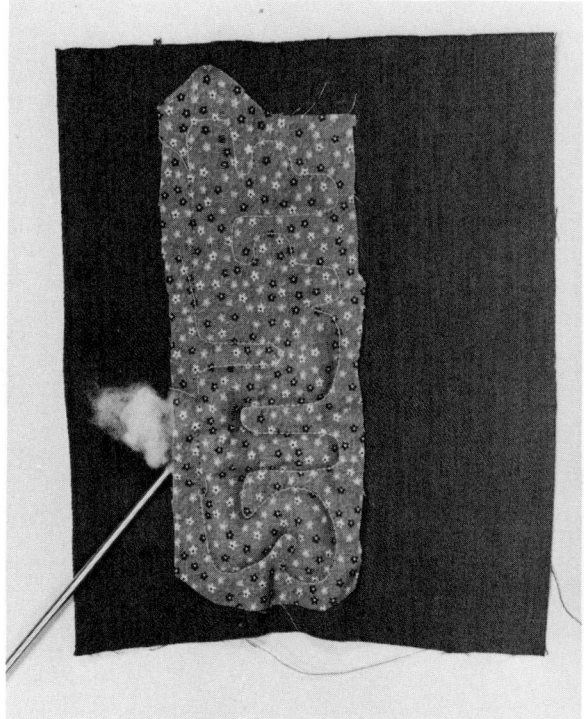

Fig. 58

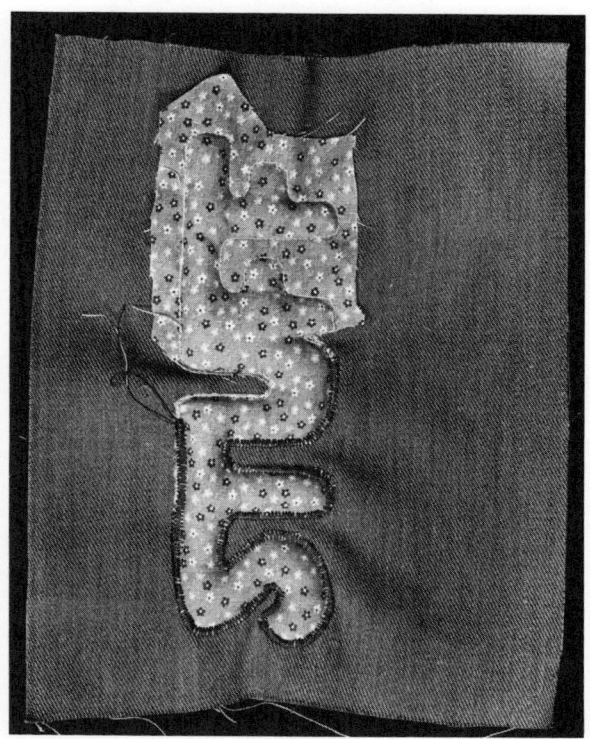

Fig. 59

STUFFED MACHINE APPLIQUÉ

Follow the steps for machine application in Figure 36, but in step b leave small openings in the stitching. Insert low stuffing (Fig. 58) and complete the stitching (Fig. 59). Since it is not necessary to slit the foundation fabric, the back of the work does not need to be further finished (Fig. 60).

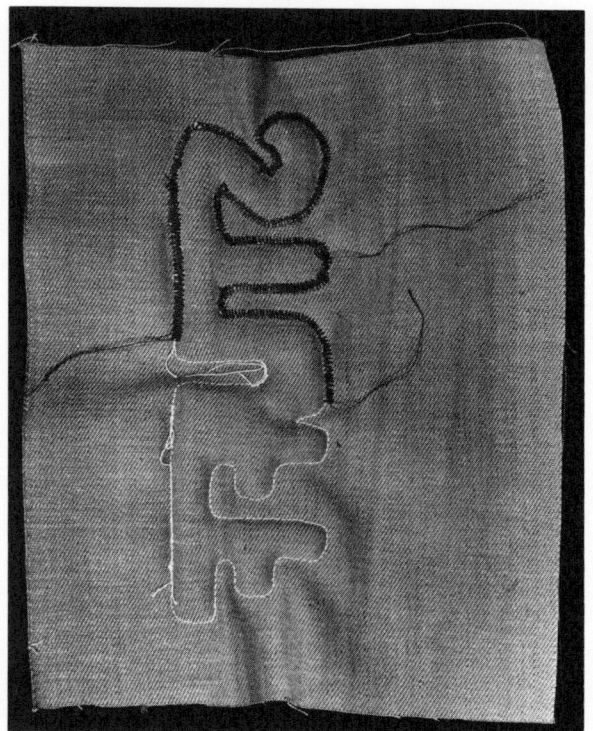

Fig. 60

50 The Complete Book of Stuffedwork

Seventeenth Century *Stumpwork Picture*
(9½" x 13½"). Silk and metal thread, purl, beads on
silk. The Metropolitan Museum of Art; bequest of
Carolyn L. Griggs, 1950.

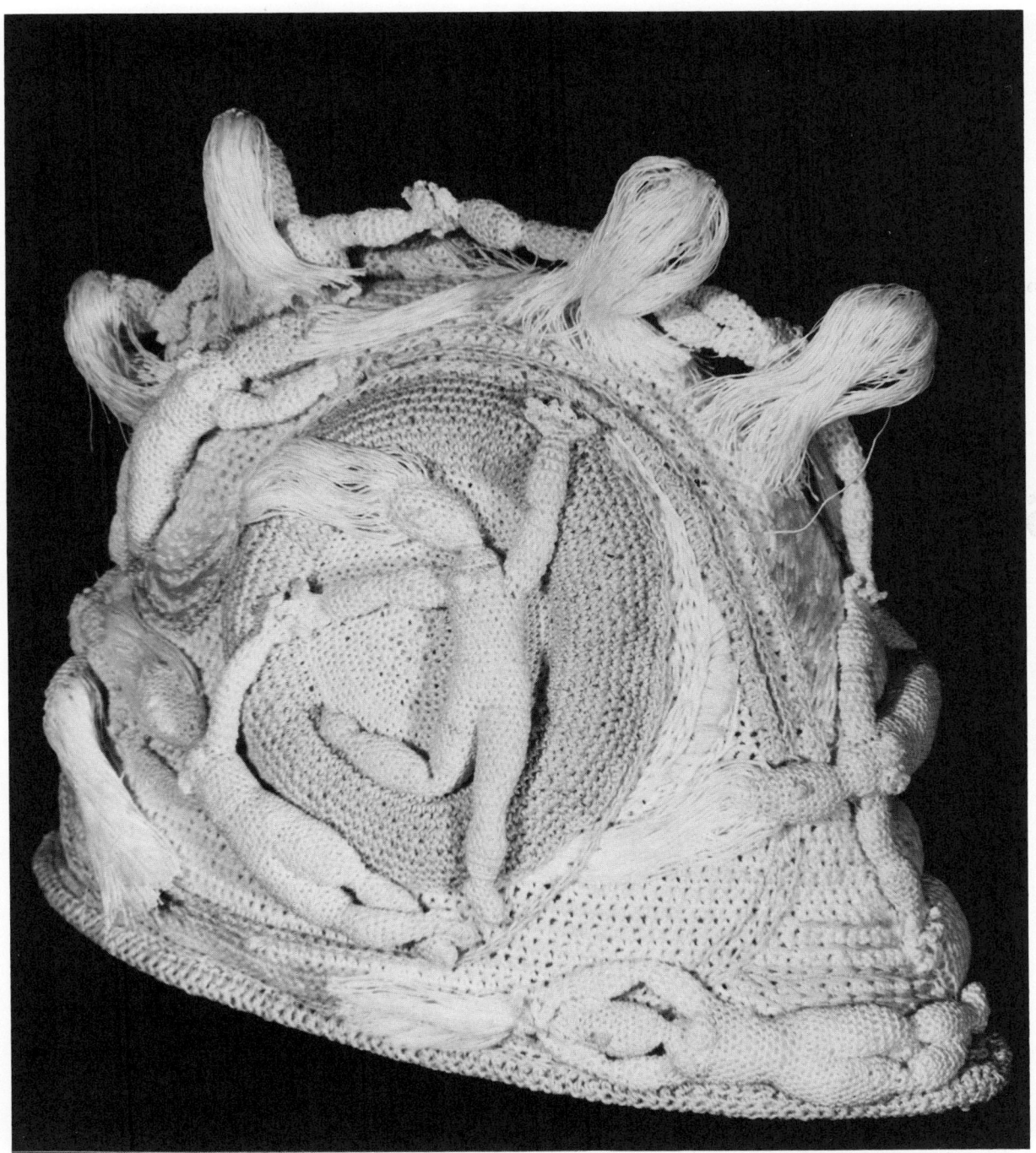

Norma Minkowitz *For Women Only* (10" x 13"), 1972. Stuffed knitted helmet form. Applied stuffed crocheted figures with hooked hair. Knitting is trapunto-quilted. Synthetic stuffing. Collection of Mrs. Kenneth Hall.

52 The Complete Book of Stuffedwork

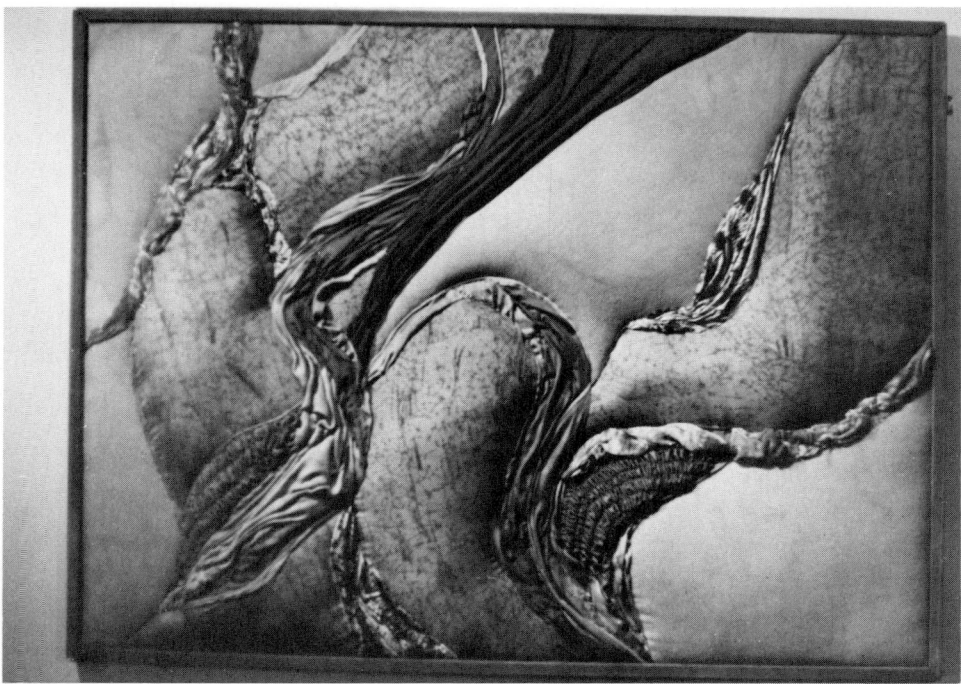

Bernice Colman *It Really Should be French*
(35" x 48"). Silk. Batik and tie dye, appliqué,
trapunto, and stitchery.

Amy Schupler *Dyed Hands* (18" x 20"). Watercolor;
cotton fabric, hand sewn with six-strand cotton;
polyester stuffing; stretcher frame.

Stuffed Appliqué 53

Amy Schupler *John Lennon and Yoko Ono*
(22" x 27"). Hand- and machine-sewn fabrics, stuffed appliqué, embroidery, yarn, wrapped cords, buttons, glasses, and stretcher frame.

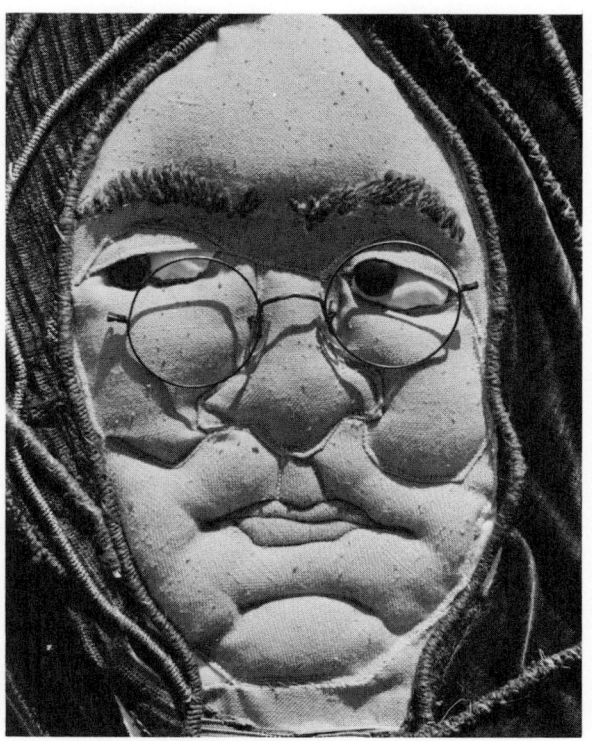

Detail of *John Lennon and Yoko Ono*

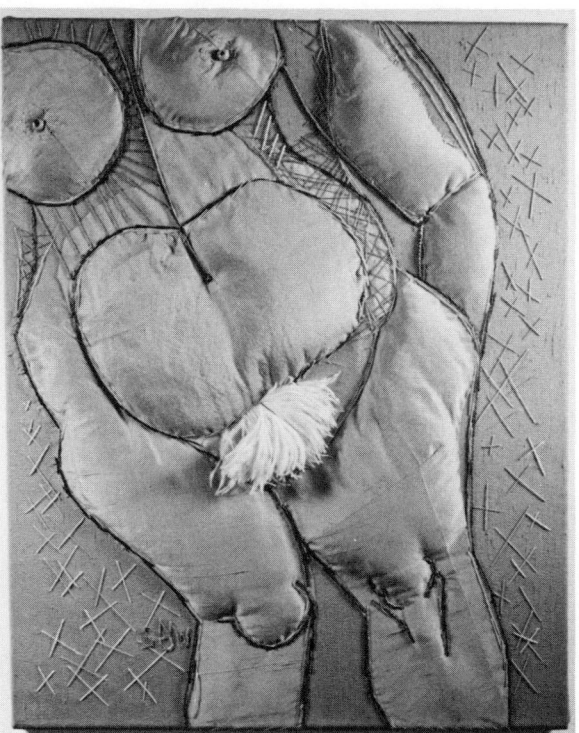

Lee Erlin Snow *La Plume de Ma Tante*.
Hot pink silks stuffed with old nylons.

Plate 4 STUFFED PLEATS AND CIRCLES

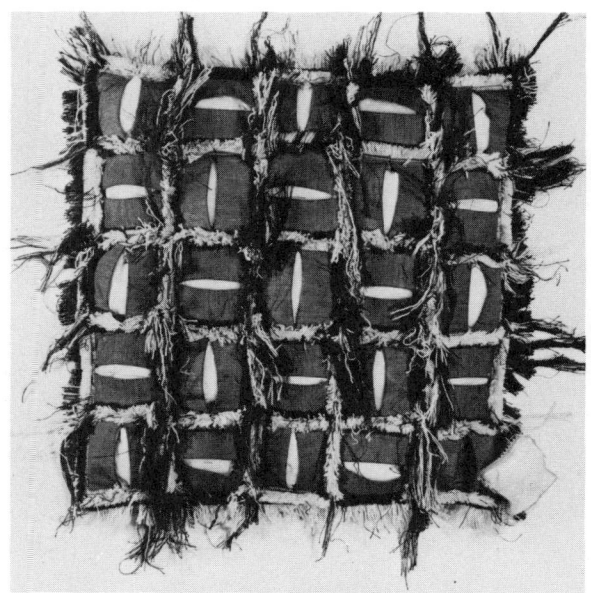

A. Denim pillow of pleated patches, joined with outside frayed seams. Plastic pillows (one is extracted) filled with synthetic stuffing are inserted into the pleats.

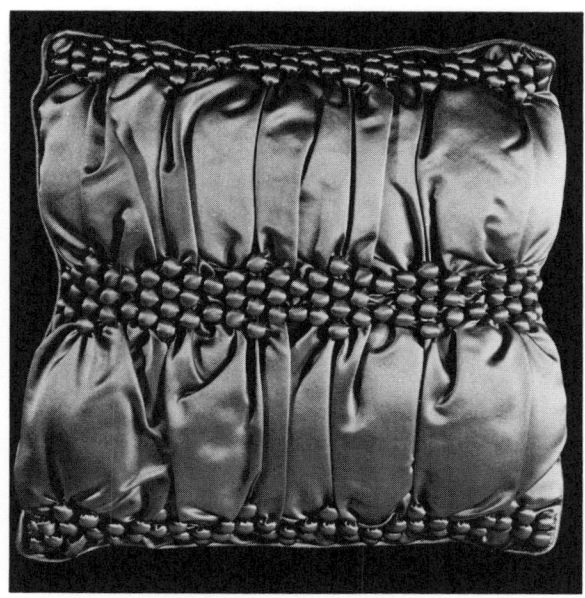

B. Satin pillow of stuffed smocking

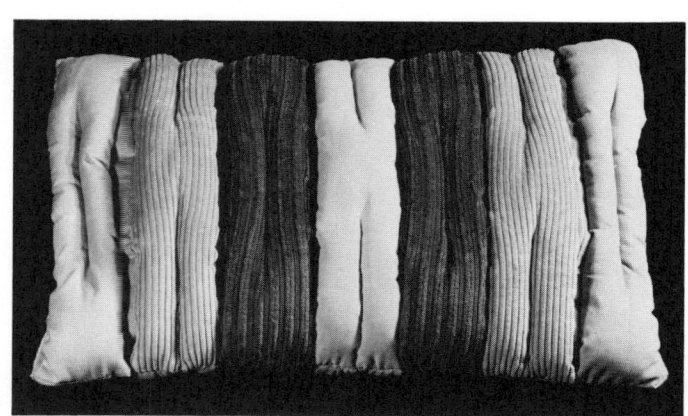

C. Corduroy pillow of stuffed pleats

D. Corduroy grape pincushion of stuffed smocking

Chapter Three
New Techniques

THE FOLLOWING techniques have the convenience of patchwork when it comes to constructing large surfaces. At the same time a high, stuffed surface — one much loftier than wadded quilting — emerges during the piecing. If the wrong side of the finished piece will be visible, as in a quilt, a piece of wider backing can be tied to the underside of the top at regular intervals and turned over the top edges to make a narrow binding. A soft preshrunk blanket can be tied between the top and the backing for additional warmth and softness.

Whether these methods are used strictly or freely, they will suggest new ways to make substantial and dramatic surfaces out of ordinary fabric.

The first three techniques are stuffed pleating, stuffed circles, and stuffed tubing and can each be made from a single piece of fabric. They can, of course, be pieced to introduce additional colors, or to extend the width of the fabric, but the structural results can be obtained without any seaming.

Stuffed pleats produce long pillowlike forms that can be broken by topstitching to vary the surface. The stuffed pleat stands away from the fabric that separates the pleats, creating deep shadows and secret spaces beneath the pleats.

Stuffed circles produce not only clusters of grapelike nodes, but also the soft, rippling surface that falls from them, as it does from traditional smocking. By working within cone-shaped outlines, even three dimensional forms can be assembled from only one piece of fabric, like the grape on Plate 4D. Consider these techniques in connection with the later section on three-dimensional forms (see Chapter 5), and other applications will occur to you.

The stuffed patchwork techniques open the way to unlimited color as well as deep, dappled surfaces. Combine them, alter them, play with them. You will enjoy using them.

STUFFED PLEATS

MARKING

When you mark a series of pleats on the fabric, allow no more than half the pleat width between

56 The Complete Book of Stuffedwork

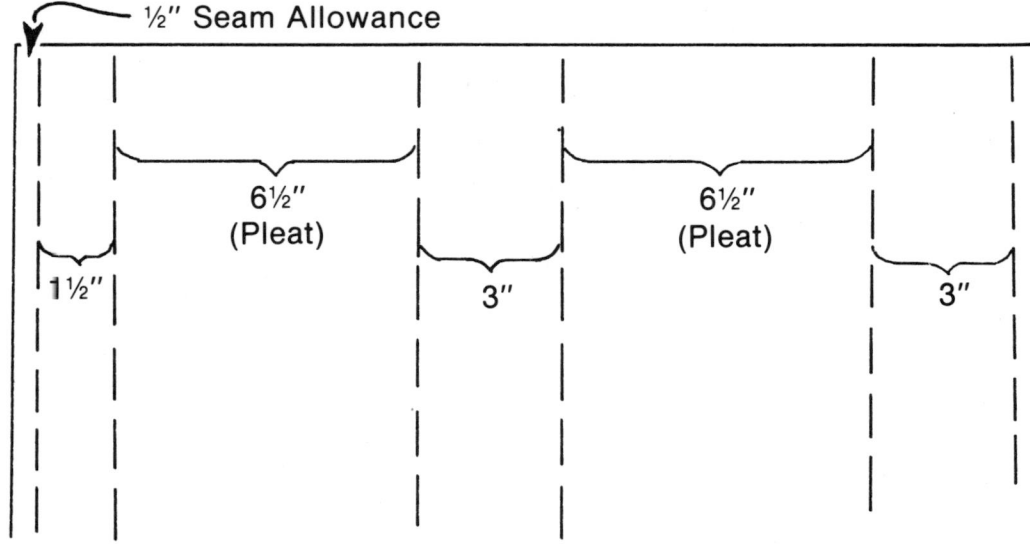

Fig. 61

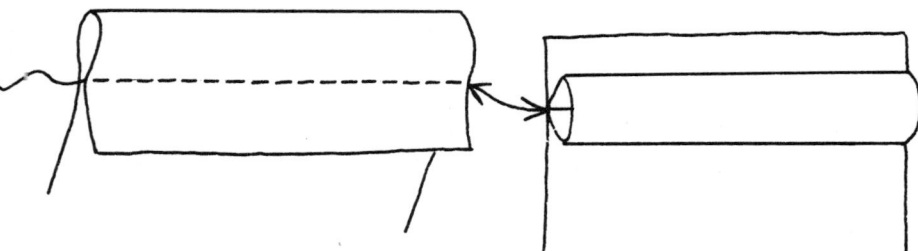

Fig. 62

each pleat. At each end, add about a quarter of the pleat width plus seam allowance (Fig. 61).

STITCHING

1. Stitch lengthwise, through a fold of fabric (wrong sides together). The pleat will lie with the stitching under the center, like a box pleat (Fig. 62). Rows of such tucks resemble cartridges (Fig. 63).
2. Topstitching along the center of a cartridge pleat will make a double channel (Fig. 64).
   When you stitch rows of alternating single and double channels, interesting patterns emerge (Fig. 65).
3. Or you can topstitch only part of the pleats (Fig. 66). In this case, alternate the topstitched portions, as these will spread less widely than the unstitched portions.

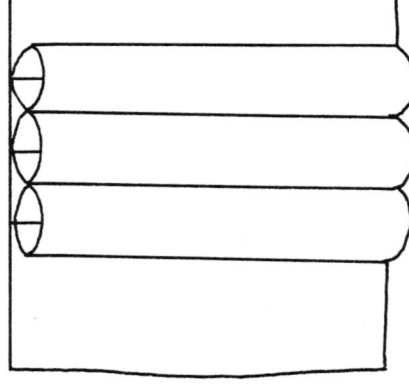

Fig. 63

New Techniques

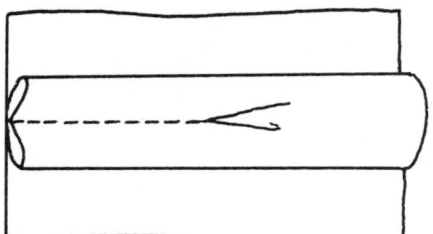

Fig. 64

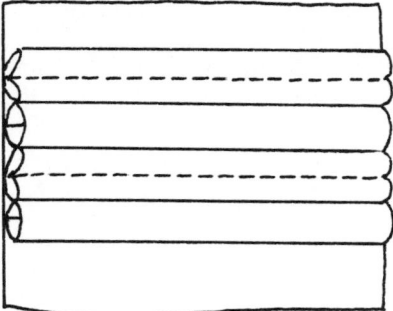

Fig. 65

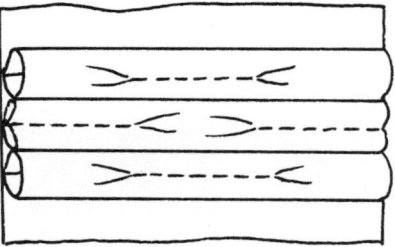

Fig. 66

STUFFING

Push synthetic stuffing into the ends of the channel with a knitting needle or similar, slender, rigid object. If the channel is too long to stuff from its ends, the stitching may be opened for an inch or two at intervals, then slipstitched to close it again after stuffing.

PIECING

Consecutive pleats in a single piece of fabric will, of course, produce a single-colored surface. Should you wish to add colors, make separate pleats, seam them together and proceed as if they were a single piece of fabric (Fig. 67).

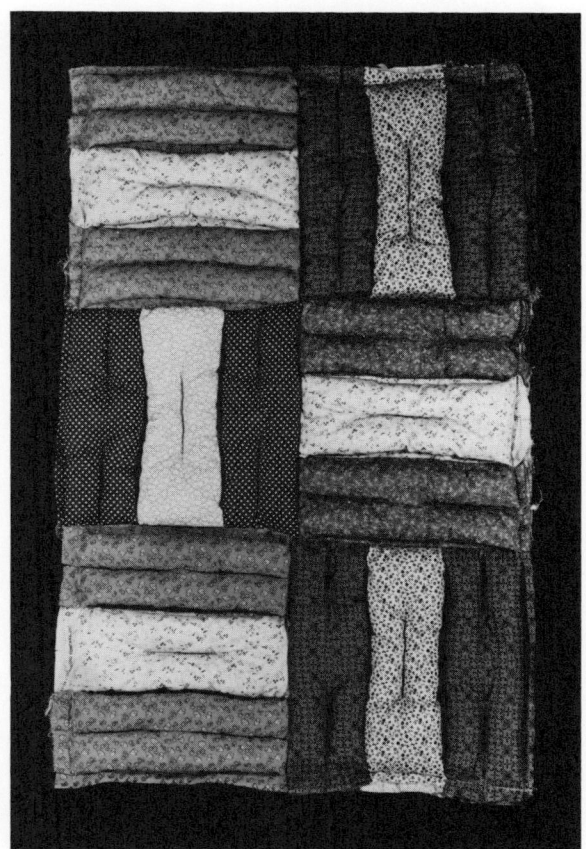

Fig. 67

58 The Complete Book of Stuffedwork

Fig. 68

Fig. 69

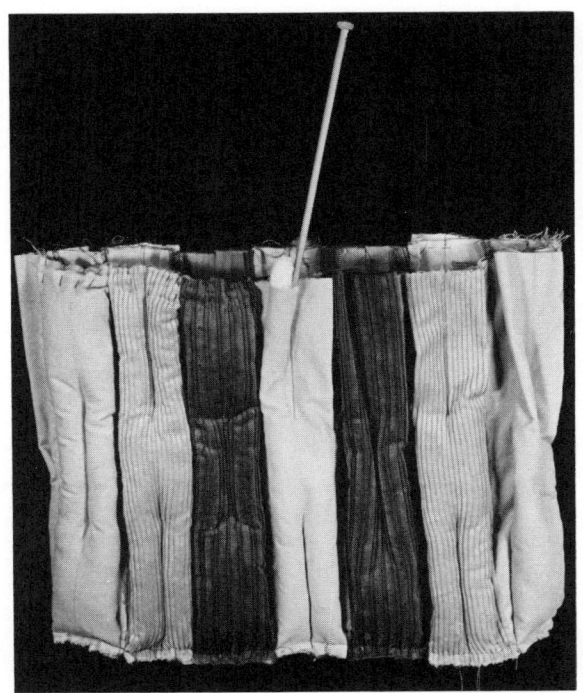

Fig. 70

DEMONSTRATION

The pillow on Plate 4C, is made with fourteen strips of corduroy, each 11½ inches wide and 17 inches long. Assemble it this way (½-inch seams are allowed):

1. Fold each strip in half lengthwise, wrong sides together. Stitch across the strip, 3½ inches from the fold (Fig. 68).
2. With naps going in the same direction, arrange the strips for the back and, beside these, the strips for the front. Pin and seam the strips together.
3. Insert three or four pins along each fold to mark the pleat center. Pin the center of the pleat to its stitching line, while spreading the fabric sideways to make a box pleat. Topstitch 5 inches in the center of an end pleat and 6 inches at each end of the next strip (Fig. 69). Continue, alternating the center with the end-stitching across the strips for the pillow back. Stitch the strips for the pillow front to match, starting with the center stitching.
4. Seam the ends to make a loop. Turn right side out. With a large knitting needle stuff each pleat, not too tightly, up to about an inch from each end (Fig. 70). Baste through the pleats about ⅜ inches from each end.
5. Matching colors and seamlines, turn in the bottom front seams over the back seams. Slipstitch. Slipstitch the top the same way, leaving an opening for stuffing. Stuff pillow and slipstitch the opening (Figs. 71 and 72).

STUFFED CIRCLES

Grapelike clusters of stuffed balls arise from circles of gathering stitches that have been drawn up around a piece of stuffing. The fabric used is about three times the size of the finished piece (Figs. 73 and 74).

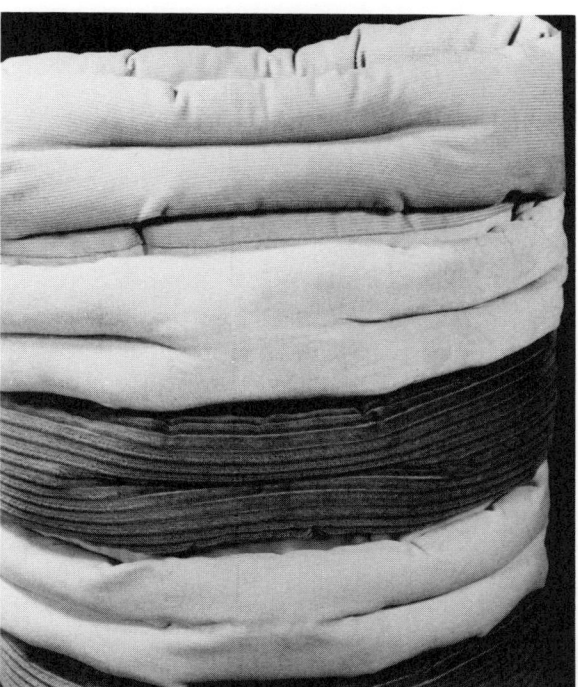

Fig. 71

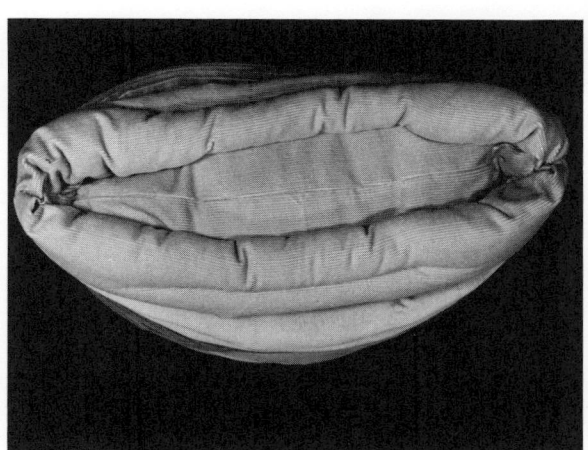

Fig. 72

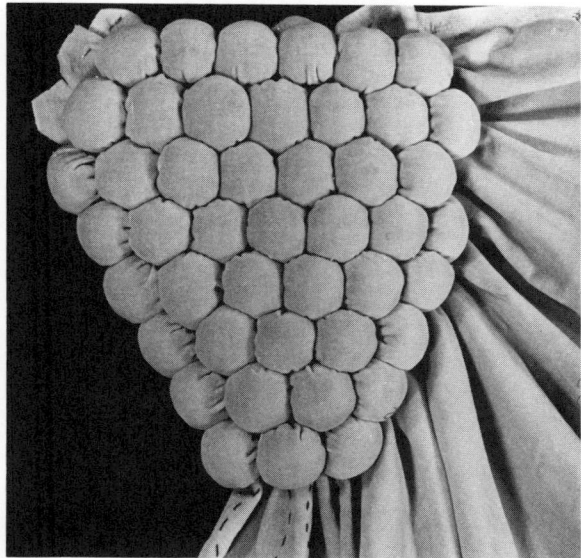

Fig. 73

Fig. 74

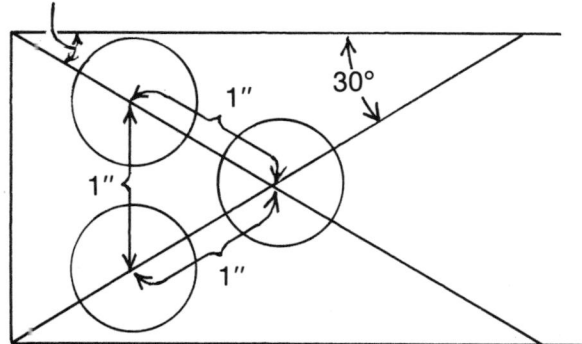

Fig. 75

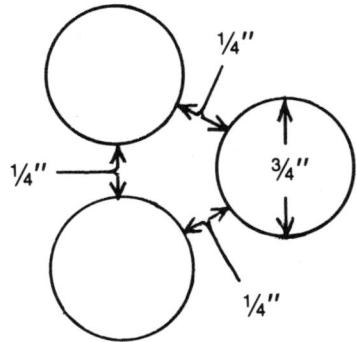

Fig. 76

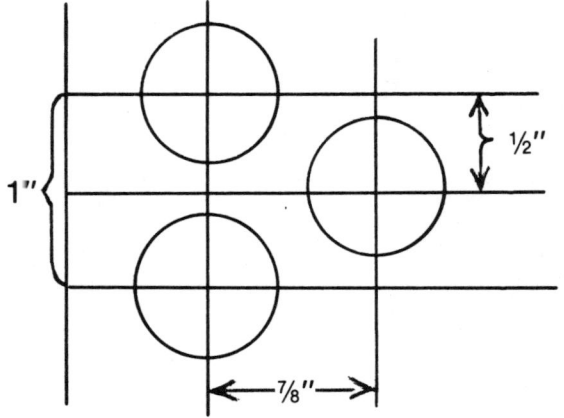

Fig. 77

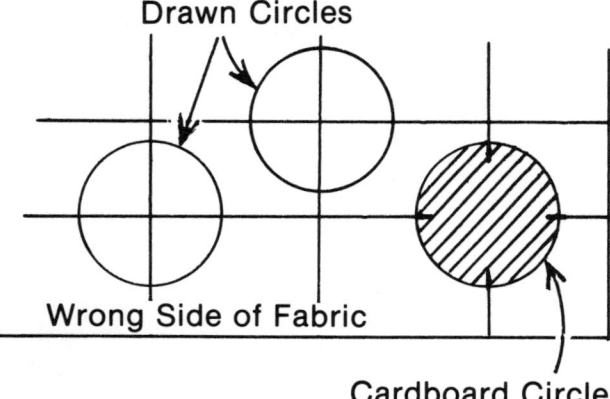

Fig. 78

DESIGN

In order to fill a space solidly, circles are drawn along intersecting diagonal rows that lie at 30 degree angles from one edge (Fig. 75).

The space between the circles is about ⅓ the diameter (Fig. 76). For three-dimensional forms, closer spacing is better — ¼ or ⅕ the diameter — since the spaces open up as the surface curves outward.

MARKING

Draw vertically and horizontally through the three centers of the distribution sample to find the grid pattern (Fig. 77).

Draw this grid across the wrong side of the fabric. With the point of a compass on the intersections, and the compass set to circle size, draw the cirles. Or cut a cardboard circle and mark the quarters at the edges. Then, matching the quartermarks to the grid lines, trace circles across the grid (Fig. 78).

SEWING

With button or carpet thread (the end need not be knotted) sew even running stitches about ¼ inches long over the drawn circle, starting and ending on the right side and leaving about 2 inches of thread at both the start and the finish of the stitching (Fig. 79).

STUFFING

With the left thumb, push a wad of synthetic stuffing against the wrong side of the circle

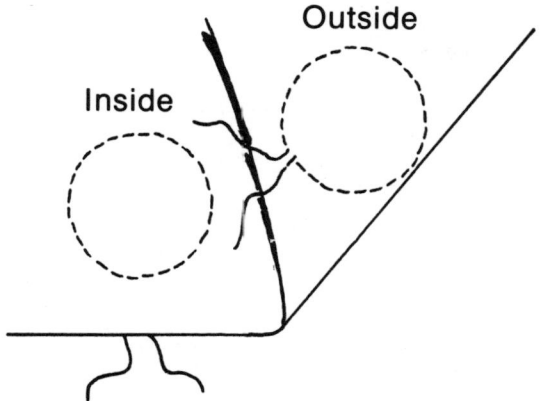

Fig. 79

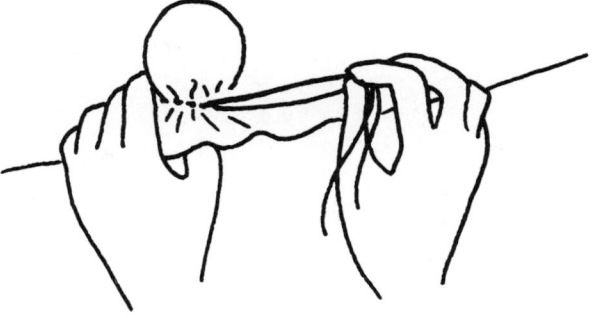

Fig. 80

while you begin to draw up the thread with the other hand (Fig. 80). When the circle is full, draw up the thread, interlace the ends and pull it closed (Fig. 81). Wrap the ends around the gathering and tie them in a square knot (Fig. 82). Trim the thread near the knot.

STUFFED SMOCKING

Continuous circles draw up fullness across the width of the fabric in the same way that smocking does. Below the circles, as below smocking stitches, the fabric is released in even gathers.

Consequently, if we omit regular segments of the overall circle pattern, gathers will take the place of the omitted circles. Matching stuffed borders that face each other, for instance, contrast strongly with the taut, controlled fullness between them, as in the silver pillow on Plate 4B.

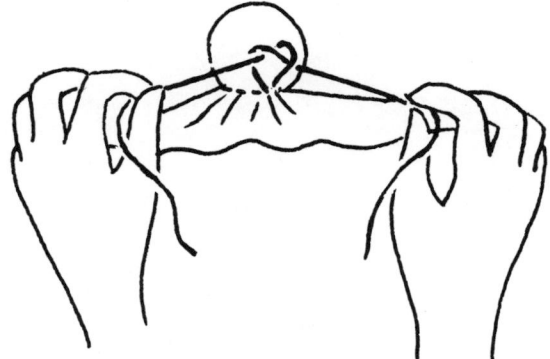

Fig. 81

Fig. 82

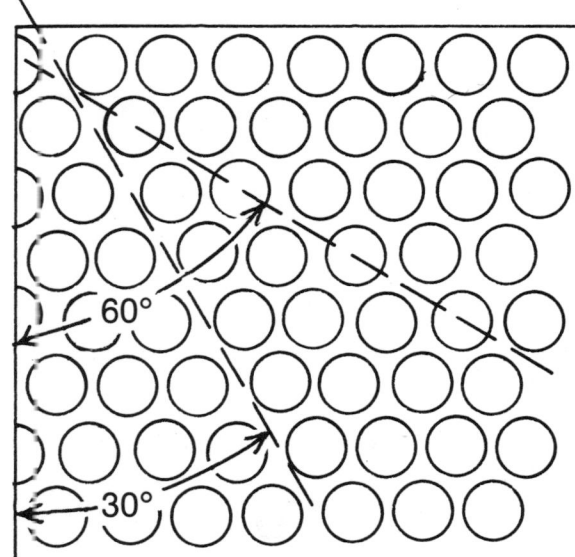

Fig. 83

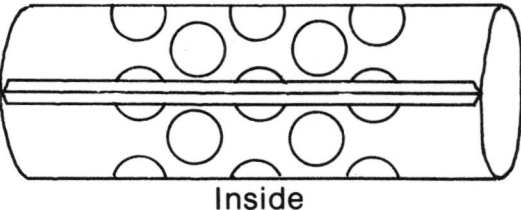

Fig. 84

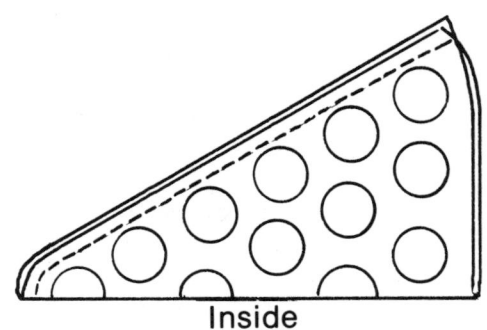

Fig. 85

ONE-PIECE SMOCKED FORMS

A surface prepared for stuffed smocking can be seamed so that a single piece of fabric makes a cone, a cylinder, or a globe.

1. The seamlines must bisect either the circles or the spaces between them to maintain a continuous field of smocking. Therefore, the seams will always lie on the horizontal or at 30, 60, or 90 degrees from it; that is, the seam will bisect all the circles, alternating circles, or the spaces between them (Fig. 83). Seam allowances are added outside such a seam, so each divided circle will complete another.
2. A cylinder, for example, is seamed through alternating circles (Fig. 84).
3. A narrow cone is seamed between the circles (Fig. 85).

DEMONSTRATION Grape Pincushion (Plate 4D)

1. Copy the circles for the stuffed grape by first ruling the grid in Figure 86b on the wrong side of the fabric. (To draw squared lines with a transparent ruler, see Fig. 157.) Then draw circles at each intersection.
2. Draw a seamline ¼ inch beyond the outside slanted rows of the triangles. Draw a cutting line ¼ inch outside the seamline and along the straight side edges. Draw another cutting line about 2 inches below the bottom edge.
3. Sew gathering stitches around all the complete circles.
4. Cut out on the cutting lines. Seam the side edges, matching the edges of the two half circles. Sew a gathering row around the seamed circle (Fig. 87).

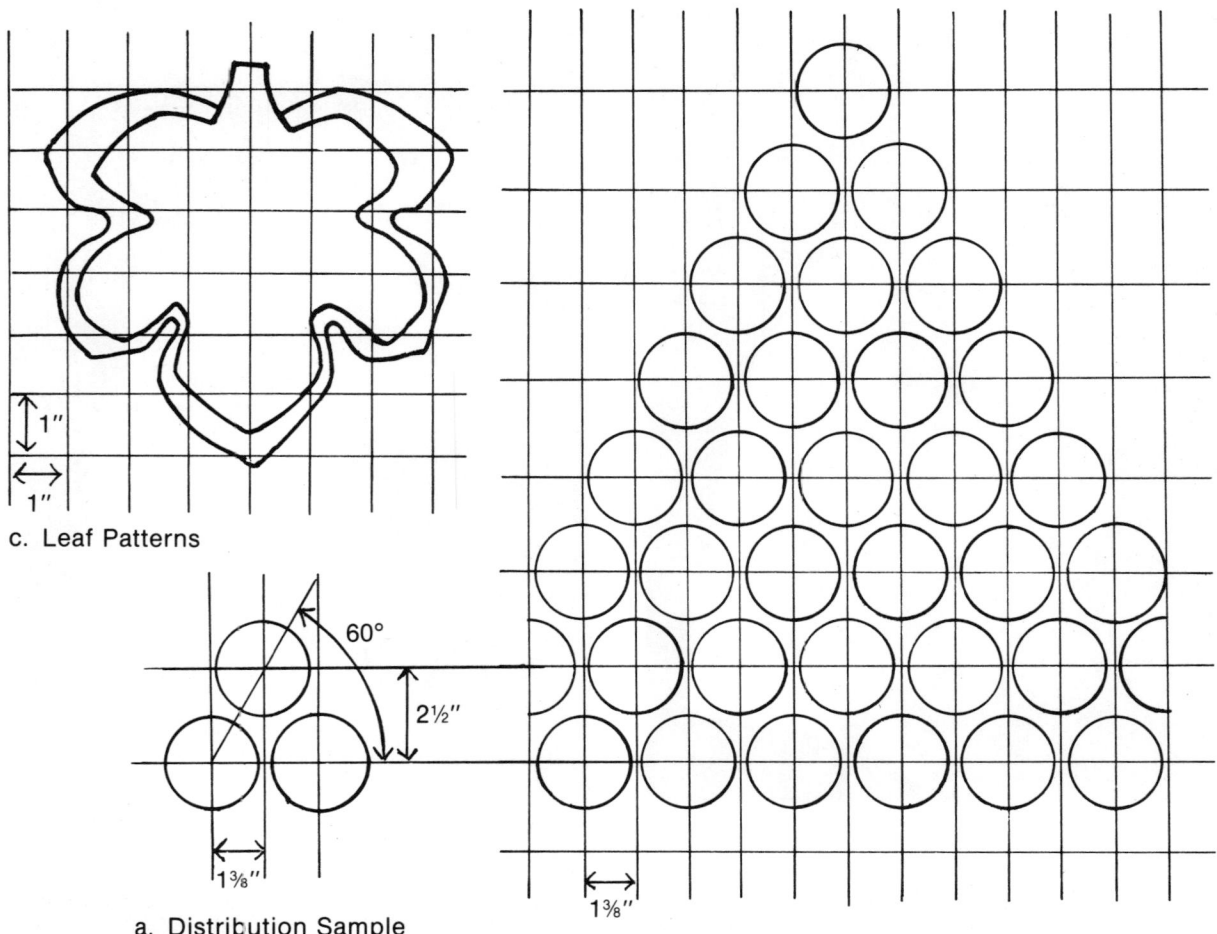

c. Leaf Patterns

a. Distribution Sample

b. Grape Circles

Fig. 86

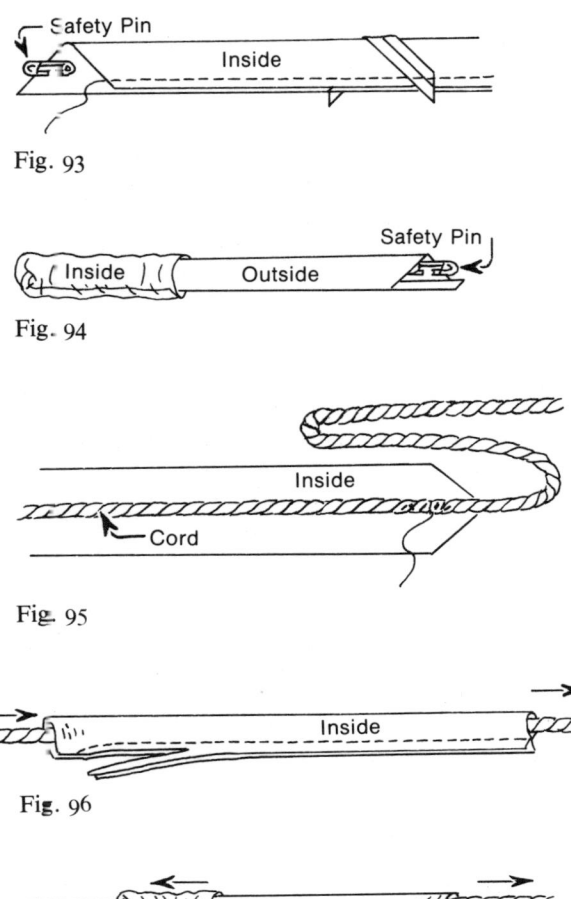

Fig. 93
Fig. 94
Fig. 95
Fig. 96
Fig. 97

clipping the thread when the stuffing is complete.

Note: For wider tubes, leave the tube seam open for an inch or so every 12 inches while you stitch. Turn it right side out. Stuff loose synthetic stuffing through an opening, slipstitch it closed, and go on to the next opening.

SIMULTANEOUS STUFFING

With narrow tubes (those with a finished diameter slightly larger than that of a filler or cable cord), the turning and stuffing can be accomplished at the same time.

1. Prepare the bias strip and trim one end to a point. Cut the cord twice the length of the strip. Stitch the center of the cord to the wrong side of the bias, sewing for about half an inch at the pointed end (Fig. 95).
2. Pull the cord forward about half an inch. Fold the bias around the cord, edges matching. With a zipper foot, stitch against the cord, tapering outward at the pointed end. Trim the seam to ⅛ inch (Fig. 96).
3. Work the bias back over the cord (Fig. 97).

STUFFED PATCHWORK

PILLOWS

When the top patch and the facing are the same size, they become, after seaming and stuffing, a little pillow. Quilts are occasionally constructed in this way. The procedure is as follows:

1. Seam the top patch to the facing, right sides together, leaving a small opening at one side for stuffing.
2. Turn the patch right side out. Stuff it and slipstitch to close the opening.
3. Continue stuffing all the patches. Join them by overcasting the adjoining edges.

DARTED PILLOWS

A rich, undulating surface comes from darting the pillow patch before stuffing it. This, of course, alters the length of one side and the

TUBING

1. Fold the prepared bias lengthwise, right sides together. Stitch ½ inch from the raw edges.
2. Turn the tubing right side out. Pin a safety pin through a single layer of fabric at one end (Fig. 93); then push the pin through the tube until it emerges (Fig. 94). Remove the pin.
3. Some materials can be carried through tubing by thread, in a blunt needle, fastened to the filler. Pushing the needle through drags the filler with it. For example, cut a piece of batting that will roll up to fit the tube. Roll it and cover it with thin muslin, edgestitched. Run strong thread through a blunt needle and knot the two ends. Sew firmly through the filler. Push the needle through the tubing,

New Techniques 67

Fig. 98

Fig. 99

shape of the patch. Alternating the direction of the adjacent patches tends to even out the overall dimensions. Two of the final edges of the whole piece will be straight, two will be zigzagged (Fig. 98).

Inside Seams: The patches may be whipstitched together by hand, as were the undarted pillows above. (A whipstitch is a slipstitch [Fig. 28] worked over two facing, rather than lapped, fabrics.) It is even possible to use a sewing machine to seam very narrowly the closed edges, taking up only about 1/16 inch. This was done in the fragment shown in Figure 99, where the patches were made as follows:

1. Cut tops and facings, each 7 inches × 10 inches (¼-inch seams allowed).
2. Seam top to facing, right sides together, leaving an opening at the end opposite the dart (Fig. 100).
3. Turn patch right side out. Fold it lengthwise, right sides together. Measure 1 inch down from the fold and 5 inches across the fold. Draw a line connecting these two points. Stitch along the line to make a dart (Fig. 101).

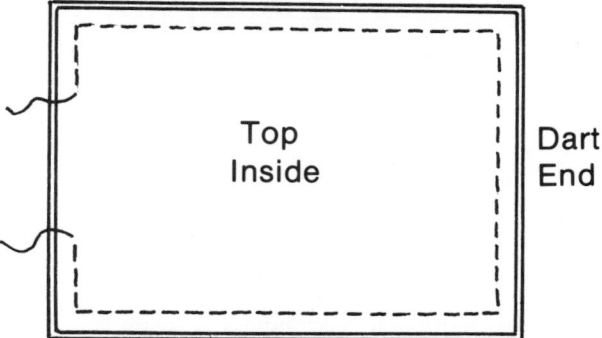

Fig. 100

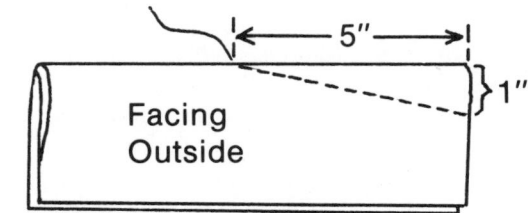

Fig. 101

68   The Complete Book of Stuffedwork

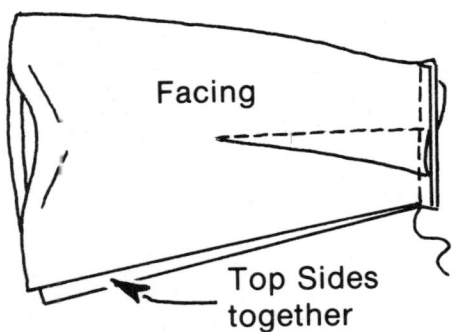

Fig. 102

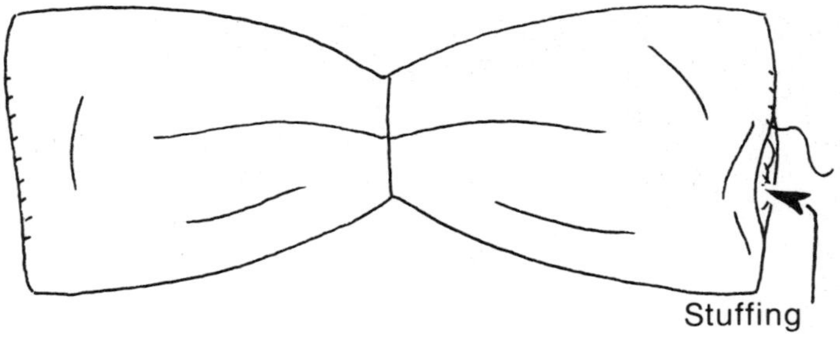

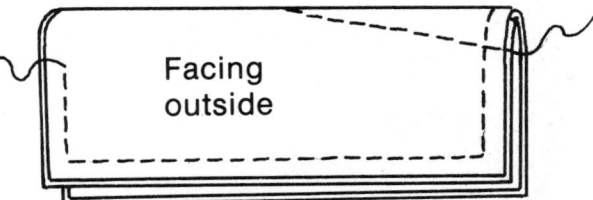

Fig. 103

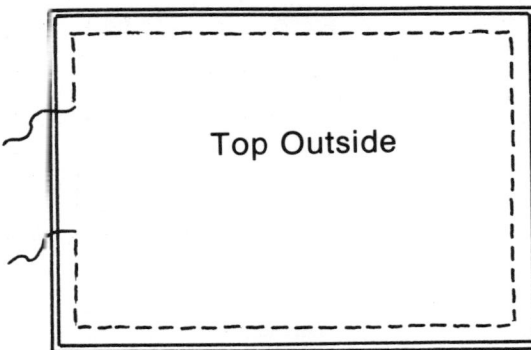

Fig 104

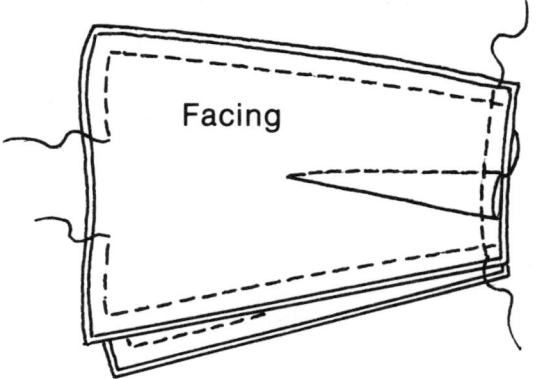

Fig. 105

Fig. 106

4. Pin two adjoining patches together at the darted ends, pressing the darts in opposite directions. Stitch a very narrow seam (Fig. 102).
5. Stuff the two patches and slipstitch to close them (Fig. 103). Continue joining patches across the row, matching similar ends.
6. Join rows with the same narrow seams, matching the wide patch ends of one row to the narrow patch ends of the adjoining row.

Outside Seams: Making the patch with outside instead of inside seams offers still another alternative. This is very quickly assembled and perfectly satisfactory when the wrong sides are concealed. The raw seam edges are visible, but barely so, since they are tucked between stuffing.

1. Using ½-inch outside seams, sew top to facing, wrong sides together, leaving an opening at the end opposite the dart (Fig. 104).
2. Fold the patch lengthwise, top right sides together. Stitch the dart (Fig. 105).
3. Stitch two adjoining patches right sides together at the darted ends, pressing the darts in opposite directions (Fig. 106).
4. Stuff the two patches. The openings can be closed at the same time that you join the next patches.

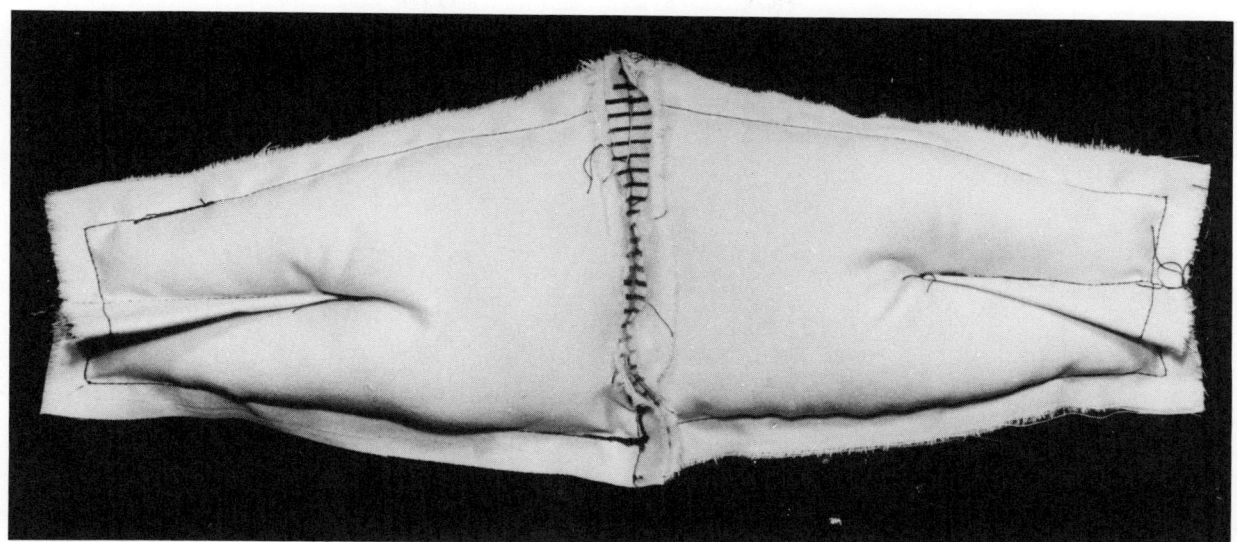

Fig. 107

DEMONSTRATION Darted Pillow Patch Tea Cozy (Plate 5C)
1. Cut twelve tops and twelve facings, each 6 inches × 9 inches.
2. Stitch each top to a facing, wrong sides together, leaving open what will be the undarted end. Fold in half lengthwise, right sides together. Mark a dart along the fold 1 inch deep and 3 inches long. Stitch dart.
3. Stitch two patches together at the darted ends, turning the darts in opposite directions.
4. Stuff the four remaining patches and stitch them together in two pairs, seaming the undarted ends (Fig. 107).
5. Seam three pairs together along the long edges (Fig. 108) for the front.
6. Stuff the middle pair of patches from each end.
7. Repeat steps 3 through 5 to make the back.
8. For the tab, cut a strip 3½ inch × 7 inches. Fold it in half, right sides together. Stitch the long edge and turn the tab right side out. Sew an end at each side of the center seam at the top of the front, with raw ends in the seam allowance (Fig. 109).
9. Pin the front over the back and stitch, right sides together, at the top and sides.
10. At the bottom, turn in the raw edge to make a narrow hem. Slipstitch.

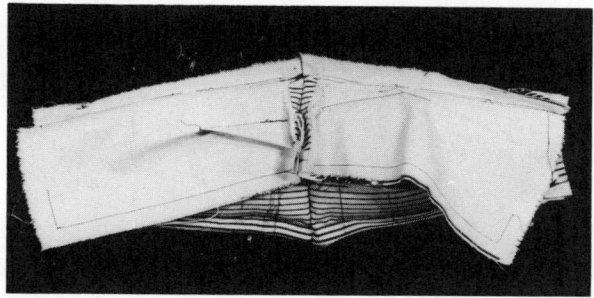

Fig. 108

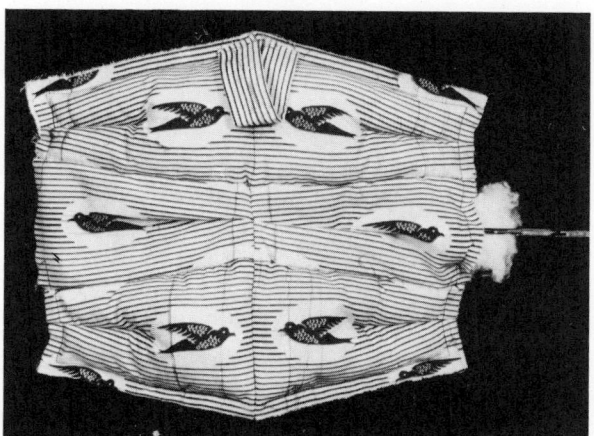

Fig. 109

Plate 5 STUFFED PATCHWORK

A. Footstool of stuffed biscuits

B. Bowl of stuffed biscuits

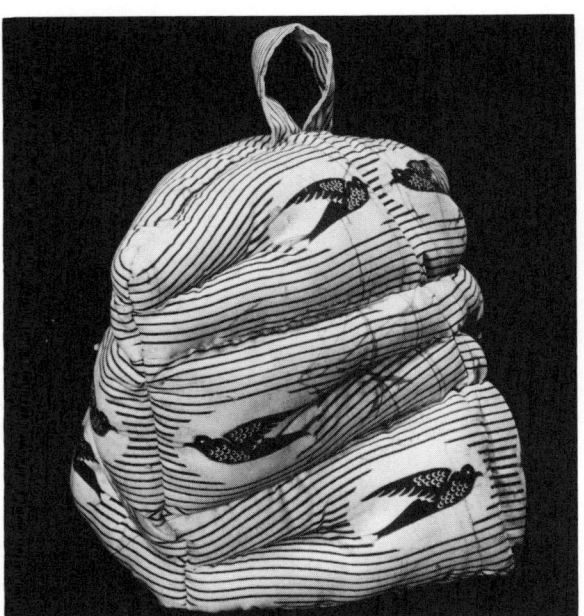

C. Tea Cozy of stuffed darted pillows

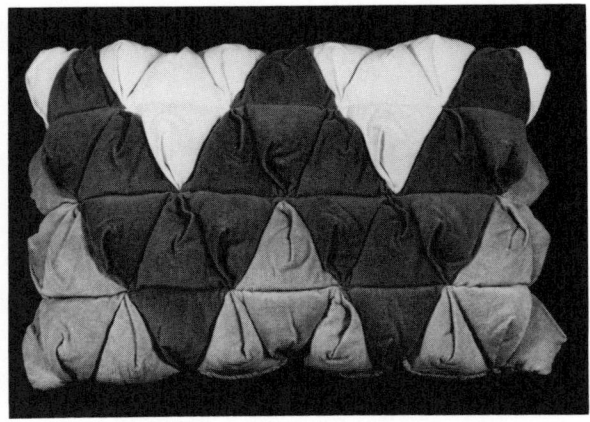

D. Velveteen pillow of stuffed triangles

E. Pillow of stuffed biscuits

F. Handbag of stuffed, darted pillows.

BISCUITS (Plate 5E)

A very high loft can be attained by cutting the top patch the same square shape as its facing but of a larger size. The top is then made to fit the facing by pleating in the excess fabric. This forms a seamless boxing, so that the patch appears to have sides.

Sometimes this technique is called biscuit quilting, because a stretch of it really looks like a pan of biscuits. The greater the difference between the top and the bottom, the higher the patch will rise. Half the difference in the widths of the squares, in fact, represents the height of the biscuit. Consequently, for quilts, the difference should be small, in order to avoid excessive weight.

For deep biscuits a box pleat is taken, as follows:

1. With right sides out, match and pin the corners of the top to the corners of the facing at one edge (Fig. 110).
2. Match and pin the centers. Centers can be marked in advance, but an eye judgment is accurate enough since the pleats, except at the perimeter of the finished object, are hidden (Fig. 111).
3. At each side of the center, take up the extra fabric in a fold, bringing the fold to meet the center pin (Fig. 112).
4. Repeat at the other three edges. Stitch ½-inch seams (Fig. 113).
   Note: For shallow biscuits, the box pleat is replaced by a knife pleat (Fig. 114).
5. Stitch the patches together to complete the whole surface.
6. Slit the facings only and stuff the patches with synthetic stuffing through these slits.

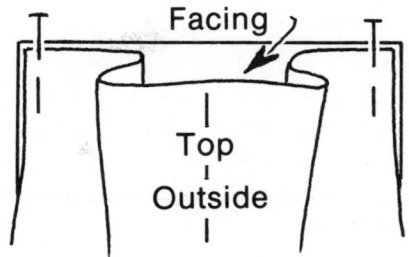

Fig. 110

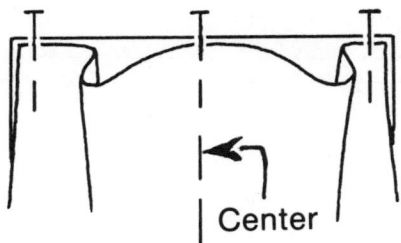

Fig. 111

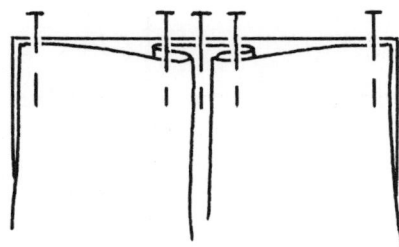

Fig. 112

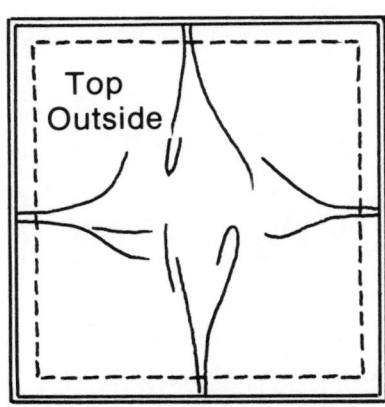

Fig. 113

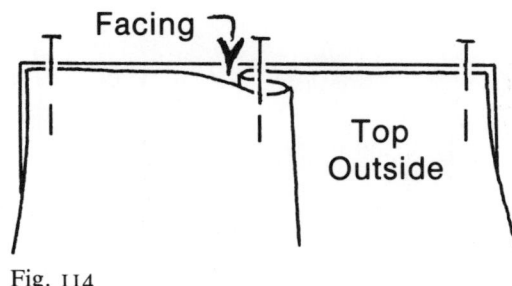

Fig. 114

QUICK BISCUIT ASSEMBLY

If the whole piece is one fabric, biscuits can be made by the following faster method, particularly suitable for the sewing machine. A patchwork piece can also be worked this way, simply by seaming the top patches to form one piece before starting to pleat.

1. Mark the fabric, leaving enough for a seam allowance at each outside edge. Between the seam allowances, draw matching "top patches" *without seam allowances*, side by side. (If the top consists of seamed patches, this step is not necessary, as the seams themselves provide the marks.) On the drawn (or seamed) line marking the edge of each "patch," mark the center between two fold lines for the pleats (Fig. 115).

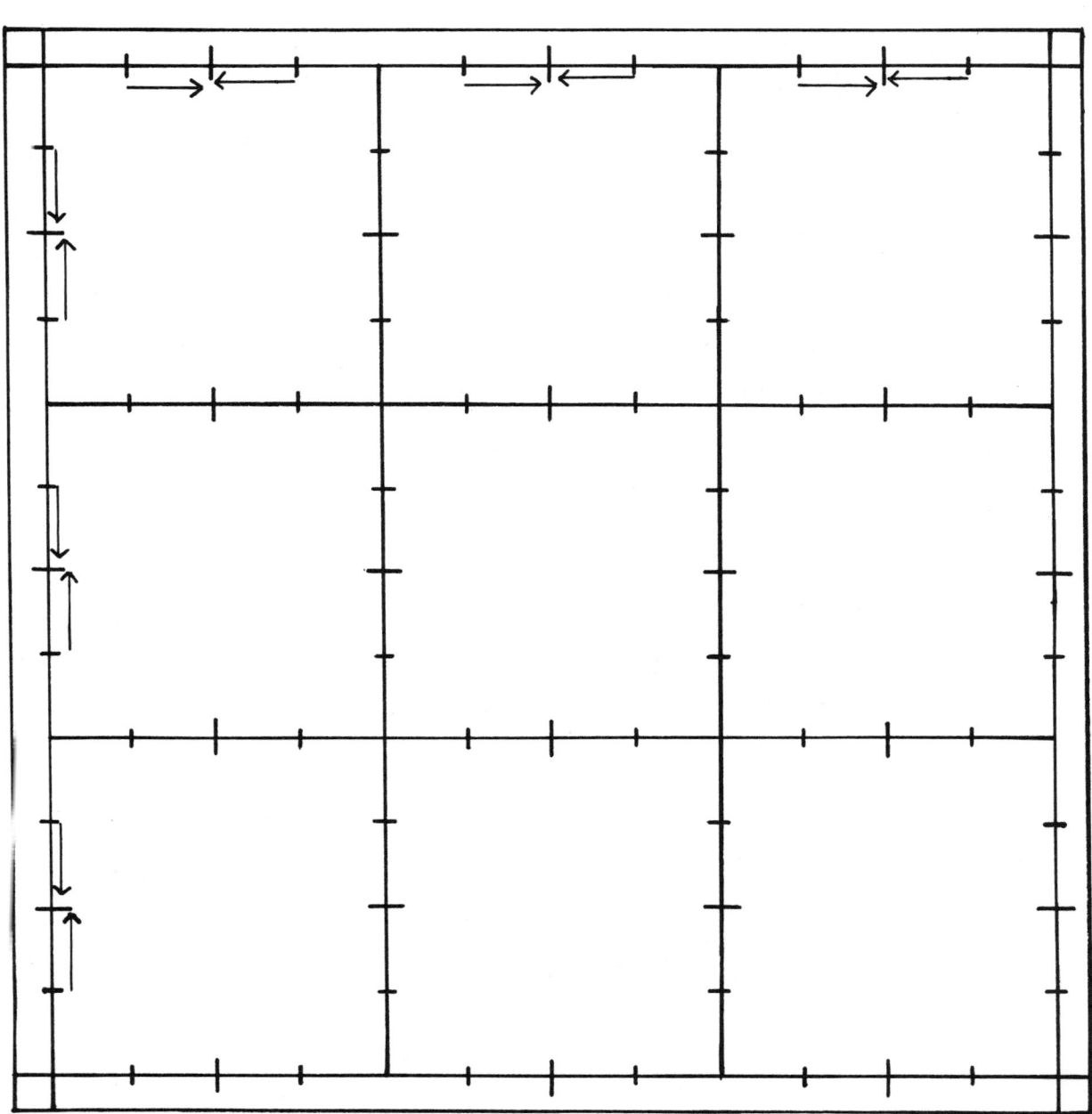

Fig. 115

New Techniques 73

Fig. 116

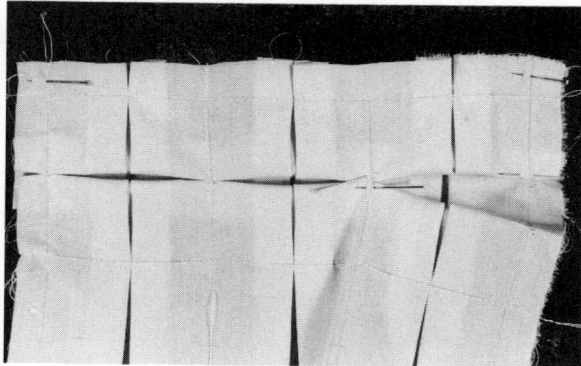

Fig. 117

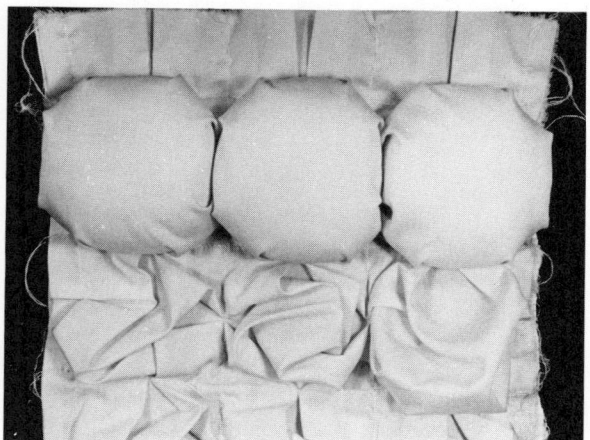

Fig. 118

2. Pin inverted pleats up and down the fabric, bringing pleatmarks to match the centers. Stitch across all the pleats on the drawn horizontal lines (Fig. 116).
3. Pin inverted pleats from side to side across the fabric. Stitch on the drawn vertical lines (Fig. 117).
4. Pin the pleated and stitched top fabric to a piece of muslin the same size. With right sides out and raw edges matching, stitch over the previous stitching through both layers.
5. Slit the backing for about an inch in the center of each biscuit. Stuff (Fig. 118). Sew across the slits or iron a small piece of iron-on fabric over the opening (Fig. 119).

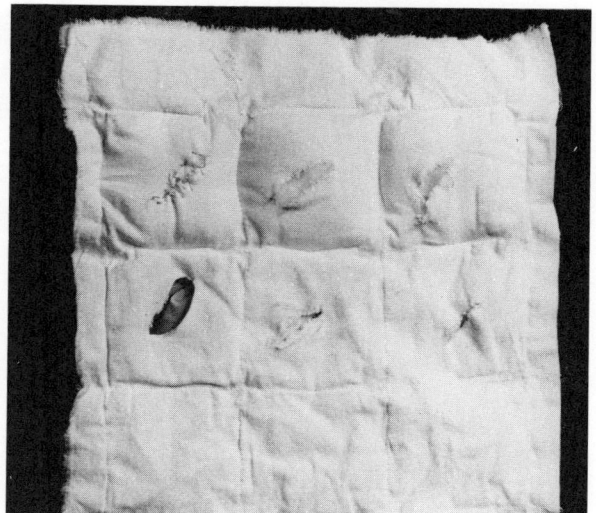

Fig. 119

74 The Complete Book of Stuffedwork

Fig. 120

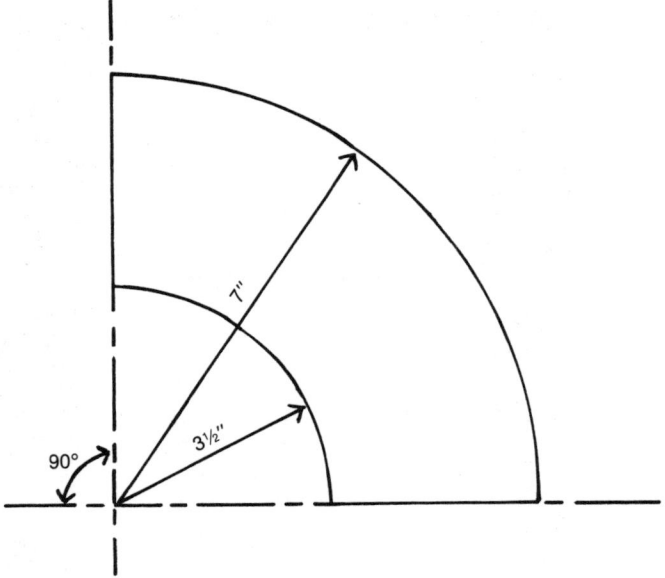

Fig. 121

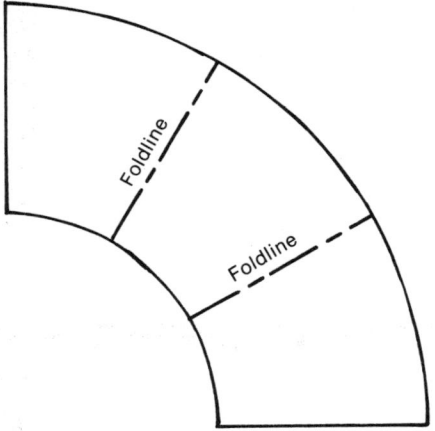

Fig. 122

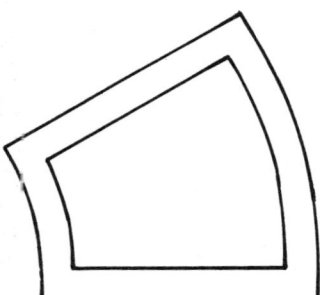

Fig. 123

DEMONSTRATION Tapered Facing — Wreath Biscuit patches may be tapered so that they will form a curve when they are joined (Fig. 120). The patches that make this wreath are pleated to wedge-shaped muslin facings, twelve of which complete a circle. The top patches are 7-inch squares.

1. Make the facing pattern as follows: draw a horizontal baseline and a perpendicular sideline. Between them, with a compass set at a 3½-inch radius, draw a quarter circle. Draw another quarter circle with a 7-inch radius from the same center outside the first one. Thus there will be 3½ inches between the circles (Fig. 121).

   Cut out on the drawn lines, including the inner circle. Turning the straight edges inward with curved edges matching, fold the quarter in three equal parts so that each straight edge meets a crease. Unfold (Fig. 122).

   Cut away one part (1/12 of the ring), trace it to a piece of thin cardboard and add ½-inch seam allowance on each edge to make the cutting pattern (Fig. 123) for the facing.

2. Seam the tops to the facings the same as you did for untapered biscuits (see Biscuits). When you pleat, you will have a very deep pleat on the inside edge and a very shallow

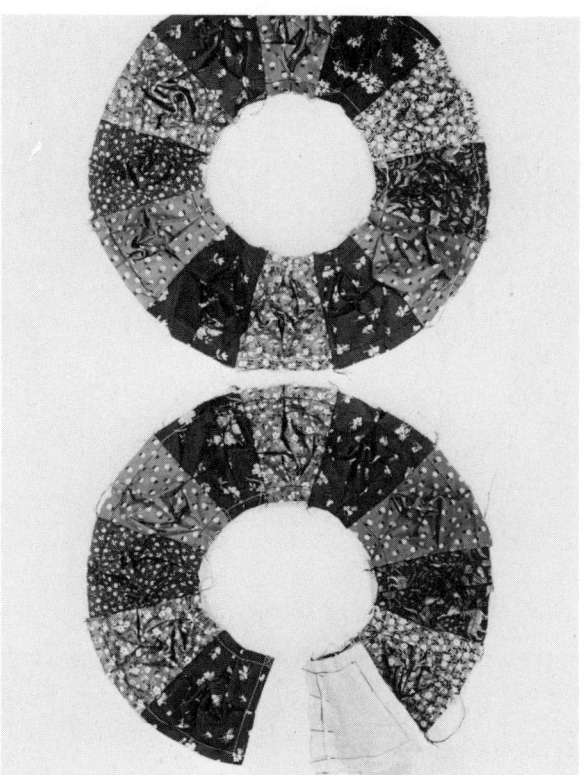

Fig. 124

Fig. 125

Fig. 126

Fig. 127

one on the outside. Stuffed, the ring will be higher in the center than at the outer edge.

3. The wreath back is the same as the front. Cut another patch in matching fabric for each of the twelve back patches and also provide twelve muslin facing pieces.

4. Arrange twelve faced patches in a ring. Seam them together along the straight edges. Repeat for the back, with colors in the same order. Press the seams open (Fig. 124).

5. Pin one ring over the other, right sides together, matching seams and colors. Stitch front to back on the outside seamline (Fig. 125). Cut a slit in each facing.

6. Turn the wreath right side out. Stuff the front patches, pushing the filling well into the corners. Stuff the back, allowing the wrong sides of the rings to come together (Fig. 126).

7. Add a little stuffing between the muslin layers. Turn in the inside edge of each ring on the seamline, pin them together matching seams and slipstitch (Fig. 127).

DEMONSTRATION Mixed Biscuits — Bowl

The bowl in Plate 5B is made from three rows of patches and a bottom. The top and bottom rows are the same as those in the wreath; between these wedge-shaped patches is a row of rectangular patches. The bottom is a flat quilted circle. Half-inch seams are allowed.

1. Cut twenty-four muslin facing wedges and the same number of 7½-inch squares in the top fabric. Pleat and seam these to make two rings of twelve faced patches each, in the same way as for the wreath.
2. Cut twelve facing rectangles, each 4 inches × 5 inches from muslin. Cut twelve top fabric rectangles, each 6½ inches × 7½ inches. Pleat these to make biscuits and seam the short ends together to make the center ring.
3. Seam the top, middle, and bottom rings, matching the seams.
4. Cut 10-inch diameter bottoms: one from the top fabric, one from nonwoven interfacing, and two from batting. Baste the fabric bottom over the batting on the interfacing. Machine stitch across the bottom in rows about 1 inch apart and around the seamline. Trim the batting to the seamline. Fold the bottom to mark the quarters. Pin it to the lower ring, right sides together, matching edges and quartermarks. Baste and stitch.
5. Slit the muslin facings (Fig. 128) and stuff the patches with synthetic stuffing.
6. Lining: Cut a bottom circle of 17-inch diameter. Cut a 4-inch-wide side strip pieced to make a strip 50 inches long. Cut the top ring 17 inches in diameter, removing an 8-inch diameter center, leaving a 4½-inch wide ring.

    Fold each lining section in half and fold again, to mark quarters on both edges. Match and pin bottom to side at the quartermarks. Pin in between and baste ½ inch from the edge, holding in the curved edge and clipping the straight edge. Stitch. Match, pin, baste, clip, and stitch the side to the top in the same way. Staystitch the seamline at the top edge of the lining. Clip to the stitching (Fig. 129).

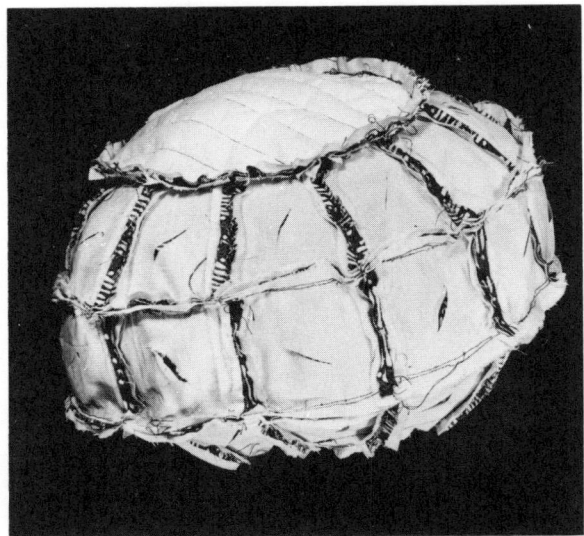

Fig. 128

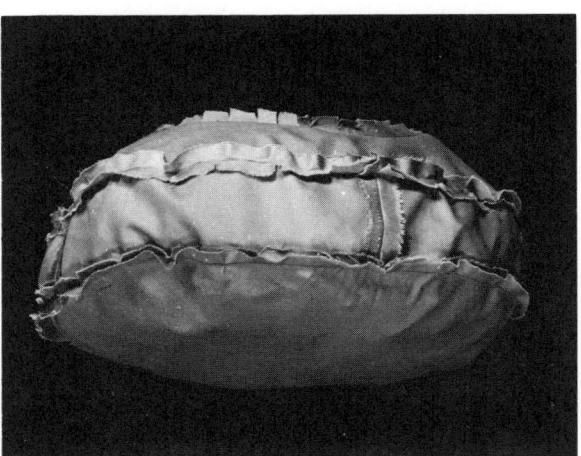

Fig. 129

7. Turn under the lining on the staystitching and pin the fold to the seamline at the top of the bowl. Slipstitch.

    Note: If you closed the open face of the bowl with another circle like the bottom, the piece could be stuffed to make a large footstool or floor cushion (see Plate 5A).

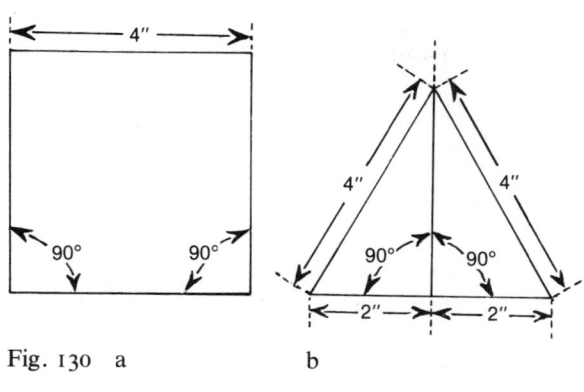
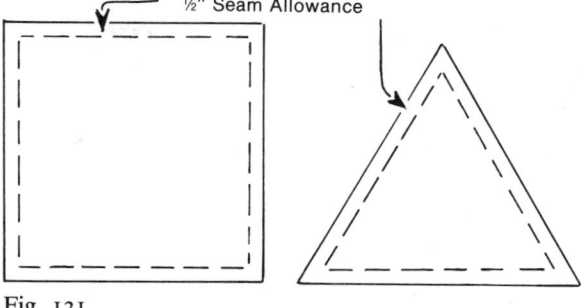

Fig. 130 a b   Fig. 131

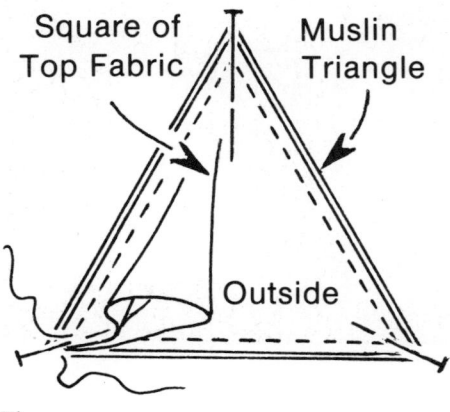
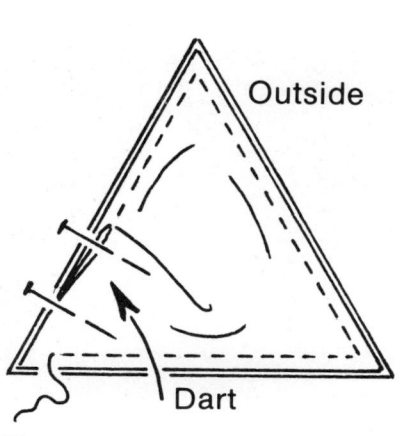

Fig. 132   Fig. 133

STUFFED TRIANGLES (Plate 5D)

To give height to a triangle, we can make the top patch a square whose edges are the same length as those of the triangular facing. The extra top edge will form a pleat and give height to the patch.

Draw a square and a triangle that have sides of the same length. Use a transparent ruler, calibrated both ways, or a drafting triangle, to square the sides of the square and to draw the center line of the triangle (Fig. 130). Add seam allowances (Fig. 131).

1. Cut squares of top fabric and triangles of facing fabric.
2. Place a square over a triangle, wrong sides together, pinning at each corner. Stitch three sides (Fig. 132).
3. Stuff through the opening made by the extra side. Lap the pleat over an adjoining side, matching edges and pin (Fig. 133). Stitch on the seamline.

Notice that the pleat can be lapped either to the left or to the right. When the patches are joined, the pleat directions contribute to the pattern, so decide the direction before you join the patches.

4. Continue, cutting and facing all the patches.
5. Row assembly: Pin the unpleated sides of two patches (facing opposite directions), right sides together, matching seam crossings. Stitch. Continue to make a row (Fig. 134).
6. Pin two rows, right sides together, matching the seam crossings (Fig. 135). Continue to make the whole piece.

78 The Complete Book of Stuffedwork

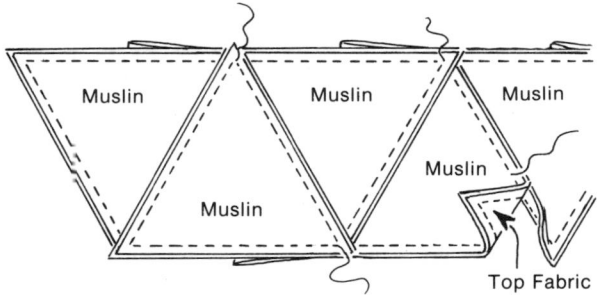

Fig. 134   Fig. 135

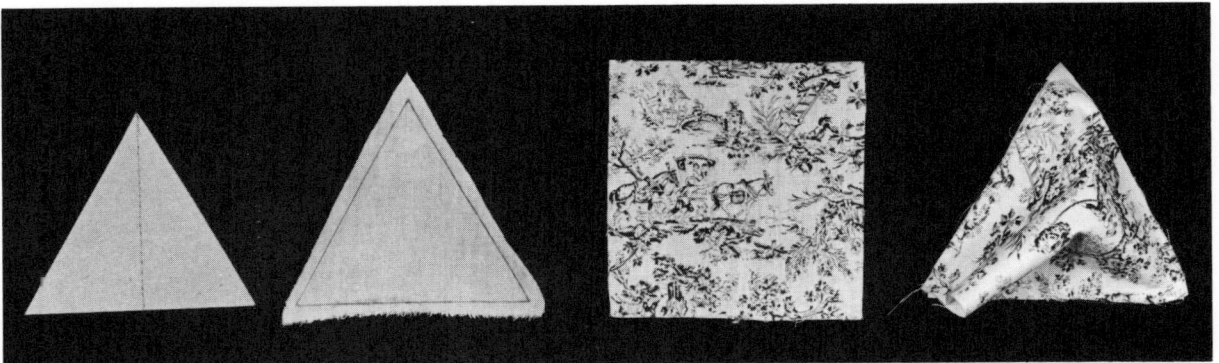

Fig. 136

Fig. 137

DEMONSTRATION Rosette Assembly — Quiltblock

We have shown triangular stuffed patches assembled in rows. It is more convenient to assemble the triangles radially, in rosettes for some designs. The following quilt patch (Fig. 140) measures about 26 inches between parallel sides. Duplicates of this block can be joined together to make a whole quilttop, which then can be faced, tied, and bound with or without a middle layer of batting.

1. Stitch three sides of the squares to the triangular facings (Fig. 136). With pleats facing the same way, stitch three triangles together, and then three more. Seam these two groups together, matching the seams at the center, to form a hexagon (Fig. 137).

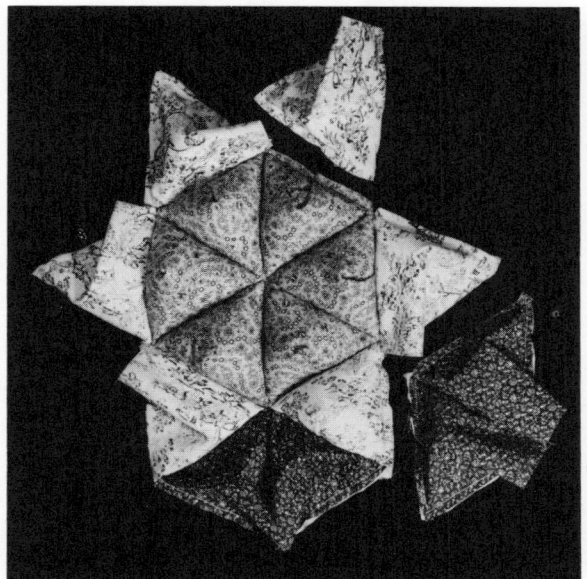

Fig. 138

Fig. 139

2. Stuff the patches. Fold over and stitch the pleats.
3. Seam a triangle to each edge of the hexagon, with pleat directions matching, to form a star. Stuff. Fold over the pleats and stitch.
4. Seam two triangles together with pleats at adjoining corners. Sew the pairs of triangles to the star edges, with pleats facing outward. Stuff. Fold over the pleats and stitch to make a hexagon (Fig. 138).
5. Add twelve triangles to form a larger star, with pleats at similar positions. Insert pairs and single triangles (shown unstuffed in Fig. 139) to complete the hexagon. Stuff and stitch (Fig. 140).

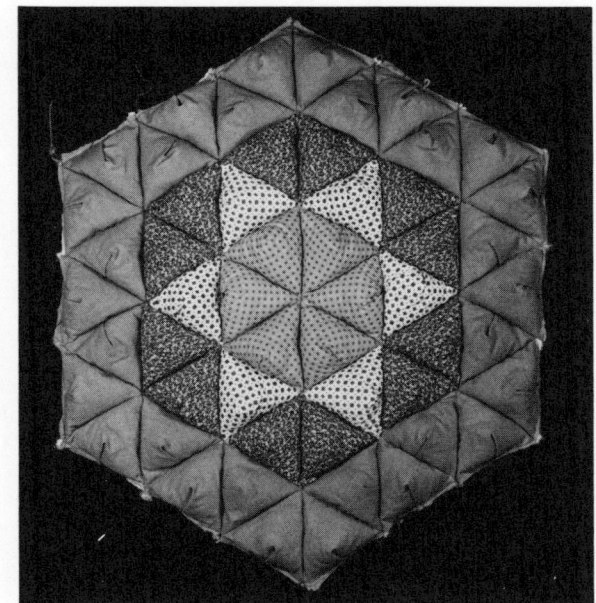

Fig. 140

80 The Complete Book of Stuffedwork

Fig. 141

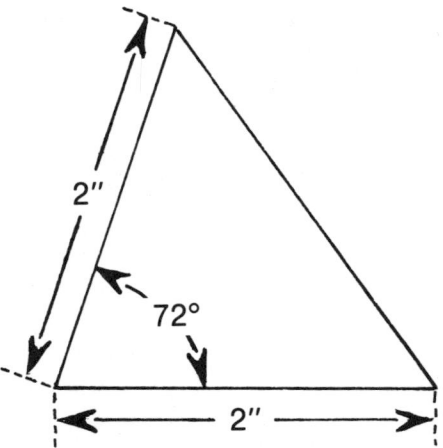

Fig. 142

STUFFED SQUARES

To give height to a square with only one (rather than the four in the biscuits) pleat, we can make the top from a pentagon whose edges match the edges of the square facing (Fig. 141).

1. Draw a pentagon as follows. Draw a horizontal line. Across it draw a short perpendicular line to mark the center. With a protractor, measure a 72 degree angle above it. Draw a line from this mark through the center. Mark off 2 inches on both lines and connect the marks to form a triangle (Fig. 142).
2. With the protractor against the line that defines the first 72 degree angle, measure a second 72 degree angle next to the first one. Mark off and draw the outer edges as before. Continue, until all five angles and edges are drawn (Fig. 143).

   Note: Once you have drawn a pentagon, you can easily change the size by drawing five new edges an equal distance from the first pentagon.

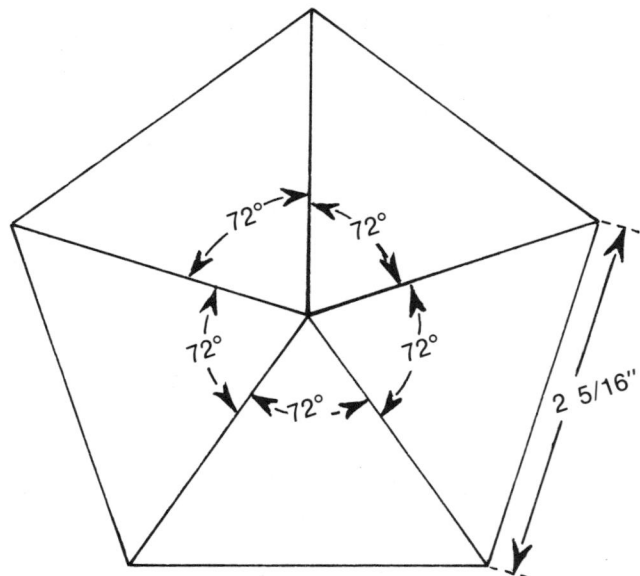

Fig. 143

3. Measure a pentagon side. Draw a square with sides of the same length (Fig. 144).
4. Add seam allowances to both the patterns. Cut a pentagon of the top fabric and a square of the muslin.
5. Place the pentagon over a square, wrong sides together, pinning the corners. Stitch four sides.

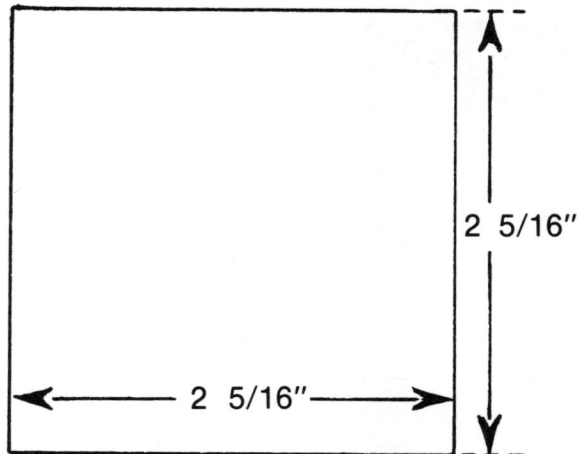

Fig. 144

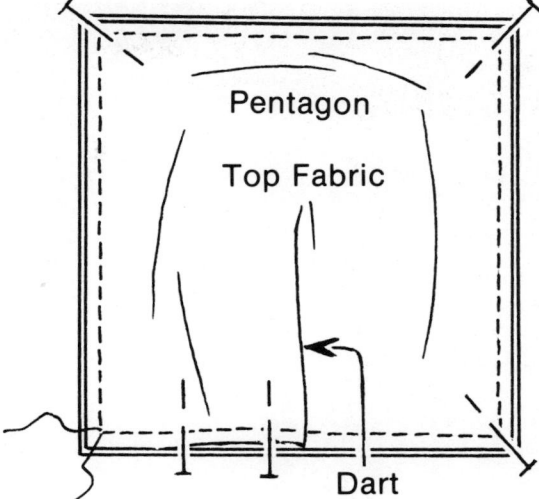

Fig. 145

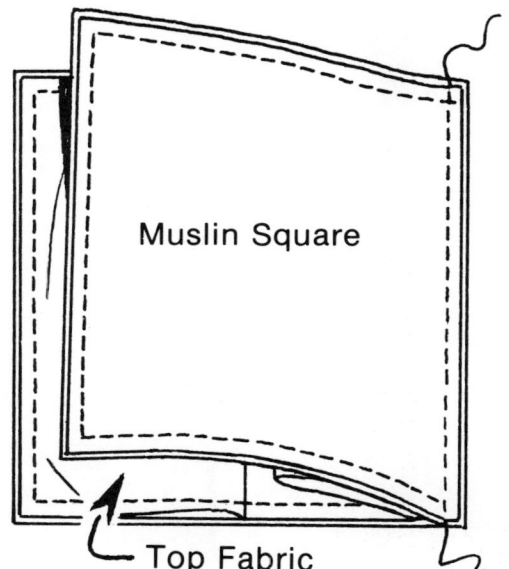

Fig. 146

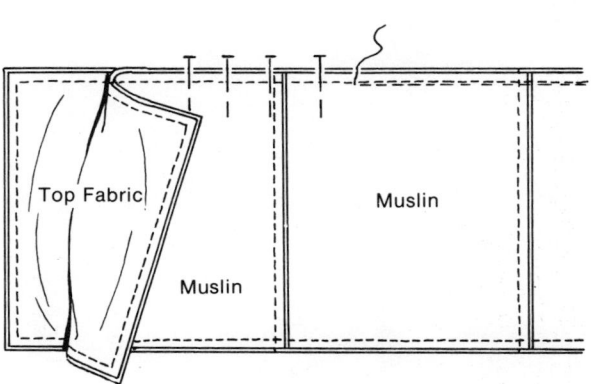

Fig. 147

6. Follow steps 3 and 4 in Stuffed Triangles, above (Fig. 145).
7. Pin two patches right sides together. Stitch (Fig. 146). Continue, making more patches and joining them, to make a row.
8. Pin two rows, right sides together, matching seams (Fig. 147). Continue joining rows of patches to make a whole piece.

82 The Complete Book of Stuffedwork

Kathryn M. Lipke *Untitled* (58 x 68), 1976.
Quilted and stuffed cotton gauze.

Detail of *Untitled*

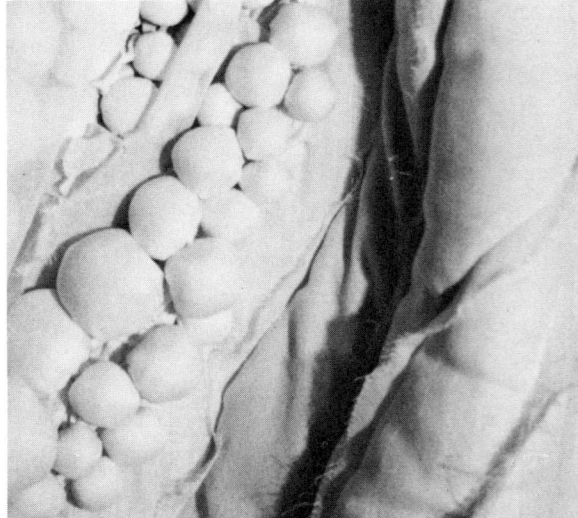

Part II
STUFFED FORMS

Plate 6 FLAT PILLOWS

View A. Knife-edged pillow

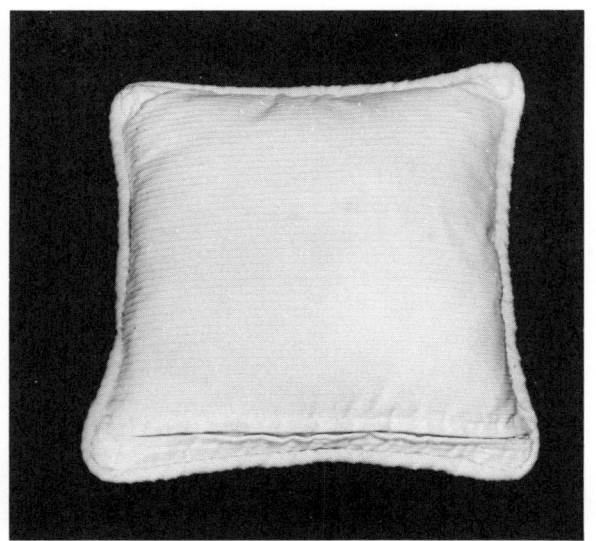

View B. Welted pillow, back view, showing zippered closing

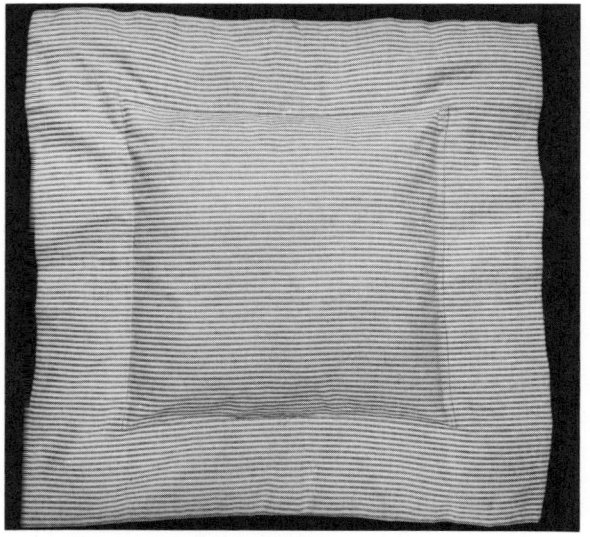

View C (front). Pillow sham

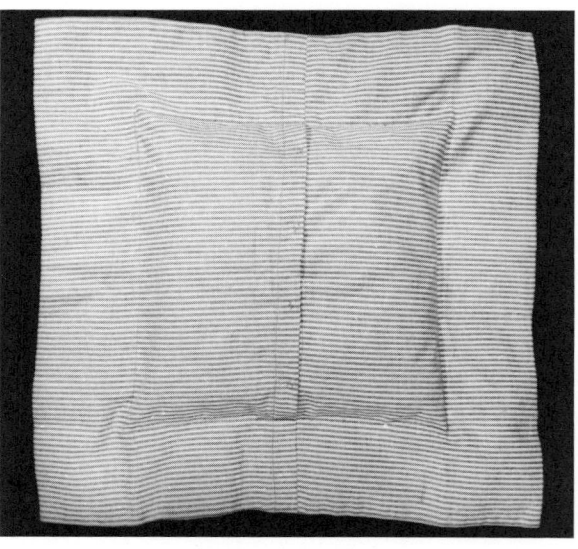

View D. Ruffled knife-edged pillow

View C (back view). Pillow sham, showing snapped closing

Chapter Four
Flat Forms

STUFFING

Characteristics such as weight, resilience, texture, and loft vary among the materials commonly used for stuffing sewn forms. The loose, synthetic stuffing, sold in plastic bags and looking like white cotton candy, is soft, lightweight, malleable, and smooth surfaced. The same kind of stuffing in cotton is more matted and less lofty. Kapok is somewhat firmer than either of these. Foam rubber slabs and pillowforms are much harder, with sharp edges and a stable form. Shredded foam rubber fills large spaces quickly but tends to look bumpy under soft fabrics. Straw and even newspaper sometimes fills large leather hassocks, such as the traditional Moroccan poufs, and this filling can be discarded for easy storage and replaced for later use. Sawdust is lightweight and firm. Old nylon stockings or shredded sheer underwear make very soft small stuffed pieces. Small sacks of sand are sometimes added inside to weight some forms and make them stand well. Feathers, down, straw, even air and water stuff mattresses and pillows.

Then there are the partially filled forms like beanbags, where the stuffing is supposed to shift, adapting itself to changing pressures and postures. Beans, rice, and birdseed fill beanbags, while Styrofoam pellets are soft and light enough for large "beanbag" chairs.

Some fillings have functions beyond stuffing the skins. Dried herbs and flowers, scented powders and pine needles occupy little pillows in order to release scent into drawers and closets. Steel filings fill small cushions that hold and sharpen pins and needles.

Except for the foam rubber forms, these stuffings are themselves shapeless and they will take the form provided by the skin. In the next three chapters, we will explore the shaping of that skin, by computation, drawing, draping, and drafting.

KNIFE-EDGED PILLOWS

Perhaps the most familiar stuffed form is a pillow. Its simplest version is made from two matching pieces of fabric, sewn at the edges, turned right side out and stuffed. This flat form is known as a knife-edged pillow. Between the edges, cording or ruffling or fringe is often inserted, framing the form.

Usually the stuffing has first been enclosed in a muslin inner case. The inner cushion or, in its absence, loose stuffing will be inserted through an opening in the pillow cover in one of several ways. Most simply, an unstitched portion of one side seam will admit the pillow and then be slipstitched closed. Openings can instead be made across the back, by cutting the back in two pieces. These are closed by a zipper or sometimes overlapped and fastened with snaps.

Illustrated in Plate 6 are four different covers for a 14-inch square inner pillow. Change the shapes and sizes to make pillows of your own choice, using whichever closing you find most convenient, and consult the assembly instructions that appear in Chapter 8.

DRAWN FORMS

Pillows lead to other two-piece flat forms in all sorts of silhouettes. Many dolls and toys are made this way, as well as pillows in irregular shapes. The patterns for pillows in Plate 6 were arrived at by *computation*. The freer forms, such as those in Plate 7, are derived from *drawing*.

Like designs for appliqué, the drawings should avoid sharp angles and small details; the stuffing will pull away from erratic contours. Subtle changes in line will disappear with the stuffing and be read simply as uncertain outlines. Slow, sure curves are appropriate for this medium.

You will have noticed that a stuffed pillow appears smaller than the drawn pattern. This is because some of the fabric must turn away from the front and back planes to accommodate the depth of the stuffing. This *wraparound* covers the thickness of the pillow: half of the needed fabric comes from the front and half from the back. In drawing your design, therefore, after the contour satisfies you, widen it to include an estimated wraparound before you add the seam allowance.

Here is a revealing experiment. Wrap a piece of paper round a finger. Mark the paper where it meets its beginning edge. Remove your finger and open the paper. This is comparable to the fabric required, before adding seam allowances, to make a skin that would match the girth of your finger. Fold the paper in half to find out what a front or back pattern would look like. Place your finger over this half-pattern. The uncovered paper is the wraparound needed for each face of a two-piece pattern to reach an imaginary seamline around the sides of your finger. In addition to this, of course, *seam allowance* has then to be added.

In relation to stuffed dolls and animals there are other practical considerations. Do not make arms and legs so narrow that they are difficult to turn inside out. One half inch between the two side seamlines is about the minimum. Also, make the neck wide and short since a thin neck will not stand but merely flop back and forth.

PATTERNMAKING

First, draw the silhouette as you would like it to look. Then draw a line outside this, to provide what you estimate will be required for wraparound. This will be the *seamline,* that is, the *finished edge.*

Finally, draw a seam allowance (¼ inch for small things or ½ inch for larger ones) outside the seamline. This line will be the *cutting line.* Label the pattern "first muslin."

MUSLIN TRYOUTS

At this point, you are ready to make the first *muslin tryout* of the pattern. Pin the pattern to folded fabric and cut along the cutting line through both layers.

If there are inner markings, transfer only the necessary ones. Marks can be transferred with dressmaker's carbon paper: Place a sheet of carbon paper face down between the pattern and the fabric, then draw a tracing wheel or a pencil over the pattern markings. Simple markings can be transferred just by perforating the pattern paper with a sharp, hard pencil, dotting the

Plate 7   STUFFED FISH

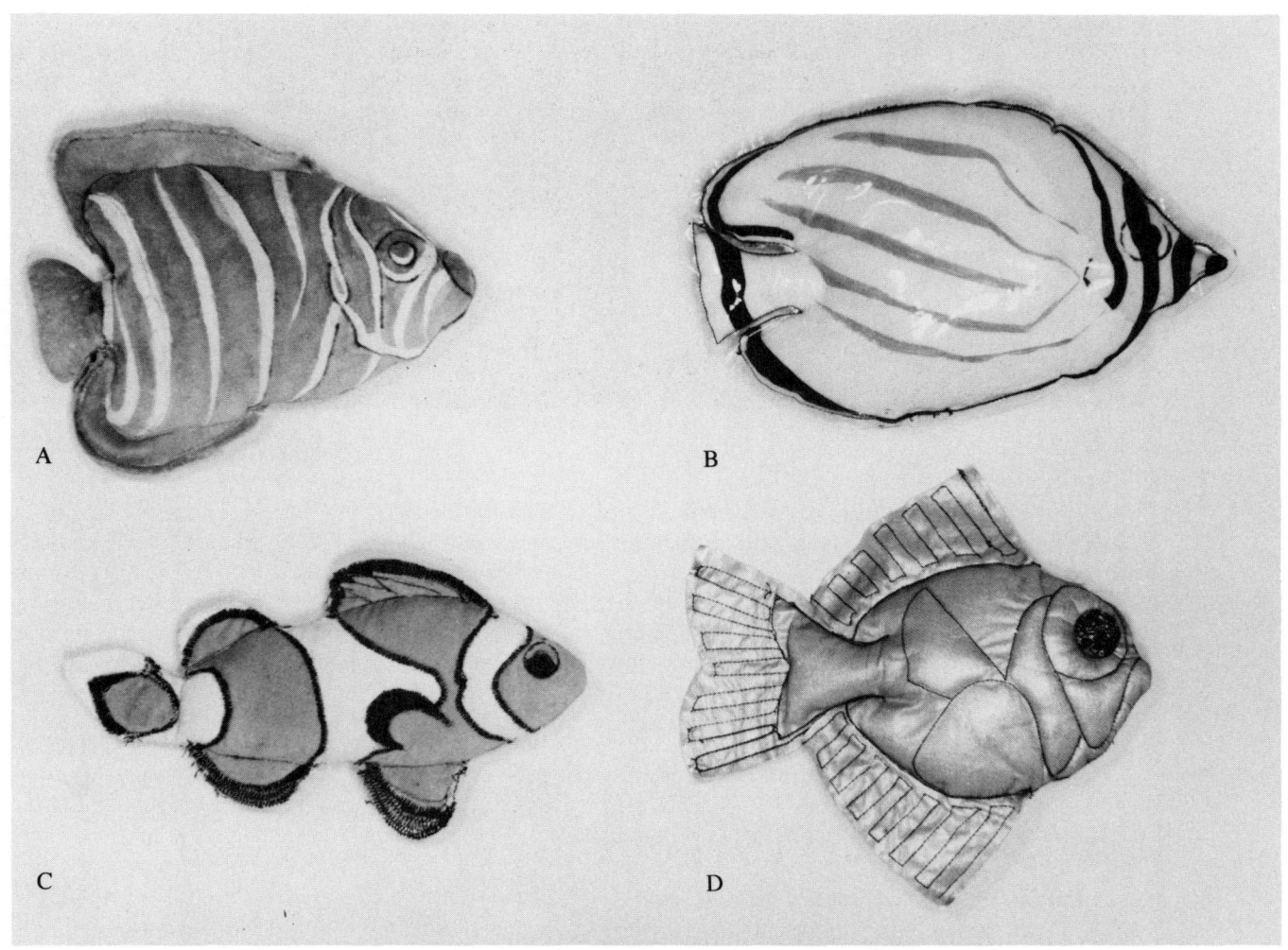

A. Dyed velveteen Angel Fish
B. Painted vinyl Butterfly Fish
C. Appliquéd Clown Fish
D. Quilted Silver Fish

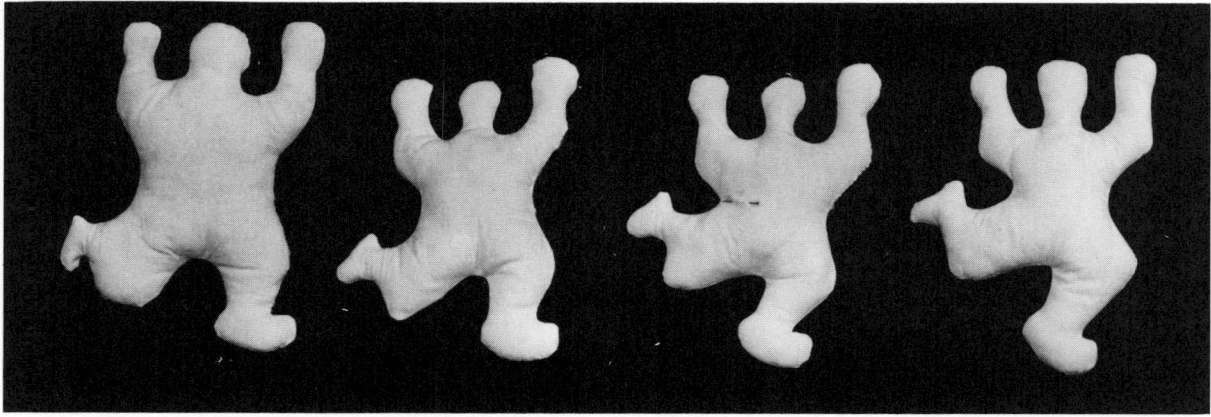

Fig. 148 a   b   c   d

fabric beneath; when the paper is removed the dots can be joined, if you like, with a continuous line.

Assemble the muslin: Seam the front to the back, right sides together, leaving an opening for stuffing. Clip to the seamline at inside corners. Turn the muslin inside out and stuff it, using a knitting needle to push the stuffing up to the edges. Slipstitch to close the opening.

PATTERN ADJUSTMENTS

After the first muslin has been sewn and stuffed, study it and make adjustments in the pattern that will improve the contours. You may make a second or third muslin tryout before you are satisfied. Above all, *save the patterns*. The final pattern (and even, sometimes, the previous patterns from earlier tryouts) will serve as invaluable reference material for future work. For new work, you can use parts of the old pattern as it is, or you can judge how much to depart from this pattern in order to obtain a different form.

The evidence accumulates as in laboratory research, and if you keep complete records, patterns, and models, you will have a ready reference to past experiences. Then you can go ahead to new results, without covering the same ground over again.

Many pattern adjustments can be made at the seam and simply by redrawing the outline of the pattern. Sometimes, however, changes intrude into the body of the pattern and these are often accomplished by *tucking*, *darting*, and *slashing*.

Three muslin tryouts for a doll (Fig. 148) and the corresponding pattern adjustments are recorded here to illustrate how to make pattern changes inside the seamlines.

FIRST MUSLIN

The first tryout (Fig. 148a and Fig. 149) was too wide and too long in the trunk. A ¼-inch tuck

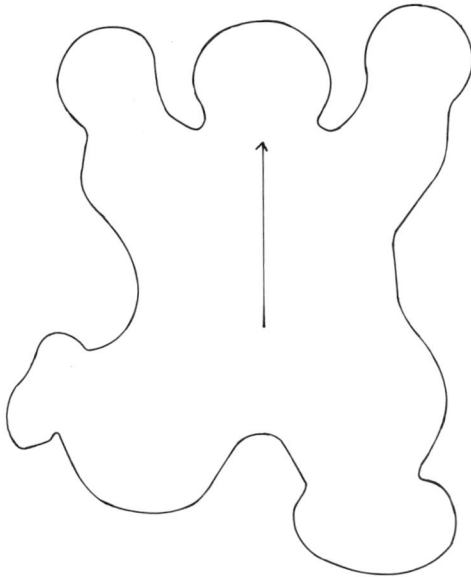

Fig. 149

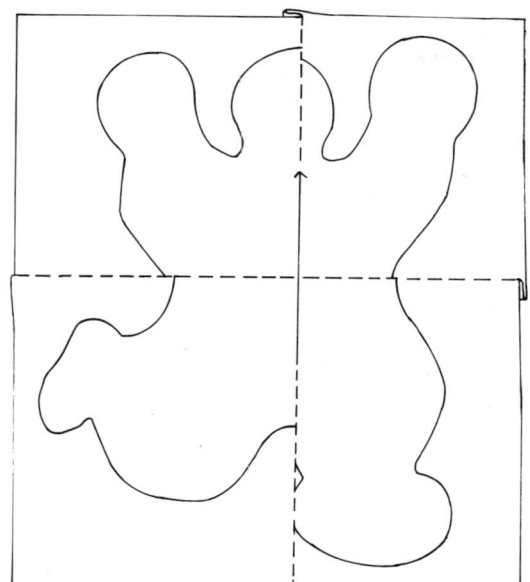

Fig. 150

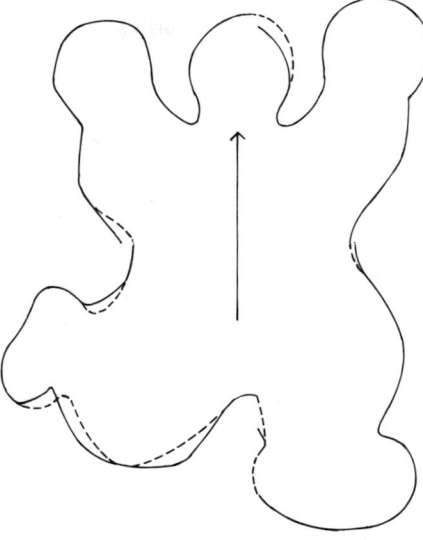

Fig. 151

was therefore folded through the whole length. To shorten it to the same degree a similar tuck was taken crosswise (Fig. 150). The tucked pattern was traced to fresh paper where the broken outlines were redrawn, as was the lifted leg (Fig. 151). This became the pattern for the second tryout.

SECOND MUSLIN (Fig. 148, b and c)

In order to lift the heel higher a dart was pinned in the muslin at the waist (c). Short pencil marks were drawn along both edges of the dart. Then the dart was unpinned and copied on the paper pattern (Fig. 152). In order to pin the paper dart, the pattern edge opposite had to be slashed until the paper would lie flat (Fig. 153). This pattern, with the dart closed and the slash open, was traced to fresh paper and the broken edges were redrawn. Other adjustments such as those at the head and the leg were made at the same time (Fig. 154).

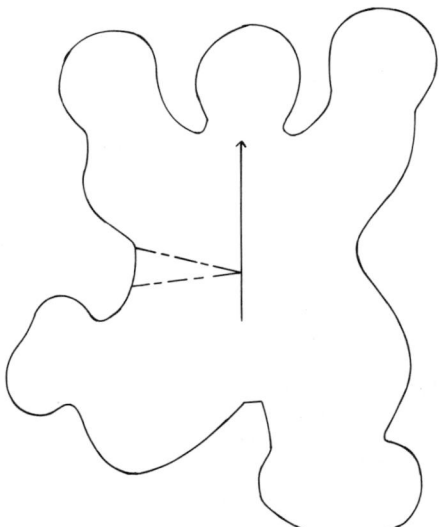

Fig. 152

THIRD MUSLIN (Fig. 148 d)

The third tryout was made and accepted without further change. The pattern was traced, seamlines were inserted (Fig. 155), and the necessary information was added in order to complete a final pattern for future use (Fig. 156).

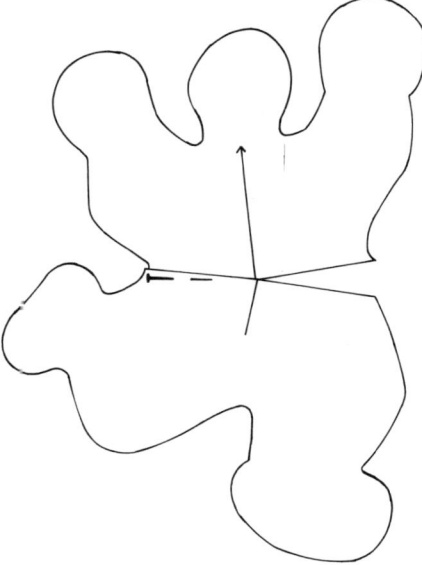

Fig. 153

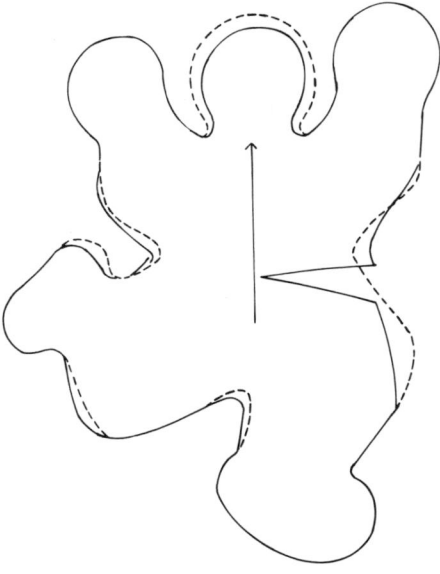

Fig. 154

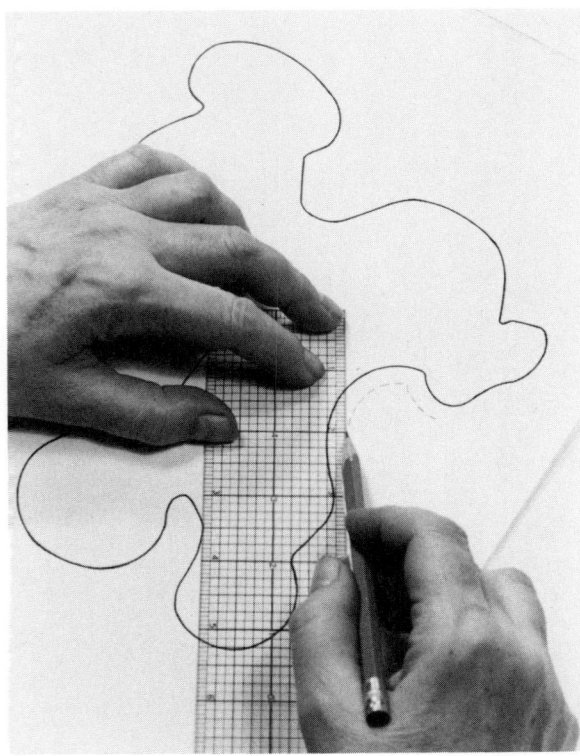

Fig. 155

PATTERN MARKS AND LABELS

The following suggestions apply to most of the patterns that you will yourself be developing.

Draw an arrow on the pattern piece to indicate the grainline. If you stood the form up against the wall, the grainline would represent a plumb line perpendicular to the floor: its position represents the center of gravity in the shape. This grainline should be parallel to the warp threads (and, thereby, to the selvage) when you pin the pattern to the fabric in preparation for cutting. If your fabric is a vertical stripe, cutting both front and back on the same grainline insures of course, true up and down stripes on both faces of the piece.

Mark two dots to indicate the ends of the opening for stuffing, choosing a fairly straight or inconspicuous edge. Draw the inner markings, if there are any. These may be facial features or outlines for paint, embroidery, or other decoration.

Label the pattern with the name of the item and the section of the pattern. Write ''¼-inch seam allowed'' or whatever is the case. (If the seamline has actually been drawn, this notation is not necessary.)

Flat Forms 91

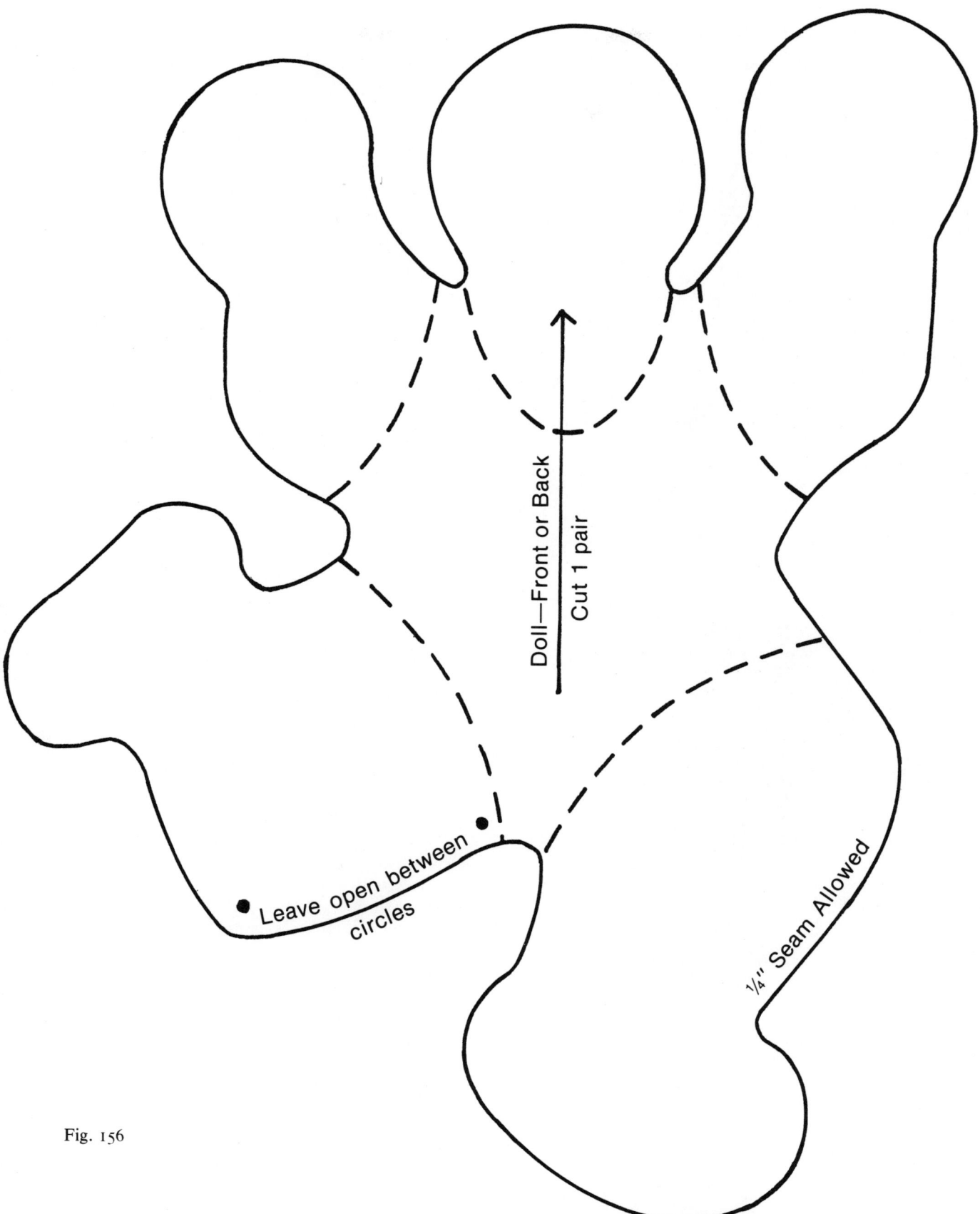

Fig. 156

Plate 8   FLAT DOLL

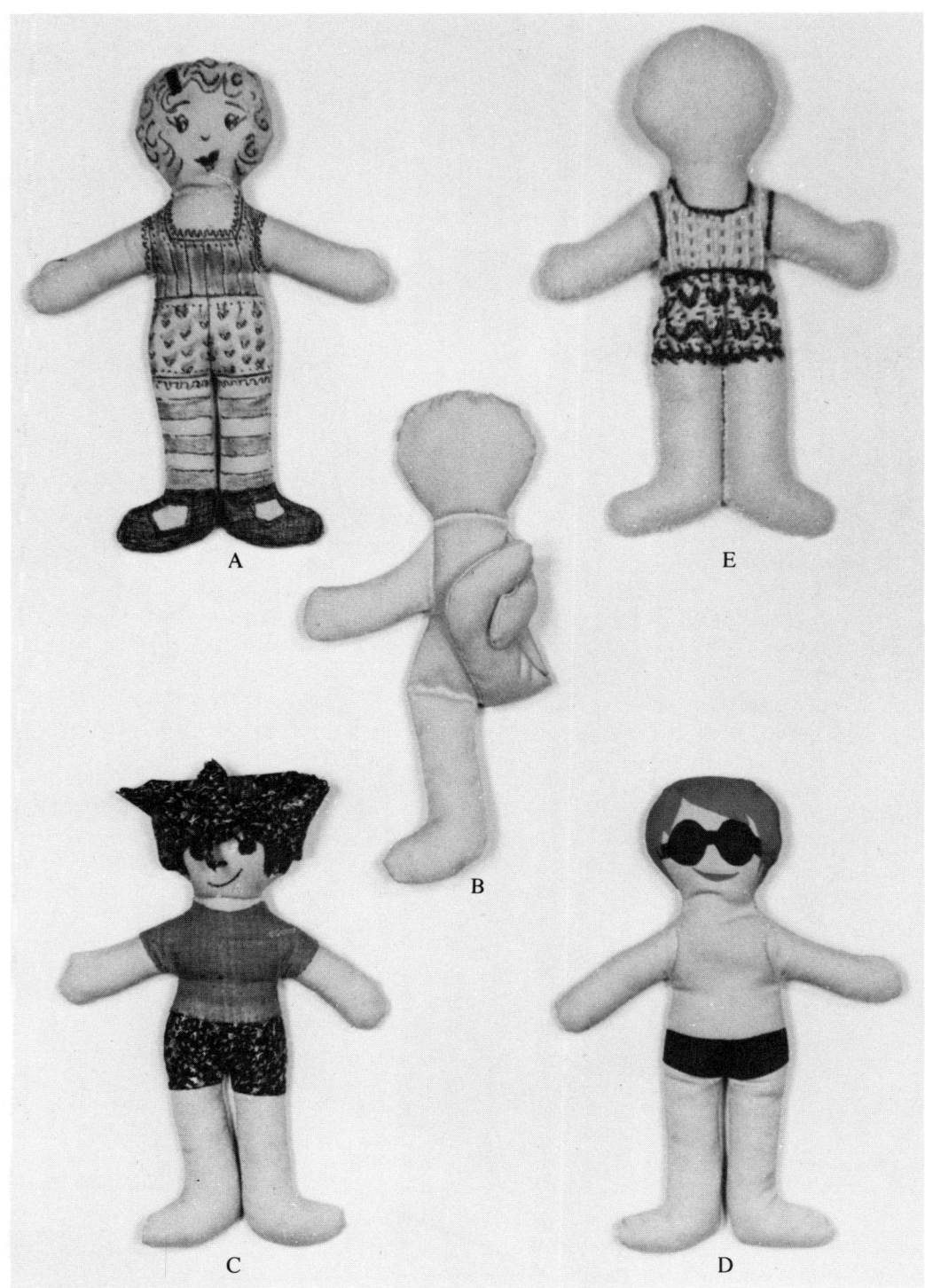

A. Painted doll
B. Jointed doll
C. Doll with fabric appliqué
D. Doll with iron-on appliqué
E. Embroidered doll

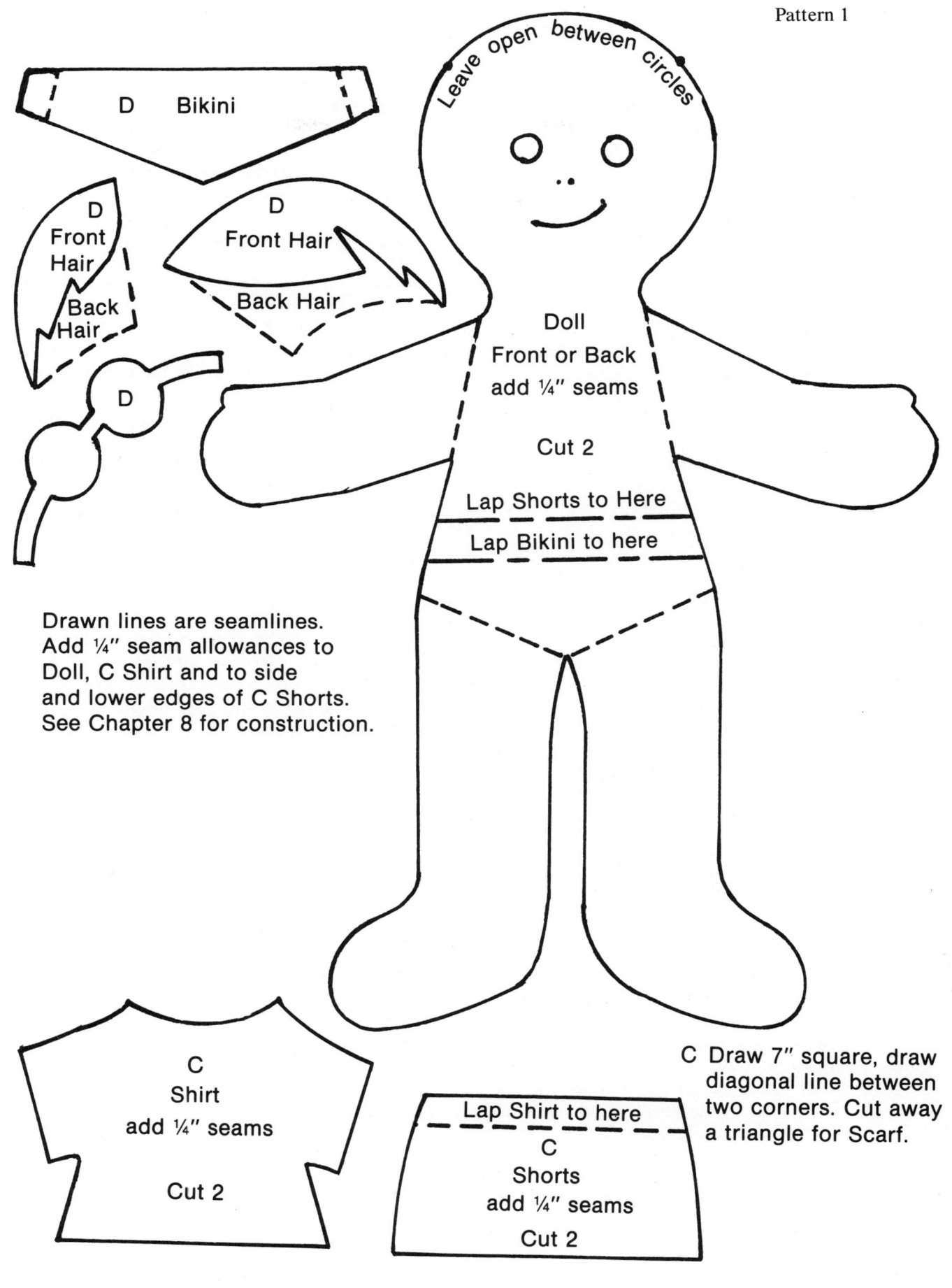

Write cutting information. If the front and the back are the same, for example, make only one pattern and label it "front or back, cut 1 pair." To cut one pair rather than to cut two indicates that the two pieces must be opposites. To cut one pair you will cut from double fabric, folded face to face. If you cut them from single fabric, the pattern must be placed right side up to cut one piece and right side down to cut the other.

When the pattern pieces are symmetrical, half a pattern is enough. The center line must then be labeled "place on fold," indicating that the piece will be cut from folded material and that the edge so labeled will match the fold. Also, with symmetrical pieces you could safely say "cut two" rather than "cut one pair."

DECORATION

Embroidery and canvas work have long histories as pillow surfaces. In the first part of this book, we have seen a number of trapunto, appliqué, and quilting techniques that also make rich surfaces for stuffed forms. Contemporary designers use many painting, dyeing, and printing techniques, as well, to color fabric surfaces. Such practices can transform a simple silhouette into a rich and complex piece.

Such embellishment is usually completed before the front and the back are assembled, or even before they are cut out. Often, as in most pillows, only the front is worked; sometimes, as in the dolls and fishes that follow, both sides are decorated with the designs meeting at the side seams so the form appears to be without seams.

Stuffed forms are usually made of firm-bodied fabrics in order to project a strong silhouette and to give the surface enough texture to balance the weight of the object. Two of the fish on Plate 7 are in napped fabric. The clown fish (C) has orange velveteen appliqués over a white corduroy body. Zigzag machine stitching provides black outlines and details. The angel fish (A) is white velveteen, "batiked" blue. The silver fish (D) is made from thin fabrics, but they are layered and stuffed to achieve a rich and sturdy surface. Gray net over gray organdy over silver lamé over muslin is stitched and "trapuntoed." The butterfly fish (B) is made of clear vinyl. Black, yellow, and orange acrylic paint is brushed on to the vinyl. This painted side becomes the inside, minimizing the brush strokes and protecting the paint. The stuffing shows through to provide the white ground color. In all cases, the surface decoration was finished before the assembly began.

The butterfly fish has been sewn entirely with outside seams. The vinyl is uncut, but stitched, around the tail. Since it is transparent, the unstuffed section disappears anyway. You will see that the other three fish have been seamed, right sides together, only around certain sections, like the nose, for instance. Then the fish are turned inside out and topstitched at the remaining edges, between the body and the fins. They are stuffed before the stitching is completed. Additional topstitching has been added to fins and tails.

The dolls in Plate 8 are made from the same pattern but illustrate four kinds of decoration: appliqué, iron-on tape, colored markers, and embroidery. Use firm cotton for doll bodies. Notice that you have a choice of stitching arm and leg joints so they will move, or of stuffing the doll firmly throughout. Step-by-step assembly directions are given in Chapter 8. Draw your own dolls and other forms and decorate them by some of the methods we have shown.

Flat Forms 95

Ghana, Africa *War Shirt* (Batakari). Leather and bone. Attached to shirt are laced amulets containing powder from a shell and bits of brass from a shell casing and also, probably, Islamic script on paper. The Museum of Cultural History, UCLA.

96 The Complete Book of Stuffedwork

Michelle Gamm Clifton *Soft U.S.A.* (6' x 10').
White duck, stenciled pencil with fixative, synthetic
stuffing. Separate states stapled to board.

Victoria Rivers *Fugitive Horizon* (6' x 4'). Procion dyes on velveteen, handpainted, screened, stuffed and beaded; three pieces are joined together.

Emily McLennan *Stuffed sculptures* (about 1' to 4' in diameter), 1974. Dyed canvas stuffed with foam rubber and synthetic stuffing. Canvas is draped over stuffing, cut, pinned, and hand-sewn with upholstery needle.

Detail of *Polish Cookie Icon*

Susan Hoover *Polish Cookie Icon*. Black fabric batik-resisted in bleach, then embroidered, lastly "trapuntoed."

Stephen Blumrich *Chess Set* (Board 26" x 26"; pieces maximum 4"), 1974. Batik on unbleached muslin. Each piece is built over a cork that has been hollowed out and filled with lead; Kapok is placed over the cork; bottom is finished with a felt circle.

Lenore Davis *Reclining Lady* (18″ high x 34″ long x 12″ deep), 1976. Direct-dyed velveteen. Squeeze bottle, brush and wash techniques. Polyester stuffing.

Morag Benepe *Reclining Woman* (60″ x 30″), 1974. Stuffed batik wall hanging. Procion dyes, muslin, stuffing.

Susan Morrison *Lady on a Ram* (about 24″ long x 22″ high), 1975. A variety of fabrics, wigs, feathers, and trims. Female figure is a stuffed nylon stocking. Ram has welded metal armature.

Susan Morrison *Wanda Rides Her Hippo* (about 32″ long x 25″ high), 1977. A variety of fabrics, wigs, feathers, and trims. Female figure is a stuffed nylon stocking. Hippo has welded metal armature.

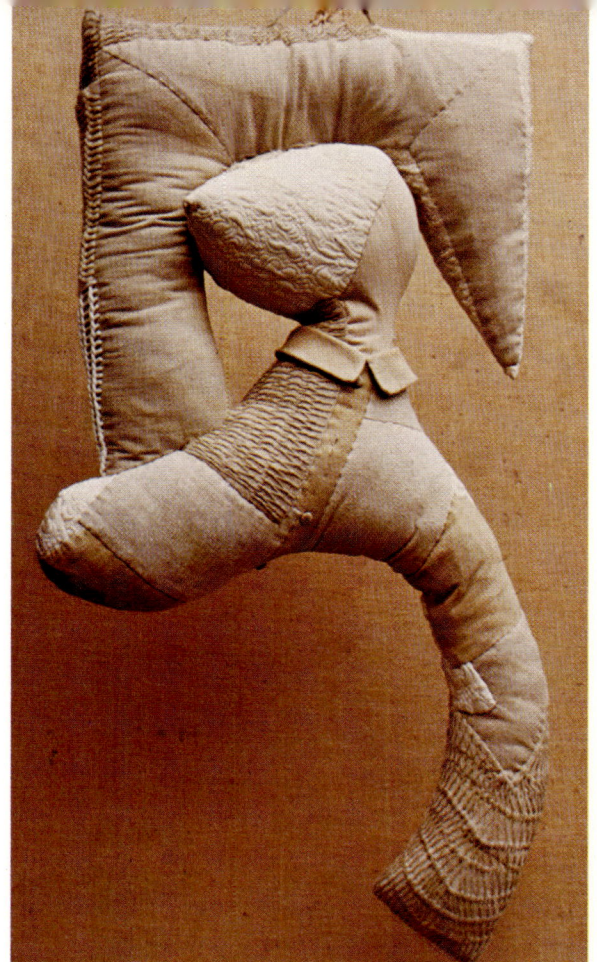

Alma Lesch *Mother and Child* (24" x 48" x 8"). Fabric sculpture.

Victoria Rivers *Flower Fantasy* (7' x 4'). Procion dyes on velveteen, beaded, stuffed, printed; in two pieces.

Cheryl A. Patton *Visitation of the Casaba Melons* (18" x 12" x 10" each), 1976. Dyed velvet, brocade and chenille, beads, crochet and tufting.

Helen Bitar   *Untitled*. Stitched, appliquéd, and stuffed fabric.

Marie Kelly   *Doll Object*. Dyed cloth, stuffed, stitched, and beaded.

Norma Minkowitz *Alligator* (3" x 14"), 1973. Crochet, knit, plastic tubing (teeth), synthetic stuffing. Collection of Arthur Edelman.

Elizabeth Lady *Pangolin* (15" x 38" x 12"). Sewn and stuffed fabric, individual stuffed scales are sewn to body in overlapping rows.

Katherine Williams *Fish* (72" long). Screen-printed cheesecloth, fabric, batting backed with cheesecloth. Batting pieces are seamed by hand to make the form, then inserted in a turned, machine-sewn fabric skin. Outer layer is screen-printed cheesecloth.

Gayle Fraas and Duncan W. Slade *American Flight Dream Reality* (36" x 40"). Photo-silkscreen printed, hand-drawn images, hand-dyed, stitched, and stuffed fabric. Silkscreen-printed covered buttons (stars), rayon flocking (clouds). Procion dyes.

Ervene Salan *Valentines,* 1976. Shoes, stuffed and beaded. Collection of Glenda Arentzen.

M. Joan Lintault *Private Thoughts as Public Events, David's Sister*. Embroidery, photograph colored with pencils, photosensitive dye on satin. Stitched and stuffed.

Polly Hope *Grey Vows* (117" x 117"), 1977.
Adjoining two-piece quilted fabric forms with stuffed appliqués, machine embroidery and applied cord, buttons, sequins, braid, medallions and beads; intervening stuffed round forms. Courtesy Kornblee Gallery, New York City.

Flat Forms 99

Marjorie Moore *Sonya Tiger Lily Lady* (24" x 30" x 7"). Dyed muslin with trapunto quilting. Heads and hands of papier-mâché.

100 The Complete Book of Stuffedwork

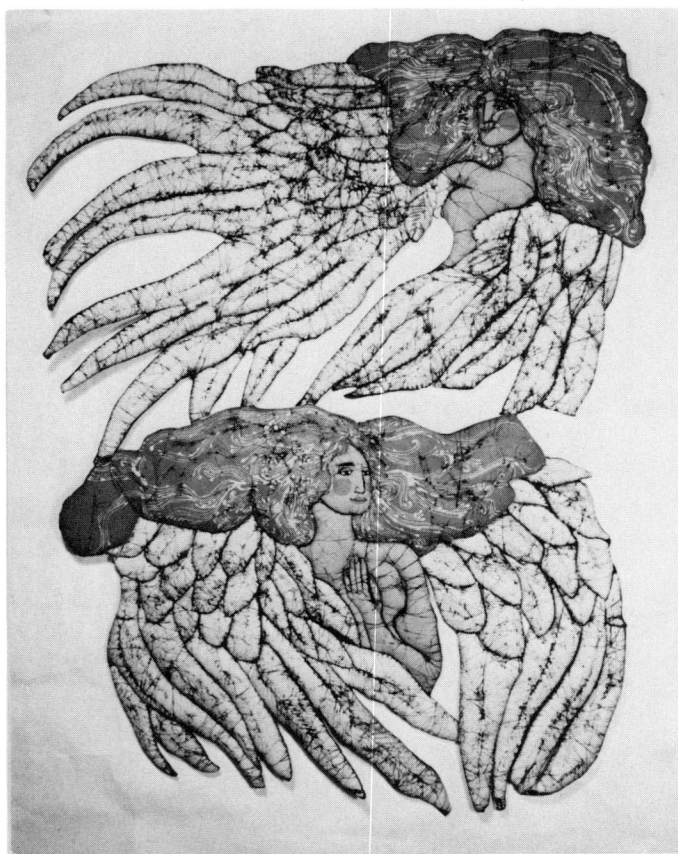

Morag Benepe *Floating Angels* (60" x 36" each). Batik on muslin, trapunto, stuffing. Colors are umbers, white, and brown.

Morag Benepe *Dancing Couple* (72" x 38"). Batik, synthetic stuffing. Colors are browns, beiges, and pinks.

Chapter Five
Geometric Forms

THREE-DIMENSIONAL PILLOWS

In Chapter 4 we examined knife-edged pillows and other flat forms. The stuffed forms were, by identification, not truly flat; they were swollen by the filling, like an overstuffed envelope. But the skin itself was two dimensional, having only length and breadth. In this chapter, we begin with pillows whose skins are cut and seamed to provide depth as well (Plate 9 and Pattern 2). They are filled with foam rubber pillowforms, each of whose planes must be duplicated by a section of the pillowcover. Although these skins cover pillows, their drafting, assembly, and closings, given in Chapter 8, will apply to other thick or boxlike forms as well.

Space for the thickness of the three square pillows, Plate 9 and Pattern 2, A, B, and E, is supplied in different ways. Pillowform A has sloping edges and the resulting curved planes are fitted by means of a dart at each corner of the front and back pillowcover. The other square pillows, B and E, have true perpendicular sides and require "boxing": a term used to describe the narrow strip of fabric that covers the thickness of a form. In E a seamed boxing, interrupted by a zippered section, is used. B demonstrates a darted "fake" boxing: full darts miter each corner and turn the front and back into side planes. This single centered side seam is frequently seen in contemporary slipcovers and, where the corners of the pillowform are curved, the extra fabric can be gathered rather than darted into the seam.

C is a round pillow and D is a bolster. At the same time D can be regarded as a cylinder and C as a slice of a larger cylinder. The boxing in C becomes the principal surface in D, but the pillowcover patterns are computed in the same way. The closing is placed on the broader surface.

The wedge-shaped pillowcover F is easily drafted by measuring the surfaces of the pillowform. Seams could occur at each change of plane, making it easy to line up the sides so that they are not askew. Here, however, one seam has been omitted at the most visible, upper front edge. In pillow E it is important that the upper and lower corners meet at exactly opposite

Plate 9 THREE-DIMENSIONAL PILLOWS

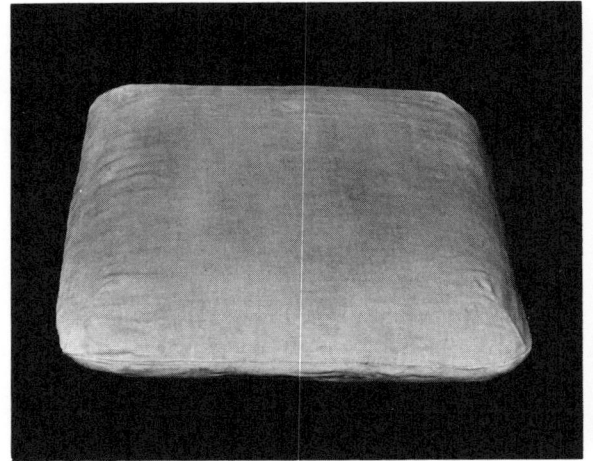

A. Pillow with darted corners

B. Pillow with darted boxing

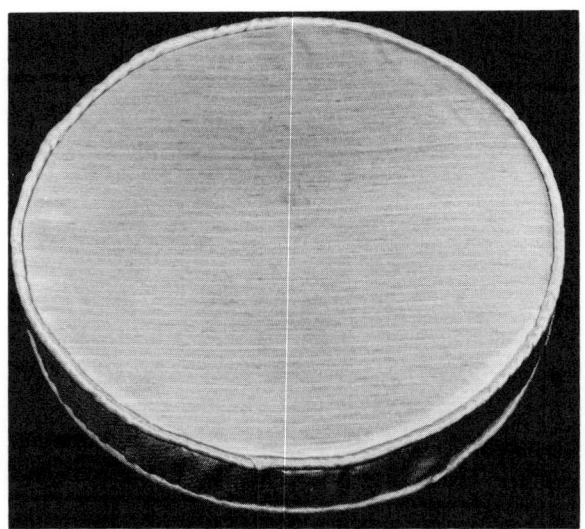

C. Round boxed pillow

D. Bolster

E. Pillow with seamed boxing

F. Wedge pillow

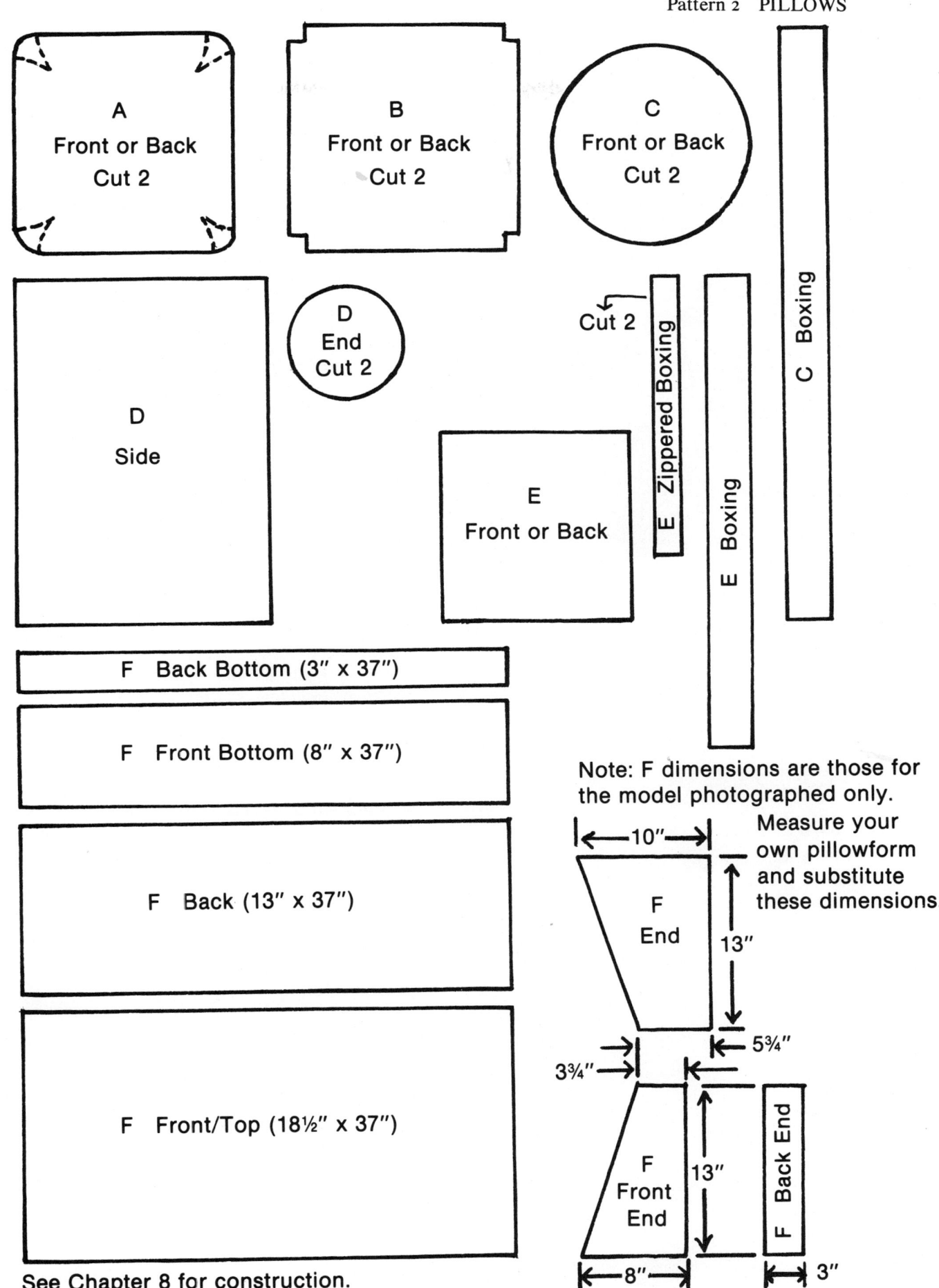

Pattern 2 PILLOWS

See Chapter 8 for construction.

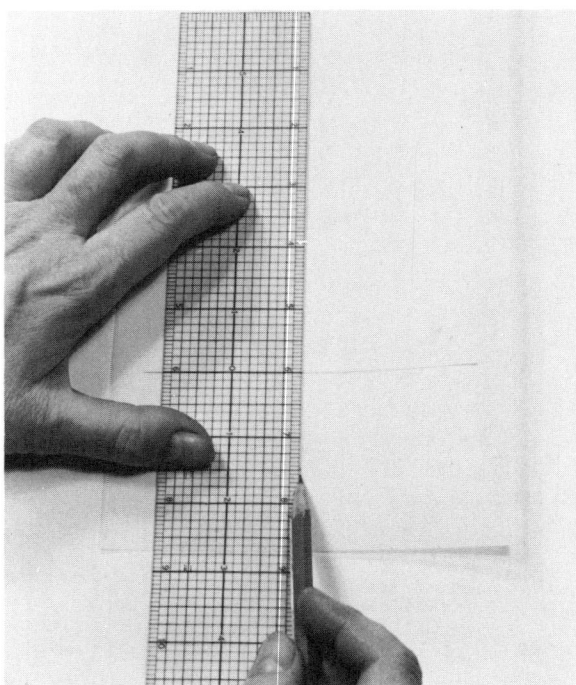

Fig. 157

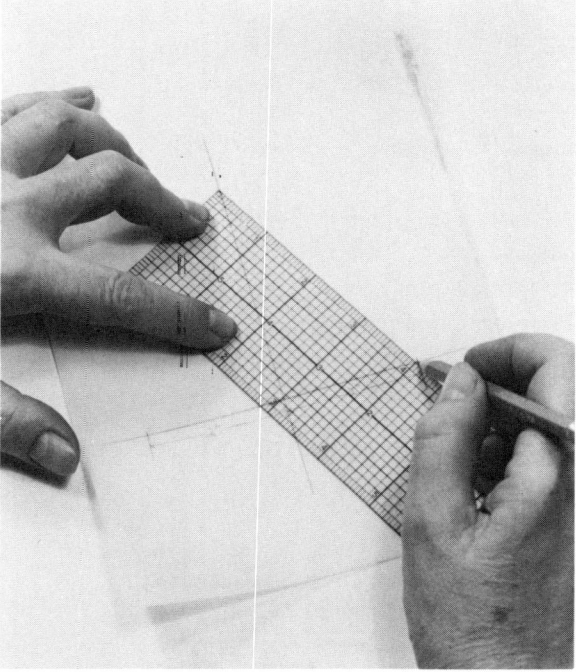

Fig. 158

sides of the boxing. It will be helpful to mark the boxing where it meets the corner seamlines before beginning to sew.

Boxed pillowcovers are often used over upholstered cushions. Therefore, the opening must extend around both corners of one side, in order to admit the unyielding form. The section of the boxings where the zippers are placed are cut in two lengthwise pieces, as in E.

GEOMETRIC FORMS

The pillow patterns just demonstrated were computed by measuring the underlying pillowforms. There are other basic forms where the patterns are based on simple geometric principles. As you look about, notice how many objects are related to *cubes* and *cones*, *prisms* and *pyramids*. Their planes can be embellished, and the forms themselves can be sliced and segmented, connected and combined in endlessly varied ways.

To experiment, cut forms like those in Plate 10 and Pattern 3, in felt or nonwoven interfacing, so that the edges can be just whipped together without taking up seam allowances. Then play with the shapes, altering and combining them freely, redrafting to make new sizes and proportions. To make final pieces, of course, you may add seam allowances and use woven fabrics.

When you draw the patterns, be sure that all perpendicular lines are truly square. Use a *transparent ruler* that has measurements marked both lengthwise and crosswise. Place any crosswise line exactly over the drawn baseline and draw its perpendicular along the ruler edge (Fig. 157). Use a sharp pencil and keep its point right against the ruler. To draw a triangle with two matching sides, erect a perpendicular in the center of a baseline. Then place the desired length of the ruler so that one end matches the end of the baseline and the other end touches the perpendicular. Draw along the ruler (Fig. 158). For the matching side, connect the other end of the baseline with the top intersection. Add seam allowances.

In Pattern 3 the cube (A) is drafted in a single pattern piece. It could also be made in as many as six pieces, with a seam at each foldline. Similar piecings can also be made at the foldlines in B, C, and D. Proportions, of course, can be altered. The cube could become a prism by lengthening equally the four sides, while keeping the top and bottom the same. The triangular sides of the pyramids can be lengthened or shortened as long as they match each other.

The *compass* is an even more magical instrument than the ruler. The same size circle can be sliced into countless different wedges, and each can be seamed to make a different cone. We have shown cones, in Plate 10, made from one third (F and G), two thirds (E) and truncated halves (H and I) of the same circle (in this case, 9-inch diameter). To draft the circles that are the base of the cones, the old principle $C = 2\pi r$ is indispensable. For π use 3.14 and compute to the nearest ⅛ inch, with the formula

circumference = 3.14 × diameter

then add seam allowances.

Note: If slight differences result between the matching edges, the longer edge can be held in slightly along the seam. Find the centers by folding each edge in half and mark each end of the fold. Match the centers when pinning the two pieces together. Then, by eye, match and pin the quarters together and continue, pinning halfway between the previous pins. This distributes the little extra fullness evenly and invisibly.

To find the diameter of the circle that will fit the base of Plate 10F, for example, measure the lower edge of the cone. If it is 9½ inches, find the diameter as follows:

$$9.50 = 3.14 \times D, \text{ or } \quad 3.14 \overline{\smash{)}9.5000}^{\,3.02}$$

Draw a 3-inch diameter (1½-inch radius) circle.

The circle that fits E (a two-third segment whose lower edge is therefore twice as long as F) is, naturally, twice F's diameter, that is, 6 inches.

BALLS

The patterns (Pattern 4) for the spherical forms in Plate 11 were arrived at by a combination of geometry and "draping" over sporting balls. Notice the seams in tennis balls, baseballs, and softballs. They are all the same. If you drape a piece of muslin over them and mark the seamline, you will arrive at a figure-8-shaped piece. Two of these pieces are joined at right angles to make the sphere.

When you look at a basketball, there are eight wedges, pointed at one end and blunt at the other. When these are joined, however, you see the same construction as the tennis ball's, except that on the basketball the figure 8 has been divided lengthwise by an additional seam. When you copy these in fabric, you will see that the 8-piece form is rounder than the 2-piece form, which tends to look a little square.

The 4-piece football is pointed at the ends. We have used half a pattern piece to make a bisected ball. The base of this section is computed with the $C = 2\pi r$ formula, after multiplying the base of this pattern by four, to find the whole circumference.

The 6-piece E has been draped as described below. The single segment F could be extended to a form whose curved sides were made up of five segments or less. In any case, its sides would be the same — a half-circle whose diameter was computed by our usual formula, after multiplying the crosswise center of the pattern piece by 6 to find the circumference.

Truncated cross sections are joined to make G. Notice, when drafting Upper G, that the outside edge is curved by drawing an arc with the point of a compass at what would have been the tip of the original segment. Otherwise, the edge would appear hexagonal rather than round. The straight lower edges of these segments are indeed hexagonal but they are not visible at the neck of the form.

The end views of the football and of the 6-piece ball may remind you of the crowns of fabric hats. As with the balls, the 6-piece crown is rounder. The greater number of seams afford more places to "dart out" the fabric, in order to change flat fabric to a spherical form.

If you visualize the pattern pieces flat, you will see how the adjoining curves cut out the excess material at the apex of each section (Fig. 159). The narrower the sections, the shallower the curves. A 6-part ball will appear rounder than a 4-part one because the same amount of excess fabric is cut out more gradually.

Plate 10 GEOMETRIC FORMS

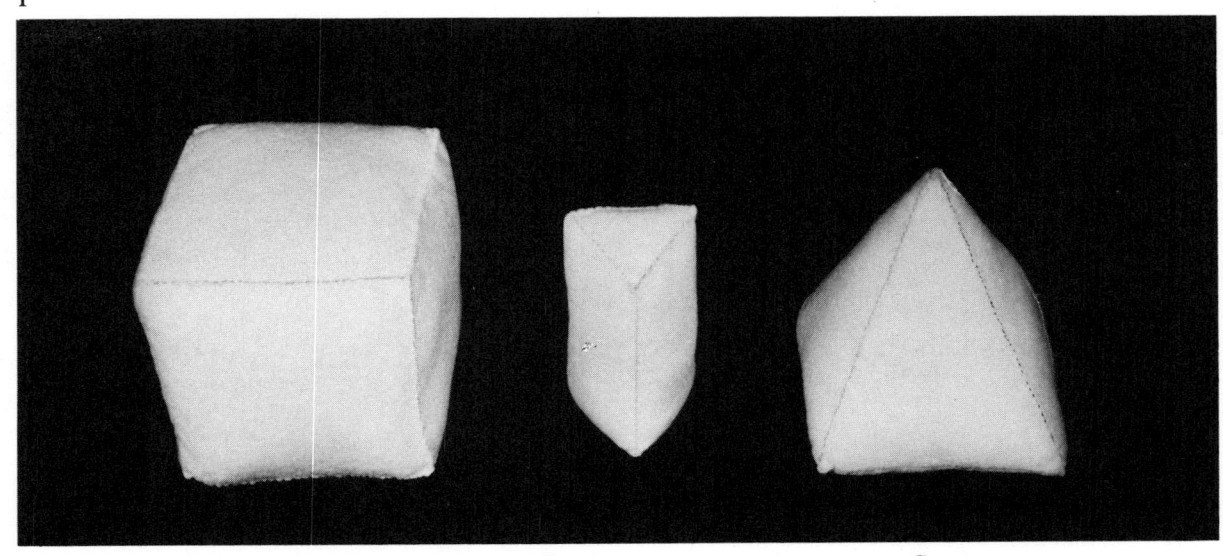

A B C

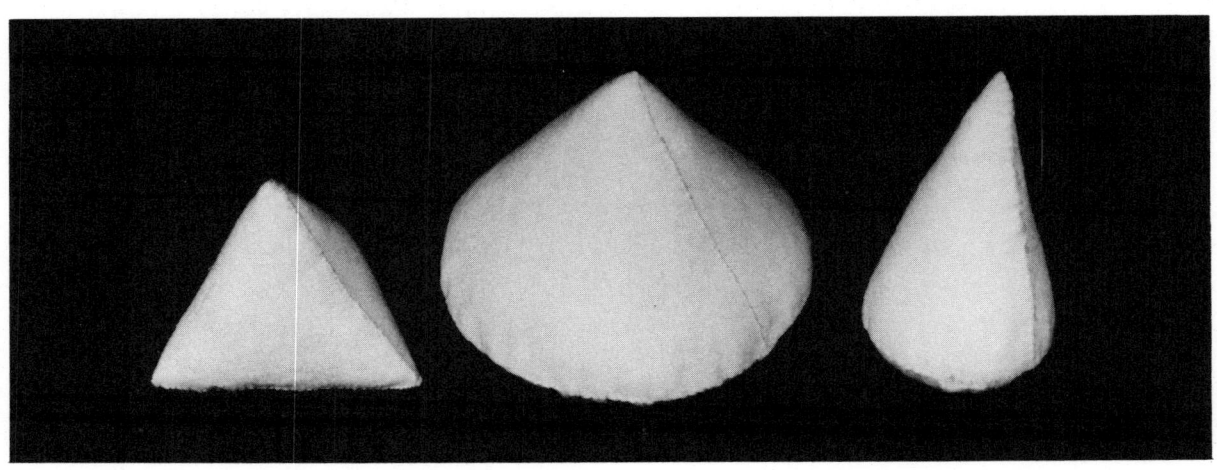

D E F

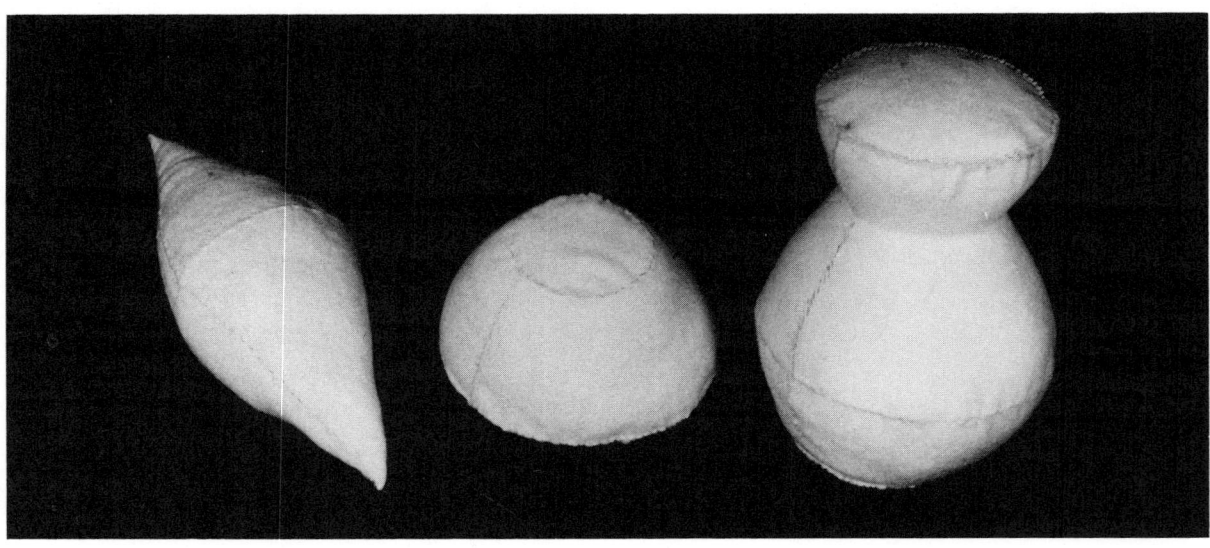

G H I

Pattern 3 GEOMETRIC PATTERNS

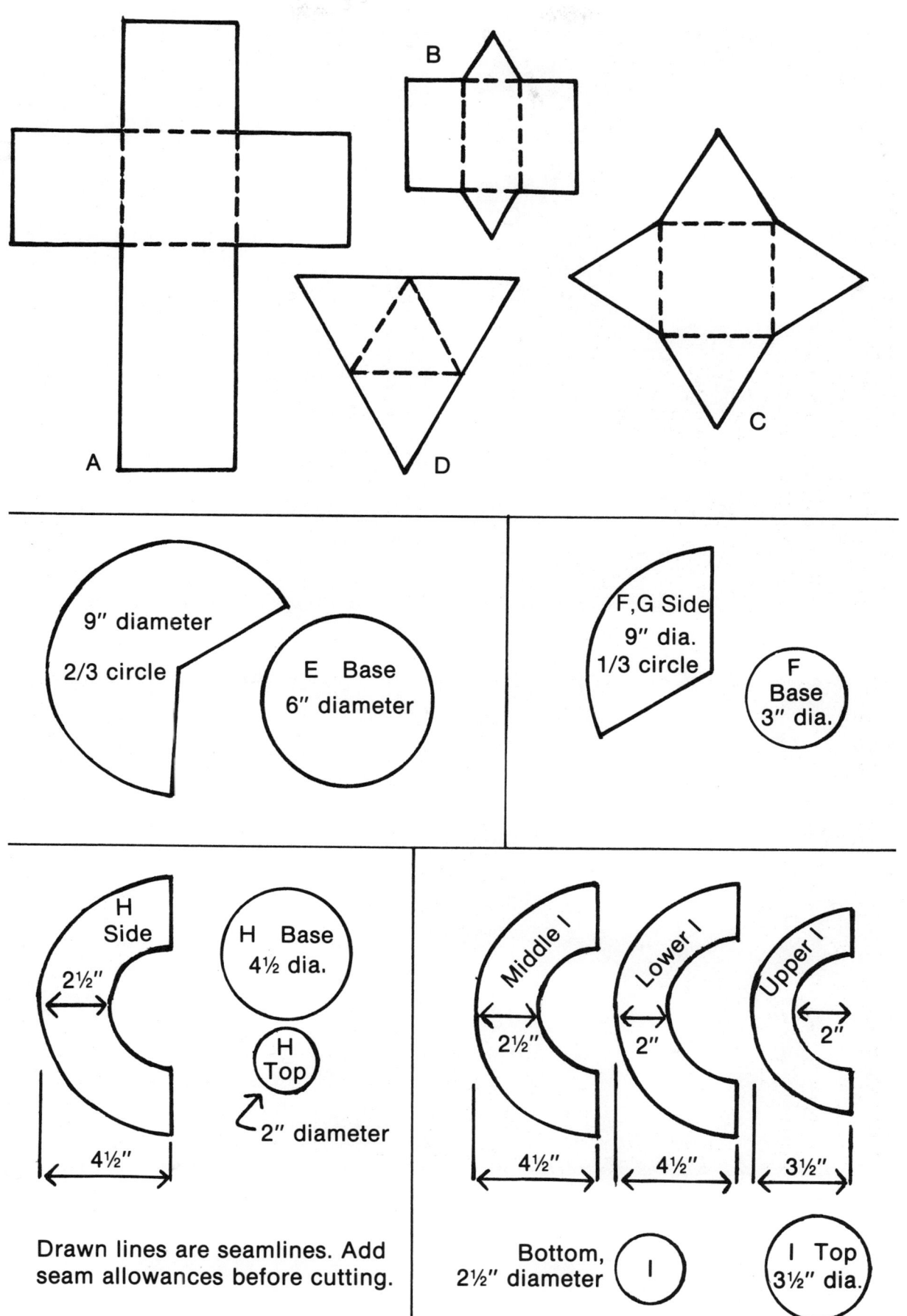

Drawn lines are seamlines. Add seam allowances before cutting.

Plate 11 BALLS

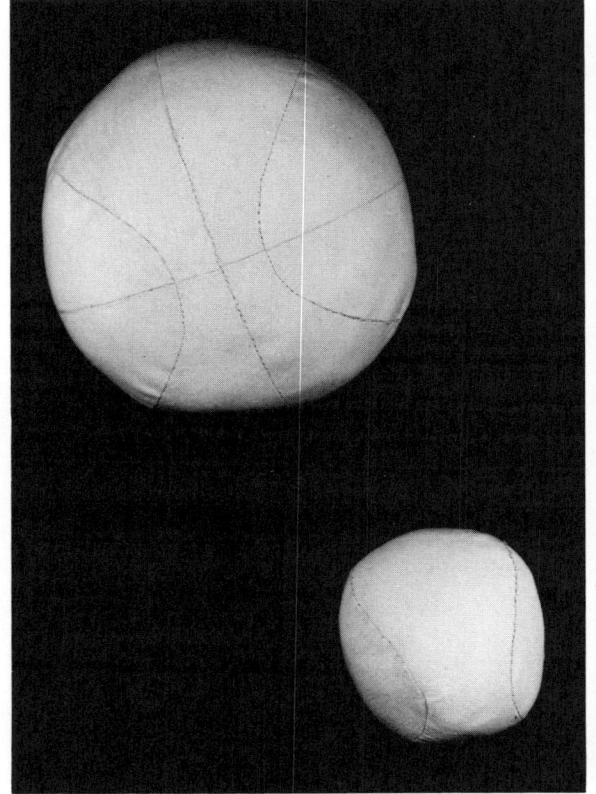

A. Basketball   B. Softball

C. Football   D. Football segment

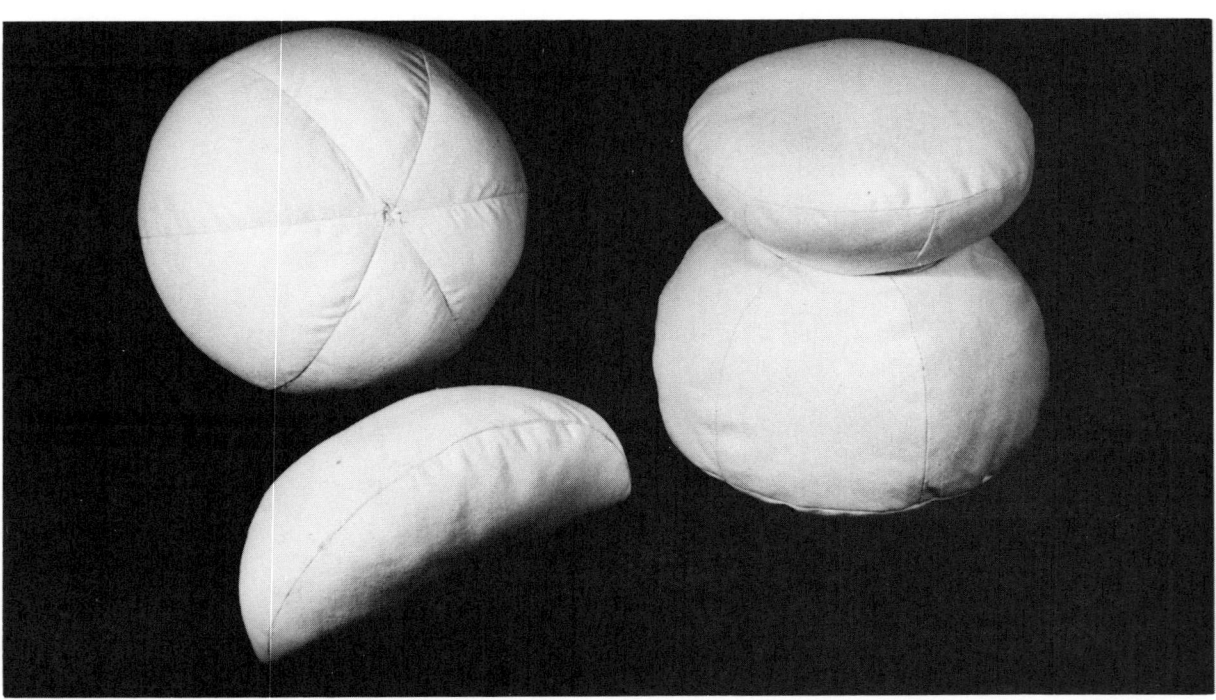

E. Sphere   F. Sphere segment   G. Truncated sphere

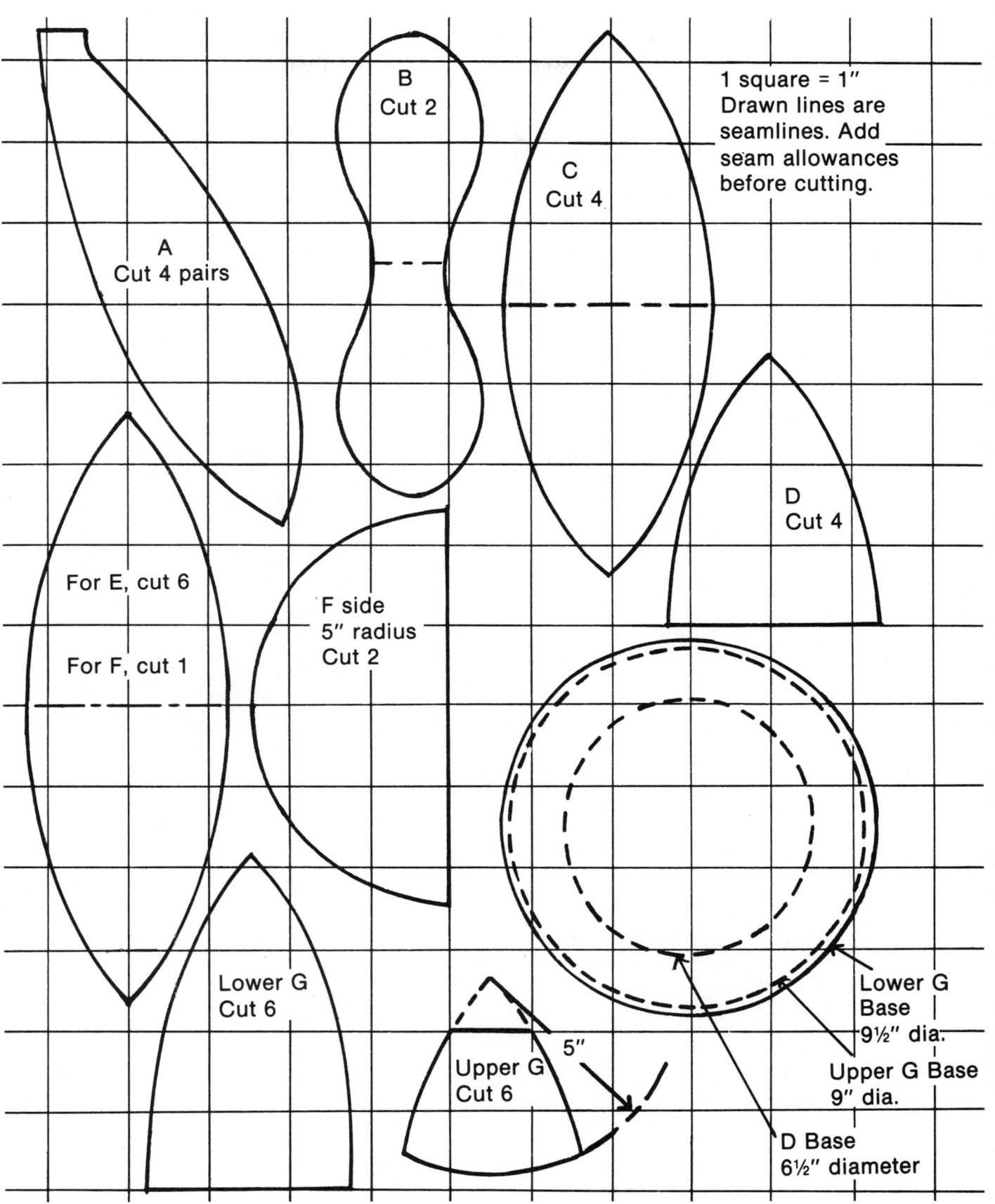

Pattern 4 BALL PATTERNS

110 The Complete Book of Stuffedwork

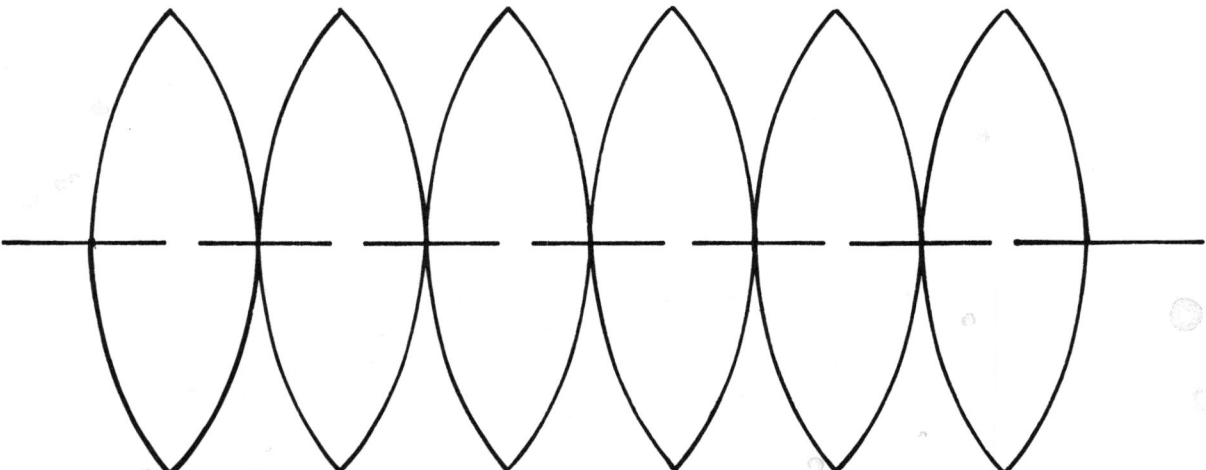

Fig. 159

You will see, if you try the draping exercise that follows, that the fabric cannot follow the form of the ball much beyond the rubber bands. You could make a fairly round 5-part ball but a 4-part ball looks more like a square.

PATTERN DRAPING

Draping is another basic method, along with computing and drafting, of arriving at a pattern. Clothing designers drape muslin over dressmakers' dummies. You can drape over any firm object into which you can push pins.

This 6-part sphere pattern was draped over an inflated rubber playground ball, which had been made of two molded halves, sealed at a center seam. We divided it into six equal sections with rubber bands (Fig. 160). (When you drape over basketballs or footballs, you need only to mark the muslin along the seamlines of one section of the ball. You can feel the indented seam through the cloth with a pin or your thumbnail.)

1. Measure the center seam of the ball to find the circumference. Divide it by 6. The resulting figure, to the nearest $\frac{1}{16}$ inch, will be the center width of each section and the baseline of the pattern. Mark off the ball seam in sixths, drawing about ½ inch each side of and perpendicular to the seam on the ball.
2. Place three rubber bands around the ball, joining opposite $\frac{1}{6}$ marks and keeping the

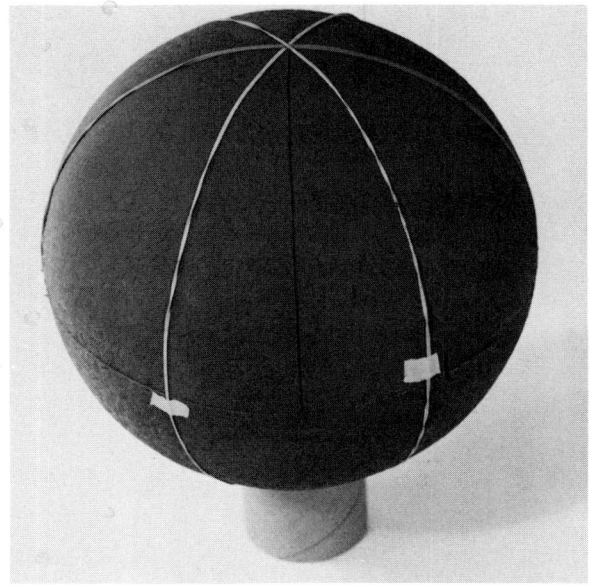

Fig. 160

bands perpendicular to the seam at the crossing. Place the tape measure along one rubber band from seam to seam and mark its center. Repeat for the other two rubber bands. Move them, if necessary, so that all the center marks match.
3. Make a mark exactly halfway between two rubber bands, on the seam. Place one edge of a tape on this mark and bring it up to the top intersection. Mark along the tape to indicate the lengthwise center of the section (see Fig. 160).

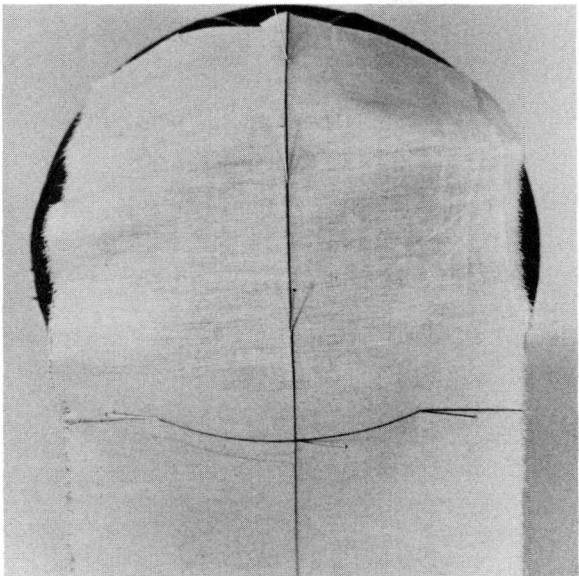

Fig. 161

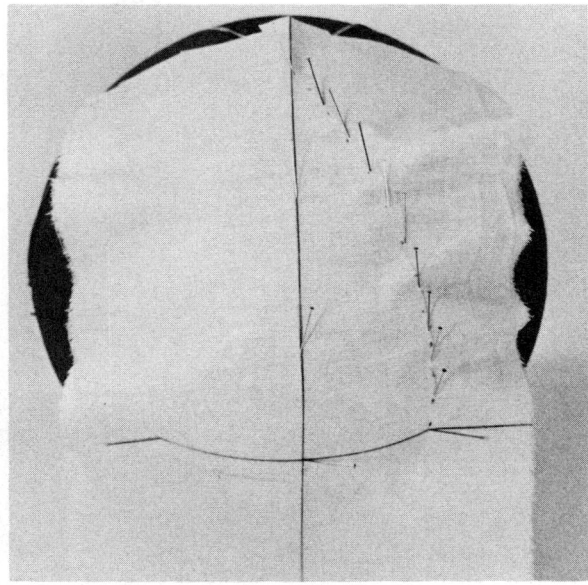

Fig. 162

4. Cut a piece of muslin larger than the section. Pull threads at each side to straighten the edges. Fold the muslin in half lengthwise, matching the edges, and press the fold to mark the centerline. Repeat, matching the other two edges, to mark the baseline. Draw along each fold with a dark pencil.

5. Place the muslin's baseline over the seam of the ball between the two rubber bands, with its centerline matching the drawn centerline on the ball. Use the tiniest bit of pinpoint (so the ball will not leak air) or masking tape to hold the muslin in place briefly (Fig. 161). Smooth the muslin over the ball and insert just the tips of pins along the rubber band, which you can feel through the muslin. Make short pencil marks along the pins (Fig. 162).

6. Remove the pattern. Connect the pencil marks with a smooth drawn seamline. (Use a French curve if you have one.) Draw a cutting line ¼ inch outside the seamline (Fig. 163).

Fold the muslin in half on the centerline, matching and pinning the baseline. Cut along the cutting line from the point to the baseline through both layers (Fig. 164).

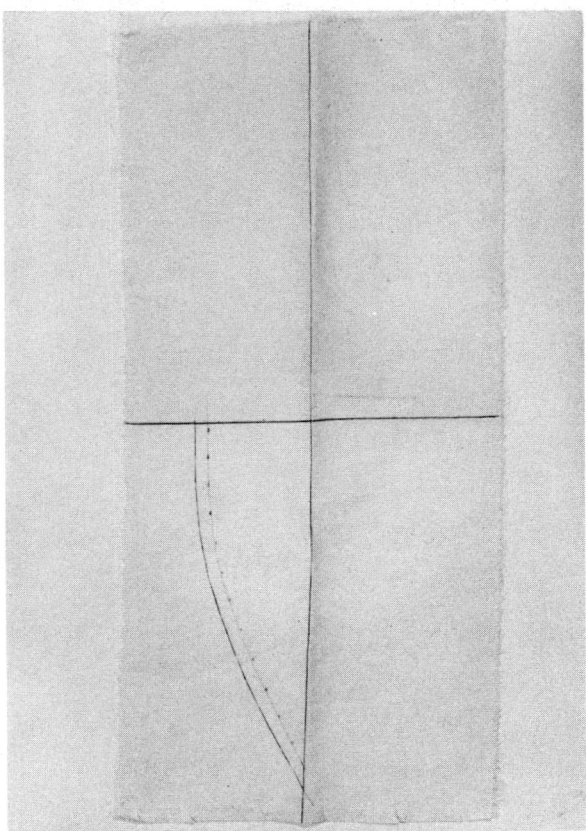

Fig. 163

Fig. 164

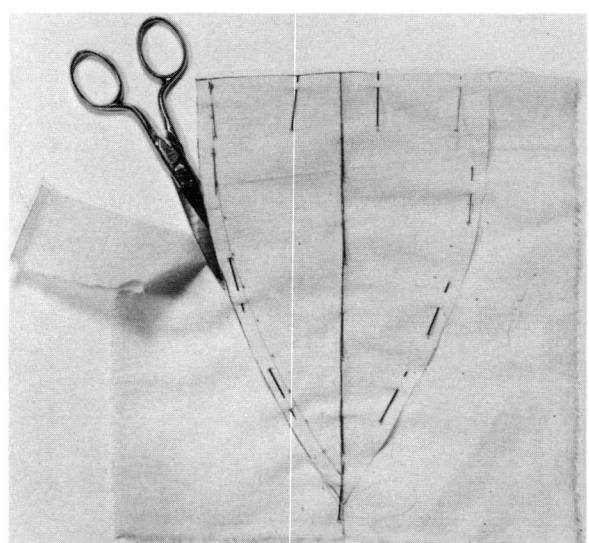

Fig. 165

Unpin the muslin. Refold on the baseline, matching and pinning the centerline. Cut the bottom layer to match the top layer (Fig. 165).

7. Unfold and press the finished pattern (Fig. 166).

Note: To make a somewhat smoother ball, the centerline of the pattern may be placed along the bias grain of the fabric when you cut out the six sections. To find the bias, see Figure 90, page 65.

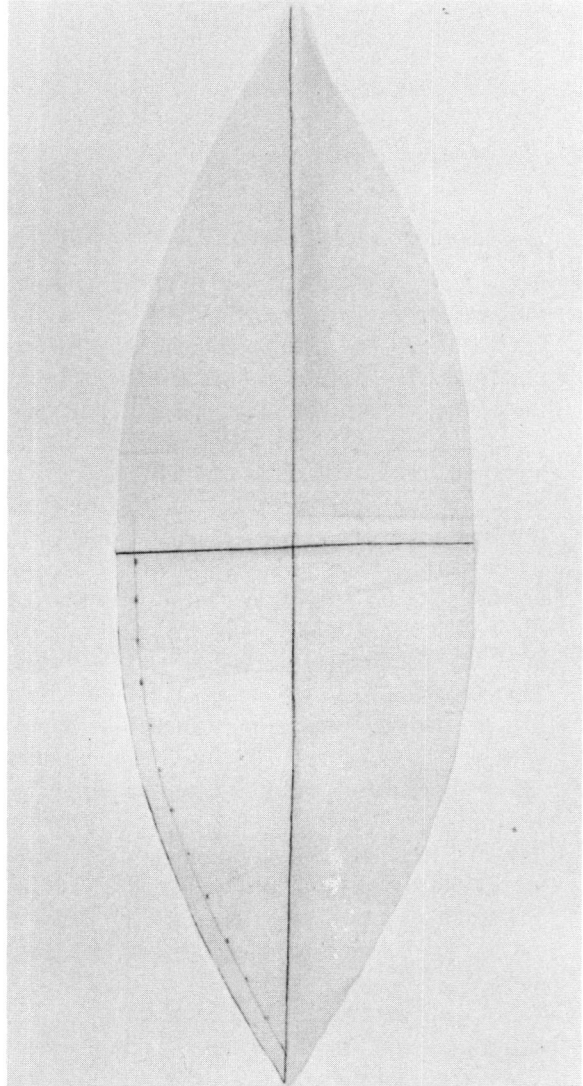

Fig. 166

Geometric Forms 113

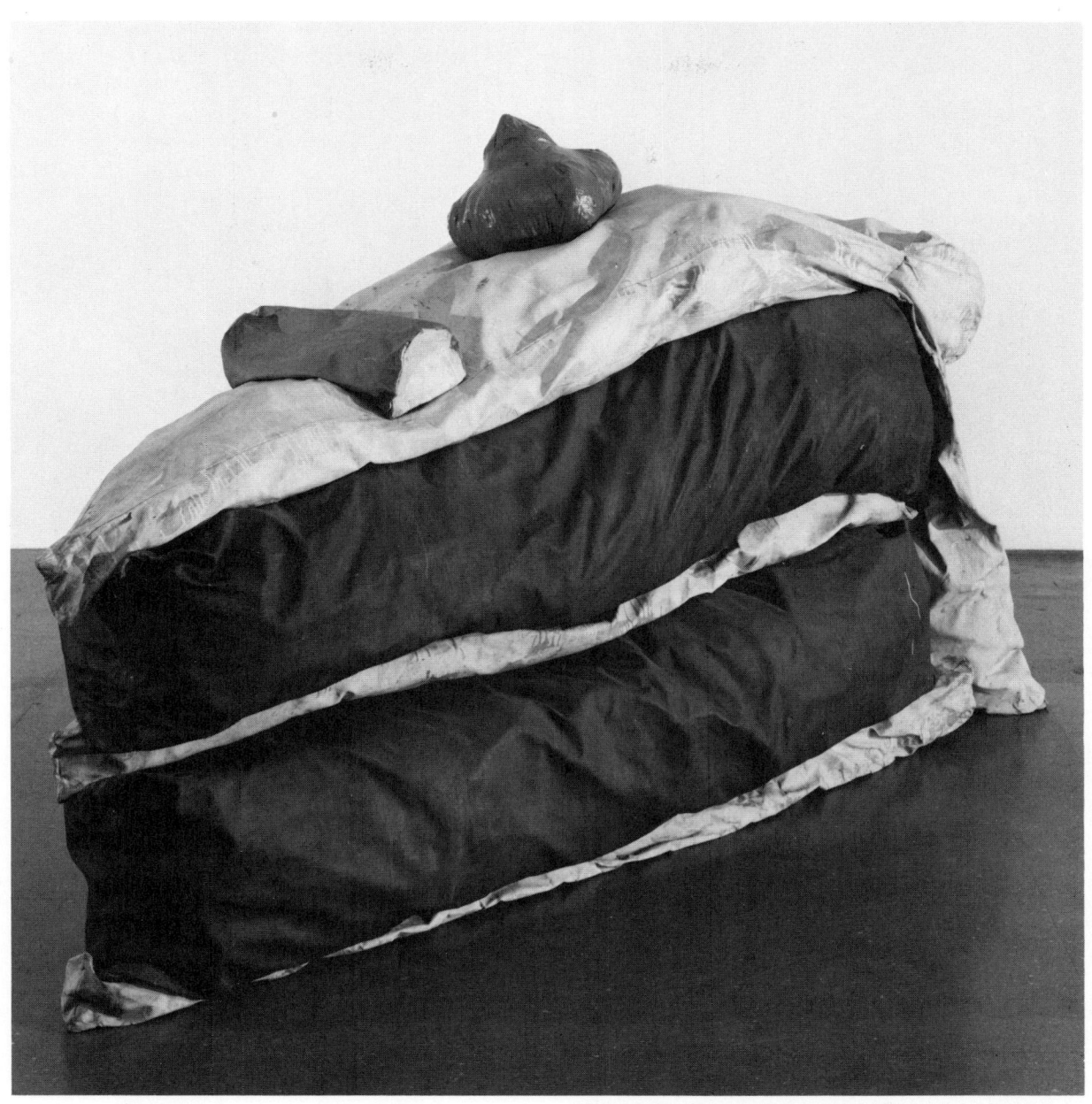

Claes Oldenburg *Floor Cake (Giant Piece of Cake)* (60" x 9' x 48"), 1962. Synthetic polymer paint and latex on canvas filled with foam. Collection, The Museum of Modern Art, New York, gift of Philip Johnson.

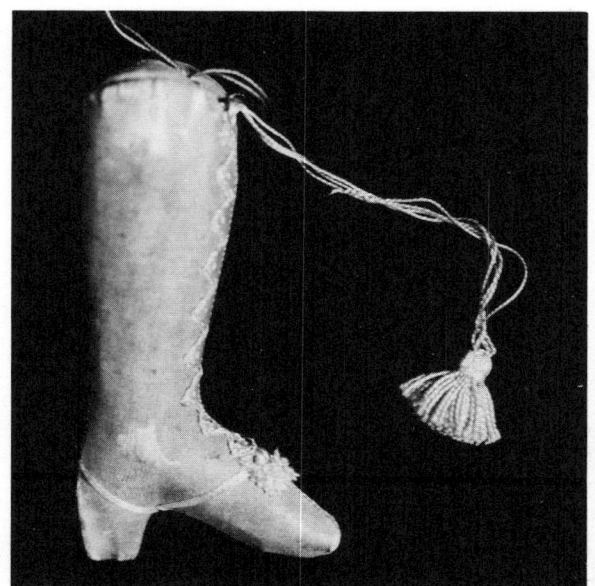

Boot-shaped Pincushion. Museum of the City of New York, gift of Mrs. Henry W. Lancer.

Norma Minkowitz *Bridal Box* (18" x 14"), 1973. Crochet, knit, trapunto, beading, plastic tubing, gasoline tubing, cardboard.

Geometric Forms 115

Michelle Gamm Clifton *Soft Fire Hydrant* (32" high), 1976. Stuffed white duck form, synthetic stuffing. Machine quilted surface, hand-sewn appliqués.

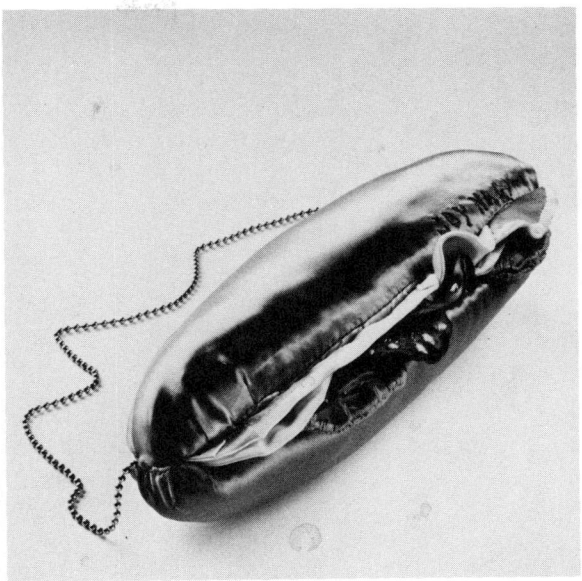

Joy Nagy *Sandwich Bag* (10" x 3½"). Satin fabric, foam rubber filling.

116 The Complete Book of Stuffedwork

Bernice Colman *Ceridwin* (44" x 34" x 32"). Fabric construction.

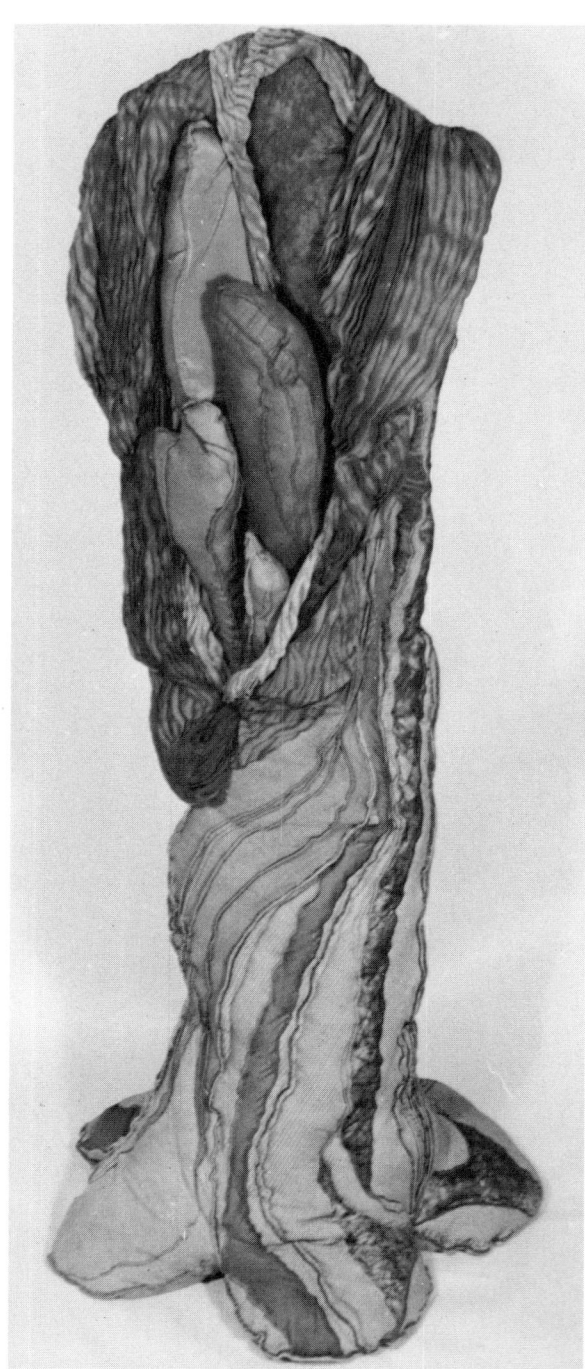

Bernice Colman *Adruinna* (50" x 20" x 18"). Fabric construction.

Tlingit Indians, Alaska *Hoonah Dolls*. The American Museum of Natural History.

118 The Complete Book of Stuffedwork

Raggedy Ann Doll, with book *Raggedy Ann and Andy and the Camel with the Wrinkled Knees* by Johnny Gruelle. Museum of the City of New York.

Geometric Forms 119

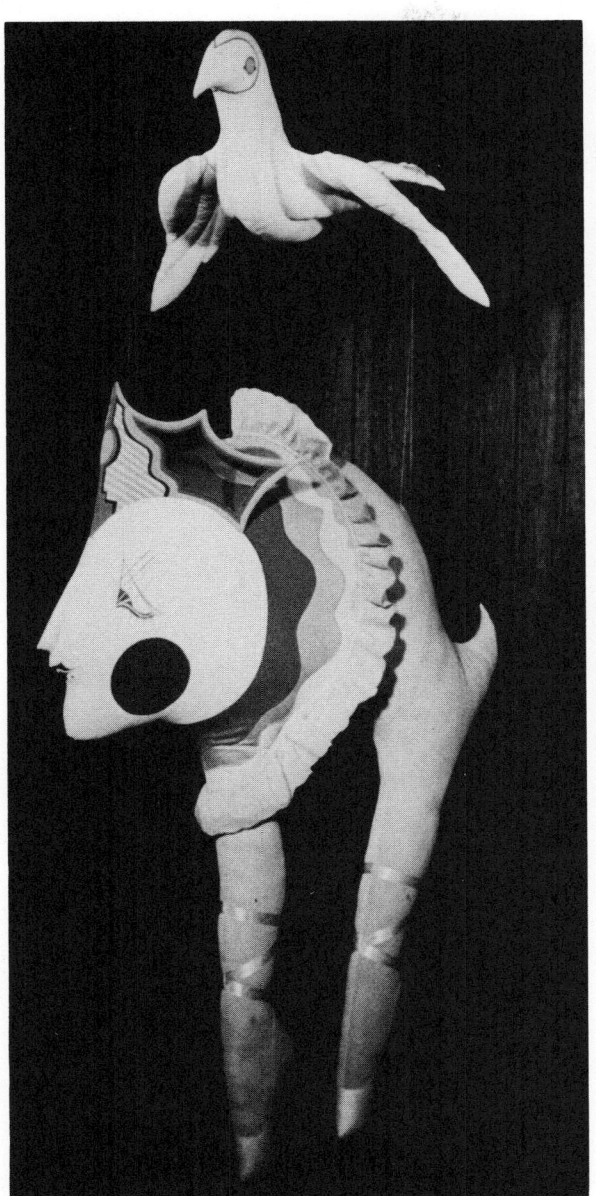

Catherine Pierce *Swan Lake* (65" x 38"). Muslin, procion dyes, acrylic paint. Double trapunto.

Diane Koppisch King *untitled* (25" x 24" x 35").
Direct dye and batik on cotton velveteen, stuffed and quilted.

Plate 12/Pattern 5A BODY A

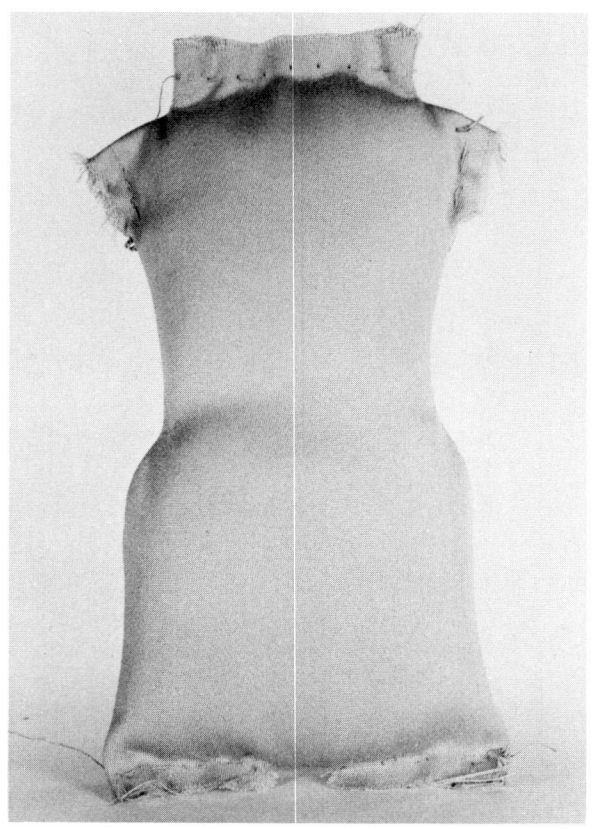

2-piece body, front view

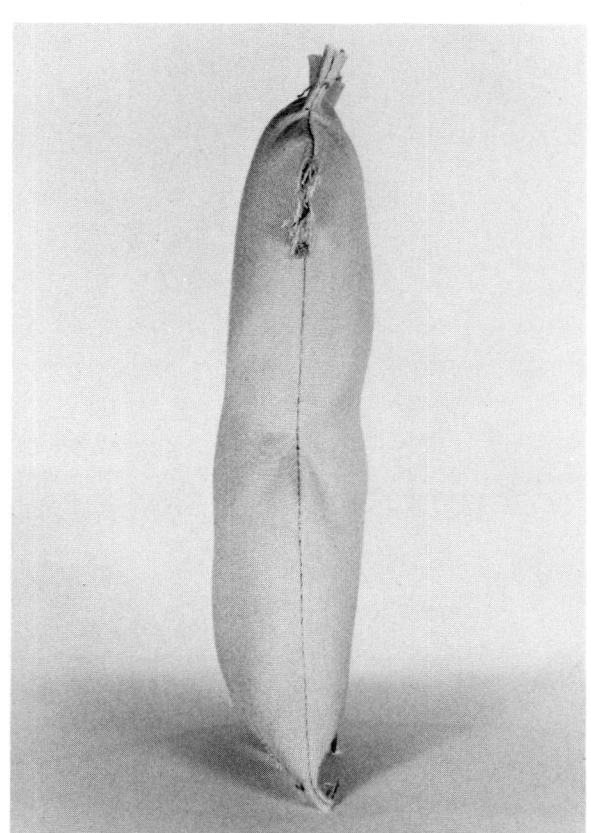

2-piece body, side view

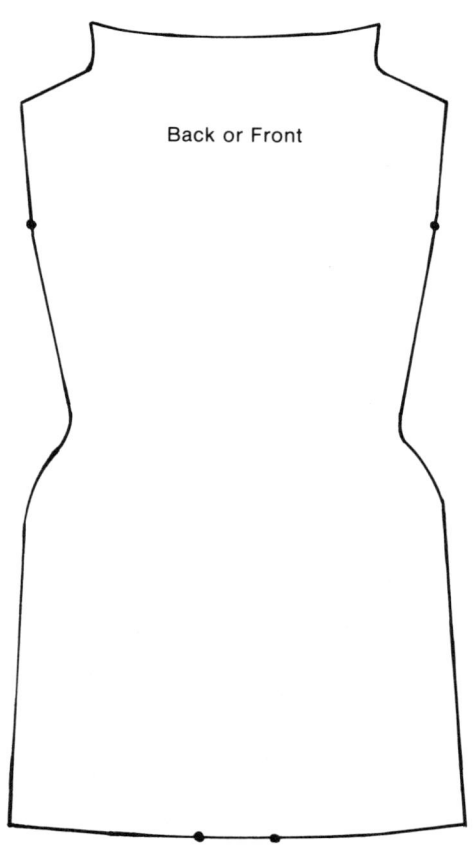

Back or Front

2-piece body, pattern

Chapter Six
Bodies

As THE FLAT FORMS in Chapter 4 have indicated, the *shape,* in sewing, is *where the seams are.* In order to have contours at the front and back as well as at the sides of a form, additional seams must be drawn.

SEAMS

ADDED SEAMS

In Plate 12 you will see a 2-piece body (Body A). The front and back are cut the same. The sides are shaped but, when you look at the side view, the body is flat.

In the pattern for Body B, the center foldline of Body A has become a center seam to which a stomach curve at the front and a lower curve at the back have been added. The new seams affect the contours that are visible in the side view.

Suppose shape were needed, not in the center front but nearer the sides, in breast position, for instance (Plate 13). Again, we could return to the Body-A pattern and divide it into thirds, adding breast and hipbone curves to the front seams and a rump to the back seams (Body C). Matching crossmarks have been placed at the breast, so that the left and right sides of the body will join the center front at the same level.

Plate 13A/Pattern 5B BODY B

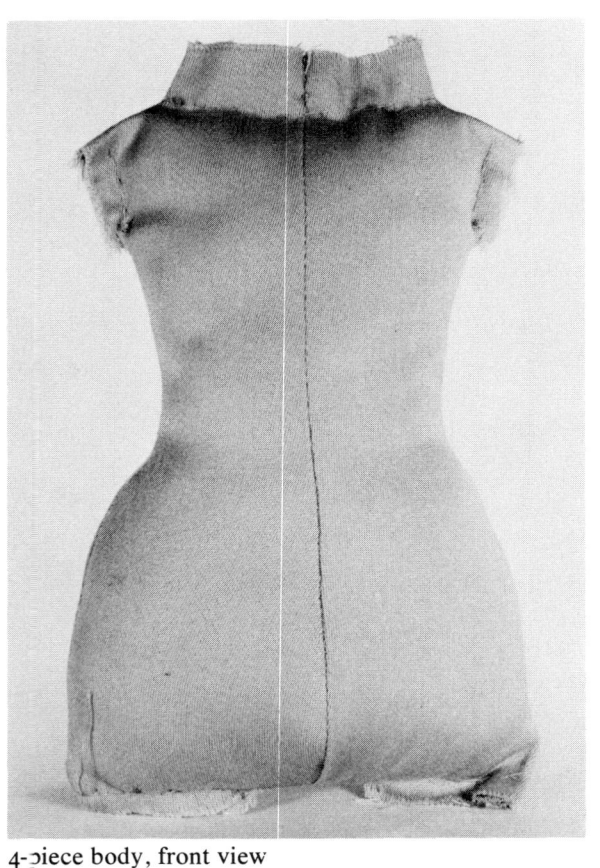

4-piece body, front view

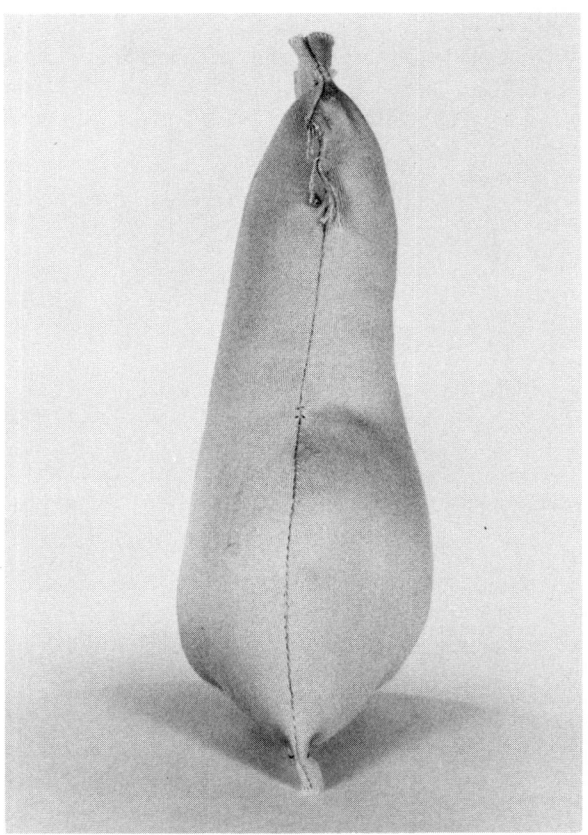

4-piece body, side view

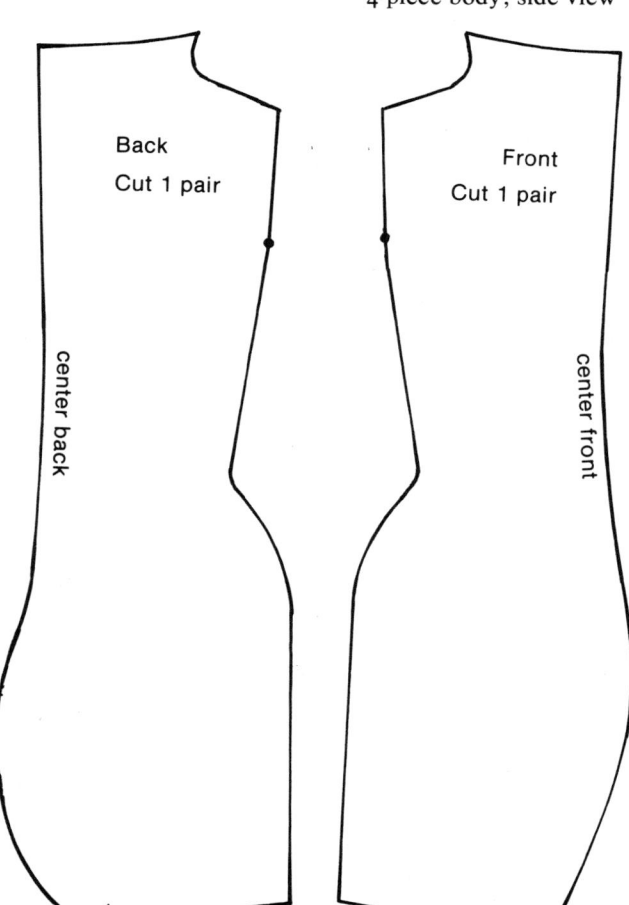

4-piece body, pattern

Plate 13B/Pattern 6 BODY C

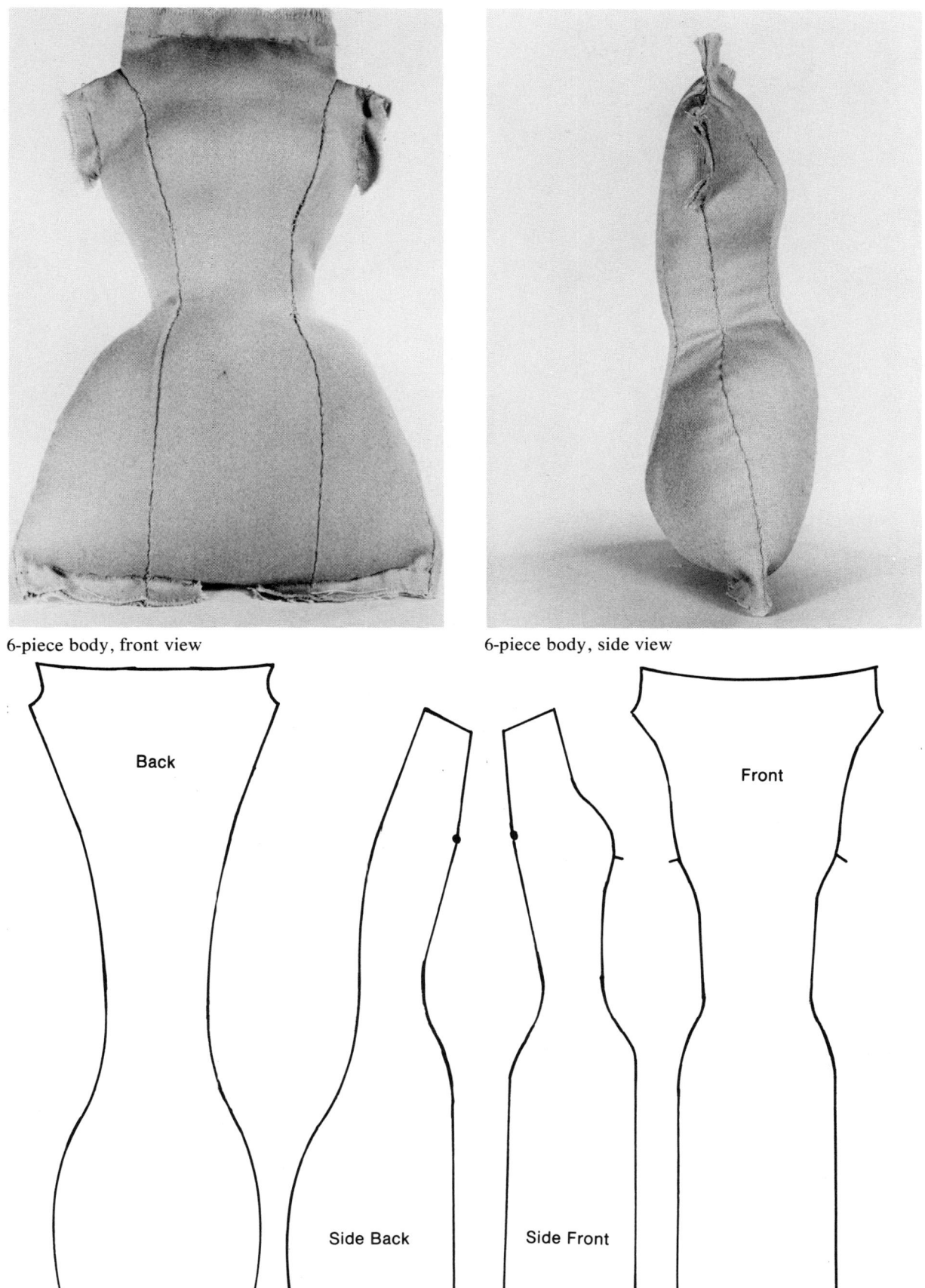

6-piece body, front view

6-piece body, side view

6-piece body, pattern

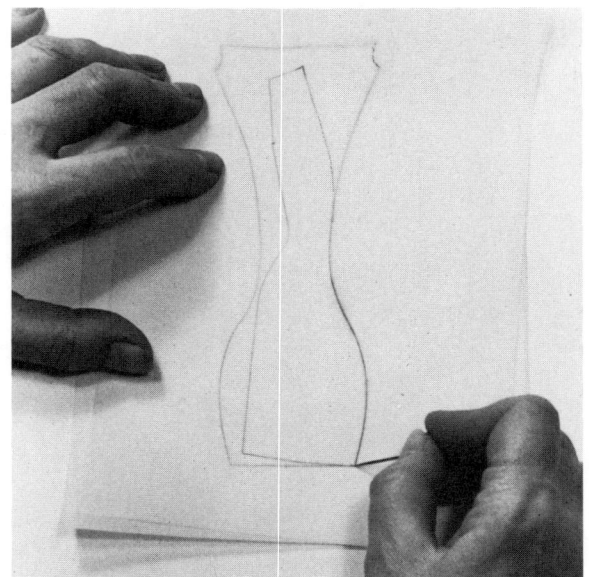

Fig. 167

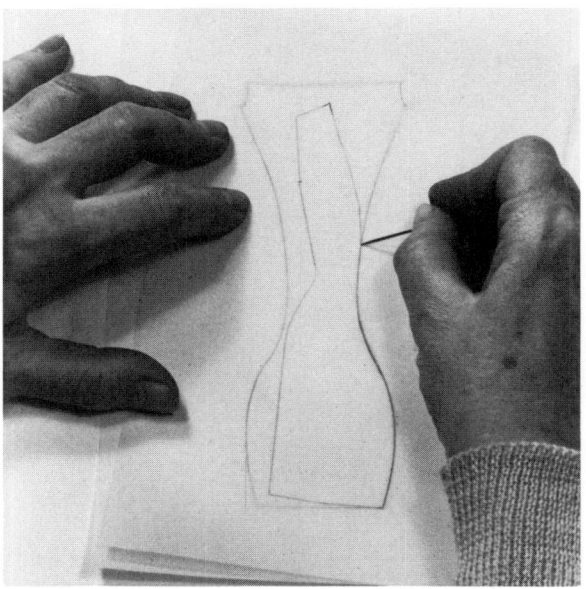

Fig. 168

PIN-TRACKING

During patternmaking, adjoining seams can be pin-tracked to see that they match. Draw the pattern pieces on transparent paper and find a darning needle or long pin. Place one pattern piece over the other, matching the beginning of two seams (Fig. 167). Where the seams begin to diverge, anchor the two patterns with the needle point (Fig. 168). Swivel the top paper until the seamlines overlap again (Fig. 169). Continue (Fig. 170) matching, anchoring, and swiveling to the end of the seam. Here, the seams should come out even (Fig. 171). If they don't, redraw them so that they do.

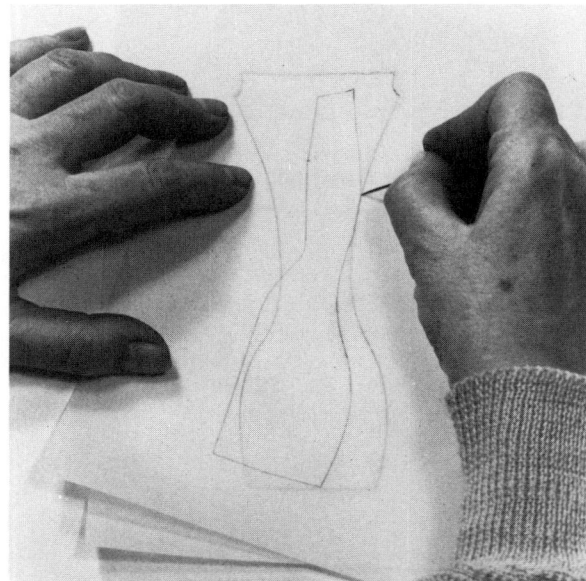

Fig. 169

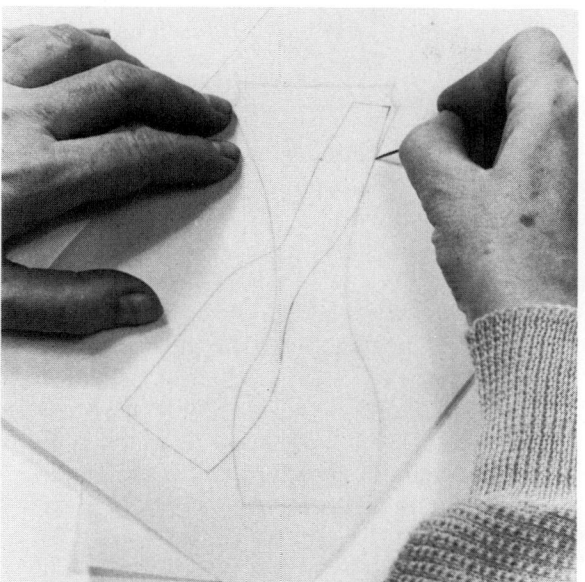
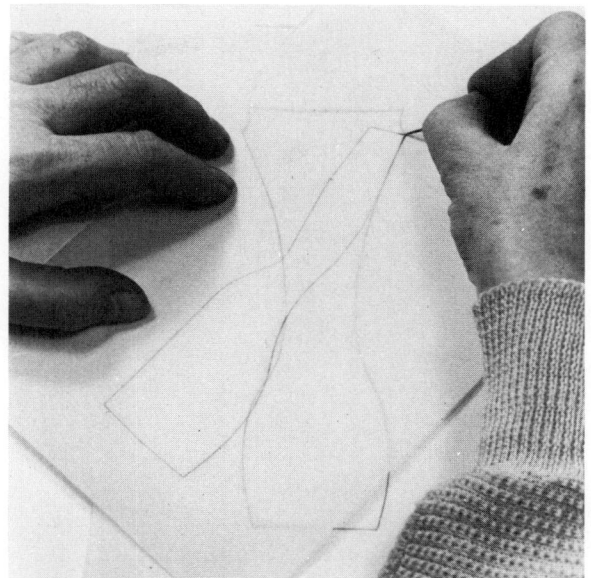

Fig. 170 Fig. 171

HOLDING IN

There are times when one seam is intentionally a little longer than the other. Here the longer seam is *held in* to meet the other. Two crossmarks have to be placed across each seam to indicate the part of the seamline where the holding in should occur. Such extra fabric provides space for breasts, bent elbows, and raised shoulders and are often encountered in clothing patterns that have to allow for body movement.

SEAM ALLOWANCES

Remember that the patterns in this book do not include seam allowances. You may add them to the pattern, drawing them outside the seamlines (Fig. 155). Or you may trace the seamlines to the wrong side of a block of fabric, with a tracing wheel through dressmaker's carbon; then cut about ¼ inch away from the traced lines (½ inch for larger pieces). When pinning the seams together, you will match the traced, not the cut lines.

Note: In order to fit the page, some pattern pieces have been drawn in two sections (Pattern 7). When you trace the pattern, match the lines that say "piece pattern here" and continue to trace the pattern, in one piece.

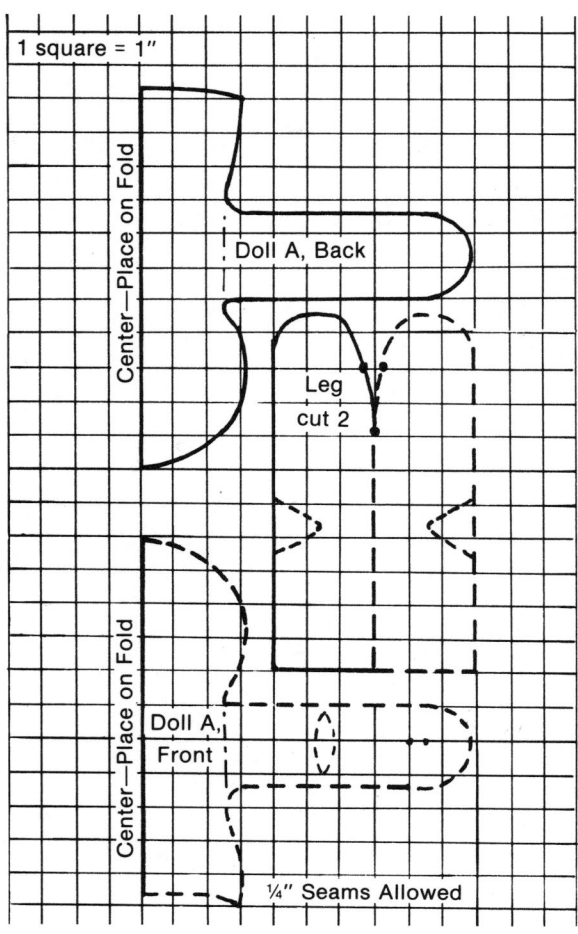

Fig. 172

DOLL BODIES

CONTOUR DARTS

Doll A (Plate 14) is drawn as a flat form, but the arms and legs are made to bend by means of contour darts known as *oysters*, stitched at the knees and elbows. The wrists and ankles are just tacked at what would be the widest point of such an oyster, achieving a similar effect. In this doll, the arms and head are cut in one piece with the front (Fig. 172). Arms like these can be pieced at the broken line — add a seam allowance to both the body and the arm if you do this — in order to save fabric. In either case, stitch across the broken line after the arm is stuffed to allow the arm to bend, then stuff the body.

Plate 14   DOLL A

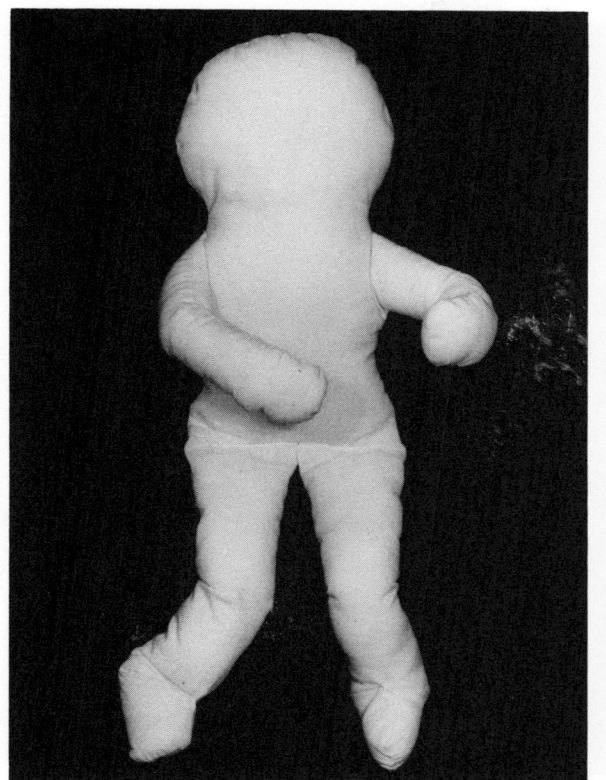
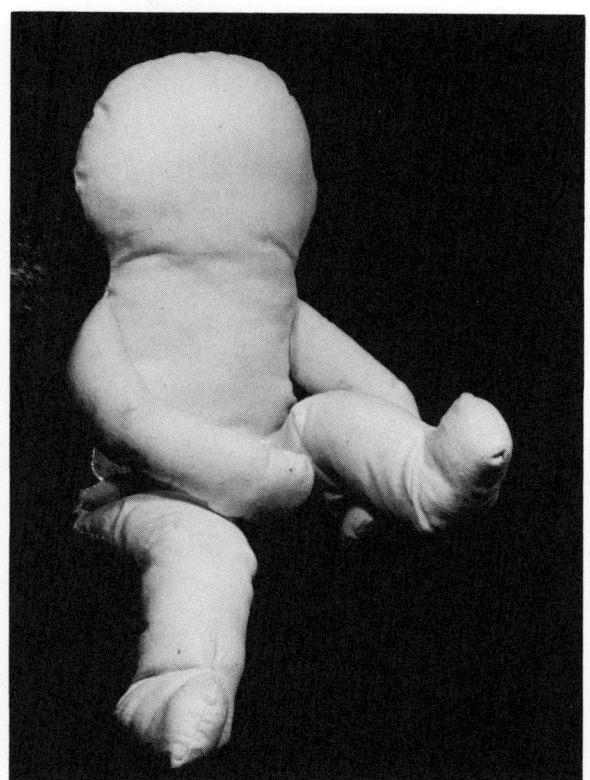
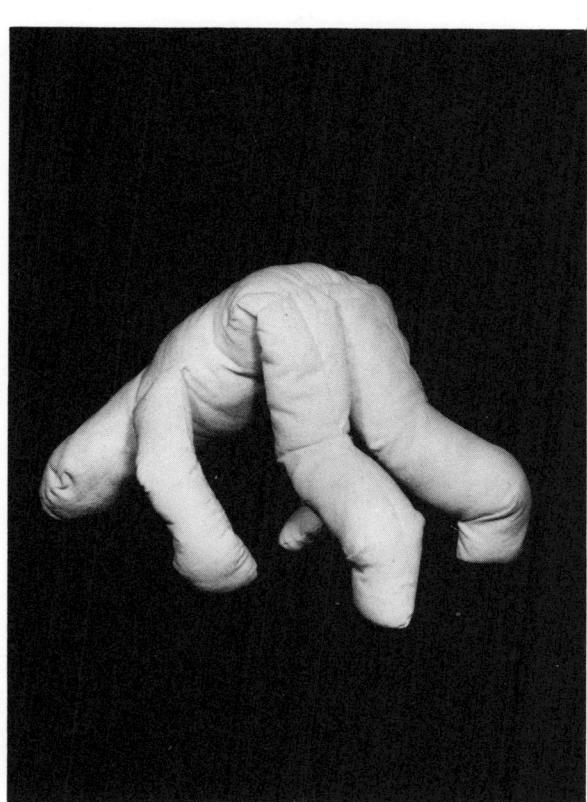

Plate 15   DOLL B

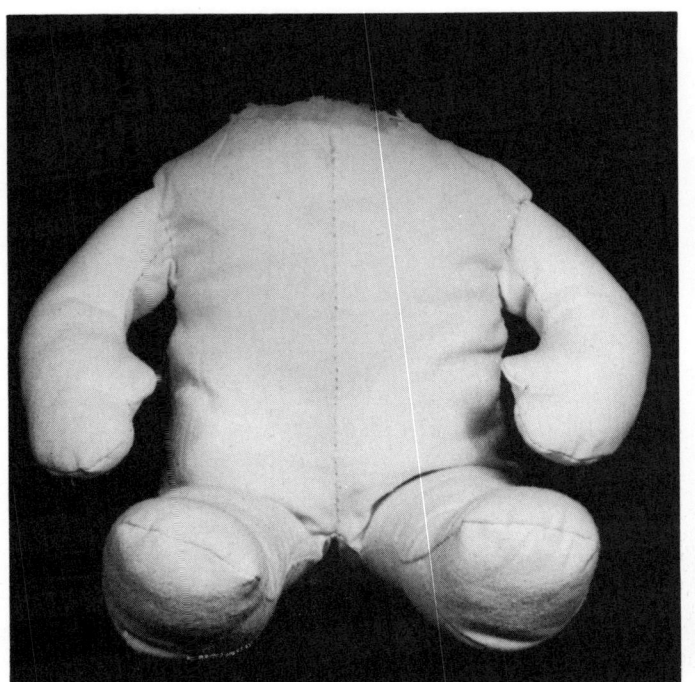
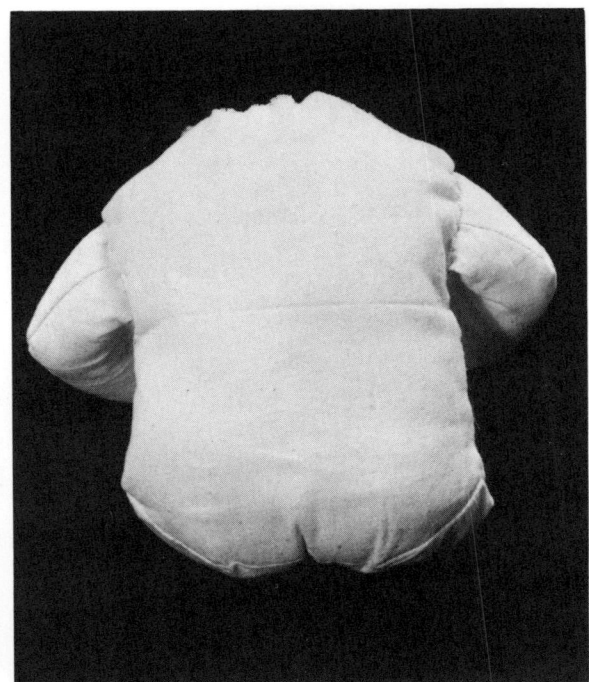
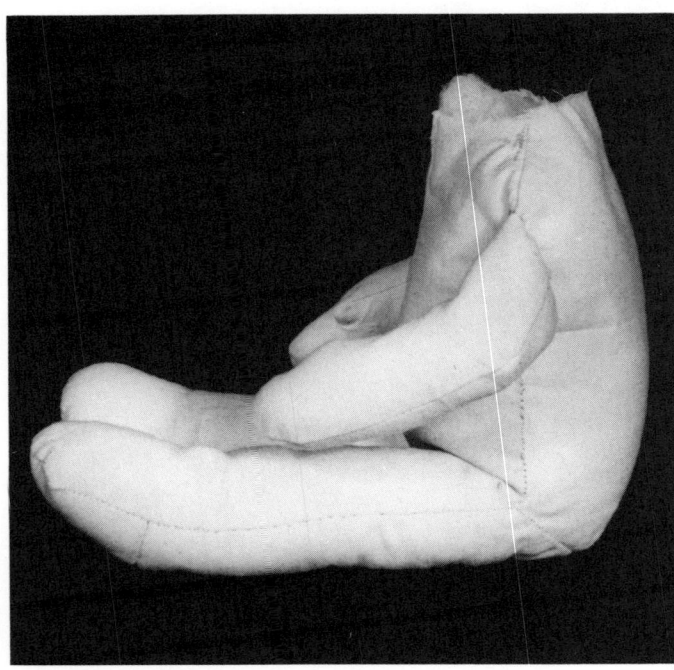

Pattern 7

piece pattern here

Doll B Back (to be pieced)
Cut 1 on center back fold

center back   place on fold

piece pattern here

Doll B   Back piecing

Doll B   Arm
Cut 2 pairs

Drawn lines are seamlines. Add seam allowances before cutting.

piece pattern here

Doll B Front
to be pieced
Cut 1 pair

Doll B Front Piecing

piece pattern here

Plate 16 DOLL C

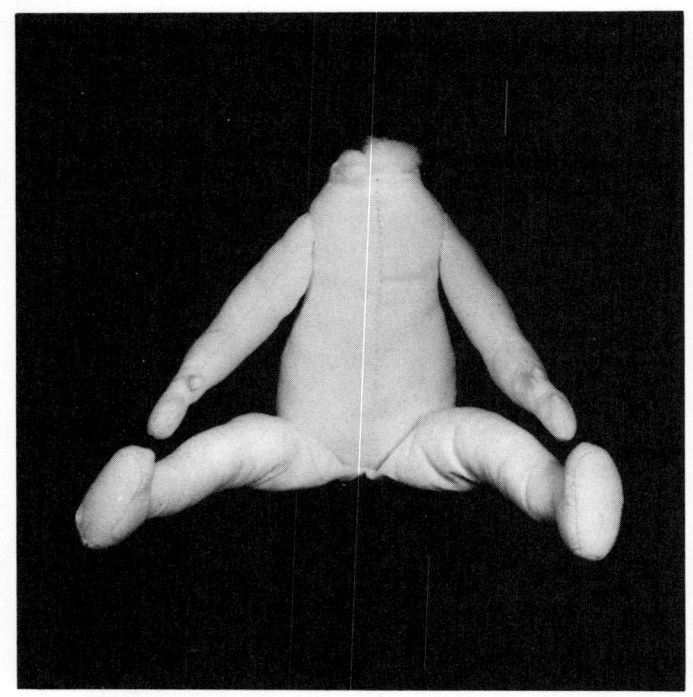
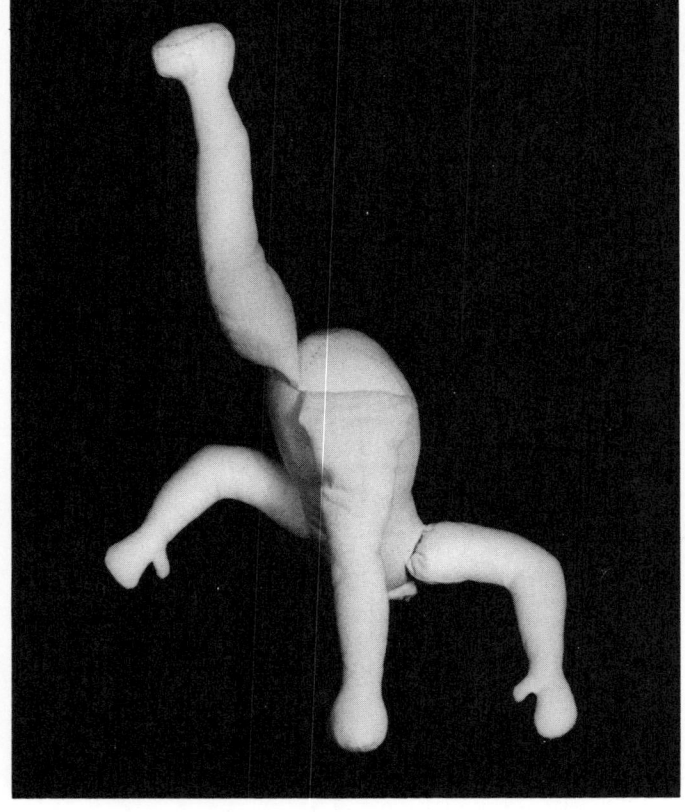
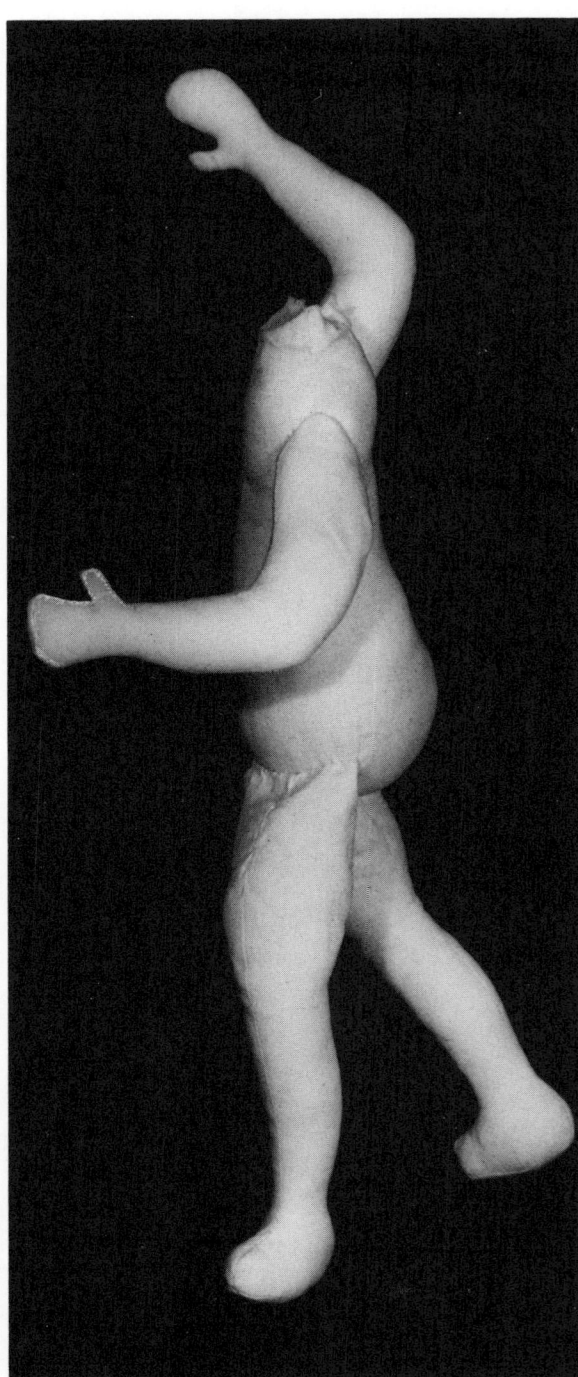

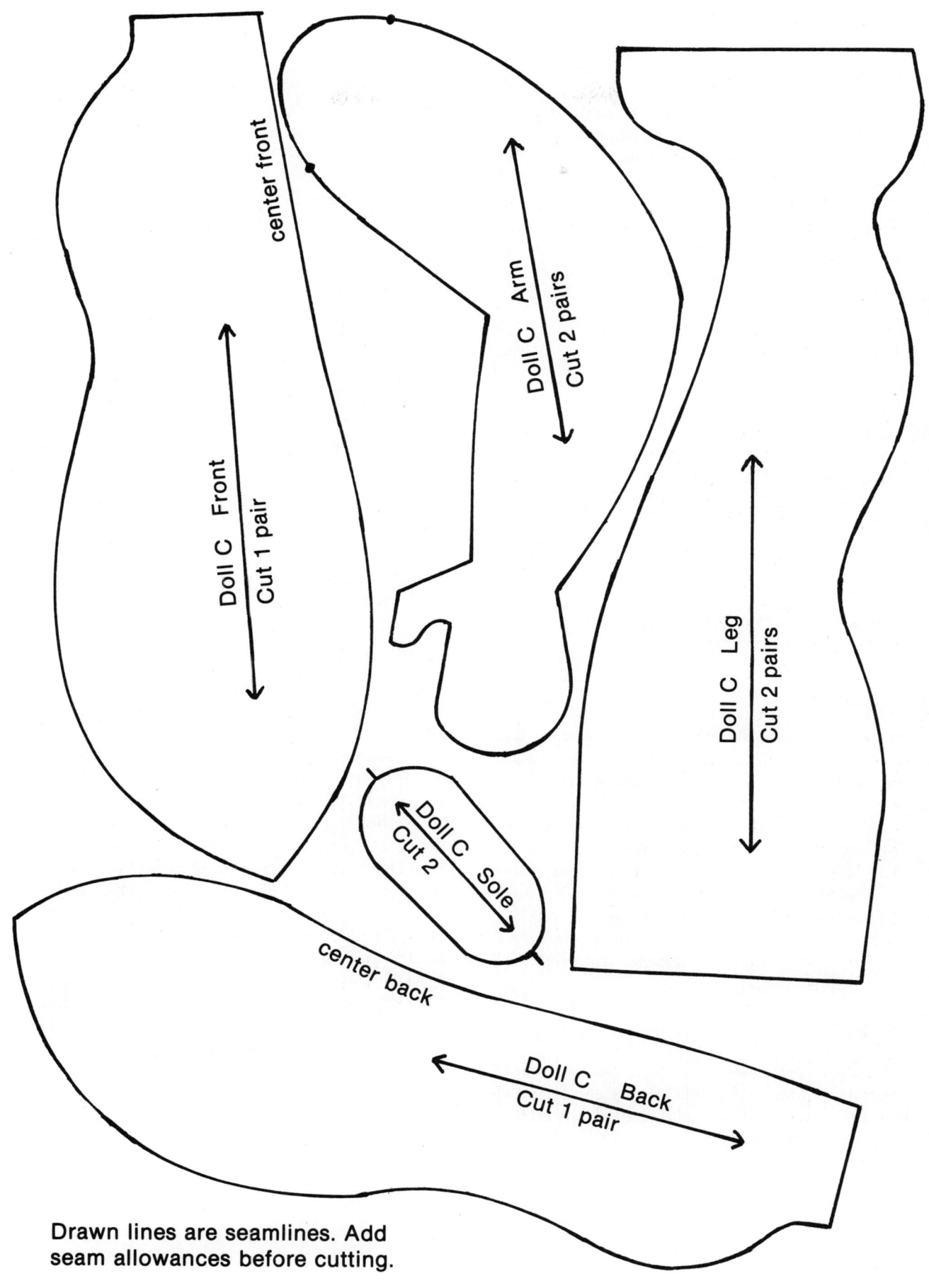

Pattern 8

Drawn lines are seamlines. Add seam allowances before cutting.

OPEN-ENDED DARTS

Doll B (Plate 15 and Pattern 7) again demonstrates the usefulness of darts, but these have only one point. The other, open end, goes into a seam. A pair of large darts makes the doll "sit" while a pair of small ones turns the foot. Also, in Doll B notice that the seams of the curved arms are brought to the center (as are the legs in Doll A) before being attached to the body.

SEPARATE LIMBS

Doll C (Plate 16 and Pattern 8) has a four-piece body without arm or leg holes, completely closed except at the neck. The arms and legs are stuffed and closed separately. They are slipstitched to the stuffed body, at the same time providing movable joints. There are soles to provide width to the feet.

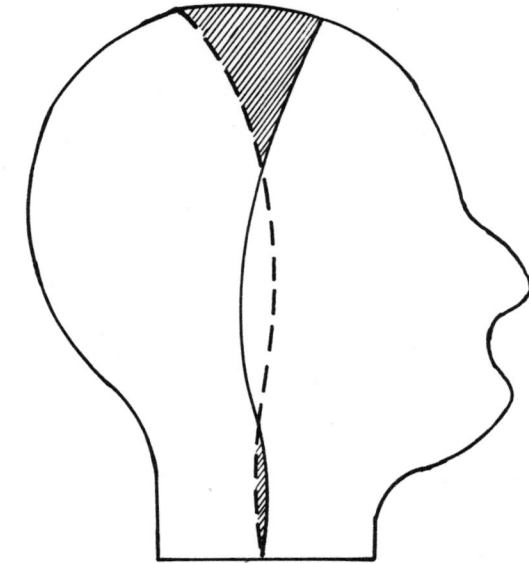

Fig. 173

DOLL HEADS (Plate 17; Patterns 9 and 10)

TWO-PIECE

In working with flat forms, we saw that two round or oval pieces sewn together will make a pillowlike form that represents the front view of a head (Plate 17, 1).

Just as we made a flat front view of the head, we can make a flat profile view (Plate 17, 5). The features must be exaggerated in the drawing, since they will be much smaller when they are turned and stuffed. Roman noses, long upper lips, sloping chins, and foreheads will hold stuffing better than snub noses, dainty lips, and sharp chins.

GATHERED

A stuffed sock makes a rounded head, closer to human contours. A gathering row can be drawn up at the eye level to make a little indentation; more gathering at the chin level begins the neck (Plate 17, 2). An alternative to the sock is a rectangle of fabric folded and seamed, then drawn up with a gathering row at the top and bottom (Plate 17, 3).

ADDED SEAMS

Four seams eliminate the gathers and allow a more realistic tapering at the top of the head (Plate 17, 4).

The flat head becomes more spherical if it is redrafted into four sections (Plate 17, 6). The 4-piece head is arrived at very much like the 4-piece body, discussed earlier. It is a combination of a front view and a side view. A center seam tapers fabric off the crown and neck and adds a little width between the ears (Fig. 173). You will recall, also, that when we discussed drafting bodies, we sometimes divided the body into thirds (p. 121). When a head is so divided, the seam can provide the full curves of a baby's cheeks (Plate 17, 7). The center sections are usually connected across the head from front to back, reducing the sections to three and avoiding a pointed crown.

STITCHING AND STUFFING

When you stitch, use short stitches (machine 11 or 12). A second row of stitching, for reinforce-

Plate 17   DOLL HEADS

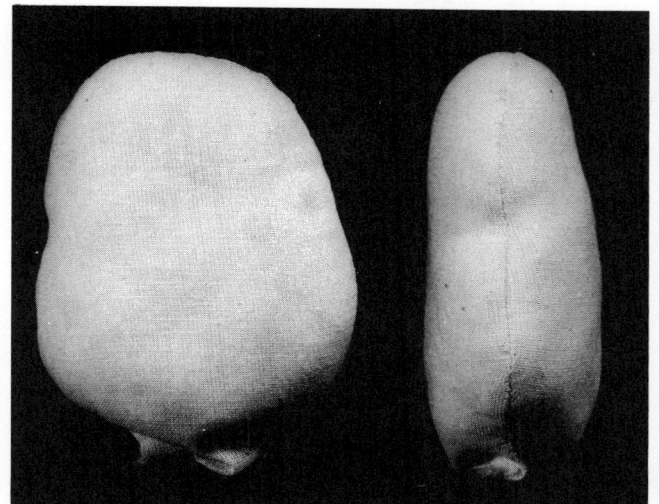

1. 2-piece head

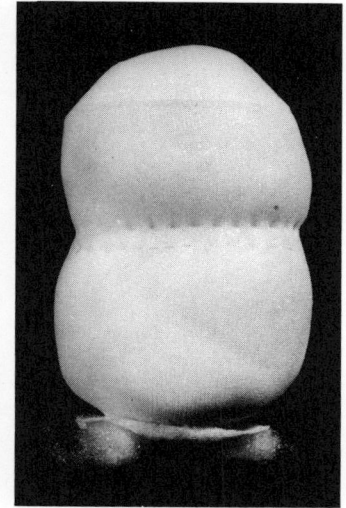

2. sock head

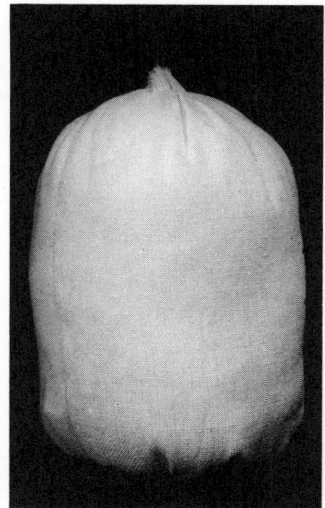

3. gathered head

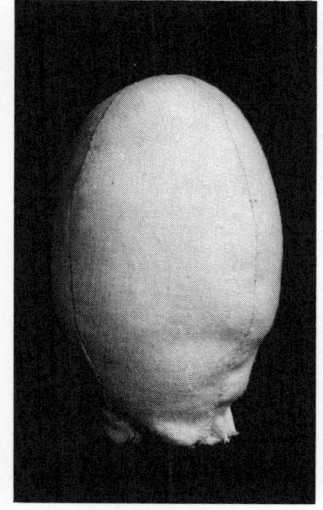

4. 4-piece head

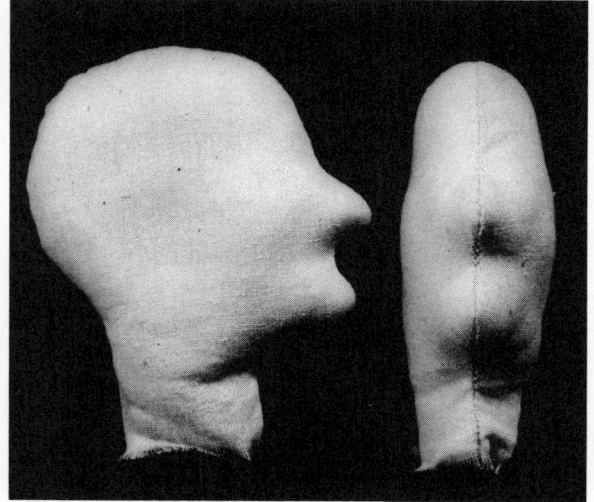

5. 2-piece profile head

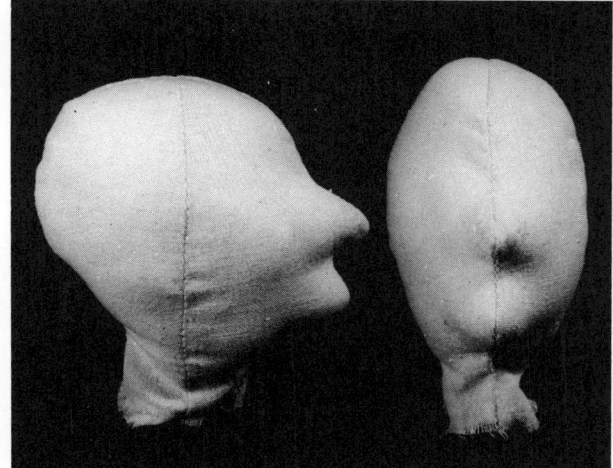

6. 4-piece profile head

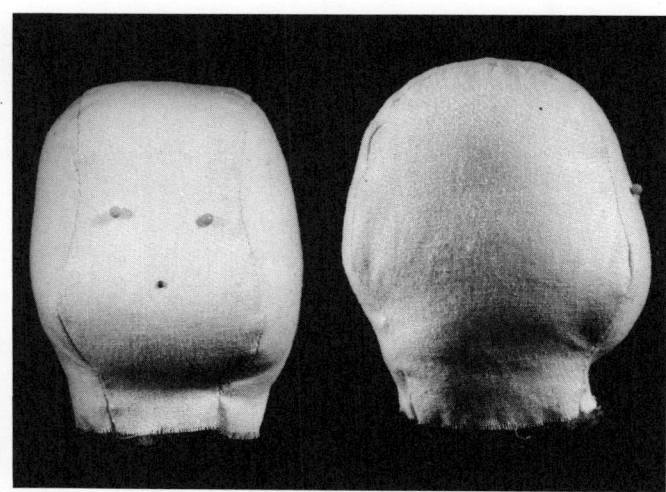

7. 3-piece head

Pattern 9

Head 5
Cut 1 pair

center front

Head 4
Side Front
Cut 1 pair

Drawn lines are seamlines. Add seam allowances before cutting.

Head 6 Side Back
Cut 1 pair

Head 6 Side Front
Cut 1 pair

Center Back

Head 4
Side Back
Cut 1 pair

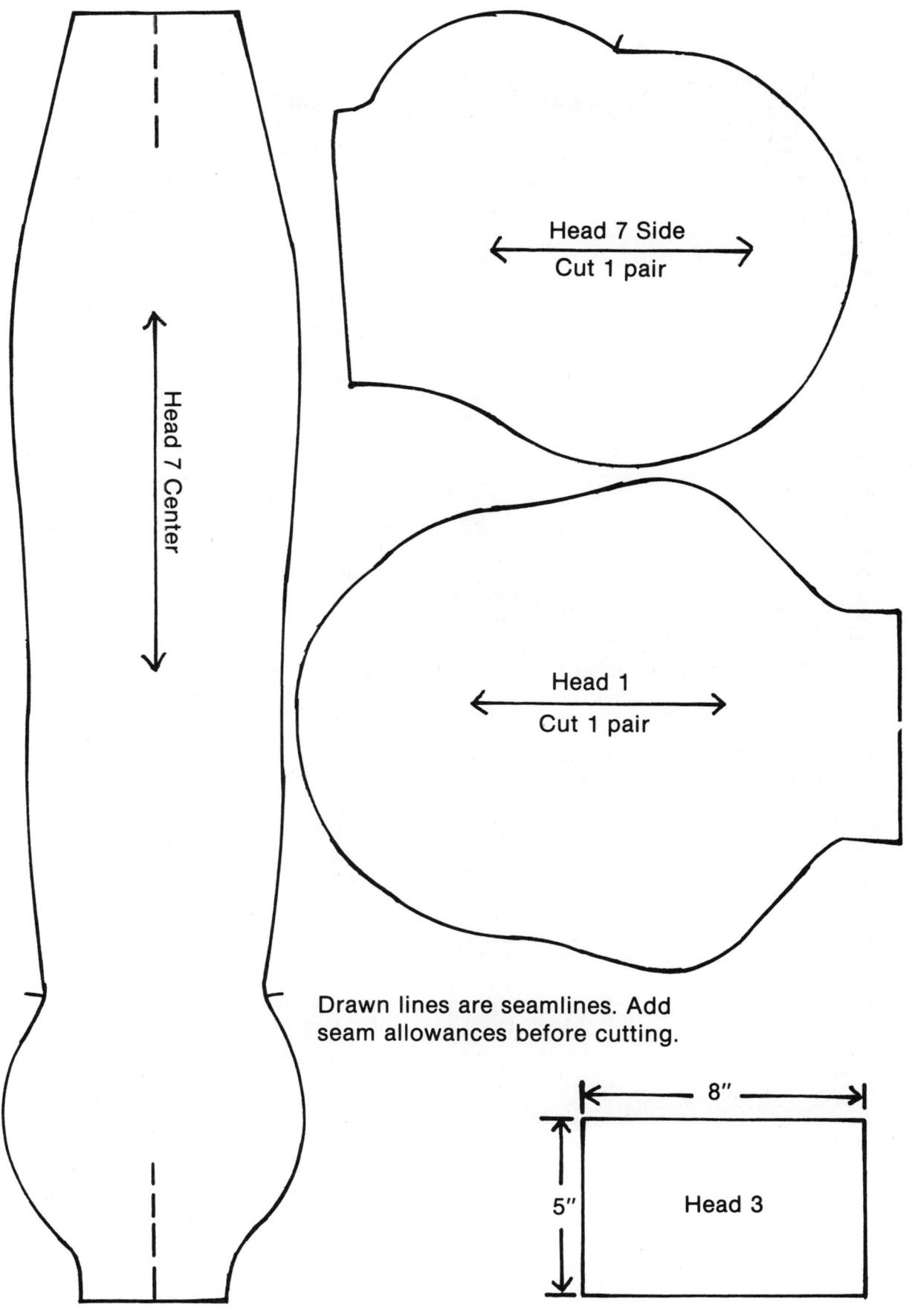

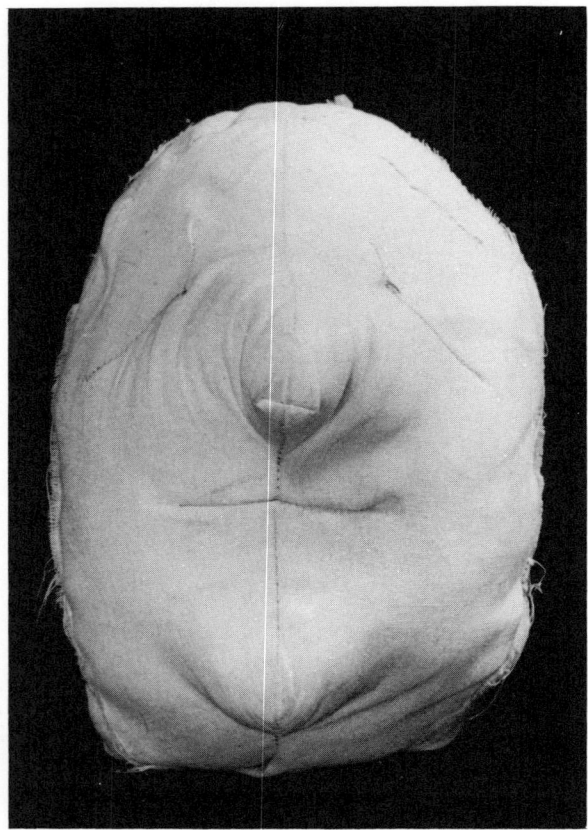

Fig. 174

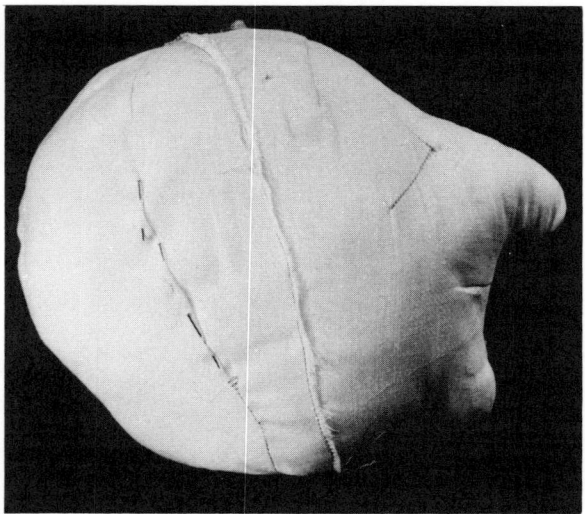

Fig. 175

ment, especially on inside corners and curves, is a good practice. When you stuff — synthetic stuffing or Kapok is usually used for dolls — use a knitting needle, running it along the inside of the seamlines to open out the spaces fully. Stuff the small spaces, like noses and chins, first. Assembly directions are in Chapter 8.

DARTS

Here a 2-piece profile head in a muslin tryout has been darted across the seam to broaden the nose and mouth. A three-cornered dart indents the eyes (Figs. 174 and 175).

ANIMALS

The patterns that follow attempt to define silhouettes more precisely. Look at the pattern and then at the photograph to see how one produces the other. Study the planes of the animal and see how the gussets and underbellies supply the width required for front, back, top, and bottom views. If you trace the patterns to transparent paper and lay one pattern piece over another, you will see how the pieces go together. Also, look at the construction diagrams in Chapter 8 to clarify the assembly. Finally, if you wish, enlarge the patterns (as explained for the grape leaf in Chapter 3). Add seam allowances and cut them out in muslin. Sew them together and stuff them to see the skin become a form. Step-by-step directions are provided in Chapter 8.

DESIGN

Collect photographs and make sketches of animals whenever you can, first establishing the profile, then the other planes of the head and the underbody. Draw all the views you possibly can: front, back, side, top, and bottom. Reduce the drawings to the essential silhouettes and draw in the seams. Usually, as you will notice from the following patterns, the underbody will come to a point at each end, meeting a center back body seam at one end and a center front head seam at the other. Decide at what place in

Fig. 176

the profile these two points (or black dots) should meet (Fig. 176) and how wide the underbody should be throughout. Decide how best the head can be constructed.

Make up a first muslin tryout for your new pattern. Don't expect it to be successful the first time. Study the results and see how you can change the pattern to make improvements; then make another tryout. Save each pattern draft and each tryout until you have made a body that suits you. Always keep this final pattern, not only because you may wish to repeat the body, but also because each pattern can teach you about other forms that you may someday wish to make. Experiment with new bodies, keeping what you need of old patterns and redrawing other parts in order to create some new creature. Pin-track your new seams to see that they will match each other.

The variety in the animal kingdom is amazing and, after you have made one good body, you may become engrossed in more attempts to capture these elusive and magnificent silhouettes.

POSITION

The following four animals represent four different positions: standing (Plate 18 and Pattern 11), sitting (Plate 19 and Pattern 12), lying on side (Plate 20 and Pattern 13) and lying on belly (Plates 21 and 22; Patterns 14 and 15). Pattern characteristics for these animals will apply to other animals in the same positions.

The principal pattern pieces of a standing animal are a side body, an underbody, and a head gusset. Gussets give width to the animal and provide space between ears and legs. You may have difficulty visualizing the top plane, but if you imagine two ears coming out of a single seam, you will see its necessity.

The underbody extends upward into the neck and hindquarters and the leg facings that are part of this piece are often copied directly from the side pattern (Fig. 176). The head gusset can be shaped to widen or narrow the head. Frequently it widens at the head top, narrows at the eyes, and widens again at the muzzle, as in the standing dog.

The side view from which you draft the pattern may be a seated, rather than a standing, animal. The same procedure applies, but the animal's width will be tilted upward and the underbody may form a wide triangular base, as in the cat.

Reclining animals can be difficult to visualize in terms of pattern pieces. In the lion, notice how one back leg comes from the side body and the other from the bottom body (Plate 20). Each leg must, consequently, be faced.

DARTS

Sometimes the ears are not set along the seam, as in the two dogs (see Plates 18, 22), but across the dart that opens out of the seam, as in the lion (Plate 20). Or the ear may occupy both the seam and a dart, to turn a corner, as in the cat (Plate 19). In the low lying dog (Plate 22), there is also a dart that broadens the muzzle.

Oysters to straighten the legs, as in the standing dog (Plate 27), and to narrow the underbelly, as in the cat (Pattern 12), are enormously helpful. Notice that the seam that indents the eye in the low dog (Pattern 15) is really half an oyster.

Plate 18 STANDING DOG

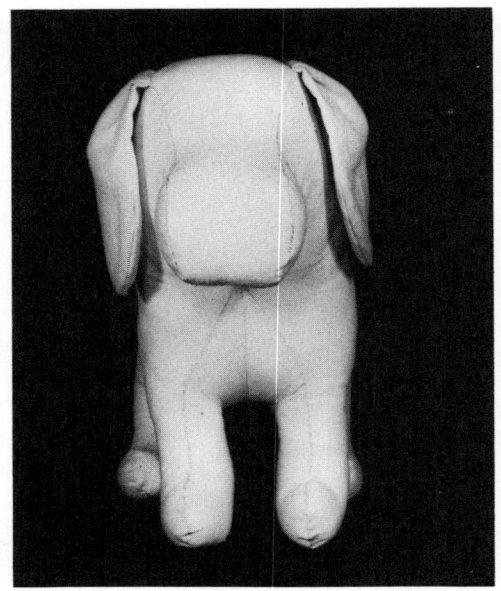
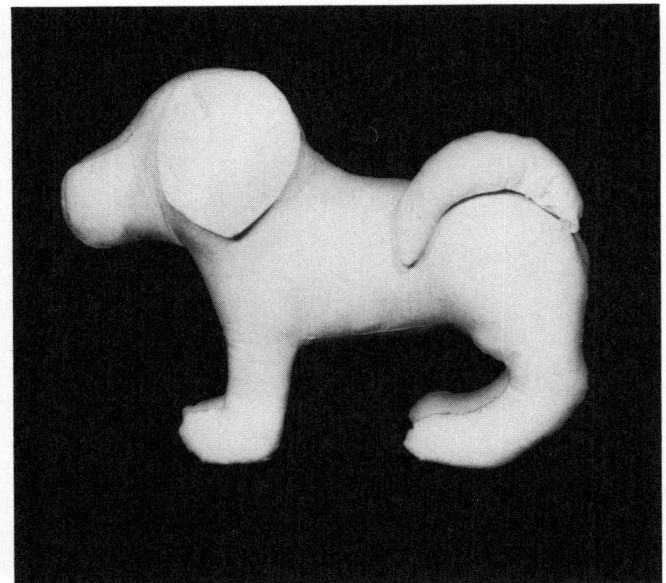
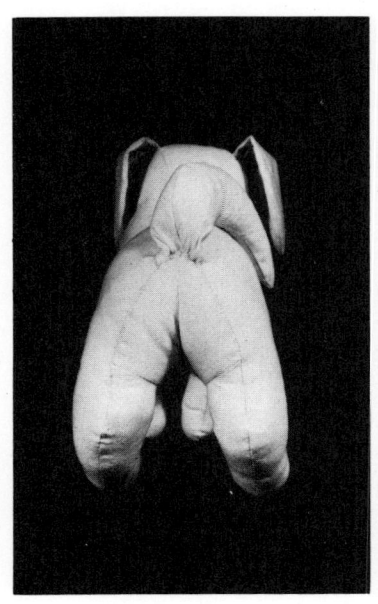
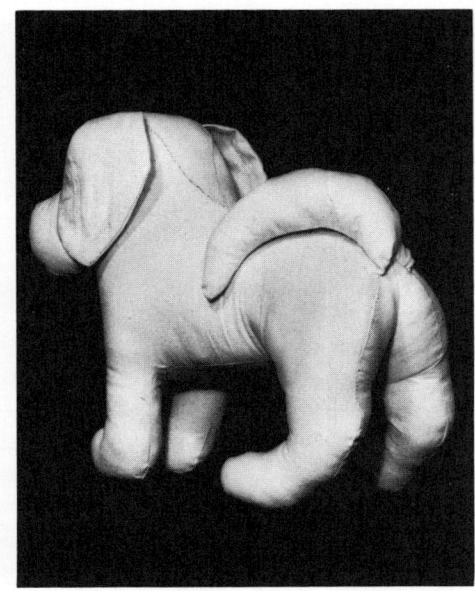
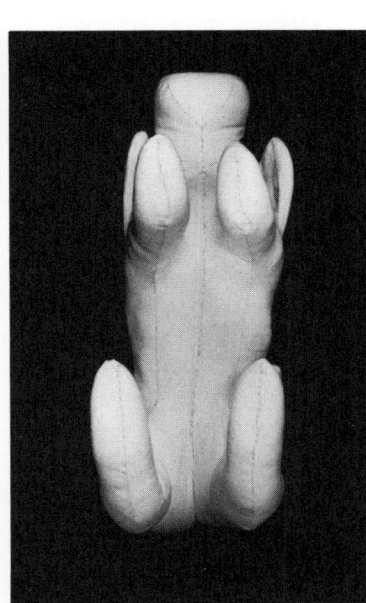

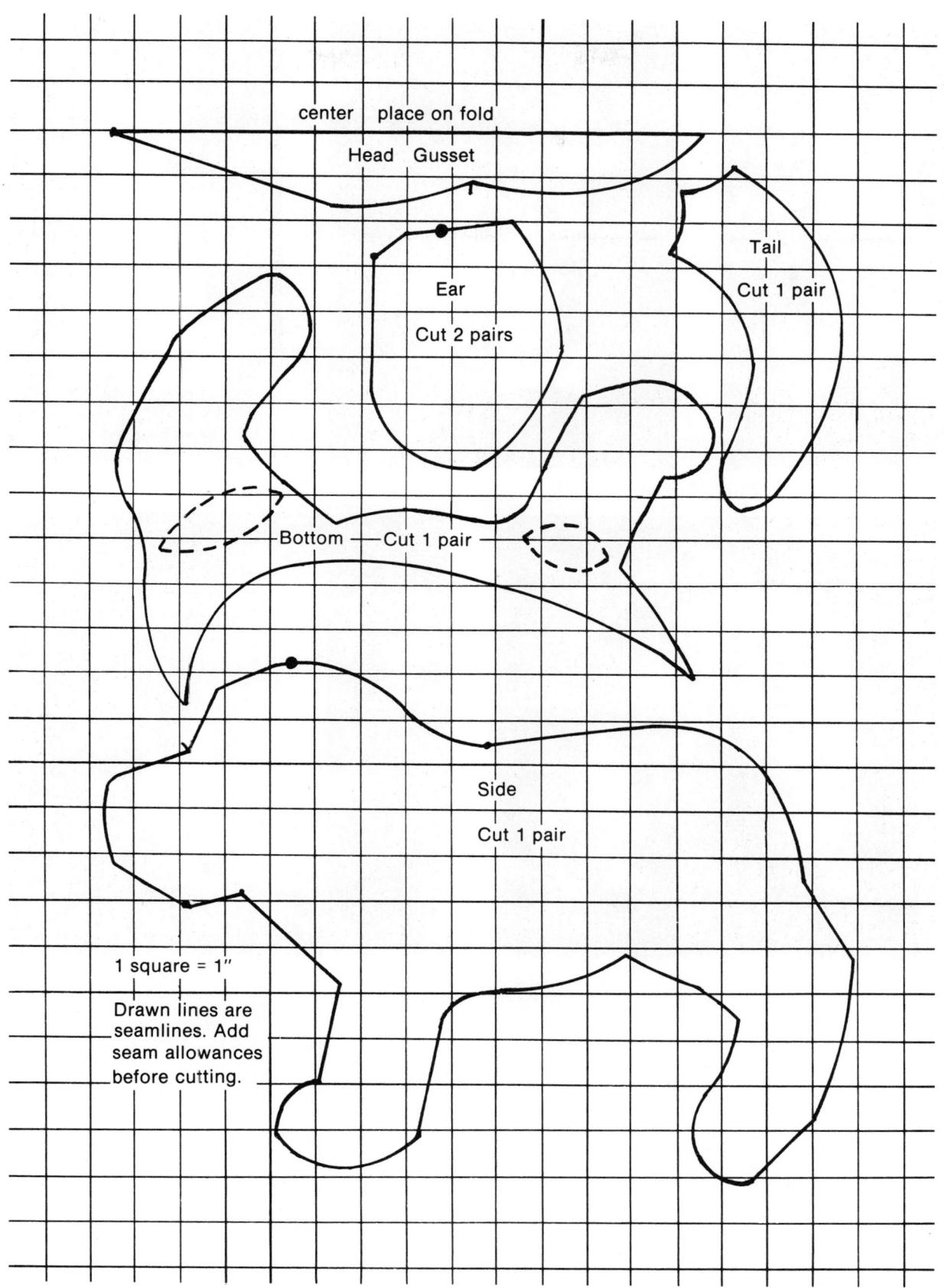

Plate 19 SITTING CAT

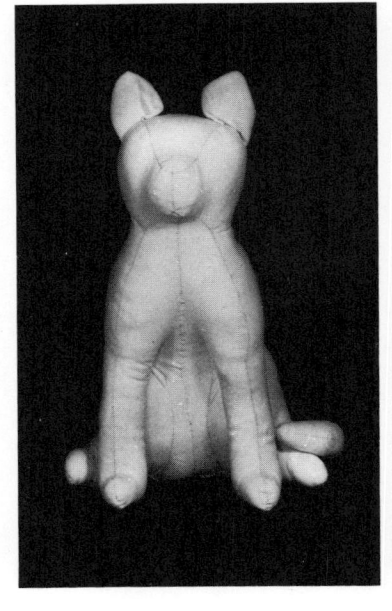
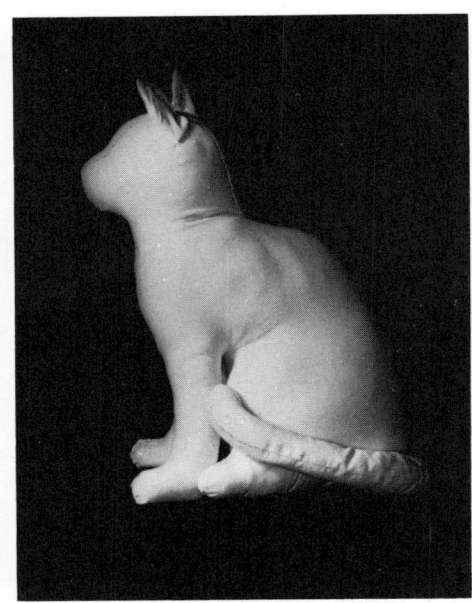
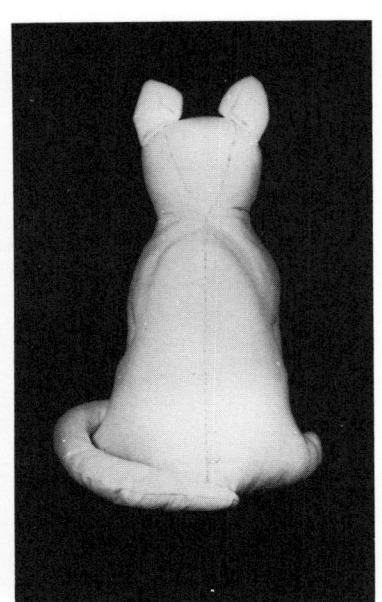
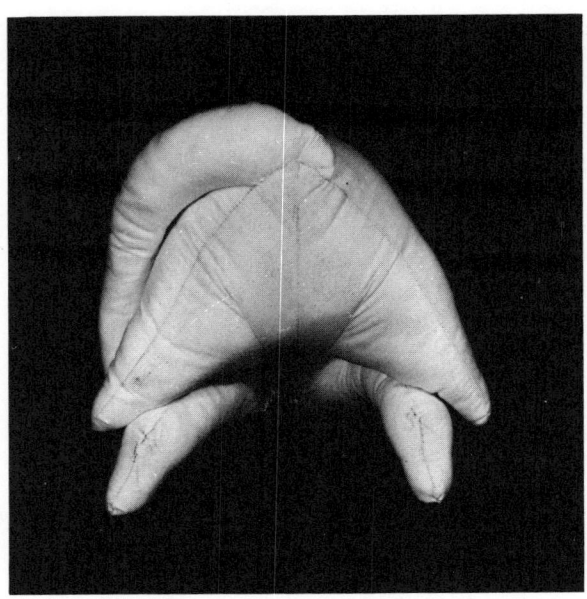
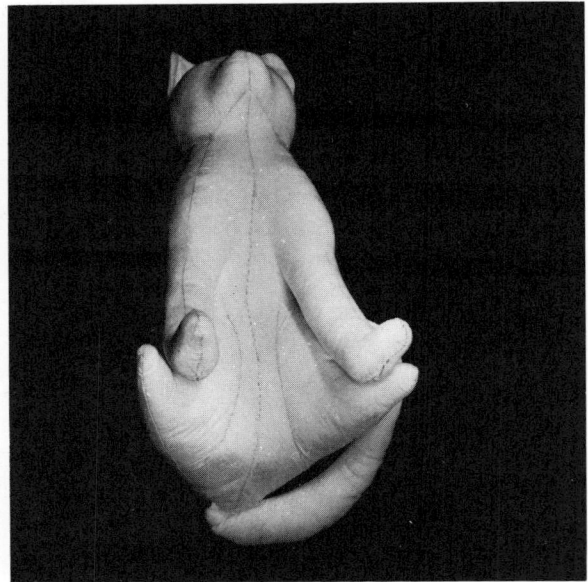

Pattern 12

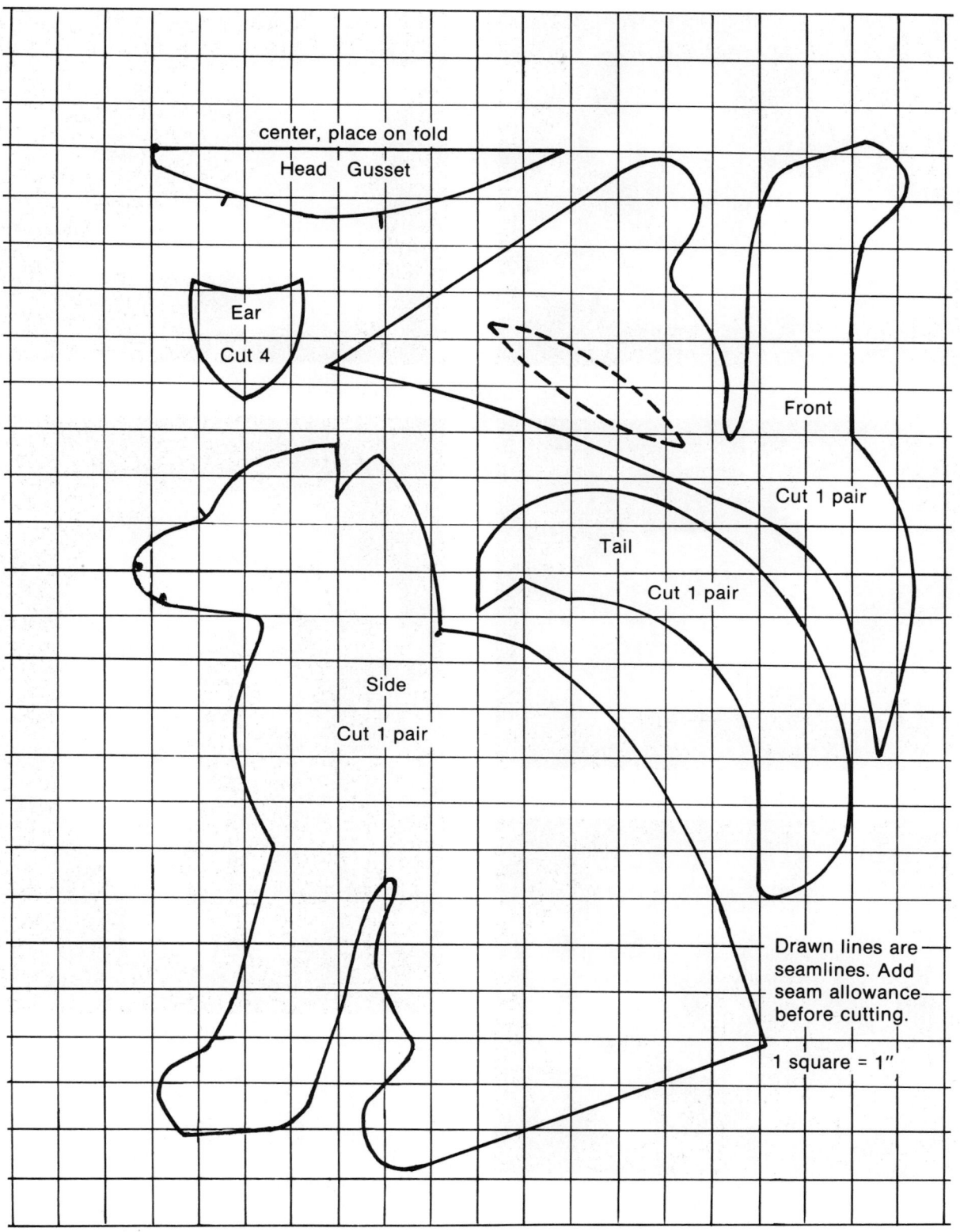

Plate 20   LION

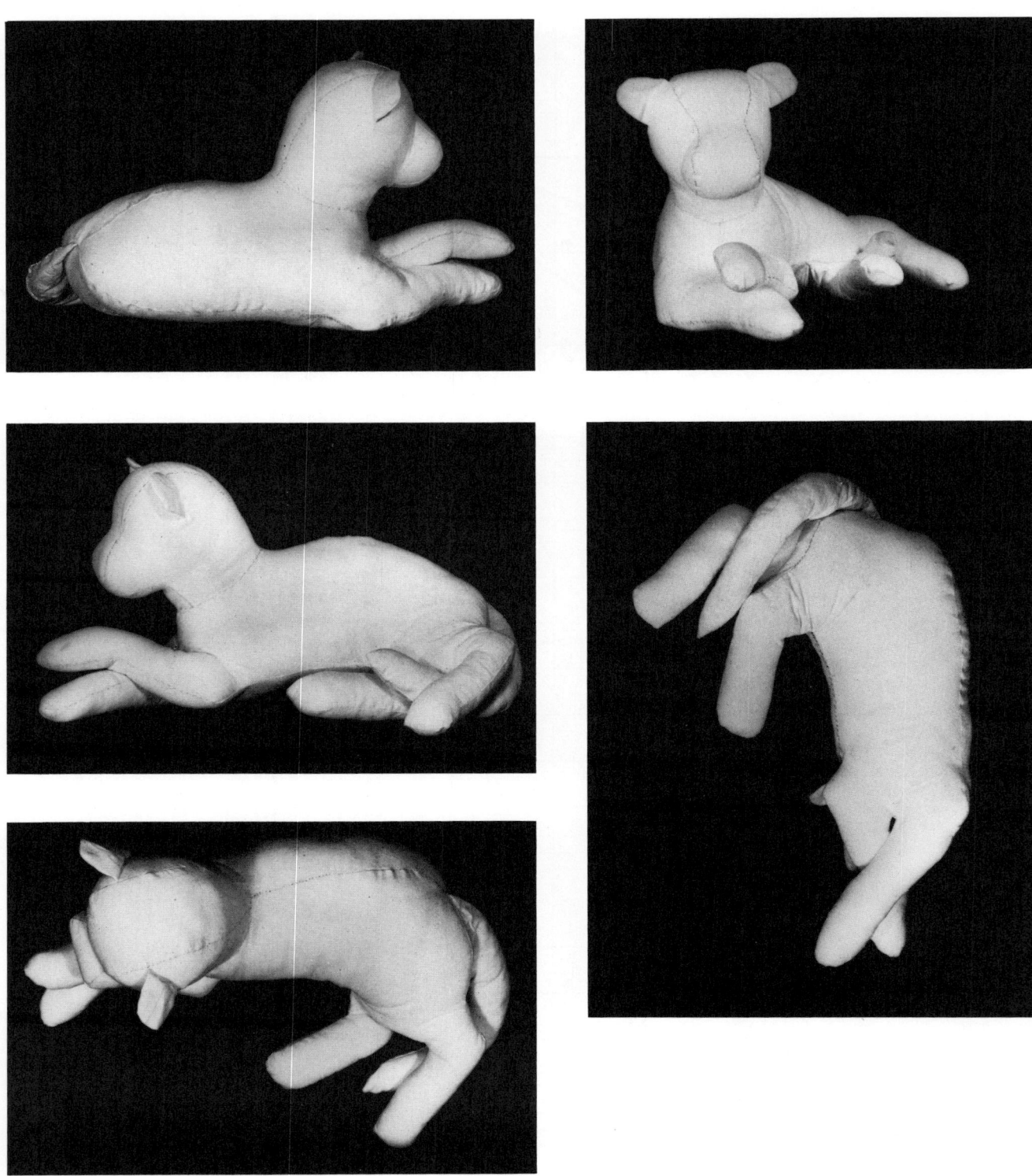

Pattern 13

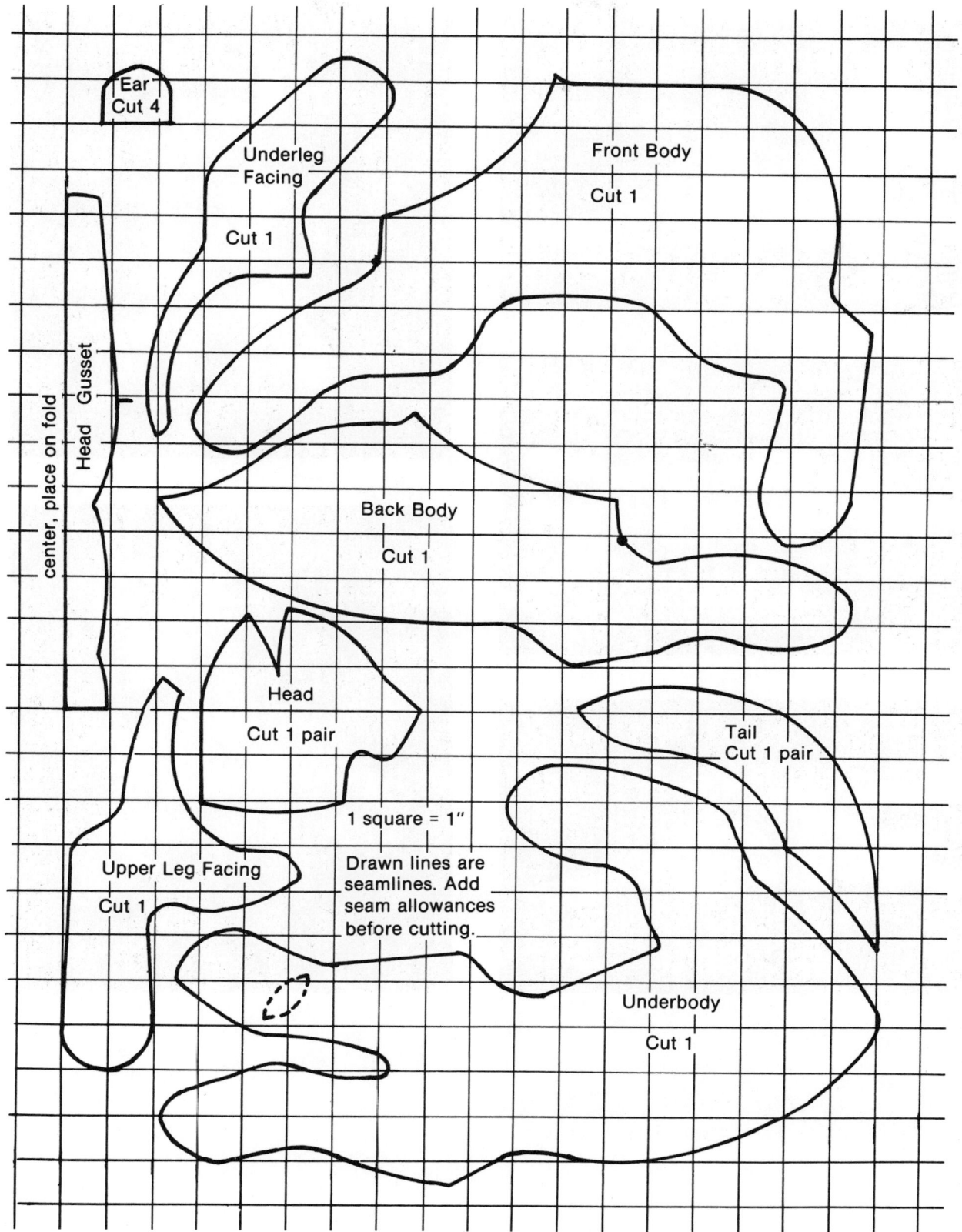

Plate 21 FOX

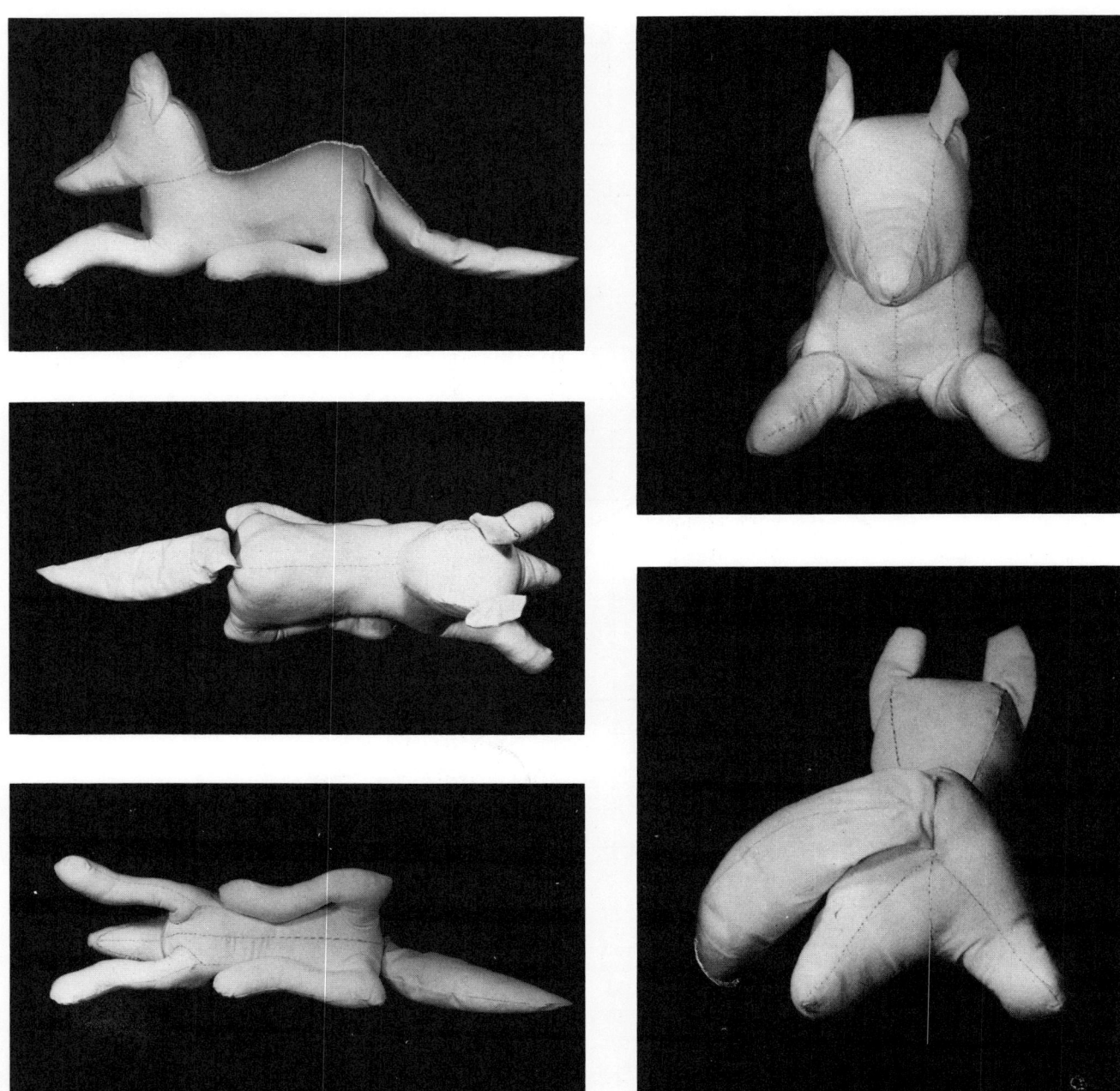

Pattern 14

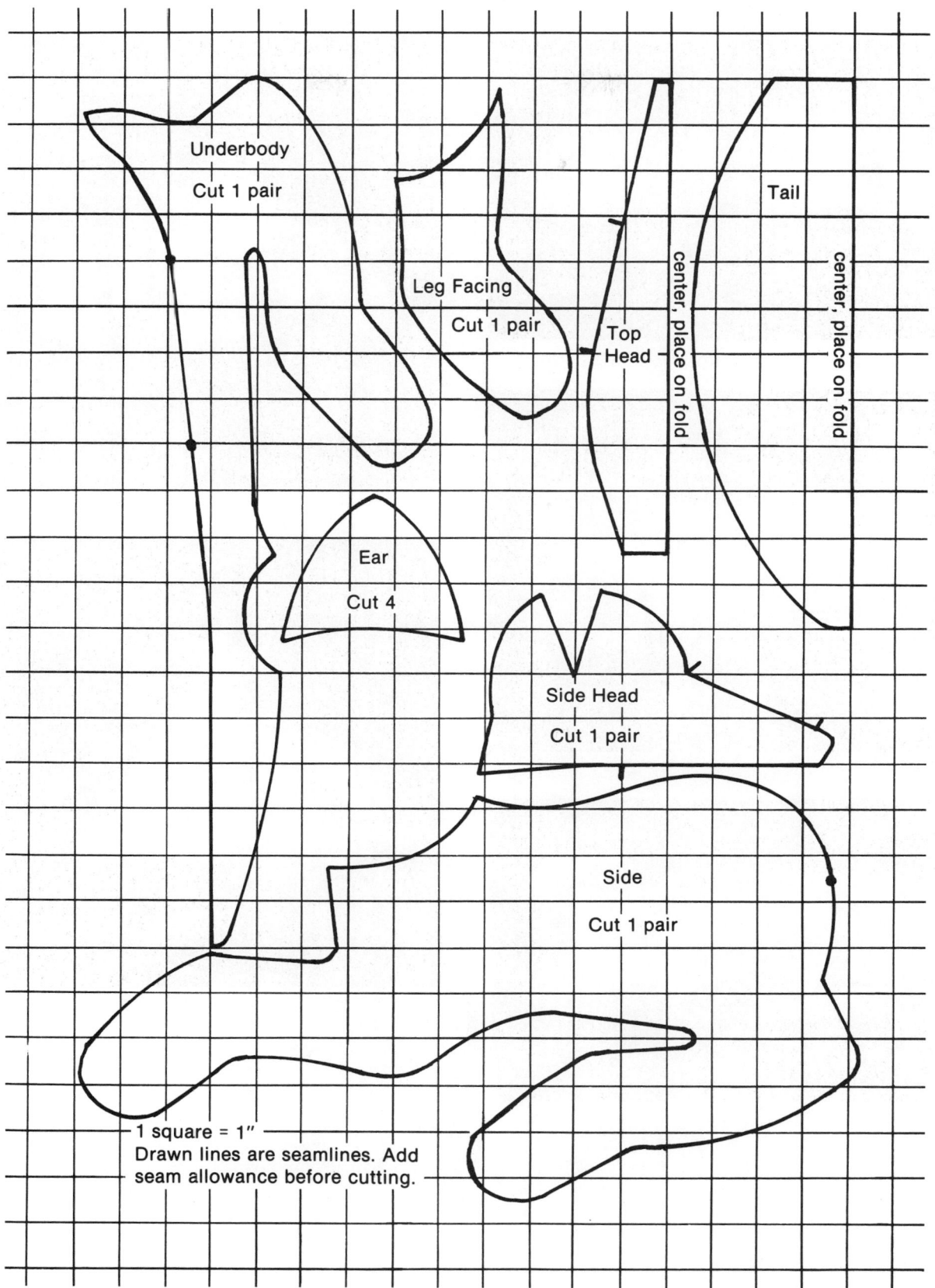

Plate 22 LOW DOG

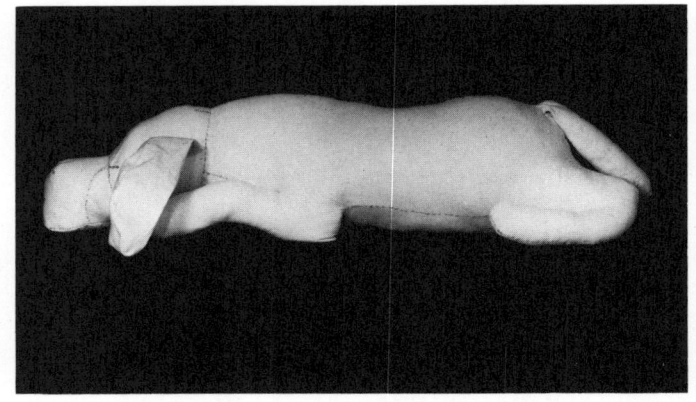
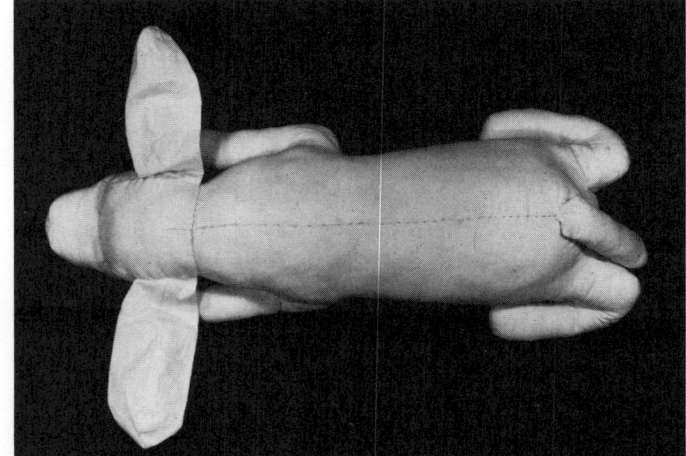
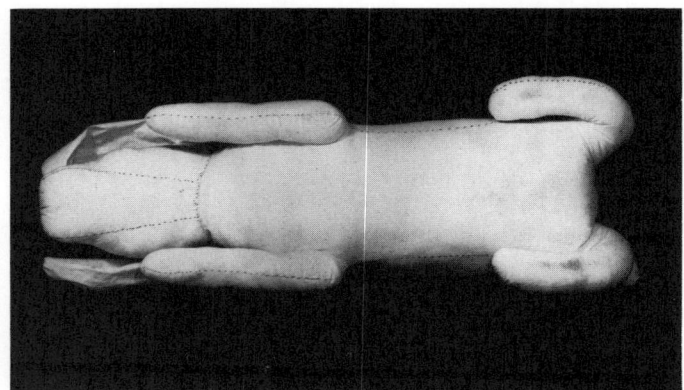
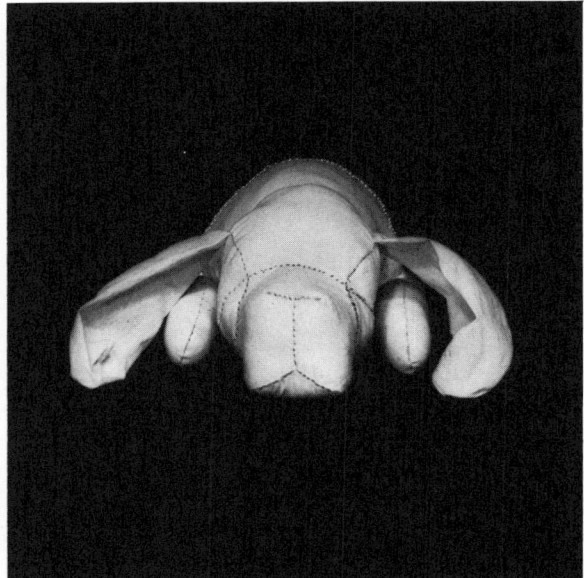
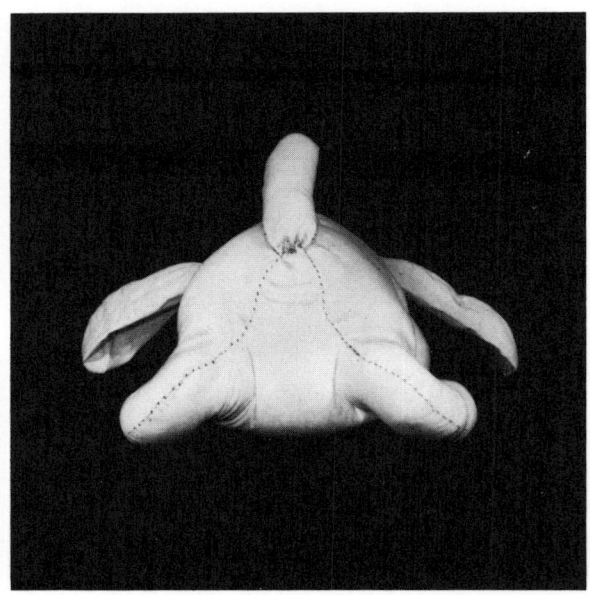

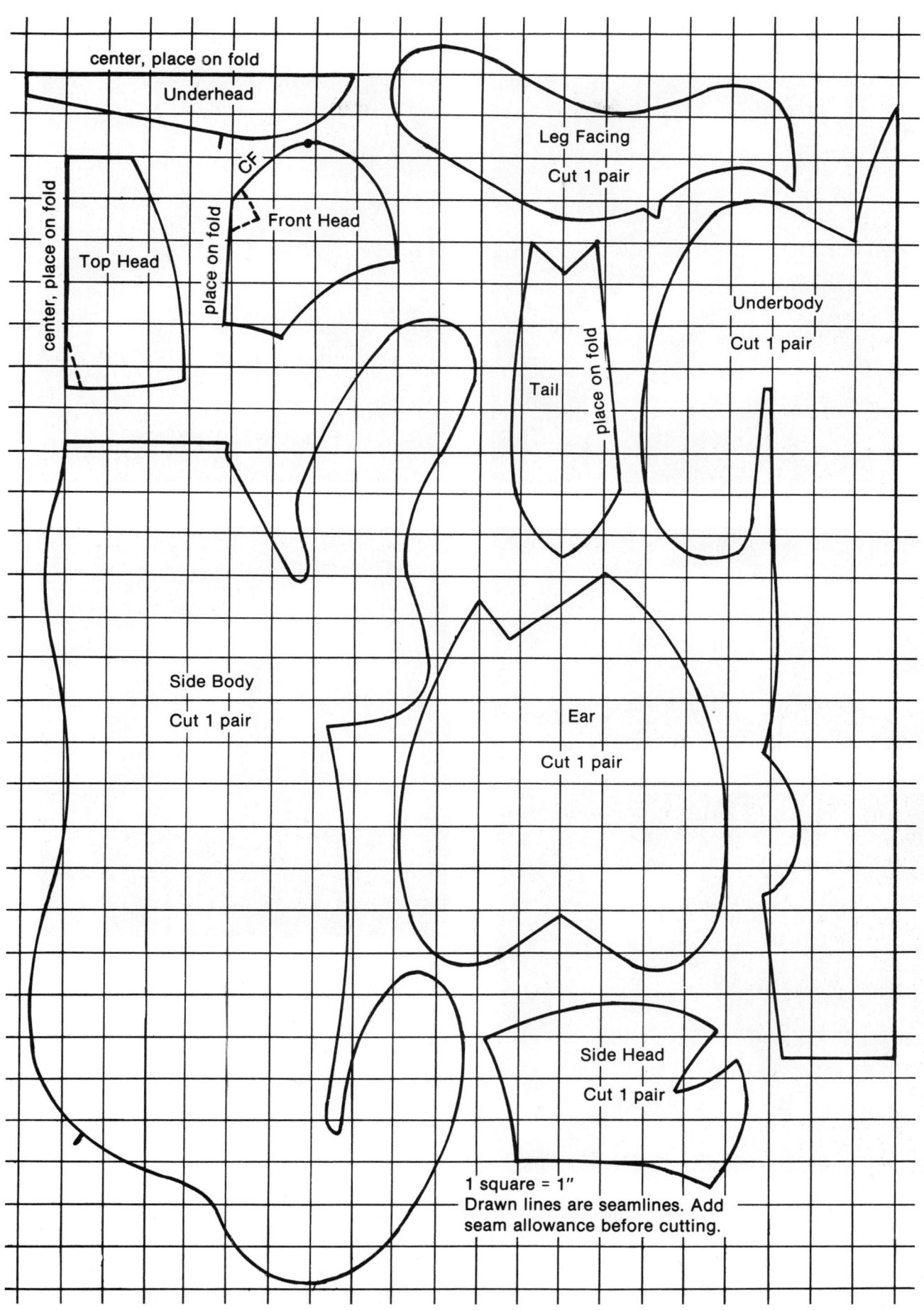

Pattern 15

Plate 23 TEDDY BEAR

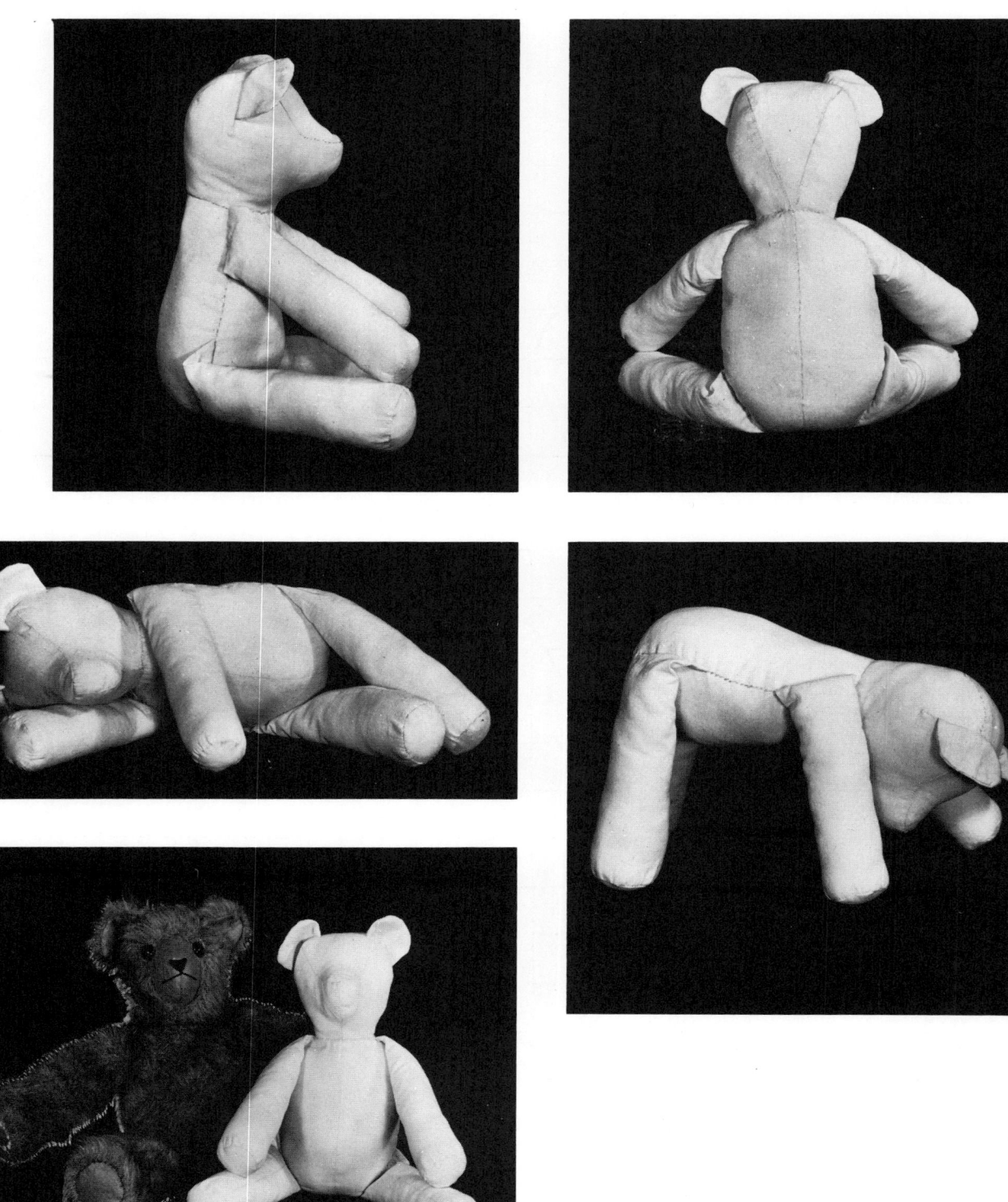

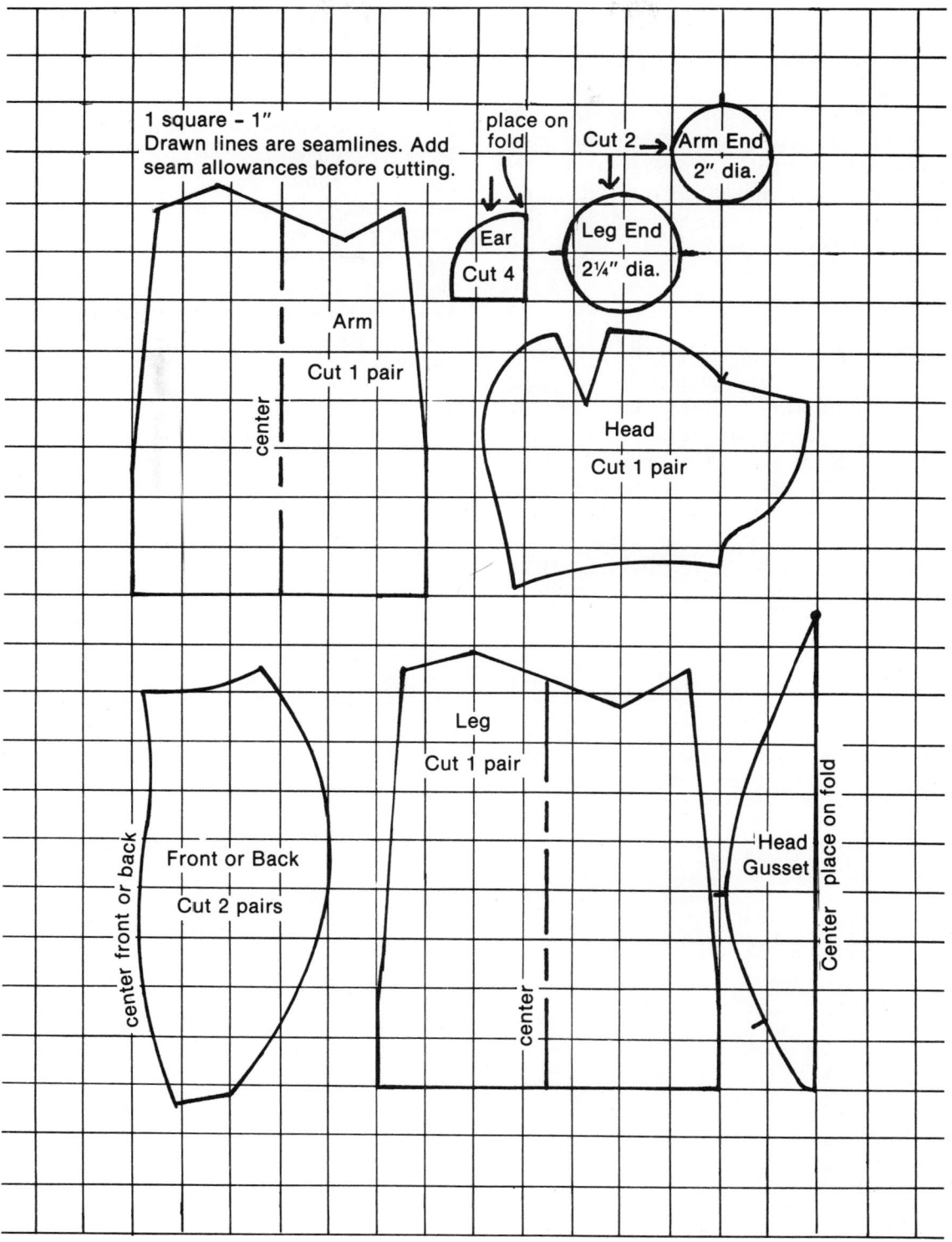

HINGED BODIES

The teddy bear (Plate 23 and Pattern 16) is a *hinged* animal. He is a more toylike version of an animal than the previous examples, for he can assume a number of somewhat human positions that make him an entertaining playmate for a child. Many toys are made with this rather neutral kind of body, relying on the head to provide its animal identification.

FURCLOTH

The animals photographed have been made in muslin. When the same patterns are cut in furcloth, the animal will appear a little larger or much larger, depending on the length of the nap. You may wish to redraw the pattern for long-napped cloth. We have shown two bears, side by side, cut from the same pattern, one in muslin and one in a fairly shallow (about ¾-inch nap) furcloth, to show the relative sizes (Plate 23).

Plate 24 shows the animals in other materials. Furcloth is frequently combined with flat fabric, as in the teddy bear and the fox. This has required piecing parts of the pattern. When you trace off the pattern you will, of course, have to *add a seam allowance at each side of the piecing lines*. Similar piecing can be used where a change of color is desired, as in the two dogs.

When you cut from furcloth, put the top of the pattern pieces at the top of the nap, so that the nap runs downward like real fur. Also, cut from the back of the cloth, sliding the scissors into the base of the nap to avoid chopping off the "fur."

Plate 24

Leather lion with jute hair

Quilted cat in cotton fabric

Corduroy dog

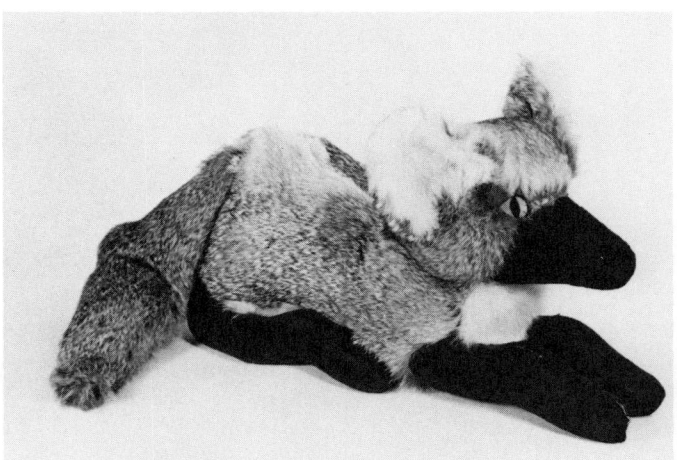

Fox in rabbit skins and suede

Velveteen dog

Vlada Rousseff *Fantasy Baby Stegosaurus*
10″ high x 8″ wide x 13″ long). Green cotton velveteen stitched, stuffed with synthetic stuffing and embroidered.

Andrea V. Uravitch *Gartenhaus* (22″ long). Crochet over wood and stuffing.

Andrea V. Uravitch *One in the Bush*, detail (tree 5′ 5″ tall, bird 22″ long). Stuffed crochet and weaving.

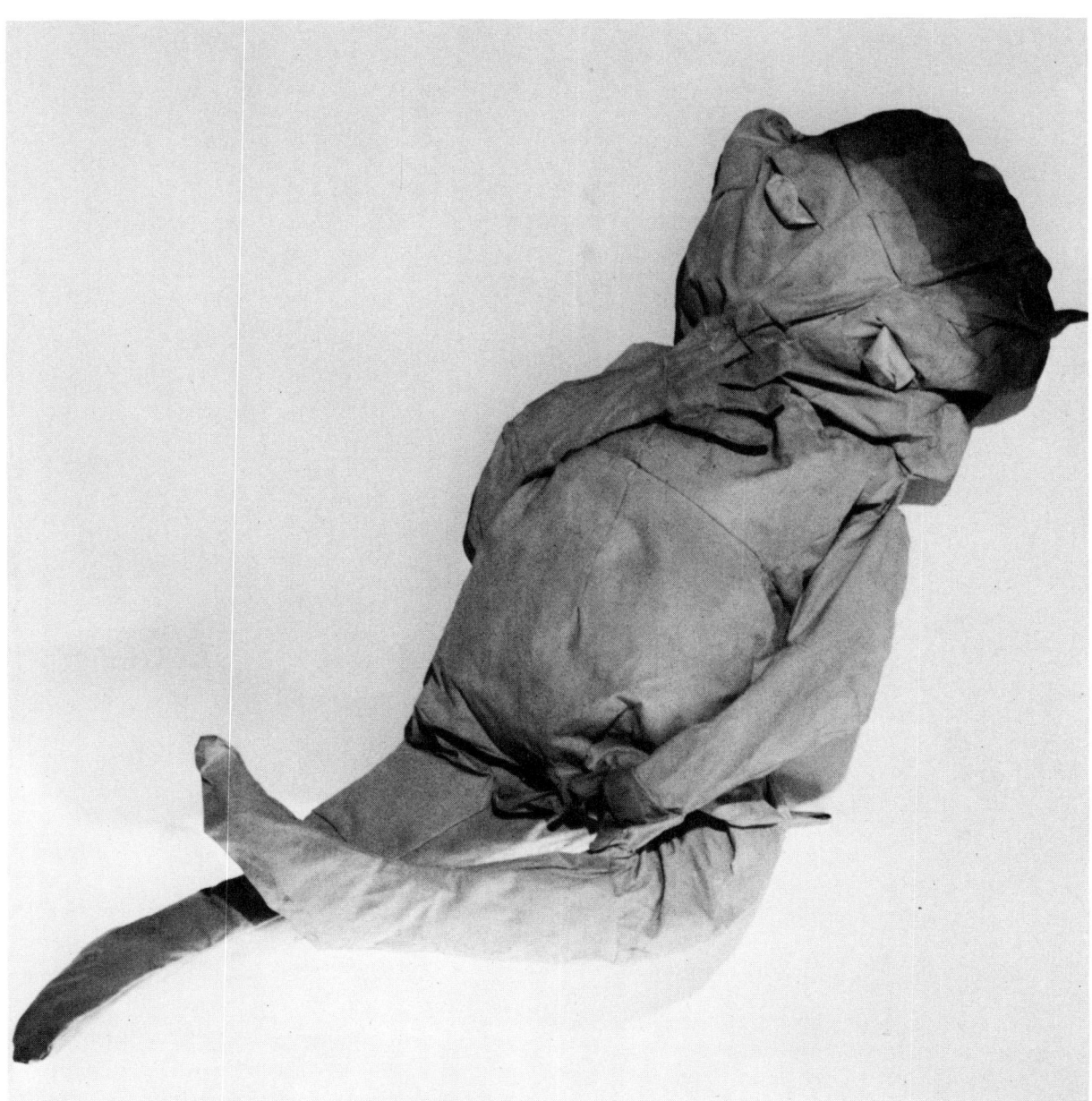

William King *Baby* (72" x 24" x 13") 1971. Painted canvas. Courtesy Terry Dintenfass, Inc., New York.

Bodies 155

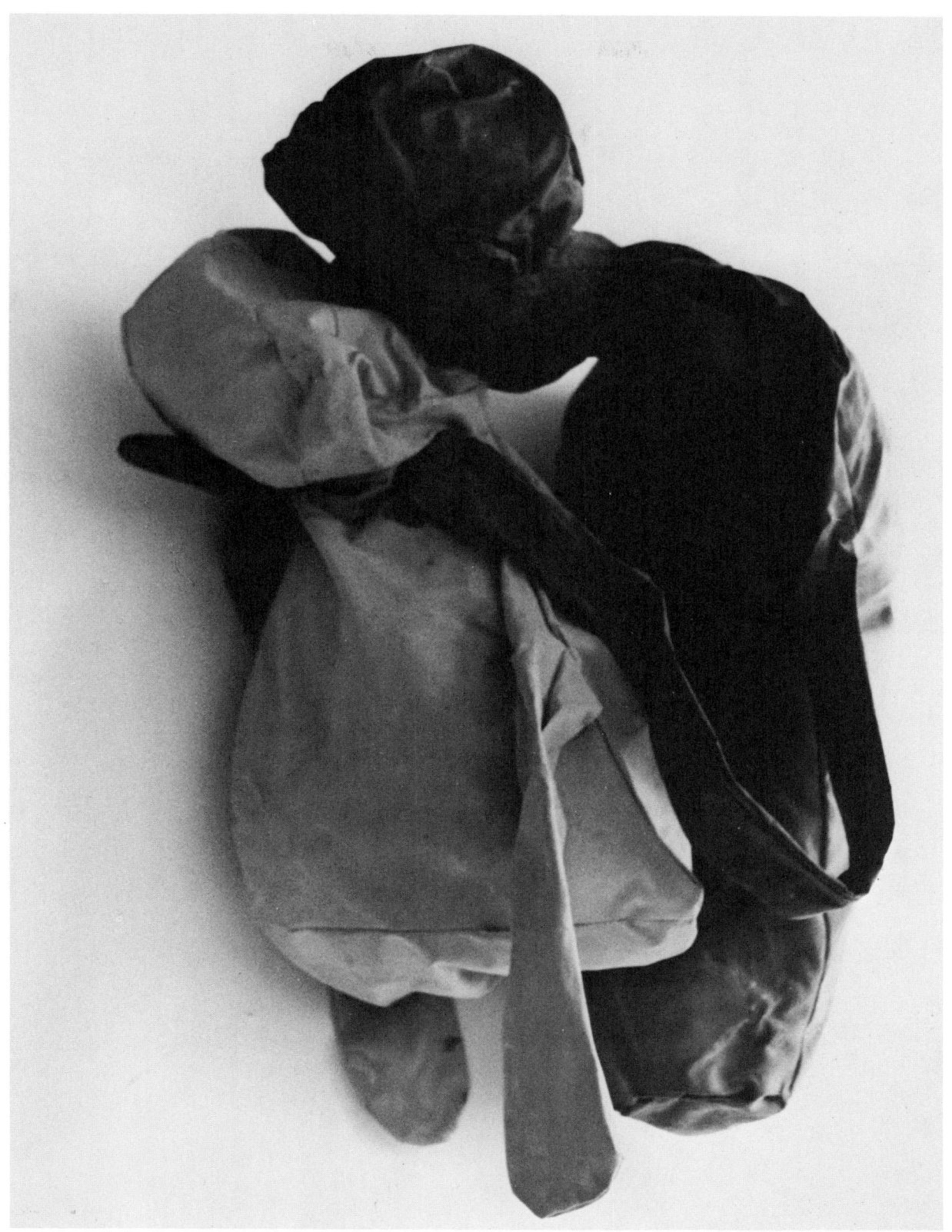

William King *Miss Mustard and Mr. Ketchup*
(40″ x 28″ x 15″). Painted canvas. Courtesy Terry
Dintenfass, Inc., New York.

156　The Complete Book of Stuffedwork

Northeastern Montana, Cow Tribe *Stuffed Effigy, Sacred Doll*. The American Museum of Natural History.

Bodies 157

Caryn Ostrowe *Hollywood Dolls* (about 10″).
Porcelain and fabric.

Elisa D'Arrigo *Harlequin Figures* (about 14" high), 1976. Stuffed leather, beads, feathers, plastic tubing, porcelain heads.

Chapter Seven
Building and Molding

IN THE SECOND HALF of this book we have been examining ways in which patterns are derived from computation, drawing, and drafting. Stuffed pieces that result from any of these methods can stand as the final form or they can be further developed by a number of improvisational methods. Whereas unlimited copies can be cut from the animal patterns in Chapter 6, for example, pieces made by the methods examined in this chapter develop spontaneously from one step to the next. We are able to give only a few examples, but similar techniques can be used to build different heads and bodies and, of course, all kinds of other images as well.

Although somewhat specific instructions accompany the following demonstrations, they are given not with the expectation that you will duplicate them, but only in order to suggest starting points for your own practice and invention.

Building over a stuffed form will be described in terms of four manipulations: *setting in, taking in, letting out,* and *building up.* All can be worked over simple flat forms or over more complex three-dimensional pieces.

Molding a stuffed nylon form can be accomplished in several ways: *pinchstitches, pullstitches, pleats, tucks,* and *drawn-up stitches.* Again, these techniques can be applied to any object: faces are especially amusing practice pieces and offer a wide variety of experience in a small object. The faces can be attached to fabric doll bodies or mounted on a cone or cylinder and "dressed" to conceal the mounting. Also, of course, the whole stocking can continue to be molded under the face to form the body. The stocking can be slashed to provide legs and cut to make separate arms.

BUILDING DEMONSTRATION

This doll (Plate 25) has been worked in chamois, making it voluptuous to touch and easy to put together. In good quality felt or chamois and other leathers, the raw edges can be simply whipstitched together.

In woven materials, on the other hand, the edges would have to be turned under at each seam.

Plate 25

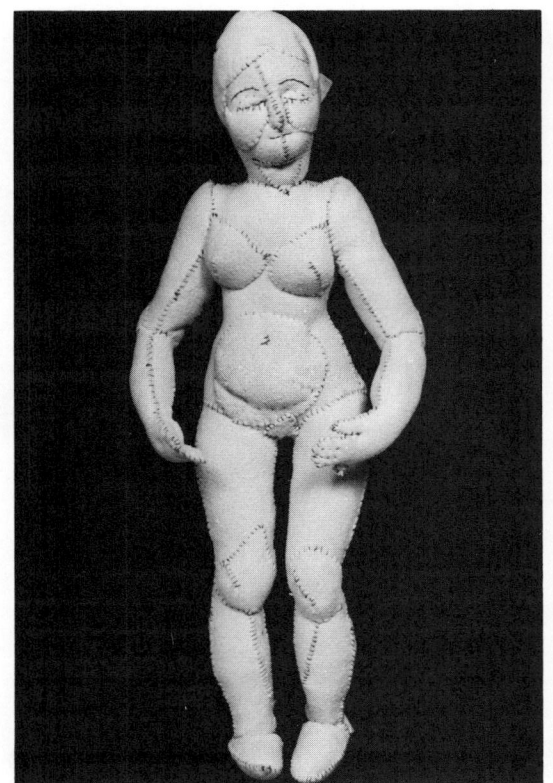

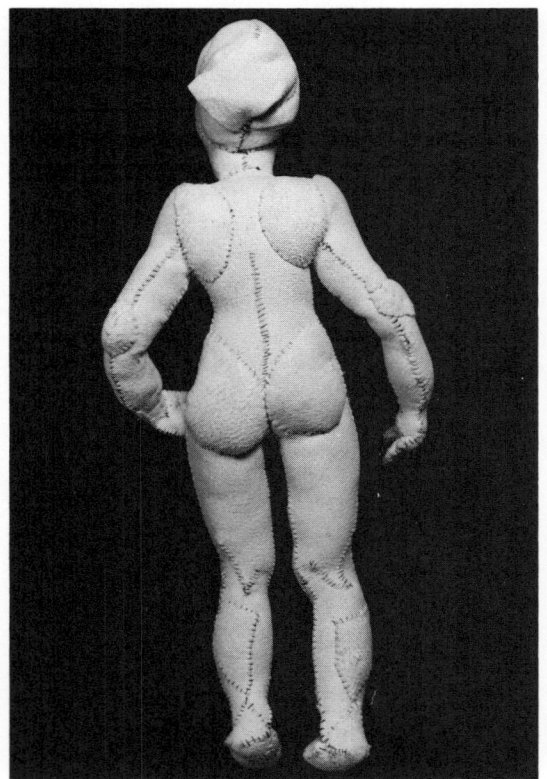

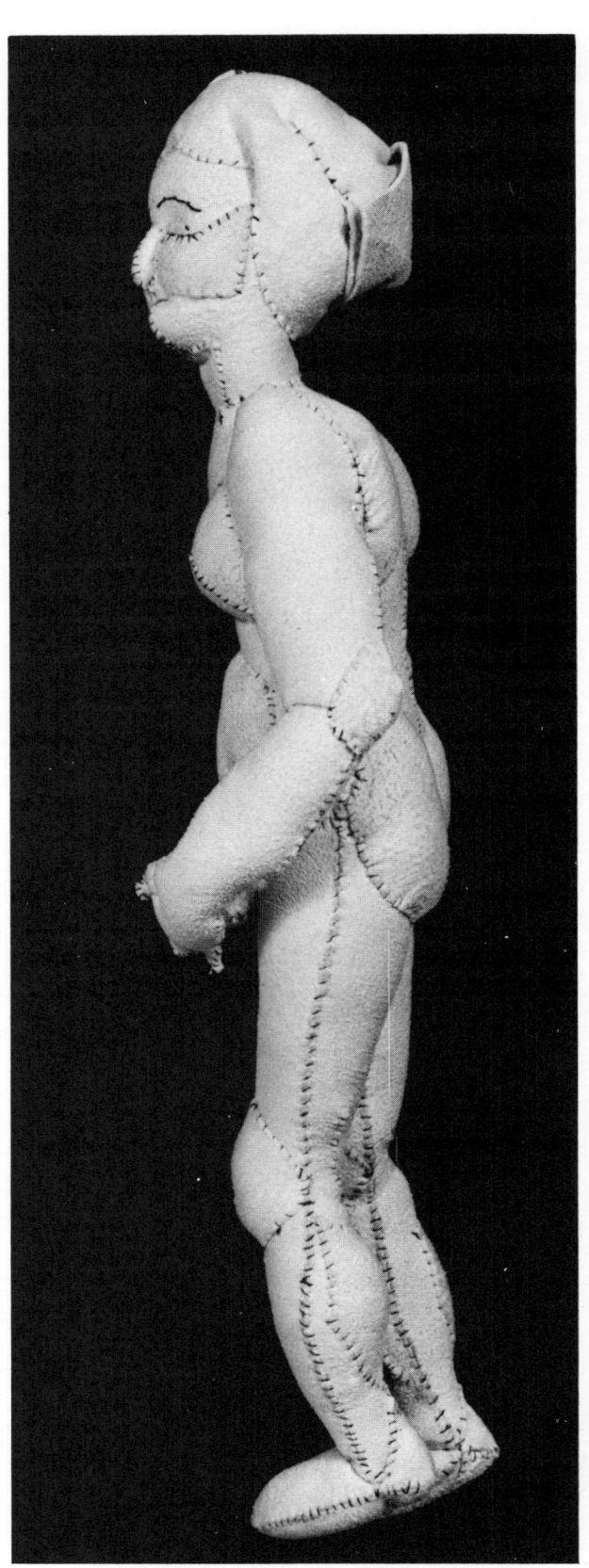

Chamois doll showing building techniques over a basic doll

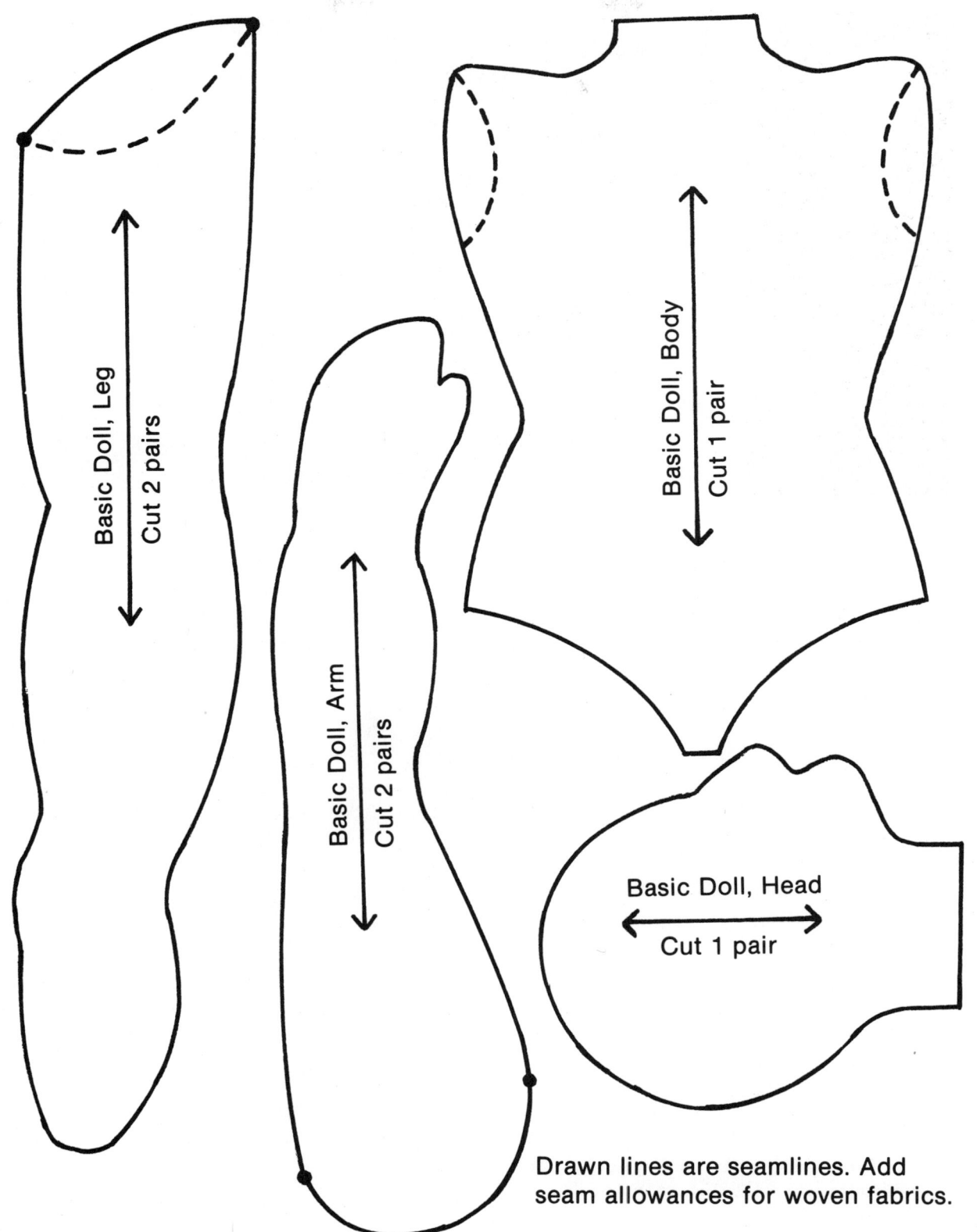

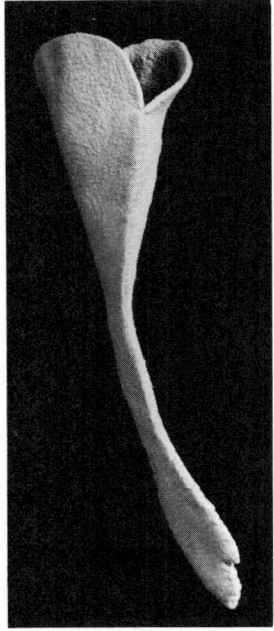
Fig. 177

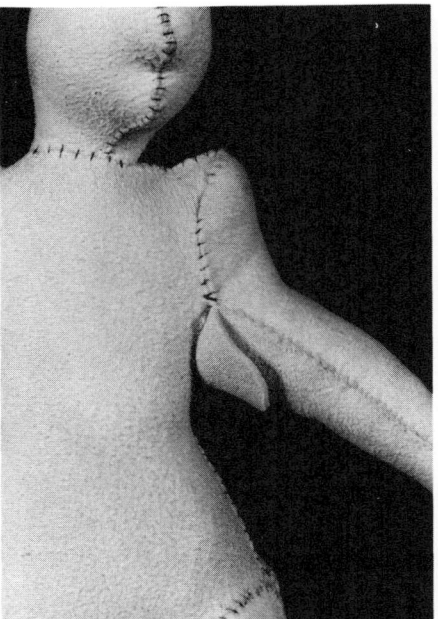
Fig. 178

Fig. 179

The basic doll has been cut from the pattern in Pattern 17. The head, legs, and arms are set in, then the figure is further developed by taking in, letting out, and building up.

SETTING IN

1. Join each pair of pieces to make the six separate parts of the basic form. Since the model is chamois, whipstitch the edges, wrong sides together, as follows: trunks except at neck and leg openings; arms and legs except between circles; and head except at neck opening (Fig. 177).
2. Stuff each seamed part.
3. Set in the legs: slipstitch their upper edges to leg openings on the trunk, matching seams and adding more stuffing before you finish.
4. Set in the head: slide it over the neck opening of the trunk and slipstitch, adding more stuffing to the neck before you finish.
5. Set in the arms: lap the top of the arm (from seam to seam) over the shoulder of the trunk. Slipstitch, adding more stuffing to the upper arm before you finish (Fig. 178).
6. Lift the arm and trim off the excess sleeve-cap underneath, so that the underarm just meets the body (Fig. 179).

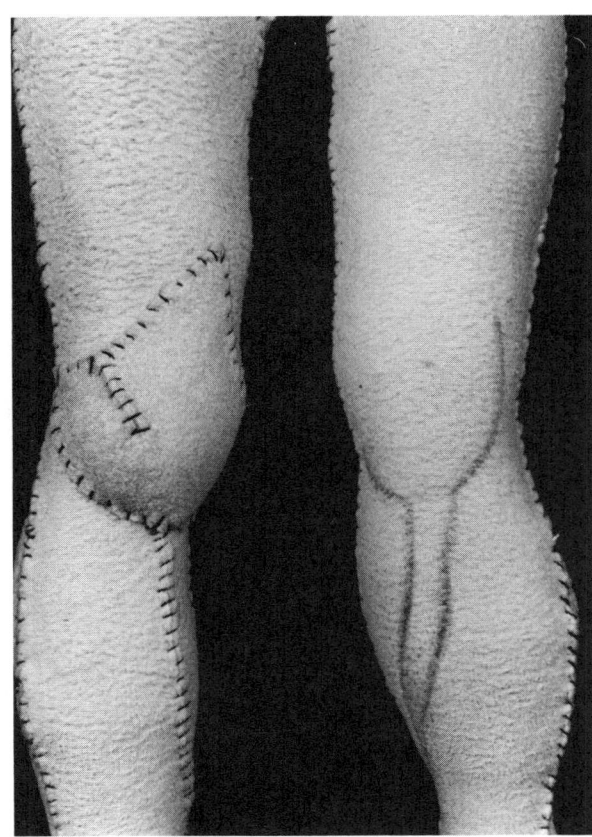
Fig. 180

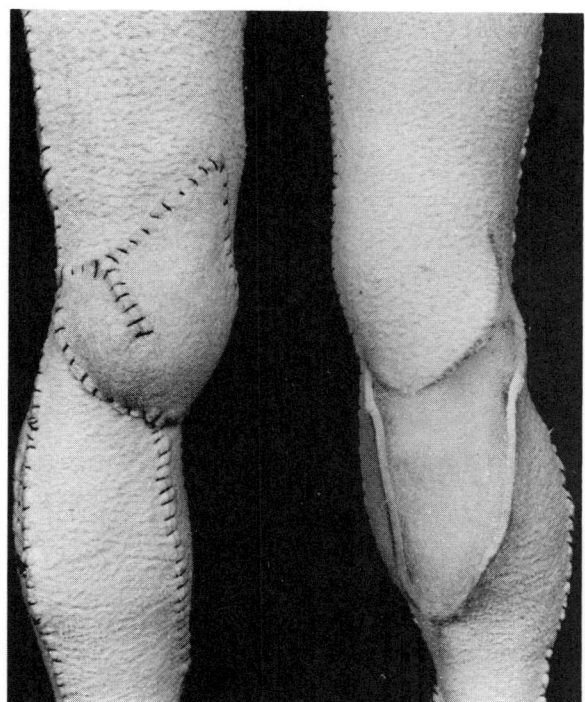

Fig. 181

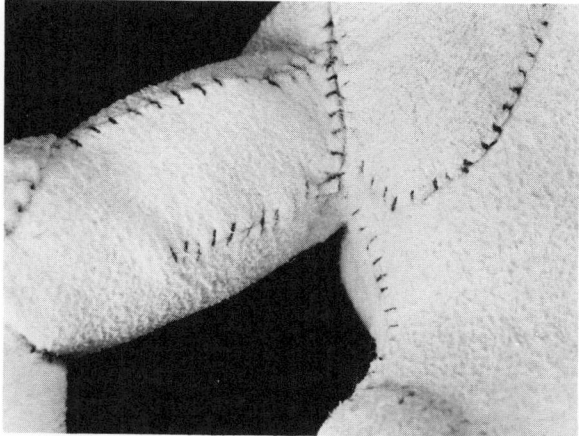

Fig. 182

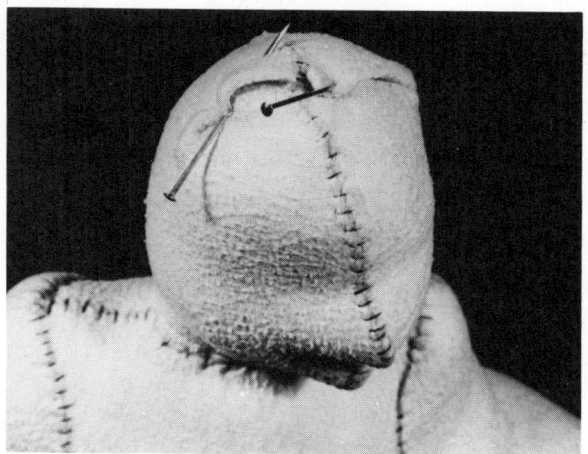

Fig. 183

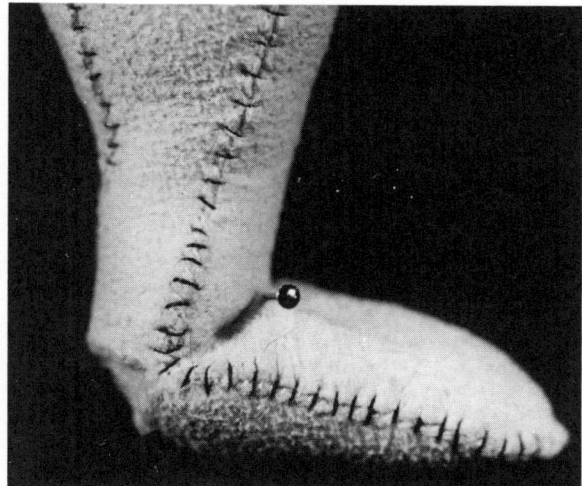

Fig. 184

TAKING IN

1. Taking in at the seamline, of course, is accomplished just by trimming the cut edges and resewing them.
2. To narrow the form at a position between the seams, however, proceed in this way. Lightly draw a dart at the place where you wish to take in the body (Fig. 180). Cut along the drawn lines. Remove a little stuffing if you wish (Fig. 181). Whipstitch the dart edges together. The resulting extra length in the kneecap can be held in over some extra stuffing, while it is restitched. The other knee has already been further built up with a patch. Darts have also been cut along the spine and at the underarm (Fig. 182).
3. Sometimes it is easier to lap than to cut out a dart, as on the head, for instance (Fig. 183).
4. Pinning a dart across a form, as at the ankle, will turn a corner, particularly if it has been let out at the opposite side (Fig. 184).

   Such darts can be slipstitched to close them, without cutting them out.

164 The Complete Book of Stuffedwork

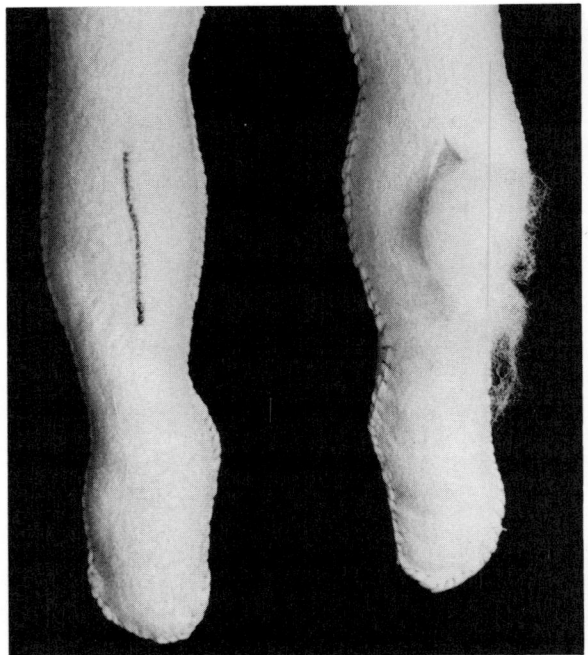

Fig. 185

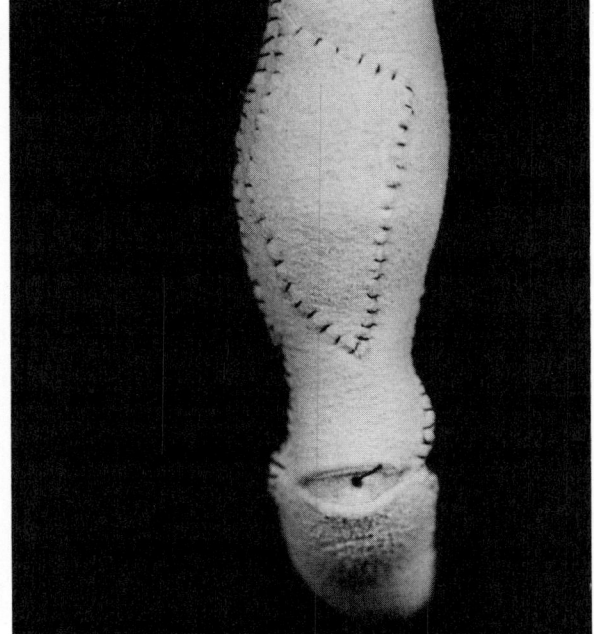

Fig. 186

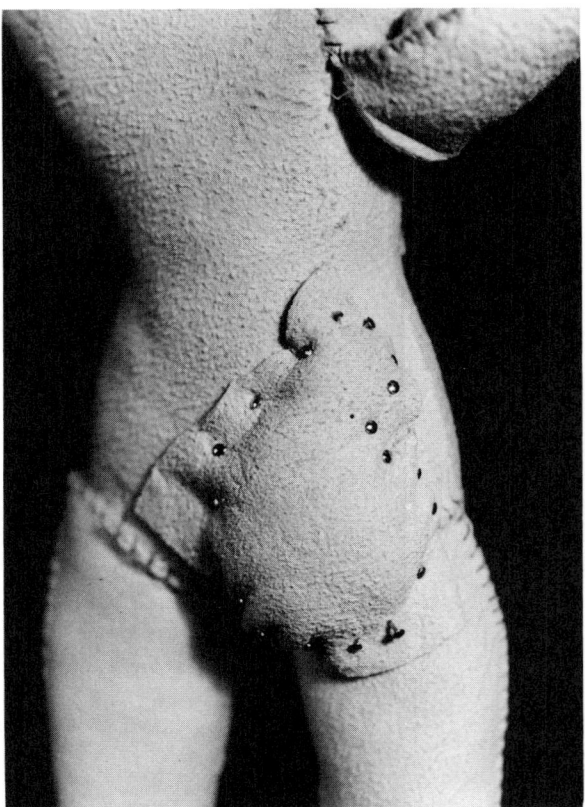

Fig. 187

LETTING OUT

Letting out increases the width between seams. Additional stuffing can be added under the patch, which is subsequently placed over the letting out, in order to improve the contours. In both letting out and building up (described next) the shapes of the patches are of great importance. Not only can they suggest the anatomy of the form, but they provide surface decoration which, along with the necessary stitching, is a significant design element.

1. Lightly draw a slash, where you wish to widen the form. Slash on the drawn line. Add stuffing if you wish (Fig. 185).
2. If the slashes are large, or if you will not patch over it immediately, crosshatching between the sewn edges will control the silhouette.
3. Cut out a patch of appropriate shape at least large enough to cover the slashed edges. Slipstitch, adding stuffing as you sew (Fig. 186).

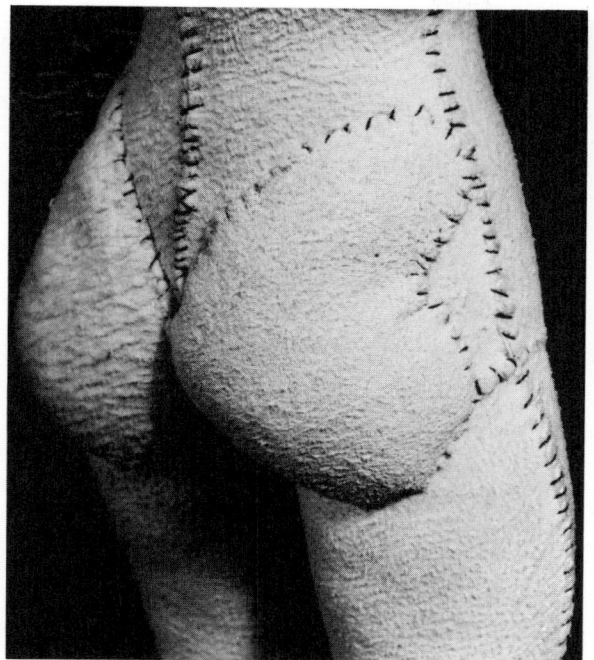

Fig. 188

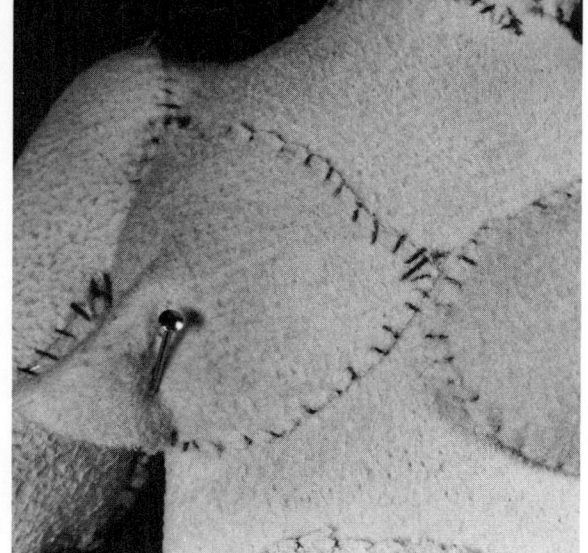

Fig. 189

Fig. 190

BUILDING UP

1. Stuffed patches build up contours wherever you want them. Place stuffing over the basic form and cover it with a scrap of chamois. Insert an outline of pins to indicate the final cut shape of the appliqué. Check the stuffed contour from all directions (Fig. 187). Cut the patch along the pinned lines, slipstitching as you go and adding more stuffing if desirable (Fig. 188).

2. Sometimes it is necessary to dart out extra fullness in the patch itself, as it was in the round pieces that were used for the breasts. Pin, cut and slipstitch around the patch as described in Step 1, pinning the excess fabric into a dart (Fig. 189).

    Cut along the pinned line of the dart. Slipstitch the edges together (Fig. 190).

3. Darts can also make a patch turn a corner, like the turn of the heel:

    Cut a square patch and pin the opposite corners above and below the heel.

    Pin the excess material into a dart at each side. Slipstitch the patch each side of the darts. Insert extra heel stuffing.

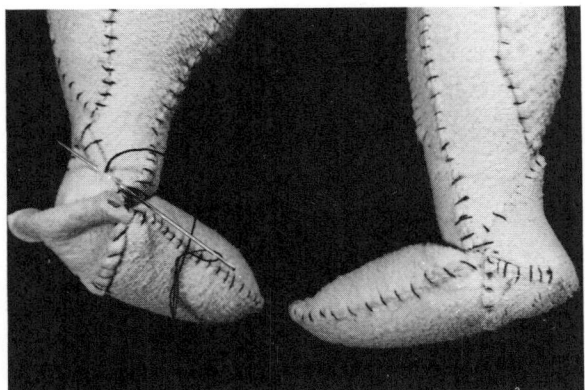

Fig. 191

Through the folded material cut a dart at each side of the heel. Slipstitch the dart (Fig. 191).

MOLDING DEMONSTRATION

The following are several faces molded from the basic head. If you are filling the toe of a stocking, proceed to step 4.

BASIC HEAD

1. Fold a 4-inch square of nylon stocking in half lengthwise and sew a narrow seam at the long edges.
2. Sew a gathering row ¼ inch from one end (Fig. 192).
3. Draw up the gathering to close the end. Stitch through the gathers several times to fasten the thread (Fig. 193).
4. Turn the head right side out and stuff it with synthetic stuffing. Sew a gathering row 1 inch from the lower edge of the head, over the stuffing. Draw up the gathering to close the end (Fig. 194). Wrap the thread several times around the stitching and the stuffing. You may unwind the thread during the stuffing, if you wish, to add more stuffing. Then fasten the end when the head is completed. The seam will be the center back of the head.

Before you mold, tie a knot at the end of a strong thread in a needle. The needle may be inserted through the neck opening or through the back of the head where it will

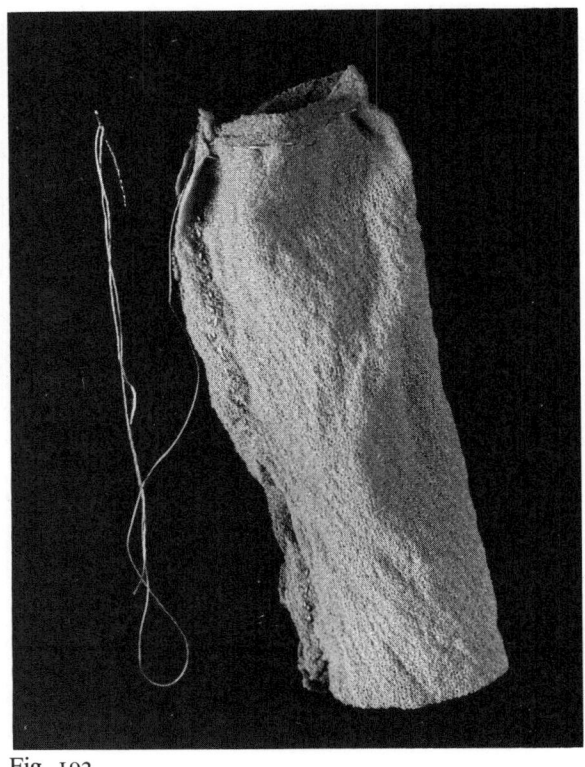

Fig. 192

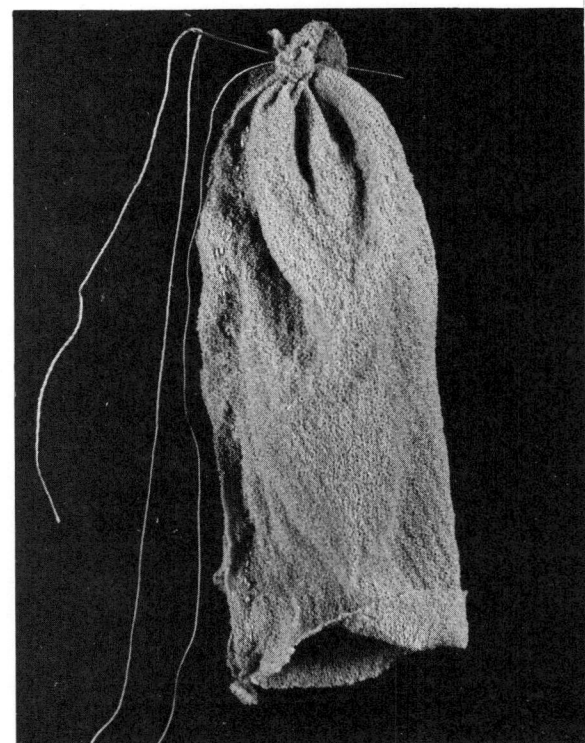

Fig. 193

Building and Molding 167

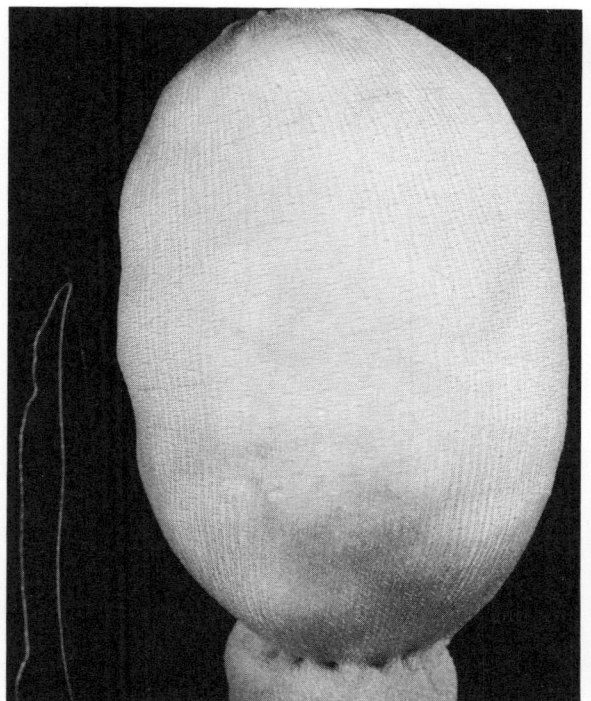

Fig. 194

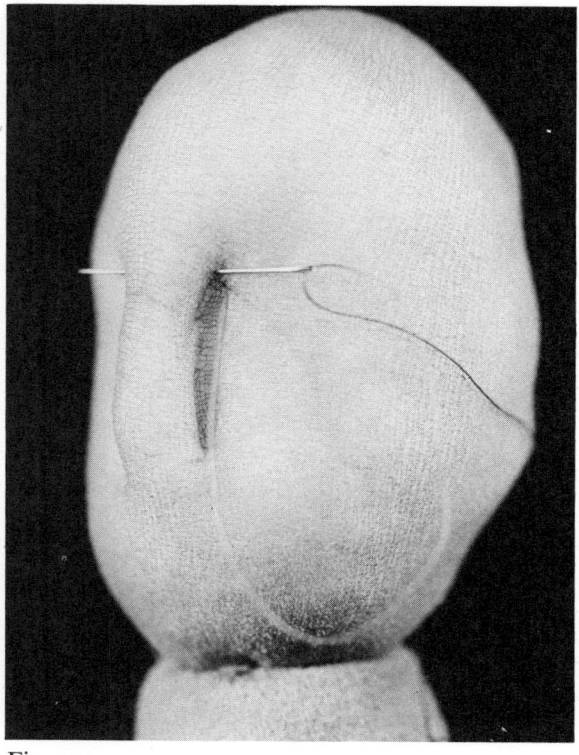

Fig. 195

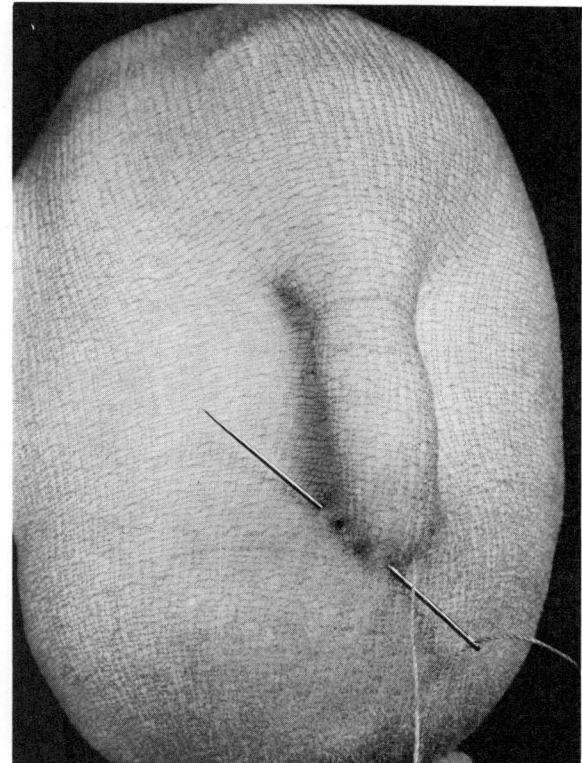

Fig. 196

later be covered by hair. After you have finished one part of the molding, the thread can be carried from one place to another through the stuffing.

FACE 1

1. *Pinchstitch* the sides of the nose at the center front. In a pinchstitch, the fabric and the stuffing is pinched up to the desired form while the stitches are taken from one side of the pinch to the other. The thread lies in the stuffing under the pinched-up form. With very little thread showing on the outside, draw the needle through the pinched form, pulling on the thread to indent the form before you take your next stitch from the opposite side. The stitches lie in the shadow of the creases. For a sharp-edged form you will pull the thread tighter than for a soft contour (Fig. 195).
2. Sew a row of small running stitches across the bottom of the nose, taking up a little stuffing with the stitches. *Draw them up* and fasten the end (Fig. 196).

168 The Complete Book of Stuffedwork

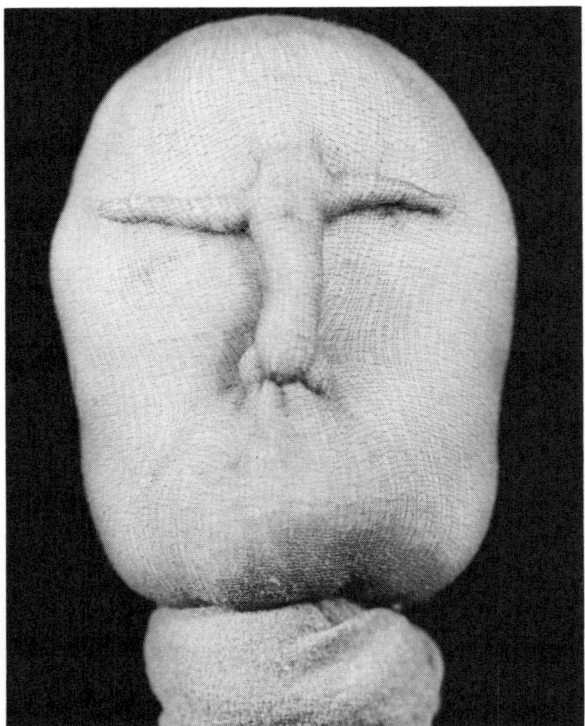

Fig. 197

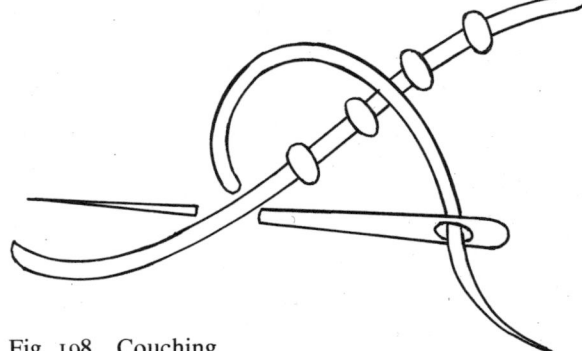

Fig. 198 Couching

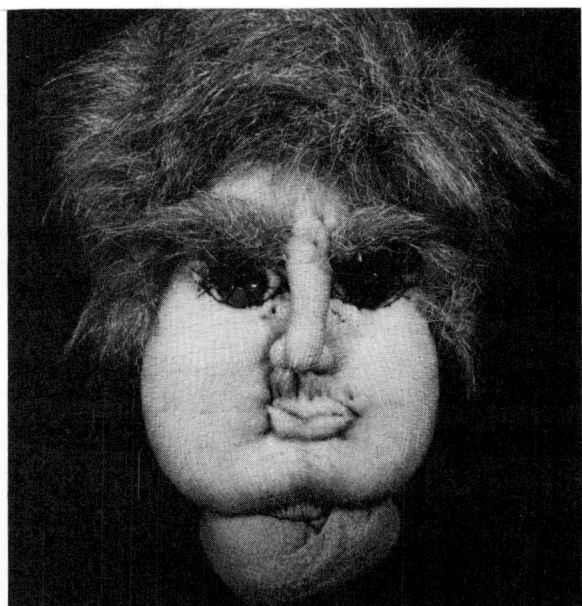

Fig. 199

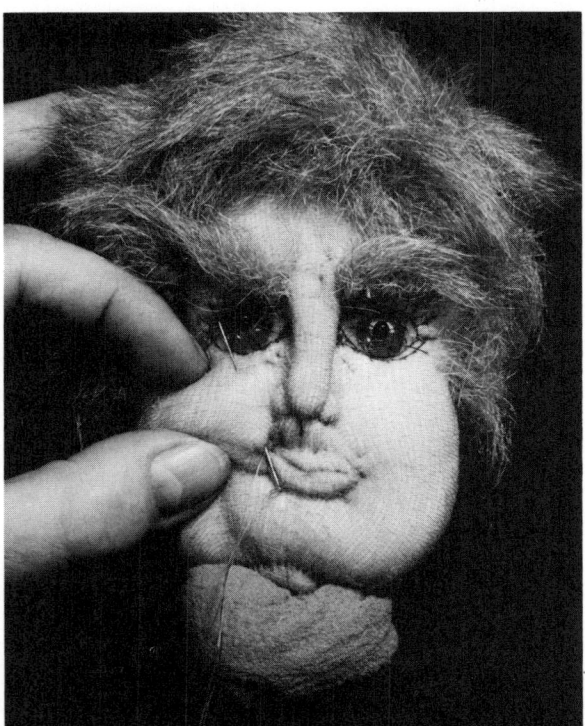

Fig. 200

3. Nostrils may be added each side of the nose. Pinchstitch from the outside of one nostril to the opposite side of the nose. Pinchstitch two eyebrows (Fig. 197).
4. In darker thread overcast beads for eyes, bringing thread through the center hole of the bead, then over the bead edge and through the stuffing (to and from the back of the head, if convenient). Repeat several times.
    "Draw" the eyelids in *couching* stitch (Fig. 198). Add straight-stitch lashes at the upper lid.
5. Slipstitch scraps of furcloth to the head, adding stuffing under the hair to fill out the back of the head.

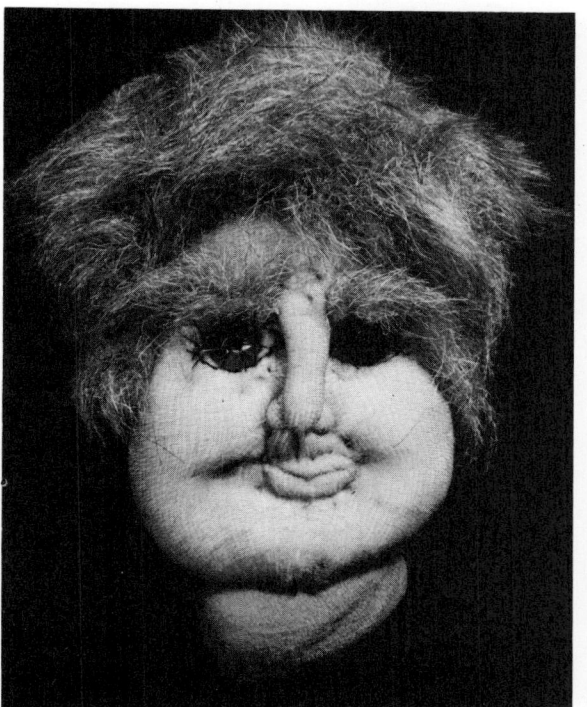

Fig. 201

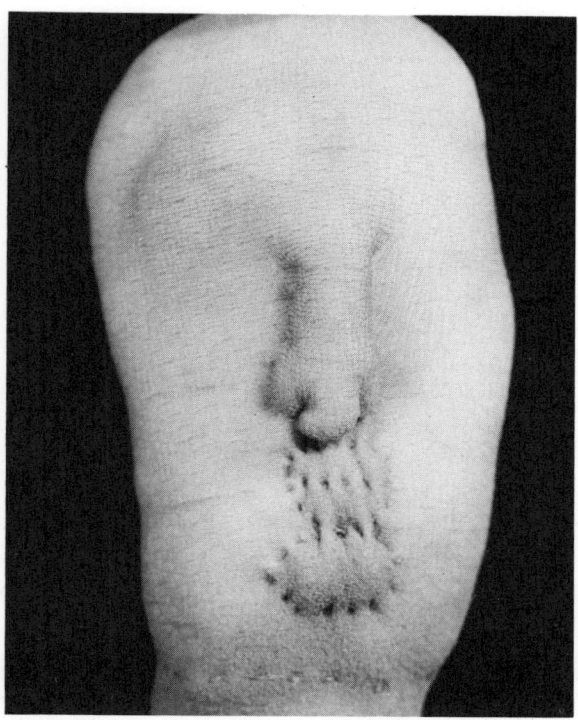

Fig. 202

Insert black plastic-headed pins in the hole of each bead. Cut narrow strips of furcloth and sew them to the eyebrows (Fig. 199).

6. Pinchstitch cheeks from the smile line to the corner of the eye (Figs. 200 and 201).

FACE 2

1. Pinchstitch a nose, wide at the bottom and narrower at the top. Work running stitches across the nose bottom, pull them up and fasten. Pinch a stitch, twice, between nostrils and fasten at the back of the head.
2. "Draw" the mouth in running stitch, outside edges first, then between the lips, picking up some stuffing with the stitch.

    Draw up the chin in the same way. Pull up the thread a little and fasten the end. With a needle point pick up a little stuffing from inside and pull it forward into the circle (Fig. 202).
3. Whipstitch over a *tuck*, picking up a little stuffing, for eyelids. Pinchstitch eyebrows (Fig. 203).
4. Pullstitch smile lines. Bring the needle from the back through the front. Take a very

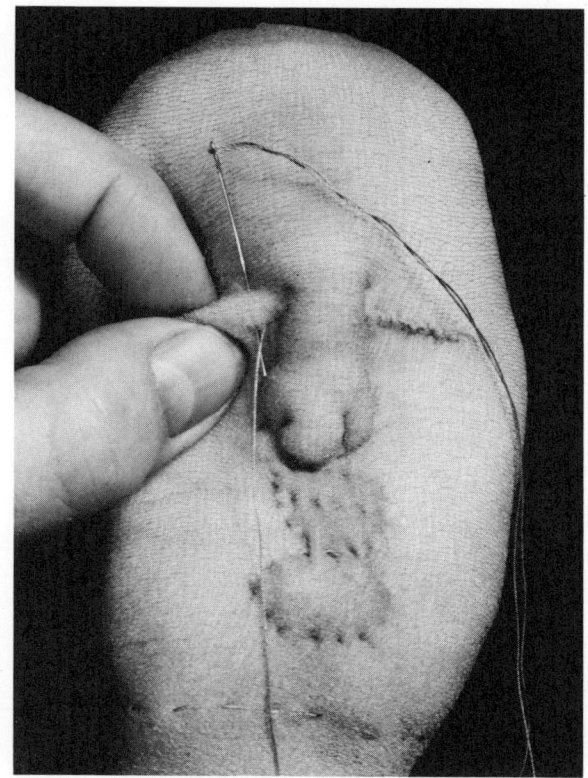

Fig. 203

170 The Complete Book of Stuffedwork

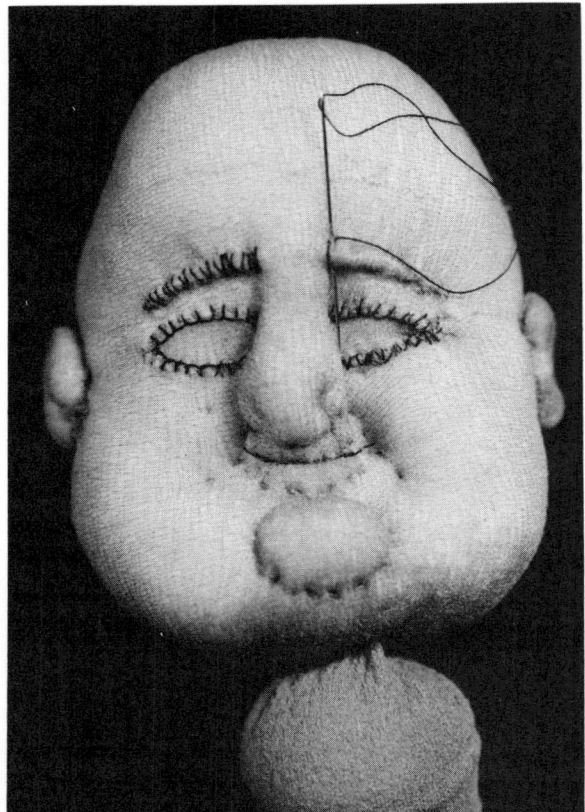

Fig. 204a

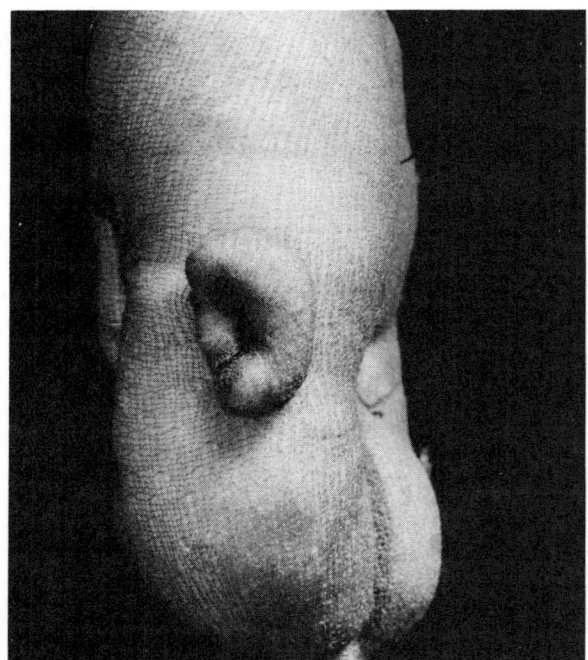

Fig. 205

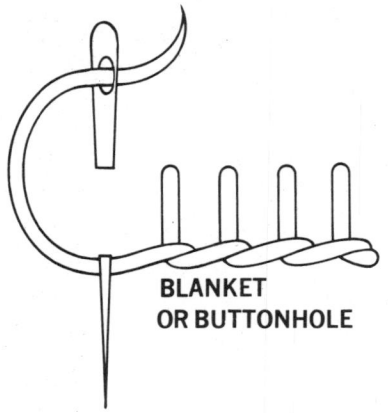

Fig. 204b Buttonhole Stitch

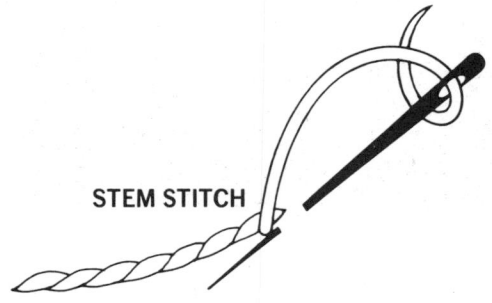

Fig. 204c Stem Stitch

short stitch and bring the needle out through the back again. Pull the thread and fasten it to make a dimple. Continue stitching, pull the thread and fasten it to indent a crease. With a knitting needle, push a little more stuffing above the pullstitching, to fill out the cheeks.

5. In darker thread, buttonhole stitch over the eyelids, overcast over the eyebrows, and stemstitch between the lips (Figs. 204a, 204b, and 204c).

6. For the ears, cut two strips of nylon about ¾ inch × 1 inch. Fold the strip in half lengthwise over a twist of stuffing. Whipstitch the

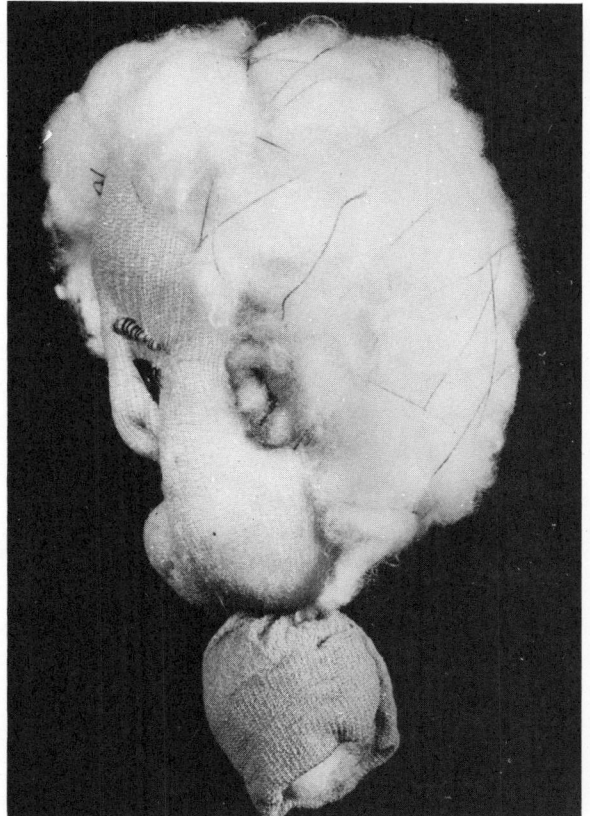

Fig. 206

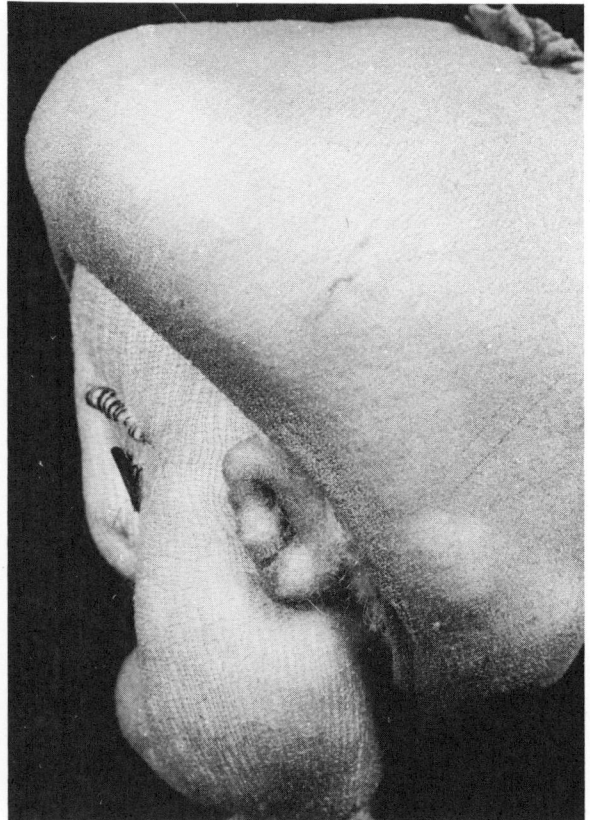

Fig. 207

long edges together. Trim the excess stuffing from each end and whipstitch them together to form a doughnut. Slipstitch each ear to the head with the seam hidden (Fig. 205).
7. Add stuffing to the head and cross it with thread to hold it in place (Fig. 206).
8. Make a nylon hat the same as the first three steps of Basic Head. Pull it over the stuffing (Figs. 207 and 208).

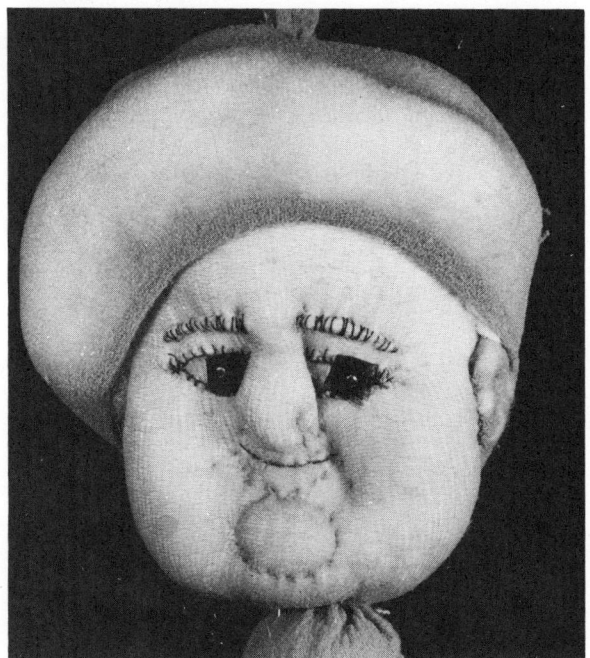

Fig. 208

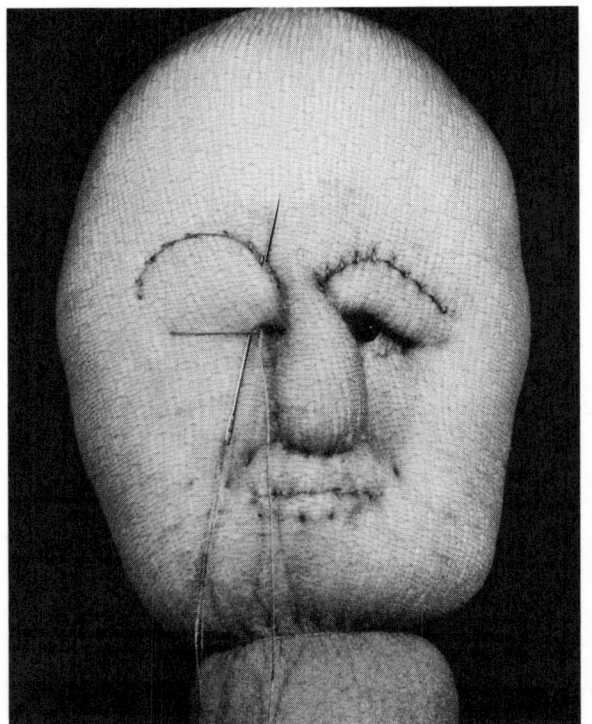

Fig. 209

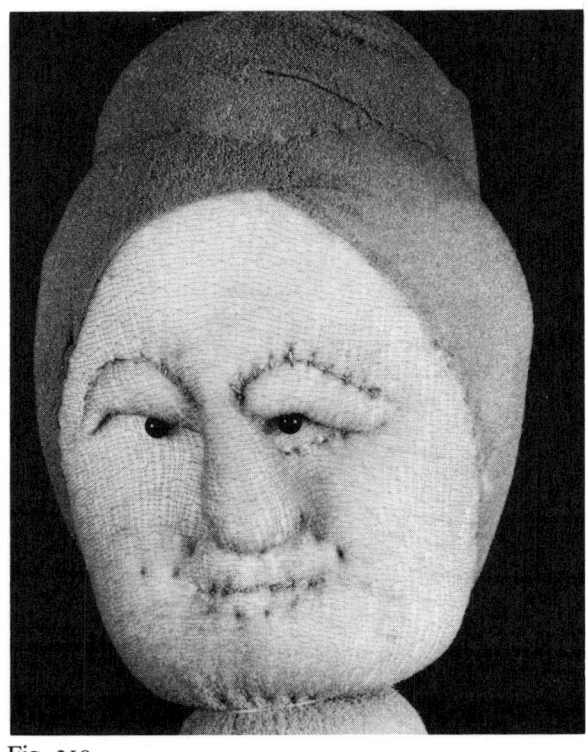

Fig. 210

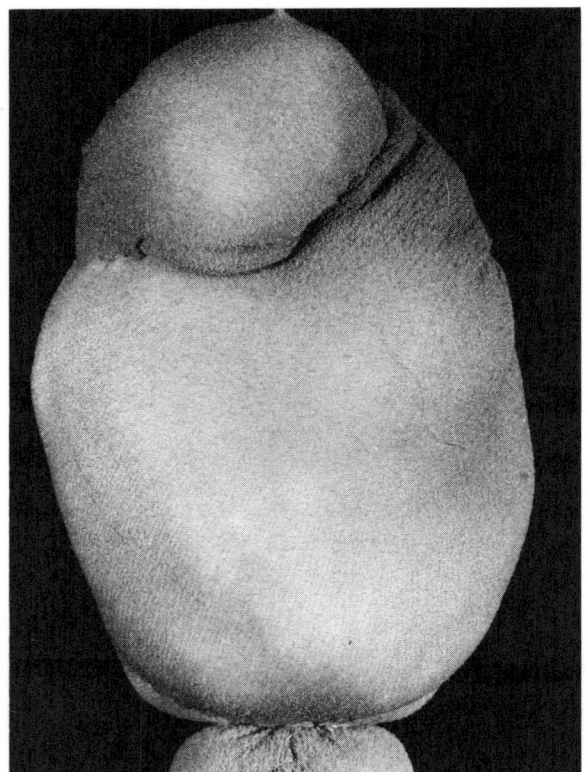

Fig. 211

FACE 3

1. Pinchstitch the nose. Sew and draw up running stitches at the bottom of the nose.
2. Pullstitch cheek lines.
3. Mark the upper edge of the eyelid with couching stitch (Fig. 198) and the lower edge of the upper lid with a long straight stitch. Pinchstitch between these two lines.
4. Work couching stitch across the mouth. Pinchstitch lightly between it and the lower lip. Pullstitch smile lines (Fig. 209).
5. Pull the toe of a stocking over the head and slipstitch it at each side of the face and across the back of the neck. Twist the extra stocking over a little stuffing to make a turban and slipstitch it in place (Figs. 210 and 211).

FACE 4

1. Work the first three steps of Face 3.
2. Couch the mouthline (Fig. 212).
3. Outline an ear with a running stitch. Draw up the thread and fasten it. Repeat for the other ear (Fig. 213).

Building and Molding 173

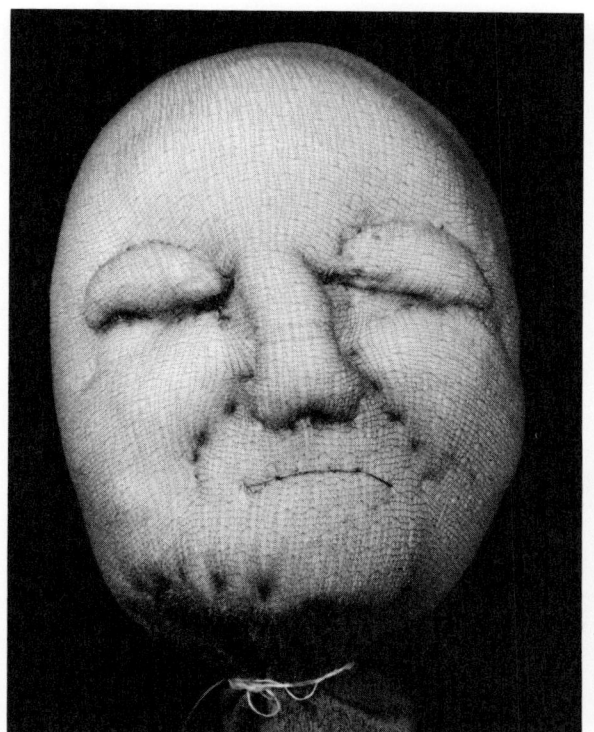

Fig. 212

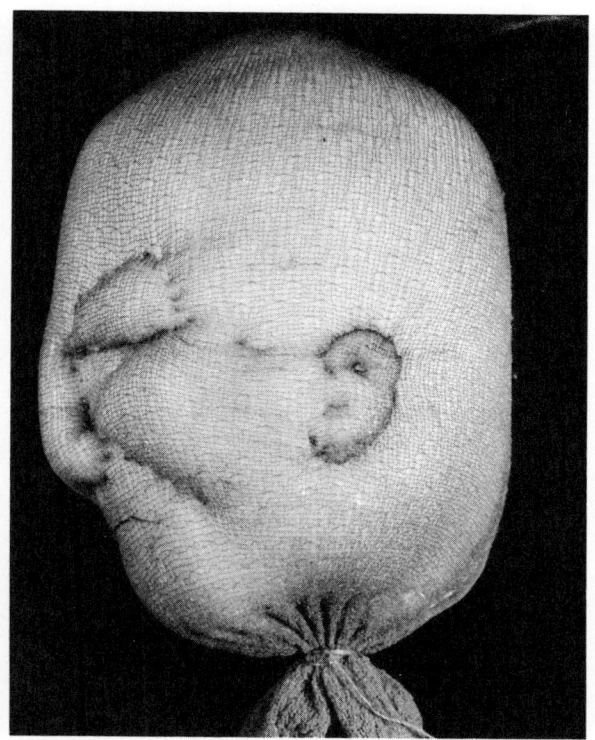

Fig. 213

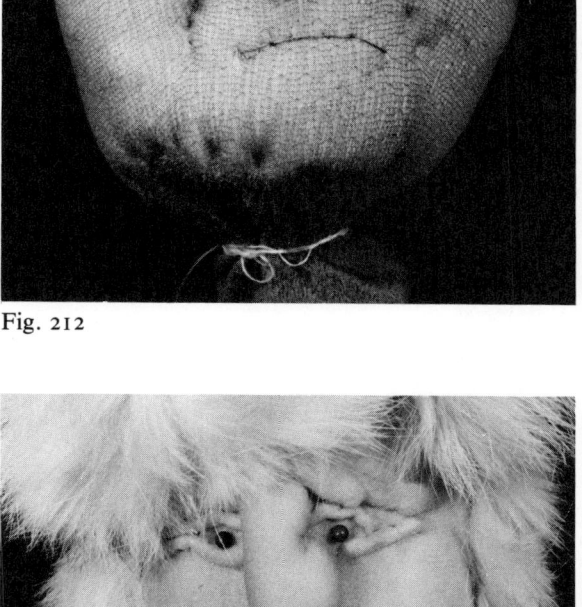

Fig. 214

FACE 5

1. Pinchstitch the nose, then gather up a running stitch beneath it.
2. Pinchstitch eyelids and eyebrows.
3. Draw up the mouth.
4. *Pleat* a chin, pushing the fabric and the stuffing upward. Slipstitch the pleat to the mouth, catching in the stuffing (Figs. 214 and 215).

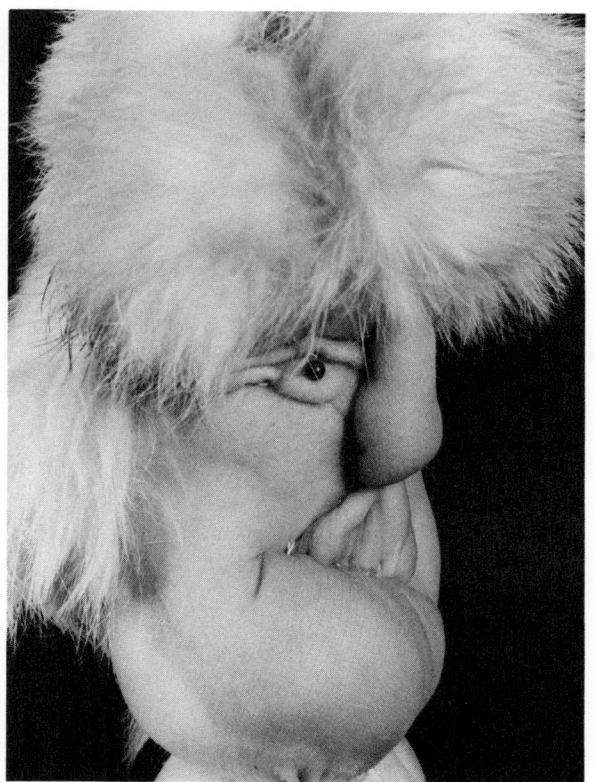

Fig. 215

Claudia Teller *Bird Man* (16" x 11"), 1977. Stuffed suedecloth body, ceramic head, cast bronze hands, veiling, beads and feathers. Courtesy Julie Artisans Gallery Inc., New York.

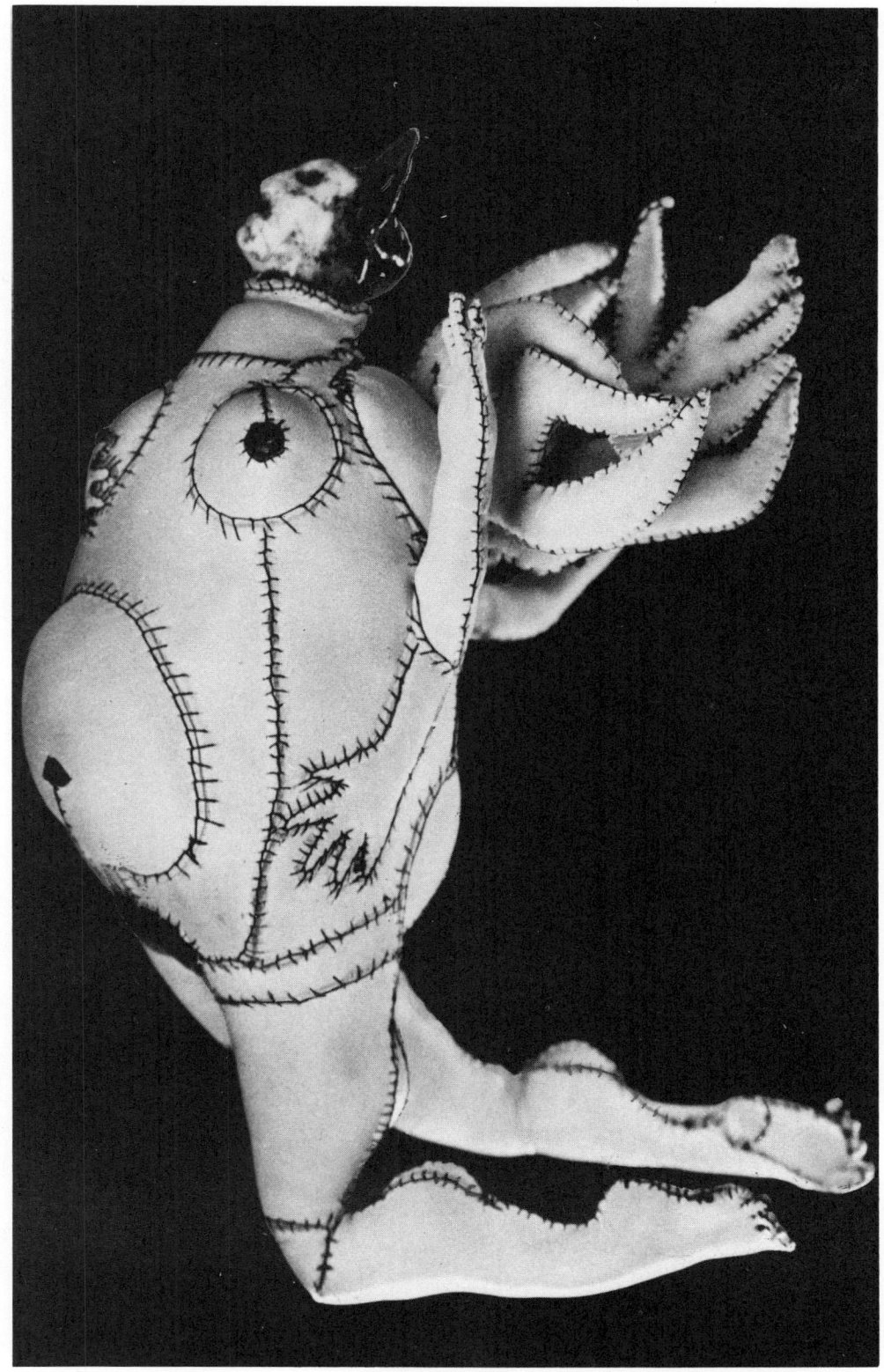

Anne Kingsbury *"Fifi"*. Leather, pieced and handsewn with blanket stitch, stuffed. Clay heads. Courtesy Synopsis Gallery.

Lenore Davis *Woman in Head Scarf, Folded Arms*
— 2 versions (26" high) 1977. Direct dyed cotton
velveteen, squeeze bottle, wash and brush
techniques, polyester stuffing.

Lenore Davis *Woman with Scarf and Hat* — 2 versions (26″ high) 1977. Direct dyed cotton velveteen, squeeze bottle, brush and wash techniques, polyester stuffing, sandbag weight in base.

Beverly Lippman, David Strauss *The Hostess* (28″).
Cotton fabric, polyester fill, yarn hair, marabou and
ostrich feathers, no armatures or wires. Courtesy
Incorporated Galleries, New York.

Building and Molding 179

Detail of *The Hostess*. Face — watercolor wash, tempera, acrylic and clear enamel.

180 The Complete Book of Stuffedwork

Beverly Lippman, David Strauss *The Can Can Dancer* (32", seated). Cotton fabric, polyester fill, yarn hair. Courtesy Incorporated Galleries, New York.

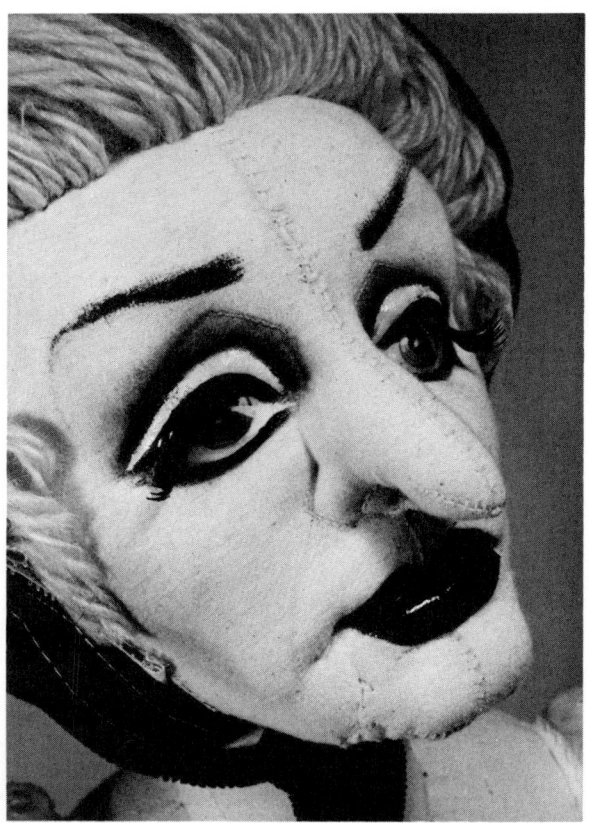

Detail of *The Can Can Dancer*. Face — watercolor wash, tempera, acrylic, and clear enamel.

Jo Ellen Trilling *Salome* (10" x 15"), 1976. Stuffed velvet body, nylon stocking hands and faces, large face and nails painted with acrylic, bead teeth, fringe hair, wire armature and synthetic stuffing. Courtesy Julie Artisans Gallery Inc., New York.

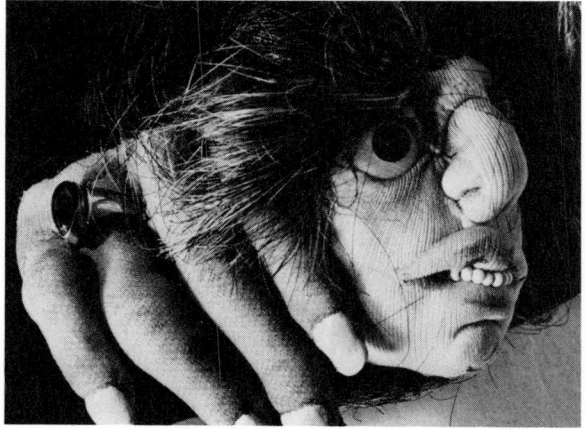

Detail of *Salome*

Jo Ellen Trilling *Elephant* (15″ x 20″), 1975.
Socks, velvet, corduroy, satin, wire armature, and synthetic stuffing.

Chapter Eight
Construction

PILLOWS (Plate 6)

All the following covers are made to fit 14-inch square pillows. Alter the cutting dimensions and materials required, as necessary, to fit other size pillows. Dimensions given in the cutting instructions include ½-inch seam allowance. To "seam" pieces, pin their right sides together and stitch on the seamline. Names of patterns or cut pieces are capitalized.

INNER PILLOW

An inner pillow is not essential; loose synthetic stuffing may be stuffed directly into the pillowcover. But later laundering is easier if you can slip out a separate inner pillow. It is cut a little larger than the pillowcover in order to produce a nice, fat filling.

Materials Required: ½ yard 35-inch wide muslin. Cut 1 Front and 1 Back, each 15½-inch square.

Assembly
1. Seam Front to Back, leaving about 5 inches open at one side. Trim corners (Fig. 216).

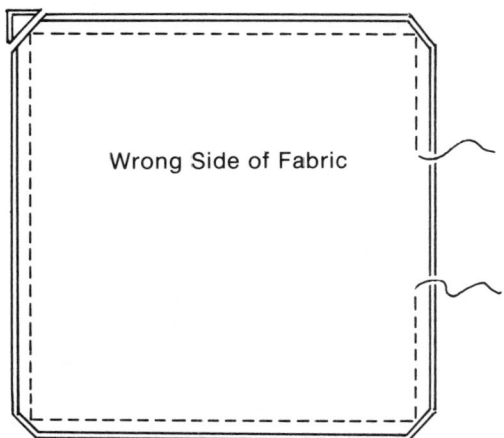

Fig. 216

2. Turn cover right side out. Insert stuffing until well filled, but not hard.
3. Turn in opening edges on seamline and pin. Edgestitch (Fig. 217).

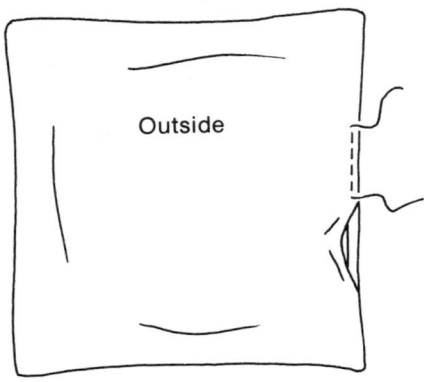

Fig. 217

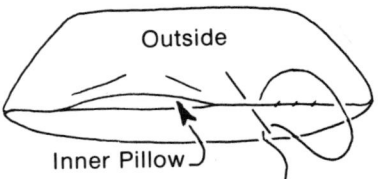

Fig. 219

KNIFE-EDGED PILLOW WITH SLIPSTITCHED CLOSING, VIEW A.

Materials Required: ½ yard 35-inch wide fabric. Cut 1 Front and 1 Back, each 15-inch square.

Assembly
1. Seam Front to Back, leaving about 9 inches open at one side. Trim the corners (Fig. 218).

CORDED KNIFE-EDGED PILLOW WITH ZIPPERED CLOSING, VIEW B.

Materials Required: ½ yard 45-inch wide fabric, 60-inch piece of filler cord or cable cord, 14-inch zipper.
Cut 1 Front 15-inch square; 1 Back 15 inches × 14 inches; 1 Back 15 inches × 2 inches and enough 2-inch-wide bias fabric to make a continuous strip 60 inches long.

Assembly
1. Turn under ½ inch at longer edge of the larger Back. Pin to a zipper tape with the fold matching the center of the zipper. Topstitch with a zipper foot (Fig. 220).

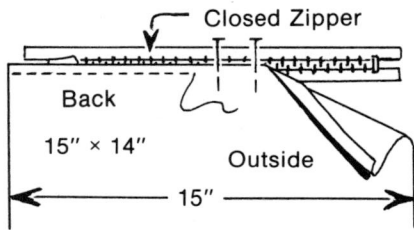

Fig. 220

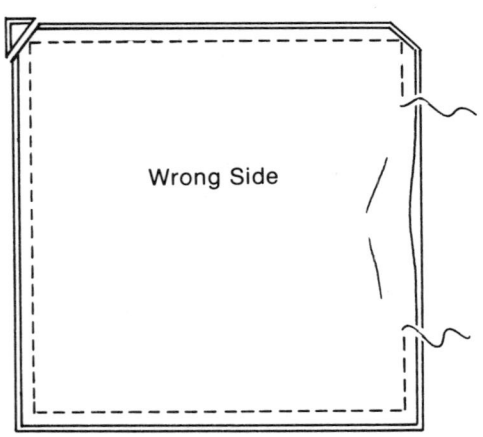

Fig. 218

2. Turn the cover right side out. Insert an inner pillow.
3. Turn in opening edges on the seamline and pin. Slipstitch to close the opening (Fig. 219).

2. Turn under ½ inch at the longer edge of the smaller Back. Pin it to the other zipper tape with folds meeting and side edges of the cover even (Fig. 221). Topstitch ¼ inch from the folds. Stitch across each end near the raw edges.

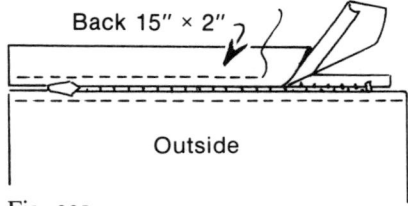

Fig. 221

3. Open the zipper (Fig. 222).

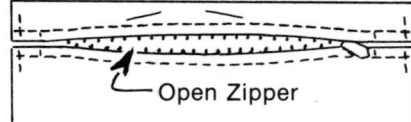

Fig. 222

4. Press open the piecing seams of the bias strip. Fold the strip over the cord, with raw edges meeting. With a zipper foot, stitch near the cord to make the piping (Fig. 223).

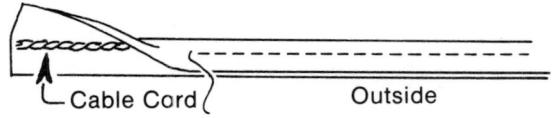

Fig. 223

5. With right sides together and raw edges matching, pin the piping to Front. When you reach a corner, clip piping seams to the stitching, in order to turn (Fig. 224).

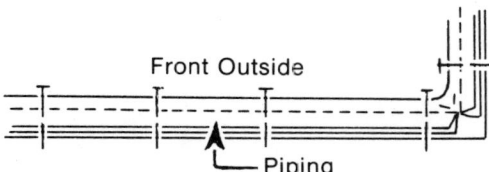

Fig. 224

6. To join the ends of the piping cut the beginning end so that both cording and fabric are flush. Pull out cord of the finishing end and trim it so that the cord ends will just meet. Trim the fabric of the finishing end ½ inch longer than the cord. Lap the final fabric over the beginning end. Turn under the raw end and slipstitch (Fig. 225).

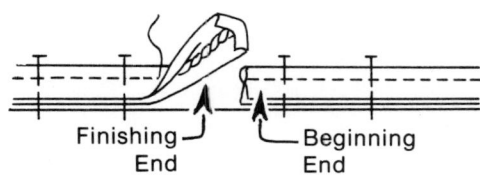

Fig. 225

7. Stitch piping to Front with zipper foot.
8. With the zipper open, baste Front to Back, right sides together (Fig. 226).

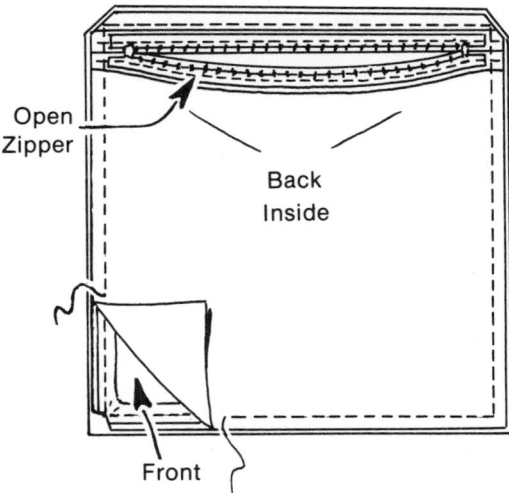

Fig. 226

9. With Front upward, stitch it to Back over the piping stitching, with a zipper foot.
10. Turn the cover right side out. Insert an inner pillow and close the zipper (Fig. 227).

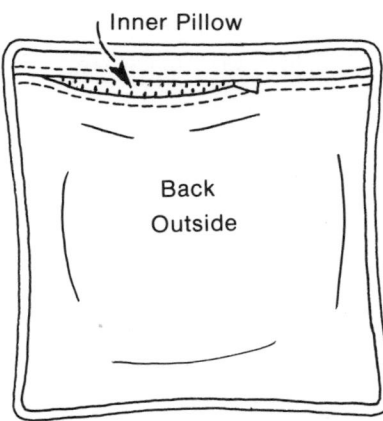

Fig. 227

PILLOW SHAM WITH LAPPED CLOSING, VIEW C.

Materials Required: ¾ yard 45-inch wide fabric and 4 snaps. Cut 1 Front 22-inch square and 2 Backs each 22 inches × 12¾ inches.

Assembly

1. Turn under ¼ inch at a longer edge of each Back. Turn under again an inch. Pin and stitch.
2. Lap one hemmed edge 1 inch over the other hemmed edge. Pin. Stitch across each end near the edges (Fig. 228).

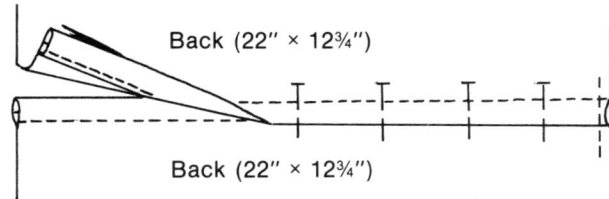

Fig. 228

3. Seam Front to Back ¼ inch from edges. Clip the corners (Fig. 229).

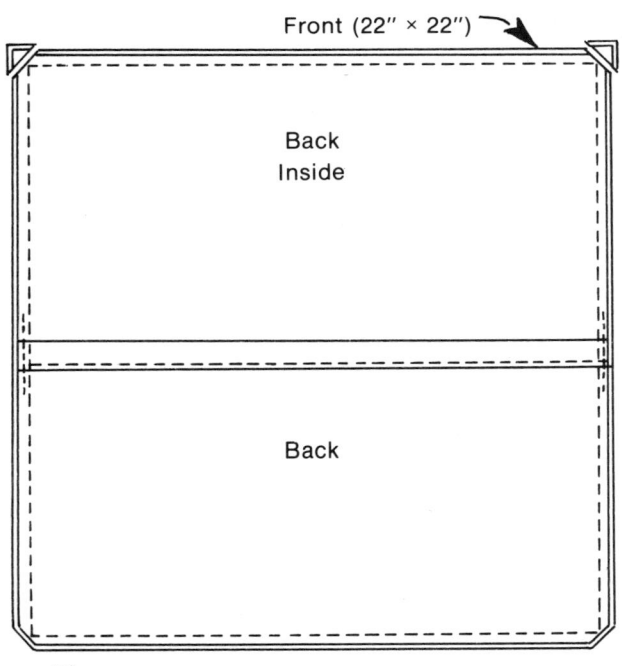

Fig. 229

4. Turn inside out. Press edges. Slipstitch the back closing for 4 inches from each edge, without catching in Front.
5. Apply two snaps 6 inches from each side, then the other two between them, evenly spaced about 3 inches apart.
6. With a hard pencil or tailor's chalk, draw a square whose sides are 4 inches from each outside edge. Stitch over the drawn lines (Fig. 230).

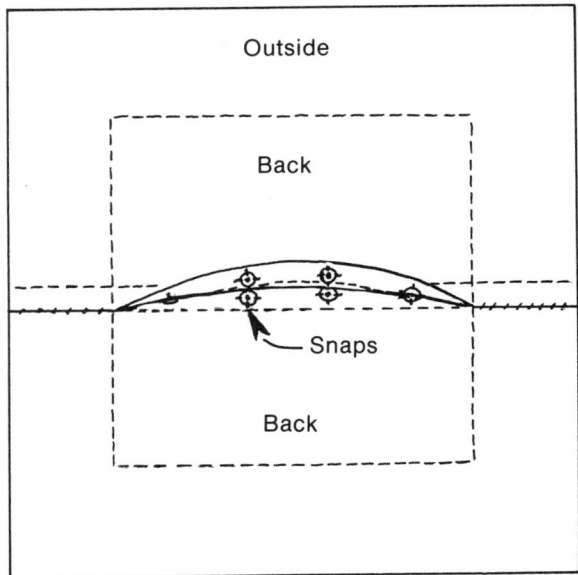

Fig. 230

7. Insert a pillow through the back opening. Snap the cover closed.

RUFFLED PILLOW WITH SLIPSTITCHED CLOSING, VIEW D.

Materials Required: ¾ yard 45-inch-wide fabric. Cut 1 Front and 1 Back, each 15-inch square. Cut 2 strips each 6 inches × 45 inches and 2 strips each 6 inches × 30 inches for the ruffle.

Assembly

1. Join short ends of the four strips with narrow seams to make a continuous loop.
2. Fold the loop in half lengthwise and pin raw edges together (Fig. 231).

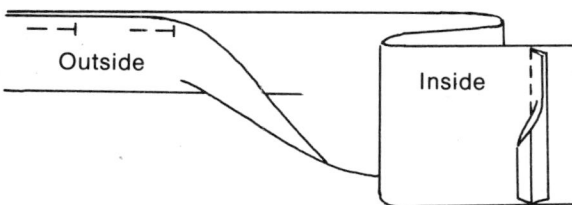

Fig. 231

3. Fold the loop in half crosswise once and then again. Mark each fold at the raw edges to indicate quarters (Fig. 232).

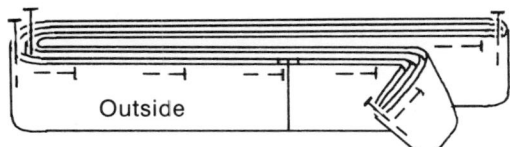

Fig. 232

4. By hand or with the longest machine stitch, run a gathering row ¼ inch from raw edges, starting at each quartermark and stopping at the next.
5. Pin each quartermark of the ruffle to a corner of Front with the gathering stitches half an inch from the edge. Clip to the stitching line of the ruffle, at each corner.
6. Pin the rest of the ruffle, pulling up the gathering row until the ruffle fits the flat edge with fullness evenly distributed. Stitch along the gathering line (Fig. 233).

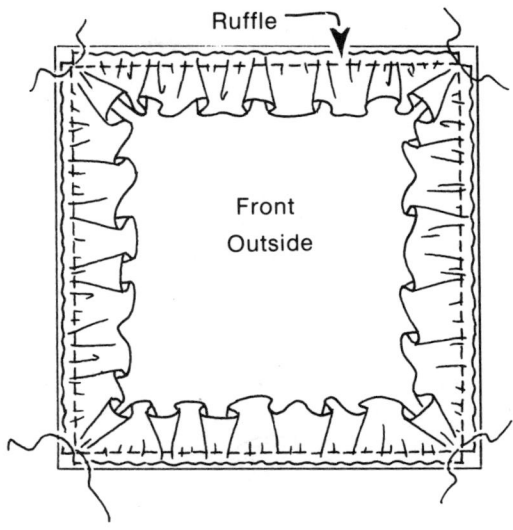

Fig. 233

7. Seam Front to Back, stitching over the ruffle stitching, leaving about 9 inches open at one side (Fig. 234). Trim the corners.

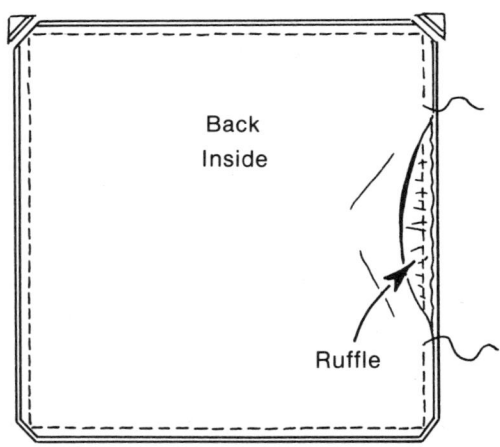

Fig. 234

8. Turn the cover right side out. Insert an inner pillow.
9. Turn in the opening edges on the seamline and pin. Slipstitch to close the opening.

188 The Complete Book of Stuffedwork

DOLLS (Models in Plate 8; Pattern 1

VIEW A

1. Trace Front to the wrong side of a piece of fabric 1 inch larger than the pattern. Pin this Front fabric to a piece of Back fabric the same size, right sides together (Fig. 235).

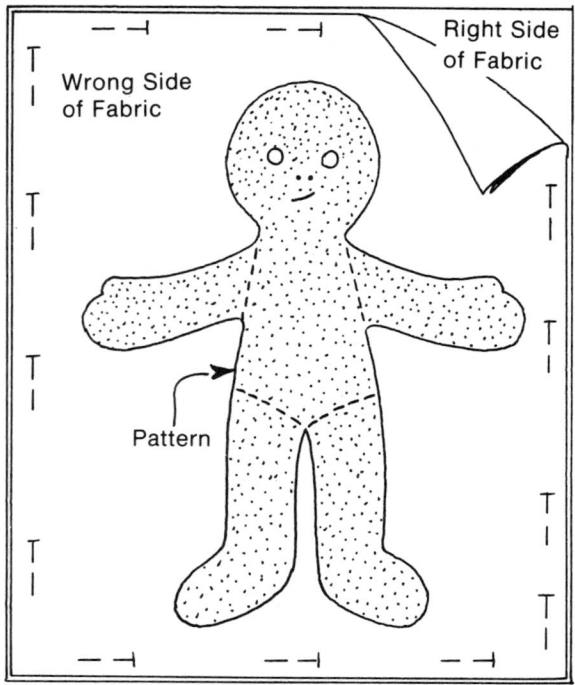

Fig. 235

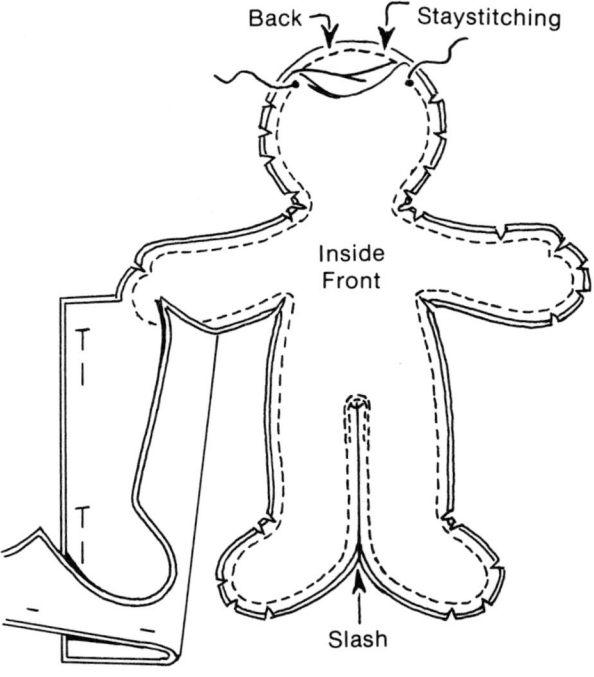

Fig. 236

2. Seam Front to the fabric for Back on the traced line, leaving the seam open between the marked dots. Stitch again at inside corners.
3. Staystitch each seamline at the head opening.
4. Trim away excess fabric, ¼ inch away from stitching. Slash between the legs. Clip almost to the stitching at inside corners and curves. Notch the seam allowance at outside curves (Fig. 236).
5. Turn the doll right side out. This doll is a little hard to turn, because it is small. Therefore push the fabric through the head opening with a knitting needle or similar instrument. When the fabric becomes congested, from the right side pick up a bit of unturned fabric with the point of a darning needle and coax the fabric out a little at a time. Do this also at the arms.
6. Insert synthetic stuffing, a little at a time, pushing it toward the outside edges until they are nicely filled. Fill the center. Turn in the opening edges on the staystitching and slipstitch them together, inserting a little more stuffing, if necessary, to fill out the head (Fig. 237).

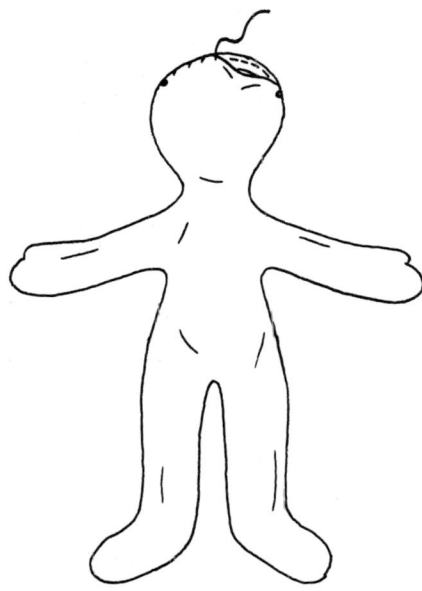

Fig. 237

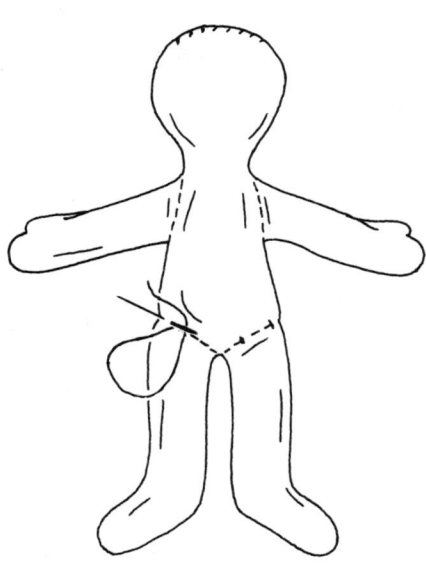

Fig. 238

7. Color with permanent markers, trying them out first on a scrap of fabric.

VIEW B

1. Follow directions for View A. However, in step 6, stuff the legs to the jointline without much stuffing near the top. Pin on the jointline. See if the doll can sit, after stuffing above the pins. If there is too much stuffing to allow the doll to sit, remove some. Follow the same procedure for the arms.
2. Topstitch across the jointlines, removing the pins, as follows. Slide unknotted threaded needle into the body, bringing the needle out at the start of the jointline and drawing up the thread until its end disappears into the body. Backstitch across the jointline, through both layers.

    Fasten the stitch and bring the thread out of the body some distance away, clipping the thread flush with the fabric.
3. Finish stuffing and close as in View A, step 6 (Fig. 238).

VIEW C

1. Follow step 1 in View A. Cut ¼ inch away from traced line through both layers. From lightweight fabric, cut out Front and Back Shirt and Front and Back Shorts. If the lower edges can be placed on a selvage, these seam allowances may be omitted.
2. Shorts: Turn under the lower edge on the seamline, unless the seamline is a selvage. Pin Shorts to the right side of Front and Back. Slipstitch the lower edge; baste the crotch, side, and top edges.
3. Shirt: Staystitch the neck seam. Clip to stitching. Turn under on stitching. Turn under the sleeve edges on the seamline. Turn under the lower edges on the seamline, unless the seamline is the selvage. Pin Shirt to right side of Doll, overlapping shorts. Slipstitch neck, sleeve, and lower edges. Baste other edges (Fig. 239).

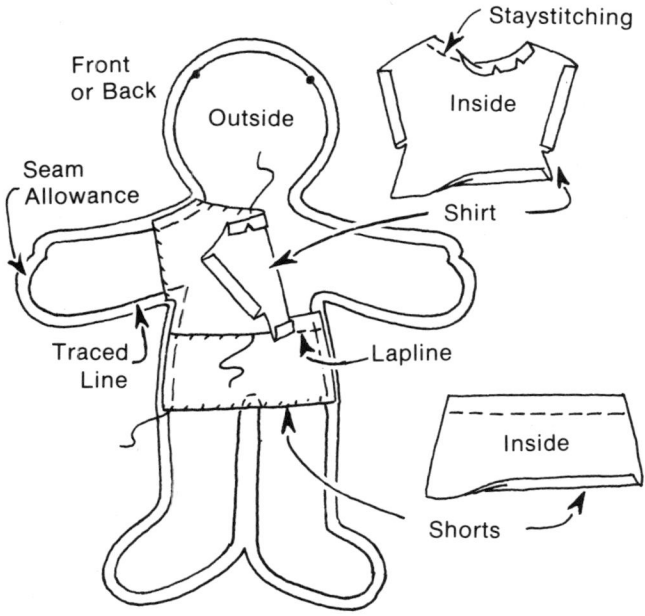

Fig. 239

4. Follow steps 2 through 6 in View A, omitting trimming in step 4.
5. Color in features with permanent markers. Cut out triangle, as indicated on pattern page, and tie it around the head.

VIEW D

1. Follow step 1 in View A. Cut ¼ inch away from traced line through both layers.
   Cut out appliqués, from iron-on tape or patches. Iron bikini to right side of Back and Front, matching at sides (Fig. 240).

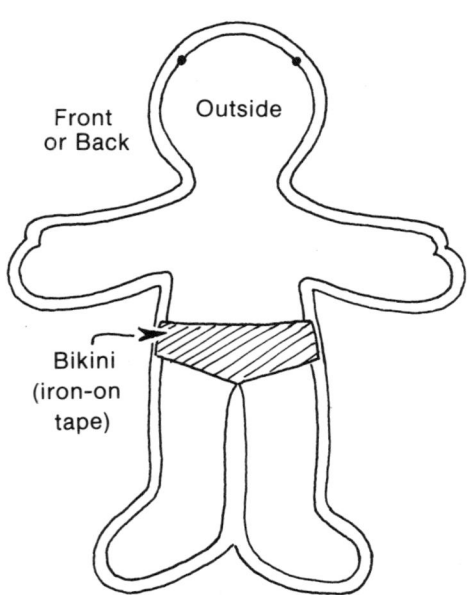

Fig. 240

2. Follow steps 2 through 6 in View A omitting trimming in step 4.
3. Iron on glasses, two pieces of the back hair, then two pieces of the front hair, overlapping the glasses. Iron on the mouth (Fig. 241).

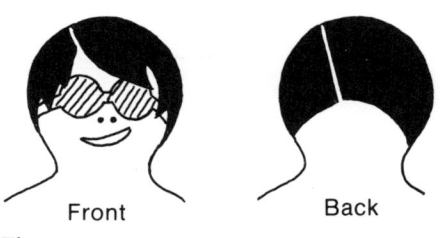

Fig. 241

PILLOWS (Models in Plate 9; Pattern 2)

PILLOW A

Some foam pillowforms are made of two pieces of foam, curved downward at the corners and glued through the center. This shaping eliminates the dog-eared corners of a knife-edged pillow (Fig. 242).

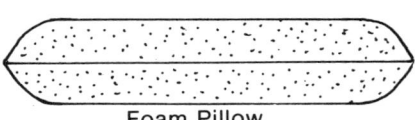

Fig. 242

Pattern

1. Place tape straight around the pillow and measure the girth. Divide this measurement in half. This is the finished size of Front or Back. Add ½-inch seam allowance all around for the cut size.
2. Cut muslin Front. Fold it diagonally, matching edges. Press fold.
3. Place the muslin over the pillow. Pin two adjoining seamlines of the muslin to the glued center edge of the pillowform.
4. Pin the extra fabric at the corner into a dart with the crease as the center (Fig. 243).

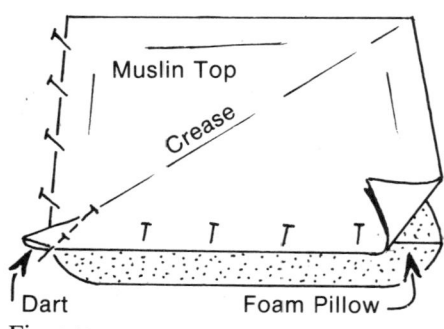

Fig. 243

With a pencil make short dashes along the pinned line.
5. Unpin and press the muslin. Trace the corner (about 6-inch square) to tissue paper. This is the pattern for the corners (Fig. 244).

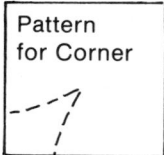

Fig. 244

Cutting

Cut Front and Back (see Pattern, step 1). Trace the dart pattern at each corner, matching the side edges.

Assembly

1. Stitch darts. Slash on the foldline to ½ inch from the point. Press open (Fig. 245).

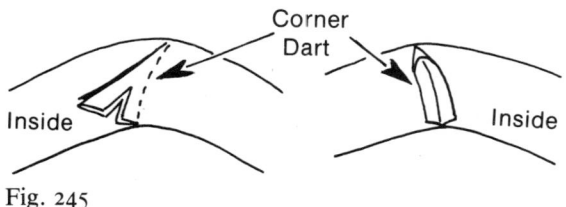

Fig. 245

2. Pin Front to Back, matching darts and edges, right sides together. Seam on three sides (Fig. 246).

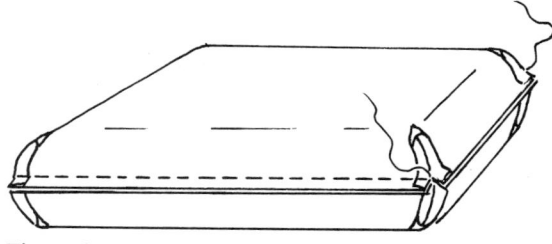

Fig. 246

3. Insert pillowform. Slipstitch to close (Fig. 247).

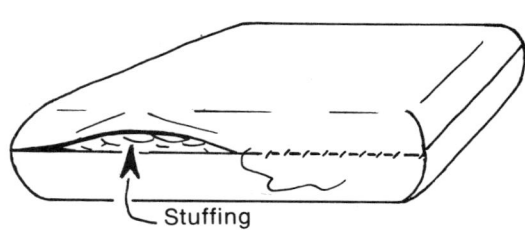

Fig. 247

PILLOW B

Pattern

1. Place tape straight around the pillow (Fig. 248) and measure the girth. Divide this measurement in half. This is the finished size of Front or Back. Add ½-inch seam allowance all around, for the cut size.

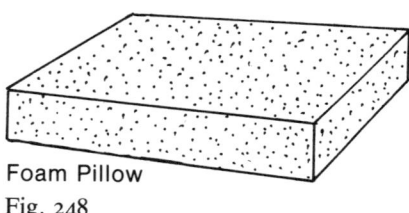

Fig. 248

2. Measure the width of the boxing and divide this in half. This is the length of each side of the corner cutouts that form the darts.

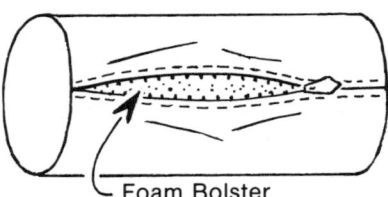

Fig. 257

4. Turn right side out. Insert foam bolster. Close zipper (Fig. 257).

PILLOW E

Pattern

1. Measure Front of the pillowform and add ½-inch seam allowance all around.
2. Measure width and length of Boxing. Subtract the zipper length (which should be a length no shorter than one side plus two Boxing widths) from the total length. This measurement times the width plus a ½-inch seam allowance all around will be the 1-piece Boxing.
3. For the 2-piece (zippered) Boxing, we need two pieces, each the length of the zipper by half the Boxing width plus a ½-inch seam allowance all around.

Cutting

Cut Front and Back the same size. Cut a 1-piece Boxing and two 2-piece Boxings. Front and Back of the pillow in Plate 9E were 14½ inches square, the 1-piece Boxing was 3½ inches × 36 inches and the 2-piece Boxings were 2¼ inches × 21 inches.)

Assembly

1. Optional purchased welting. Apply to Front and Back, as you did the covered welting in pillow C (see in Plate 10, page 106).
2. Turn under the seam allowance at one long side of each narrow Boxing strip. Pin each side to the zipper, with the folded edges meeting at the center of the zipper. Stitch (Fig. 258).

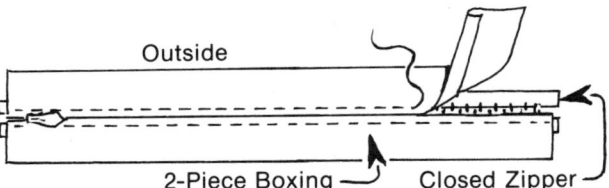

Fig. 258

3. Seam the zippered Boxings to the wide Boxing to make a continuous strip. At Boxing edges mark the center of the zipper. Mark half a finished side length on each side of this center, then a full finished side length each side of that.
4. Open the zipper. Pin Boxing to Front and Back, clipping the marks to the seamline, then matching the clips to Front and Back corners. Stitch (Fig. 259).

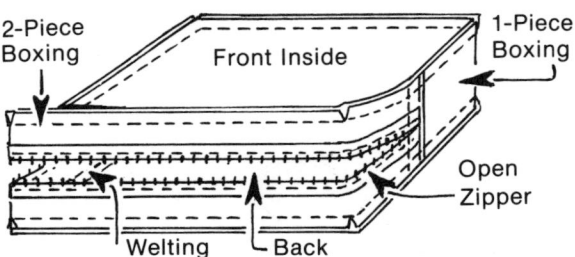

Fig. 259

5. Turn right side out. Insert the pillowform. Close zipper (Fig. 260).

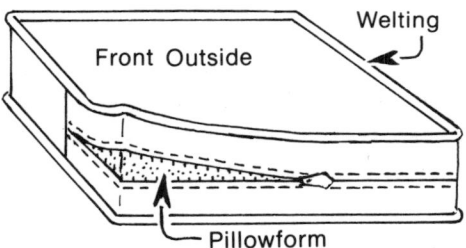

Fig. 260

PILLOW F (Pattern 2)

Pattern
Measure the pillowform as follows:
Measure Back plus seams.
Measure End plus seams.
Measure Front and Top plus seams.
Measure Front Bottom minus 2 inches plus seams.
Measure Front End minus 2 inches plus seams.
Measure Back End: height of End times 2 inches plus seams.
Measure Back Bottom: length of bottom times 2 inches plus seams.

Cutting
Cut the seven pieces described, to fit your pillowform.

Assembly
1. Seam Front End to Front Bottom and Back End to Back Bottom (Fig. 261).
2. Seam Front Bottom to Back Bottom up to the zipper opening. (Zipper reaches down one end and across more than half of the bottom.)

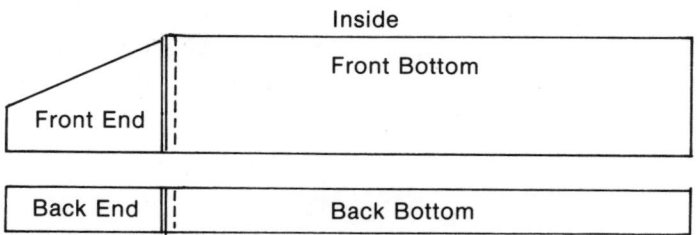

Fig. 261

3. Turn under the remaining seam allowances and stitch to the zipper tape, with folds meeting at center of zipper (Fig. 262).
4. Seam the other End to Bottom. Seam Back and Front/Top to Bottom (Fig. 263).

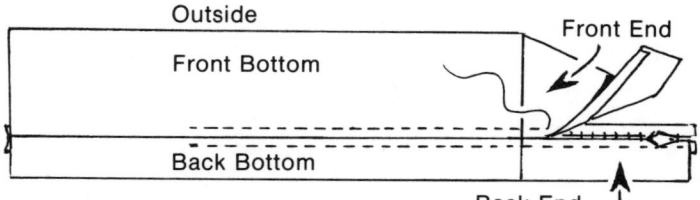

Fig. 262

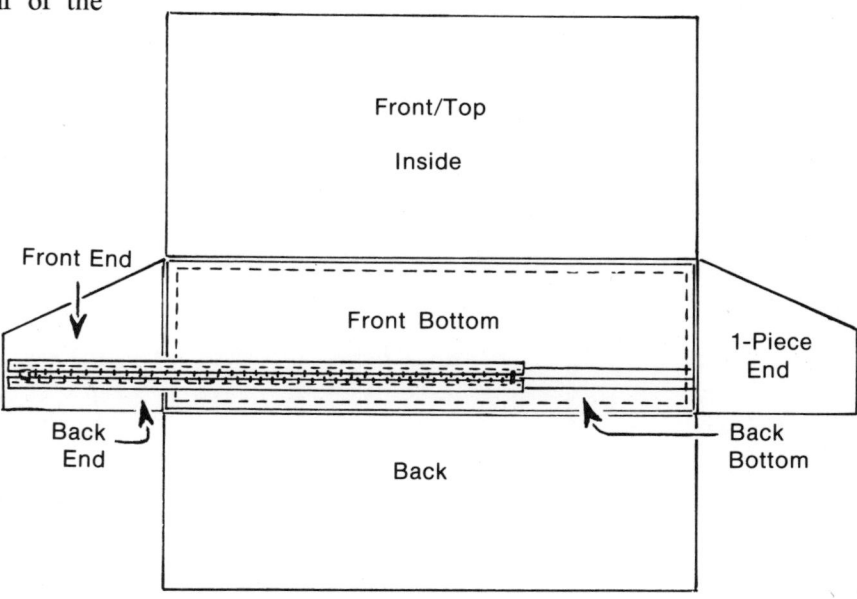

Fig. 263

5. Stitch the Ends to Back and Front/Top, clipping at corners. Stitch Front/Top to Back with the zipper partly open for turning (Figs. 264 and 265).

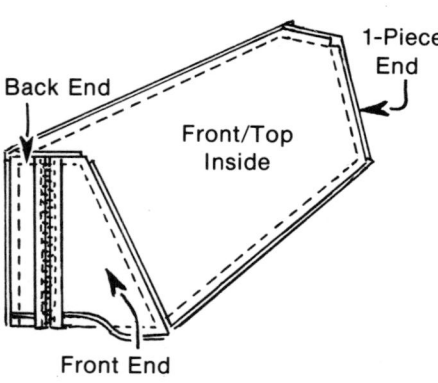

Fig. 264

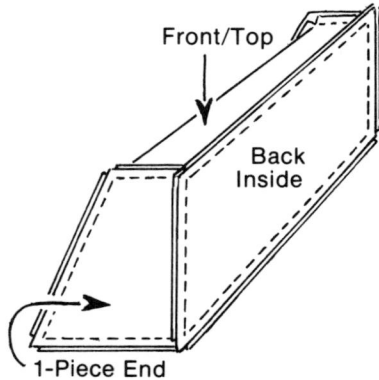

Fig. 265

6. Turn right side out. Insert the pillowform. Close zipper.

BALLS (Models in Plate 11; Pattern 4)

SPHERE (Plate 14E)

1. Seam three Sections, then the other three Sections (Fig. 266).

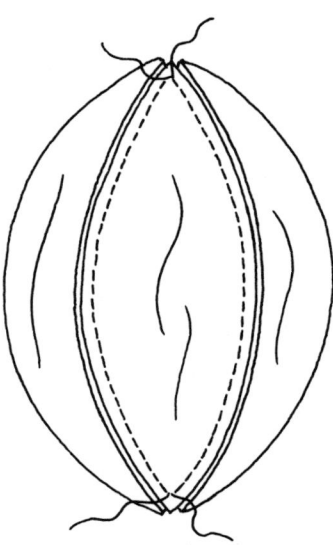

Fig. 266

2. Seam the two halves, leaving an opening for stuffing (Fig. 267).

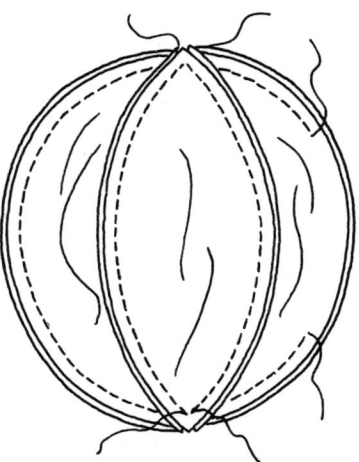

Fig. 267

3. Turn right side out. Stuff. Slipstitch to close the opening (Fig. 268).

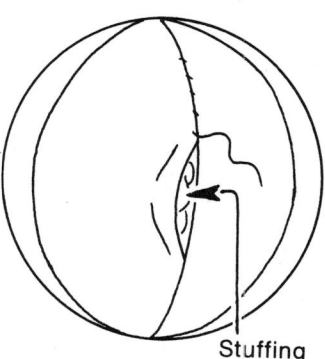

Fig. 268

SPHERE SEGMENT (Plate 11F)

1. Seam the curved edges of two Sides to Sphere Section, matching centers.
2. Seam the straight edges of Sides, leaving an opening for stuffing (Fig. 269).
3. Turn right side out. Stuff and slipstitch to close the opening (Fig. 270).

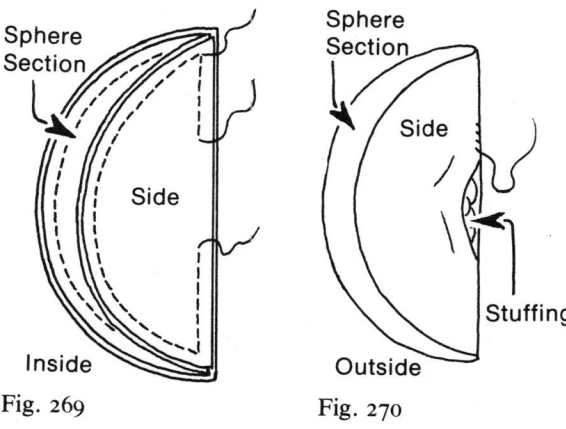

Fig. 269

Fig. 270

TRUNCATED SPHERES (Plate 11G)

1. Seam 6 Upper Sections (Fig. 271), then 6 Lower Sections (Fig. 272).

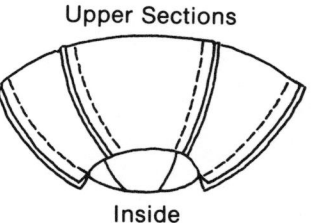

Fig. 271

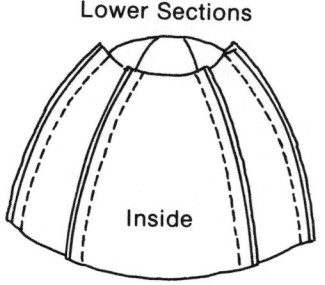

Fig. 272

2. Seam upper part to lower, matching seams.
3. Seam Top to upper part and Bottom to lower part, leaving a 5-inch opening at Bottom for stuffing (Fig. 273).
4. Turn right side out. Stuff. Slipstitch to close the opening.

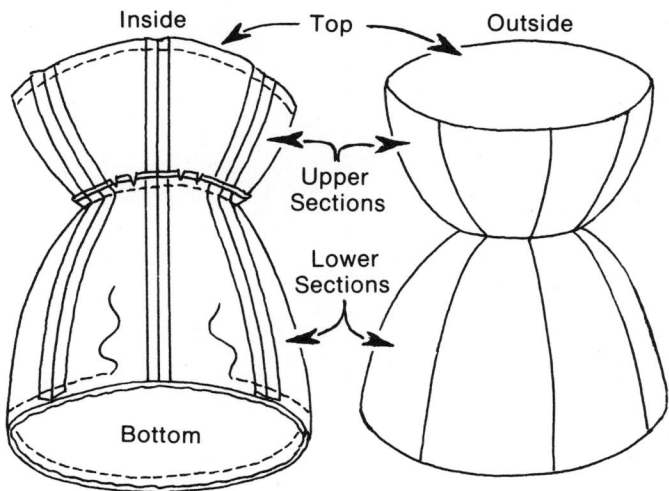

Fig. 273

BASKETBALL (Plate 11A)

1. Seam 4 pairs of Sections (Fig. 274).

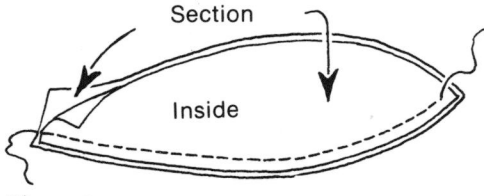

Fig. 274

2. Stitch two pairs of seamed Sections at the straight ends (Fig. 275).

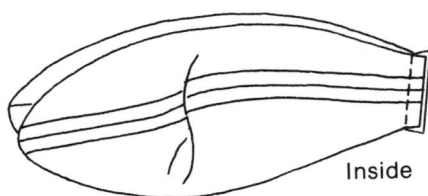

Fig. 275

3. Pin the inside curve of one piece to the outside curve of the other, matching seams. Stitch, leaving an opening for stuffing (Fig. 276).
4. Turn right side out. Stuff. Slipstitch to close opening (Fig. 277).

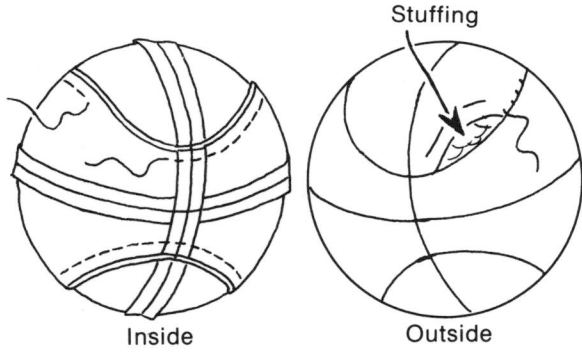

Fig. 276   Fig. 277

FOOTBALL (Plate 11C)

1. Seam 4 Sections together, matching edges, leaving an opening at one seam, for stuffing (Fig. 278).

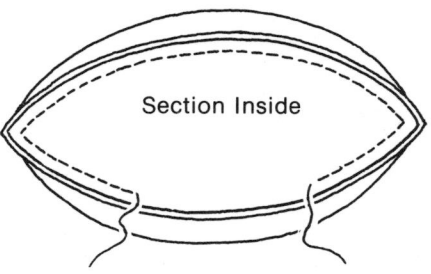

Fig. 278

2. Turn right side out and stuff. Slipstitch to close opening (Fig. 279).

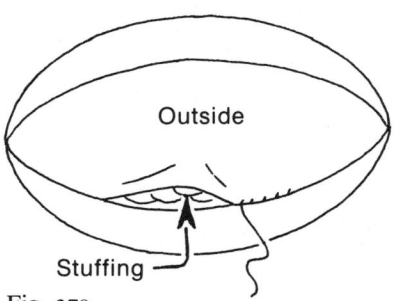

Fig. 279

SOFTBALL (Plate 11B)

1. Pin the center of the inside curve on one piece to the center of an outside curve on the other piece. Continue pinning the two pieces together, matching centers (Fig. 280). Stitch, leaving an opening for stuffing (Fig. 281).
2. Turn right side out. Stuff. Slipstitch to close the opening (Fig. 282).

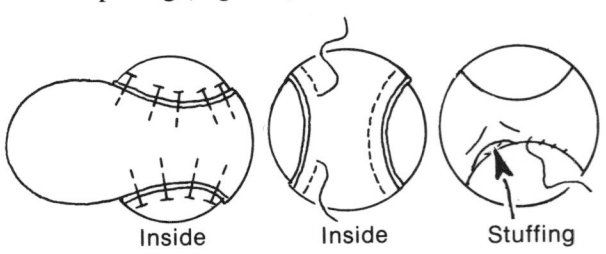

Fig. 280   Fig. 281   Fig. 282

DOLLS (Plates 14, 15, and 16)

DOLL A (Pattern in Fig. 172)

1. With right sides together, fold each Leg in half lengthwise and seam side and bottom edges (Fig. 283).

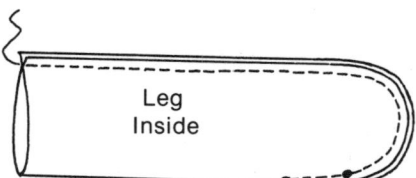

Fig. 283

2. Press the seam open. Fold across the seam and bring the dart lines together. Pin and stitch the dart (Fig. 284).

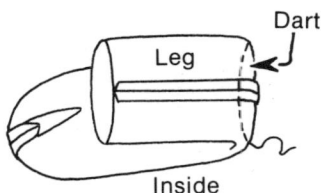

Fig. 284

3. Turn right side out and mark dots at the ankle. Stuff the toe. Fold the leg forward at the ankle to bring the dots together, pin and tack securely. Stuff firmly up to the knee, then loosely to the top. Bring the seam to the center at the top edge. Stitch across the top (Fig. 285).

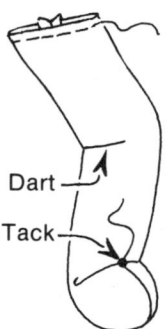

Fig. 285

4. Repeat for the other Leg.
5. With right sides together, seam Front to Back, except at the lower edge.
6. Pin and stitch the elbow darts through Front only (this is more easily done by hand). Clip seam allowance at inward curves and notch outward curves (Fig. 286).

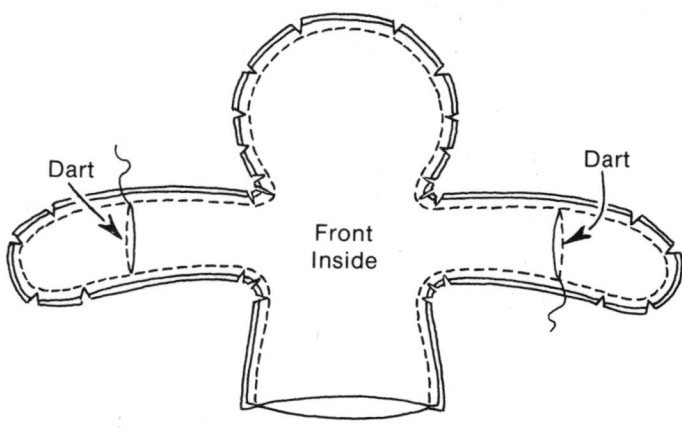

Fig. 286

7. Turn the body right side out. Mark dots to form the wrists.
8. With right sides together pin Legs to the lower front edge of Front only. Stitch.
9. Stuff the hands. Fold them forward to bring the wrist circles together. Pin and tack securely.
10. Stuff the arms. Stitch on the broken line at the shoulder to make a joint (Fig. 287).

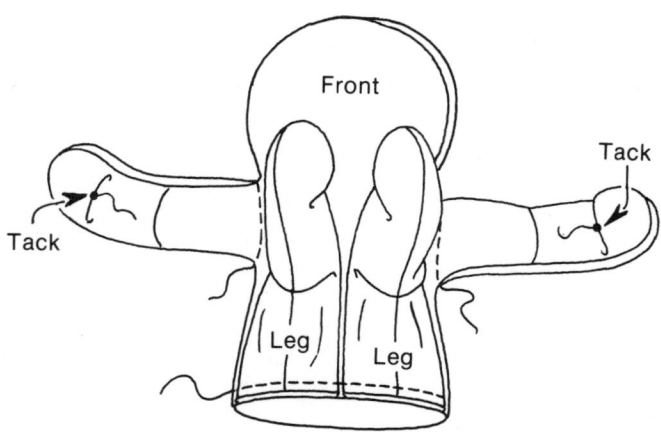

Fig. 287

11. Complete stuffing the doll. Turn under the lower back edge ¼ inch and pin it over the leg seams. Slipstitch to close (Fig. 288).

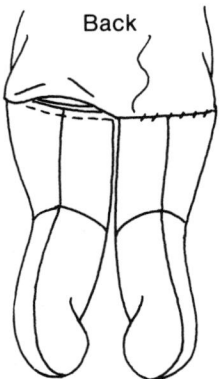

Fig. 288

DOLL B (Pattern 7)

1. Stitch the 6 darts in Back (Fig. 289).

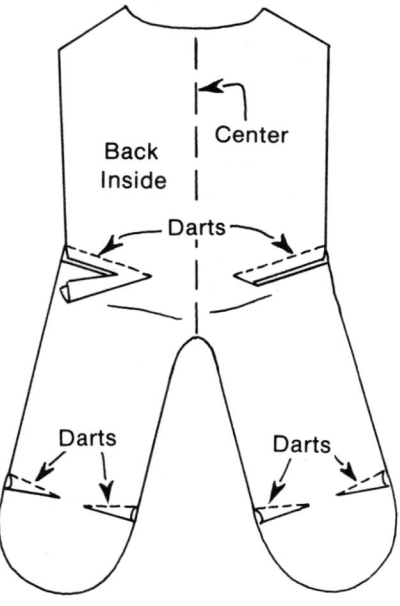

Fig. 289

2. Pin Front to Back, right sides together, matching edges. Stitch the shoulders. Stitch the sides and the legs between the dots (Fig. 290). Turn right side out.

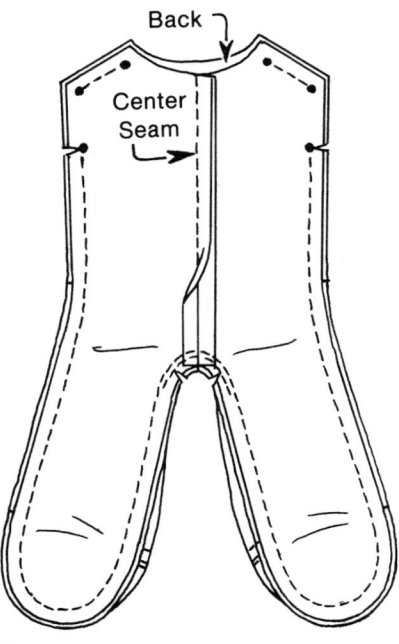

Fig. 290

3. Pin each pair of Arms, right sides together. Stitch, leaving an opening at the straight edges. Clip at the inside corners and curves (Fig. 291). Turn right side out.

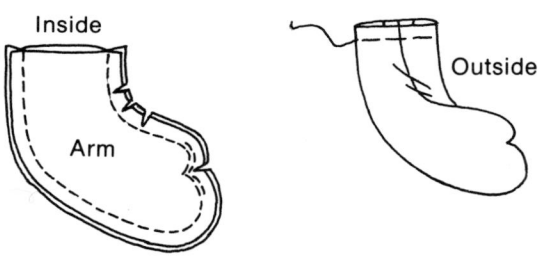

Fig. 291   Fig. 292

4. Stuff Arms firmly to the elbow. Bring the seams together and continue stuffing the arm softly. Baste across the straight edges with seams matching (Fig. 292).

5. Insert Arms in the armholes. Turn the front armhole in ¼ inch and slipstitch it over the basting. Turn in the back armhole ¼ inch and slipstitch it to the arm (Fig. 293).

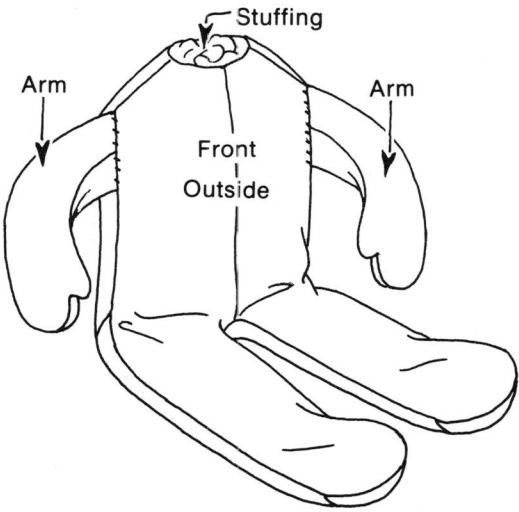

Fig. 293

DOLL C (Pattern 8)

1. Seam each pair of Legs except at the top and bottom edges (Fig. 294). Press the seams open. Clip at the inside curves.
2. With right sides together, pin Sole to Leg, matching crossmarks to seams. Stitch (Fig. 295).

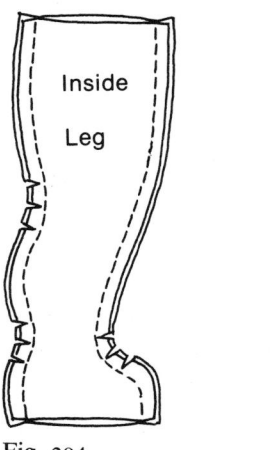 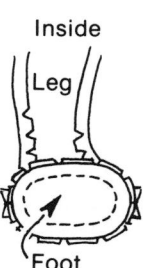

Fig. 294 Fig. 295

3. Turn right side out. Stuff Legs firmly below the knee and softly above, so that the doll will "sit." Bring the seams together at the center. Turn in the top edges on the seamline and whipstitch (Fig. 296).
4. Seam each pair of Arms except between the dots at the top. Restitch the inside corner at the thumb for reinforcement. Press the seams open. Clip at the inside curves and corners (Fig. 297).

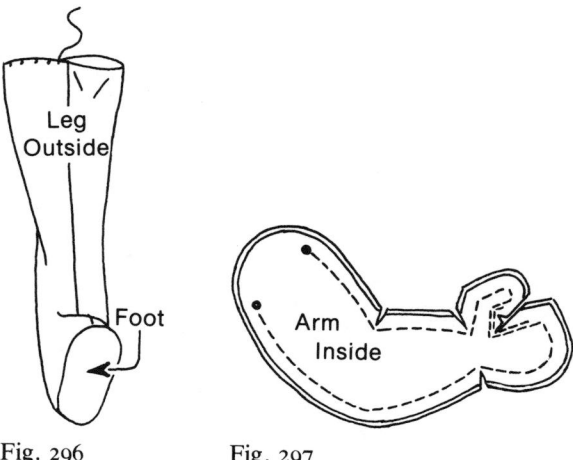

Fig. 296 Fig. 297

5. Turn right side out. Stuff firmly, then softly near the shoulder. Turn in on the seamline between the dots and whipstitch (Fig. 298).

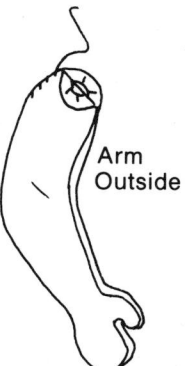

Fig. 298

6. Seam the center front and the center back seams (Figs. 299 and 300). Press them open.
7. Seam Front to Back at all but the neck edges. Press the seams open. Clip at the inside curves (Fig. 301).

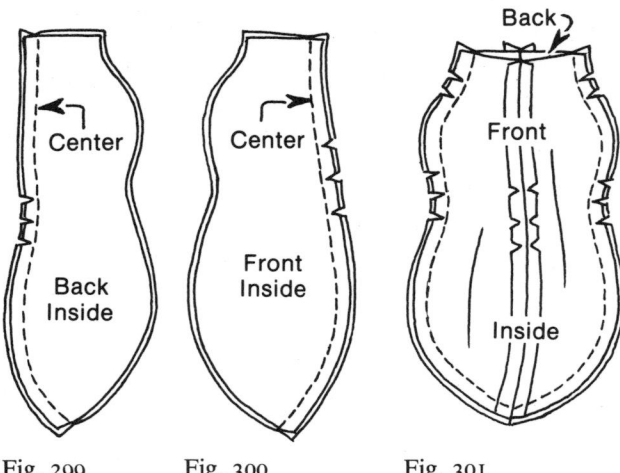

Fig. 299 Fig. 300 Fig. 301

8. Turn right side out and stuff firmly.
9. Pin Legs on the front above the bottom seam. See if the doll can "sit," changing placement if necessary. Securely whipstitch Legs to the front. Also, whipstitch top of Arms, between the seams, to the body (Fig. 302).

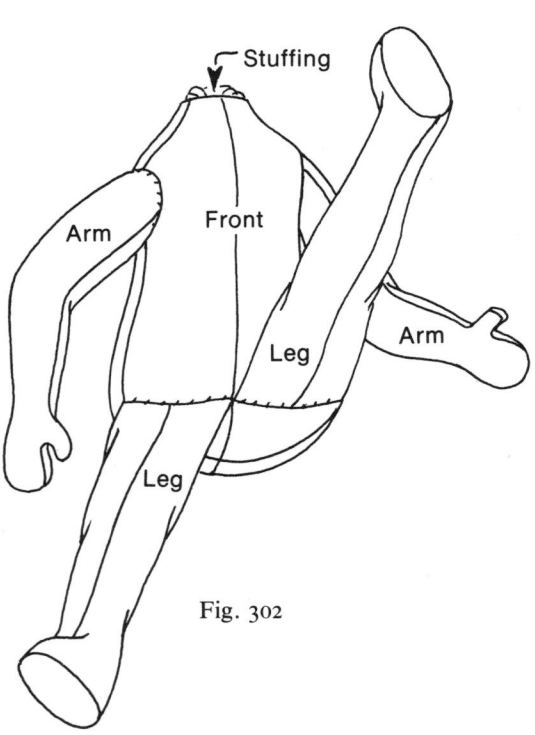

Fig. 302

HEADS (Models in Plate 17; Patterns 9 and 10)

VIEW 1

1. Seam Front to Back. Clip to inside corners (Fig. 303).
2. Turn right side out and stuff (Fig. 304).

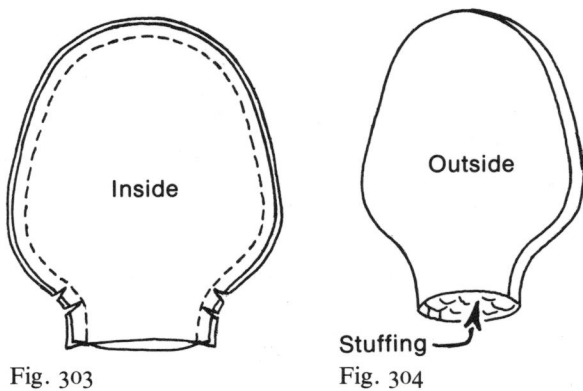

Fig. 303 Fig. 304

VIEW 2

1. Stuff sock. (Sock shown is children's size 4–5.)
2. About halfway down the desired depth of the head (at eye level) run a gathering row around the sock. Draw it in slightly and fasten the end. Repeat, about ⅛ inch below that row.
3. Repeat at the neckline. Draw up the gathering row tightly over the stuffing (Fig. 305). Wind the thread several times around the neck and fasten the end.

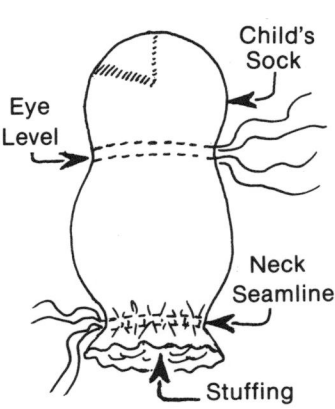

Fig. 305

4. Run another gathering row ¼ inch above this and draw it up slightly. This will be the neck seamline. Trim away the excess sock half an inch below the lowest gathering.

VIEW 3

1. Cut a rectangle of fabric (Plate 23 shows one that is 5 inches × 8 inches, including ¼-inch seams). Fold the long edges in half, right sides together, and seam at the center back (Fig. 306). Turn right side out.

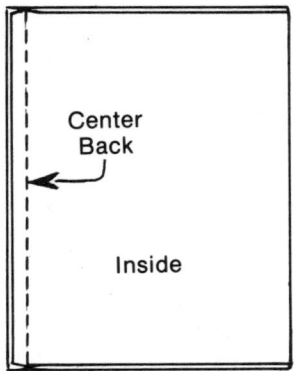

Fig. 306

2. Starting at the center back, run a gathering row ¼-inch from the top edge. Draw up to close and fasten the end. Stuff.
3. Run a similar gathering row at the lower edge (Fig. 307). Draw up to close and fasten the end. The body will join the head about an inch above the lower edge. The top gathering will be concealed under the hair.

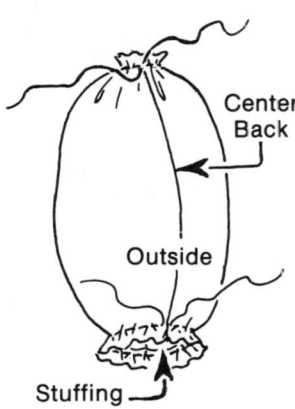

Fig. 307

VIEW 4

1. Make a mark at the bottom of the center back in the seam allowance to distinguish the back from the front after it is stuffed.
2. Seam pair of Backs along the center back seam and a pair of Fronts along the center front. Clip inside curves and press seams open.
3. Stitch, clip, and press Back and Front at the side seams, in the same way (Fig. 308). Turn right side out and stuff (Fig. 309).

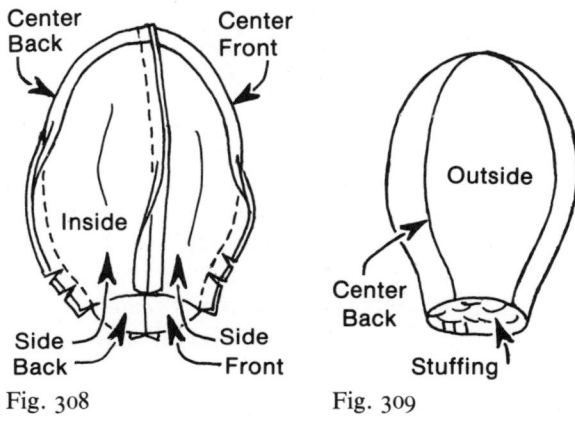

Fig. 308   Fig. 309

VIEW 5

1. Seam two Heads together. Clip to inside corners and press seams open (Fig. 310).
2. Turn right side out and stuff (Fig. 311).

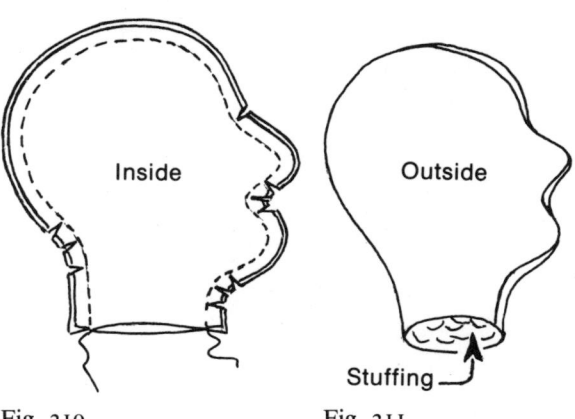

Fig. 310   Fig. 311

VIEW 6

1. Seam pair of Side Fronts along the center front and pair of Side Backs along the center back seam (Fig. 312).

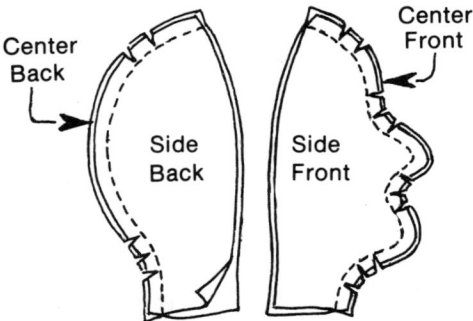

Fig. 312

2. With right sides together, pin Fronts to Backs, matching seams. Stitch side seams (Fig. 313).
3. Clip to inside corners and press seams open.
4. Turn right side out and stuff (Fig. 314).

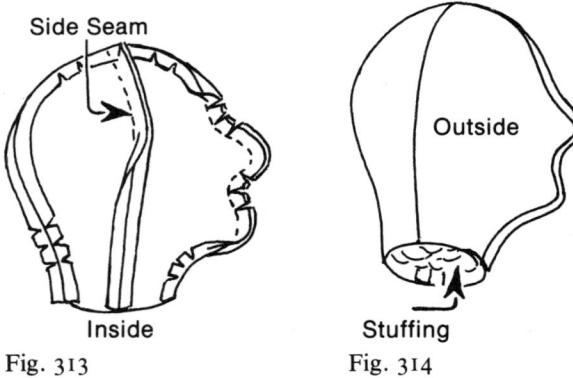

Fig. 313   Fig. 314

VIEW 7

1. Starting at the front, pin Sides to Center carefully, matching seamlines. Baste and stitch. Clip to inside curves (Fig. 315). Press seams open.
2. Turn right side out and stuff (Fig. 316).

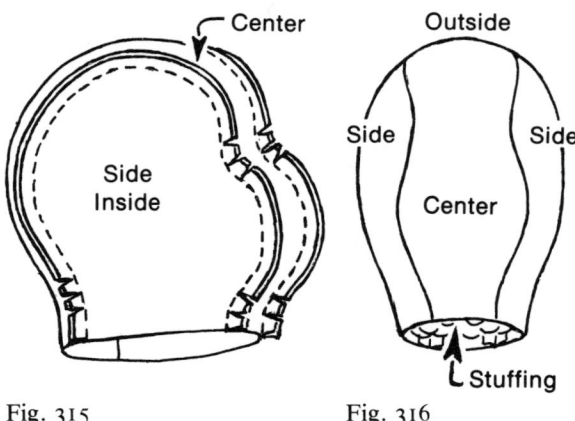

Fig. 315   Fig. 316

ANIMALS

STANDING DOG (Model in Plate 18; Pattern 11)

1. Stitch interfacing to wrong side of Ear, along the seamline. Trim interfacing close to stitching. Seam Ear to Ear Facing, leaving an opening at the upper edges (Fig. 317). Turn right side out. Bring the large circle to meet the small circle. Pin pleat and stitch edges (Fig. 318).

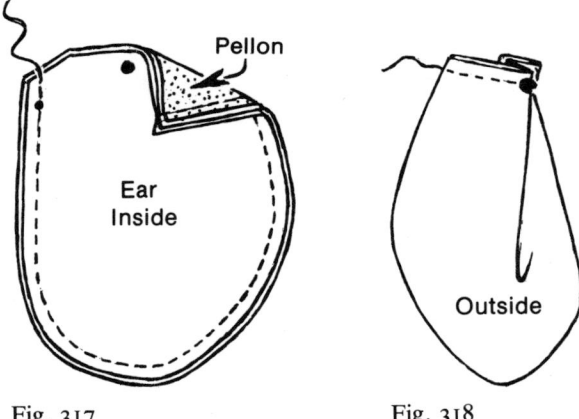

Fig. 317   Fig. 318

2. Pin Ears to Sides, matching large circles and raw edges, with the pleat at the front. Stitch on the seamline.
3. Seam Sides, right sides together, between the pairs of small dots at the center back and under the chin (Fig. 319).

Construction 205

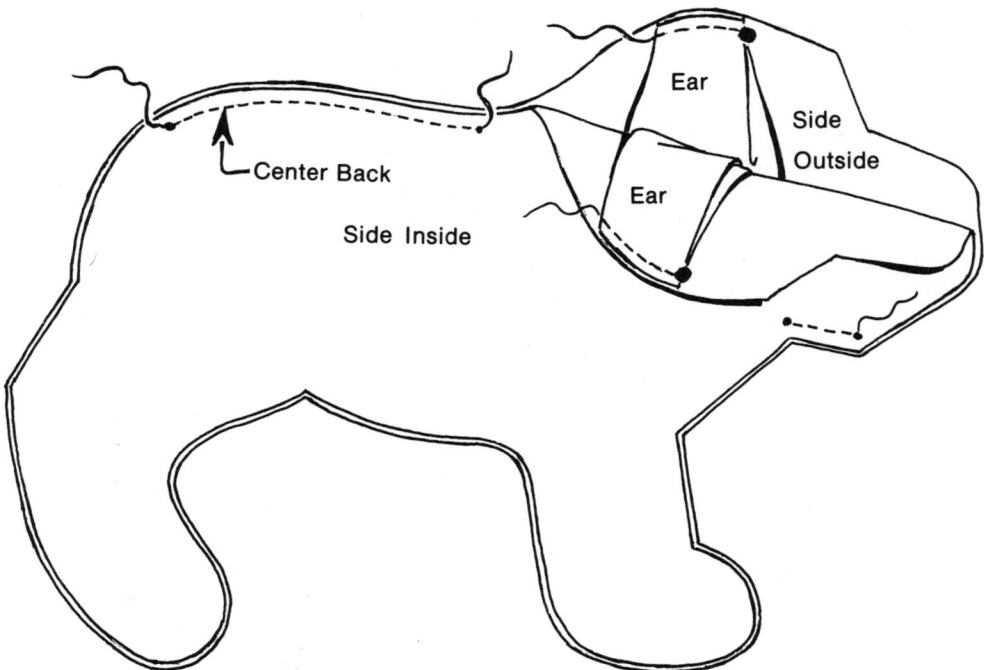

Fig. 319

4. Clip Sides to the seamline at the crossmark and the small circles. Seam Head Gusset to Sides with the dot at the center back, matching crossmarks (Fig. 320).

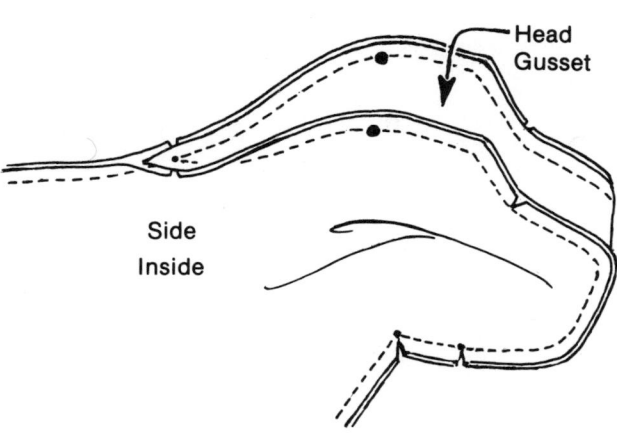

Fig. 320

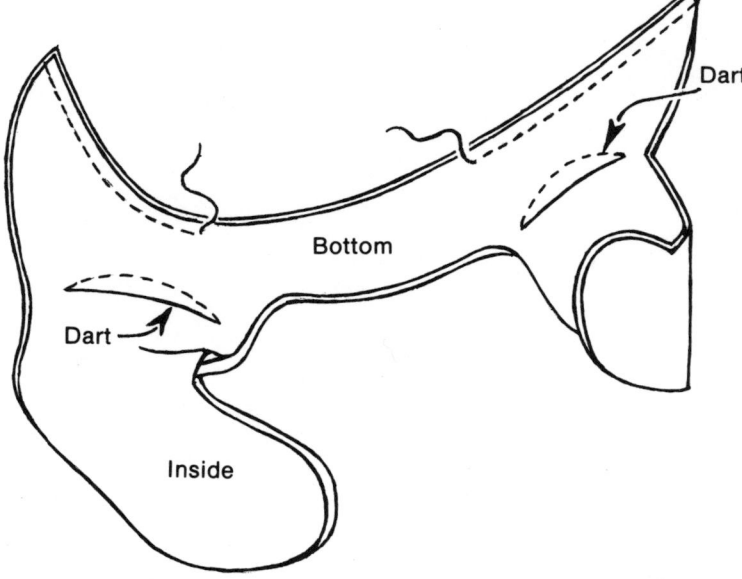

Fig. 321

5. Stitch darts in Bottoms. Seam Bottoms at the center, leaving open about 5 inches for stuffing (Fig. 321).

206   The Complete Book of Stuffedwork

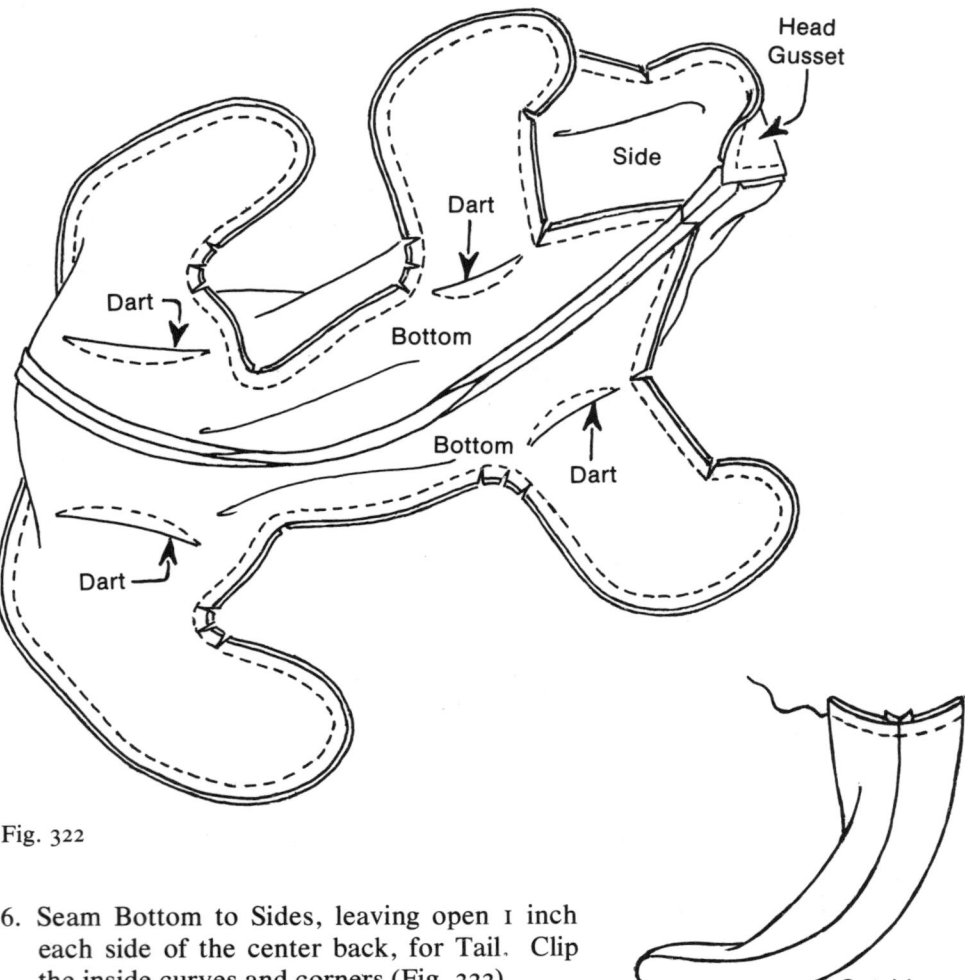

Fig. 322

6. Seam Bottom to Sides, leaving open 1 inch each side of the center back, for Tail. Clip the inside curves and corners (Fig. 322).
7. Turn right side out and stuff. Stuff legs tightly, the rest moderately. Slipstitch to close the bottom opening.
8. Seam pair of Tails, leaving an opening at the upper end (Fig. 323).

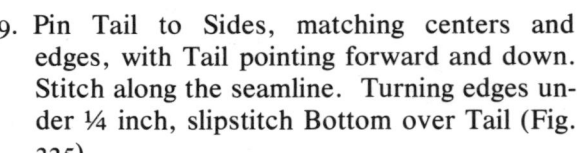

Fig. 324

9. Pin Tail to Sides, matching centers and edges, with Tail pointing forward and down. Stitch along the seamline. Turning edges under ¼ inch, slipstitch Bottom over Tail (Fig. 325).

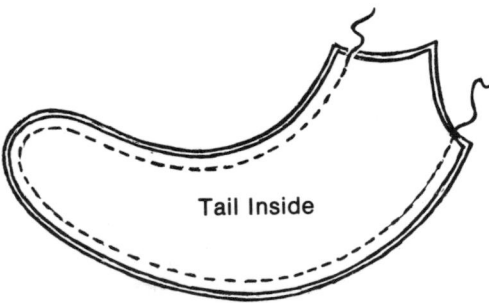

Fig. 323

Turn right side out and stuff tightly. Fold at the ends so that the seams match at the center. Pin, matching edges. Stitch on the seamline (Fig. 324).

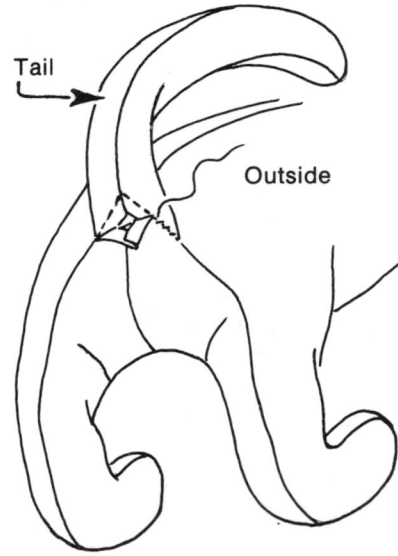

Fig. 325

SITTING CAT (Model in Plate 19; Pattern 12)

1. Seam each pair of Ears, leaving open at the bottom edges (Fig. 326). Turn right side out. Stitch along open edges (Fig. 327). Fold each ear in half and clip fold to the stitching (Fig. 328).

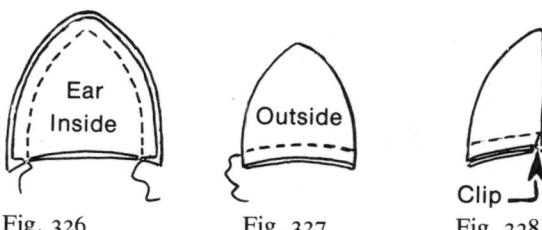

Fig. 326   Fig. 327   Fig. 328

2. On Sides, staystitch along dart seamlines at the point for reinforcement. Slash dart to ⅛ inch from the point. Pin a clip on ear to the front corner of the dart on Side. Continue pinning ear to the dart edge, matching seamlines. Stitch. Swivel ear at the clip and pin the remaining ear edge to the top seamline. Stitch (Fig. 329).

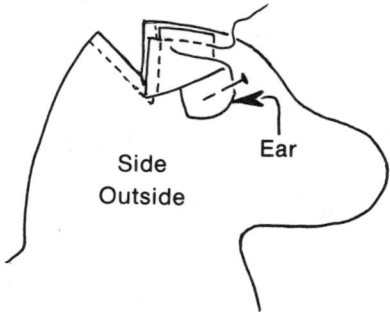

Fig. 329

Fold the other dart edge over ear and stitch through all layers. Repeat at the other Side.

3. Seam Sides at the center back, to the dot at the neck. Seam the nose between the two dots. Clip to the dot on the neck (Fig. 330).
4. Stitch darts in Fronts. Seam the center front, leaving an opening between the dots for stuffing (Fig. 331).

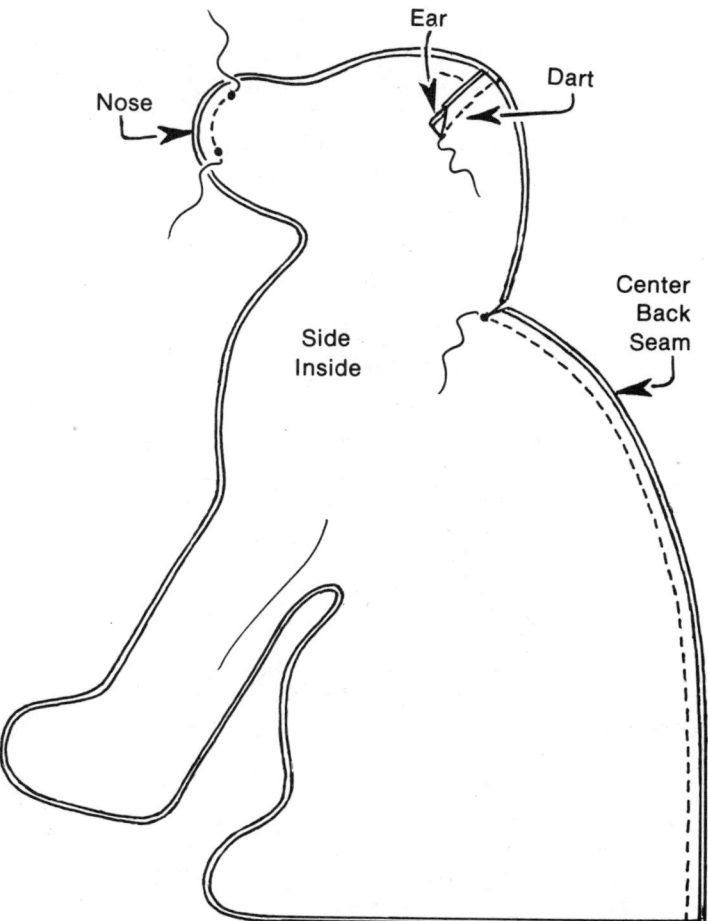

Fig. 330

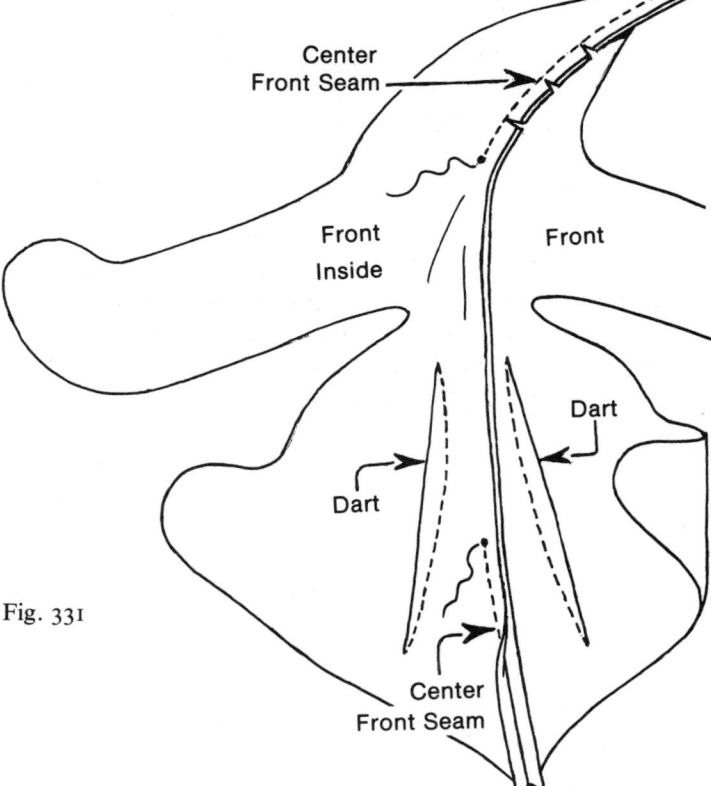

Fig. 331

5. Seam Front to Sides, matching centers. Stitch, leaving 1¼ inches open at each side of the center back at the bottom for tail. Reinforce the inside corners with a second row of stitching (Fig. 332).

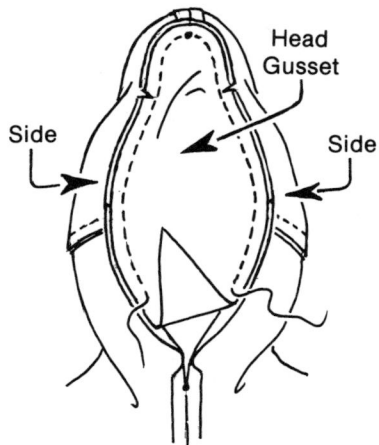

Fig. 333

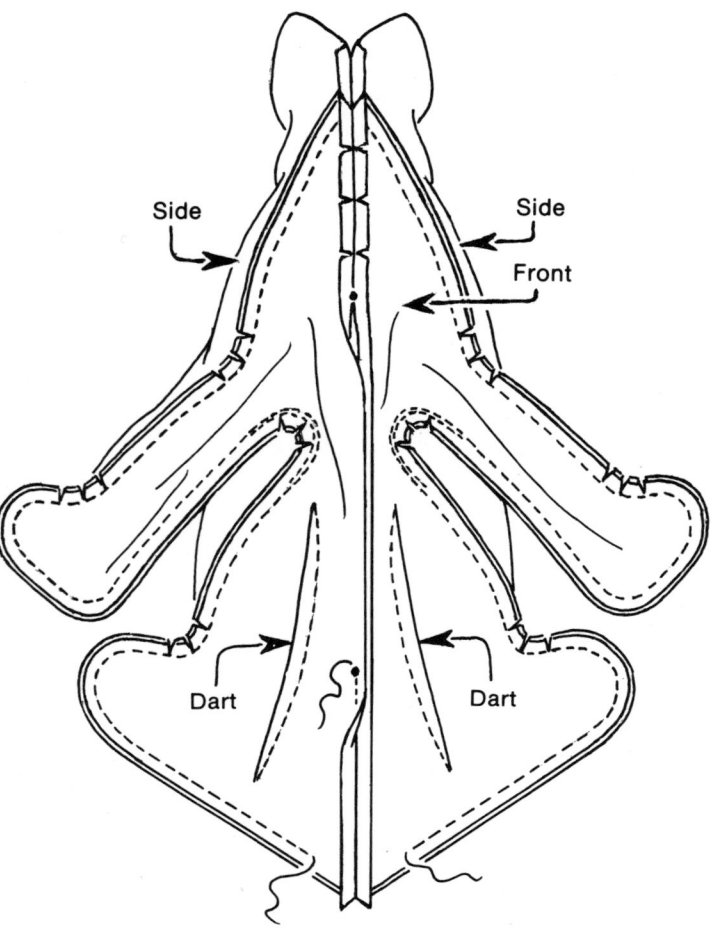

Fig. 332

6. Pin Head Gusset to Sides with the dot at the center front, matching crossmarks and centers. Stitch, clipping at crossmarks. Baste the nose section first, or stitch it by hand (Fig. 333).

7. Turn right side out and stuff the legs firmly. Continue stuffing halfway up the body. Pin the lower part of the opening to close it. Continue stuffing carefully so that the sides are filled equally.
8. Tack each ear at its inside edge about ½ inch inside the gusset.
9. Seam pair of Tails, except at the upper end (Fig. 334). Turn right side out and stuff tightly except near the upper end. Stitch top edges (Fig. 335). Pin tail to Sides, matching

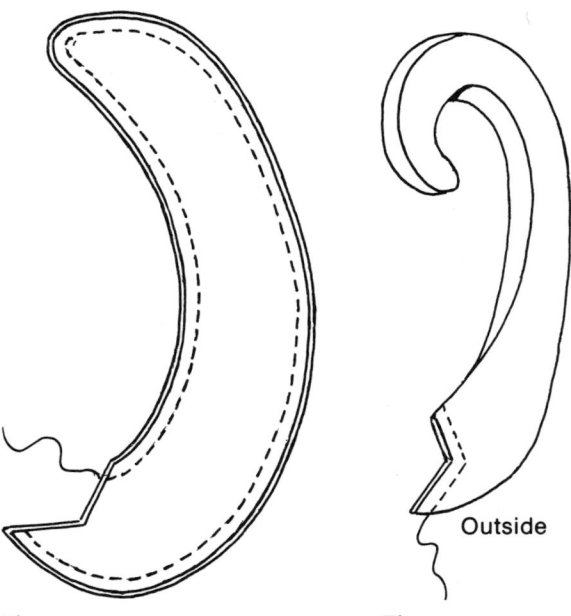

Fig. 334   Fig. 335

centers and edges, with tail curling sideways and downward. Sew along the seamline. Turning edges under ¼ inch, slipstitch Front over tail (Fig. 336).

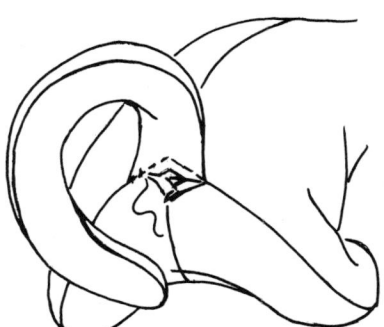

Fig. 336

LION (Model in Plate 20; Pattern 13)

1. Seam Underleg Facing to Underbody (Fig. 337).

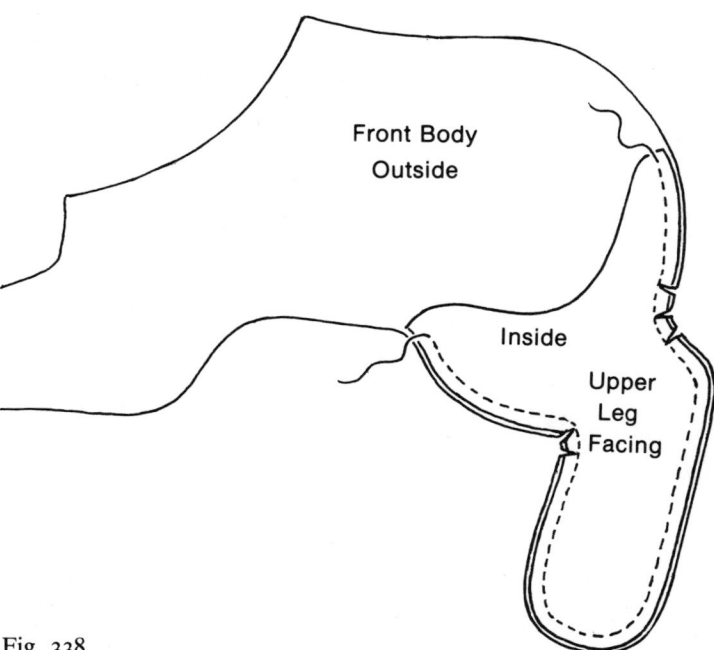

Fig. 338

Seam Upperleg Facing to Front Body (Fig. 338).
2. Seam Back Body to Front Body at the center back and at the front neck to the marked dot (Fig. 339).
3. On Underbody staystitch along the seamline between legs for reinforcement. Stitch an oyster in leg.

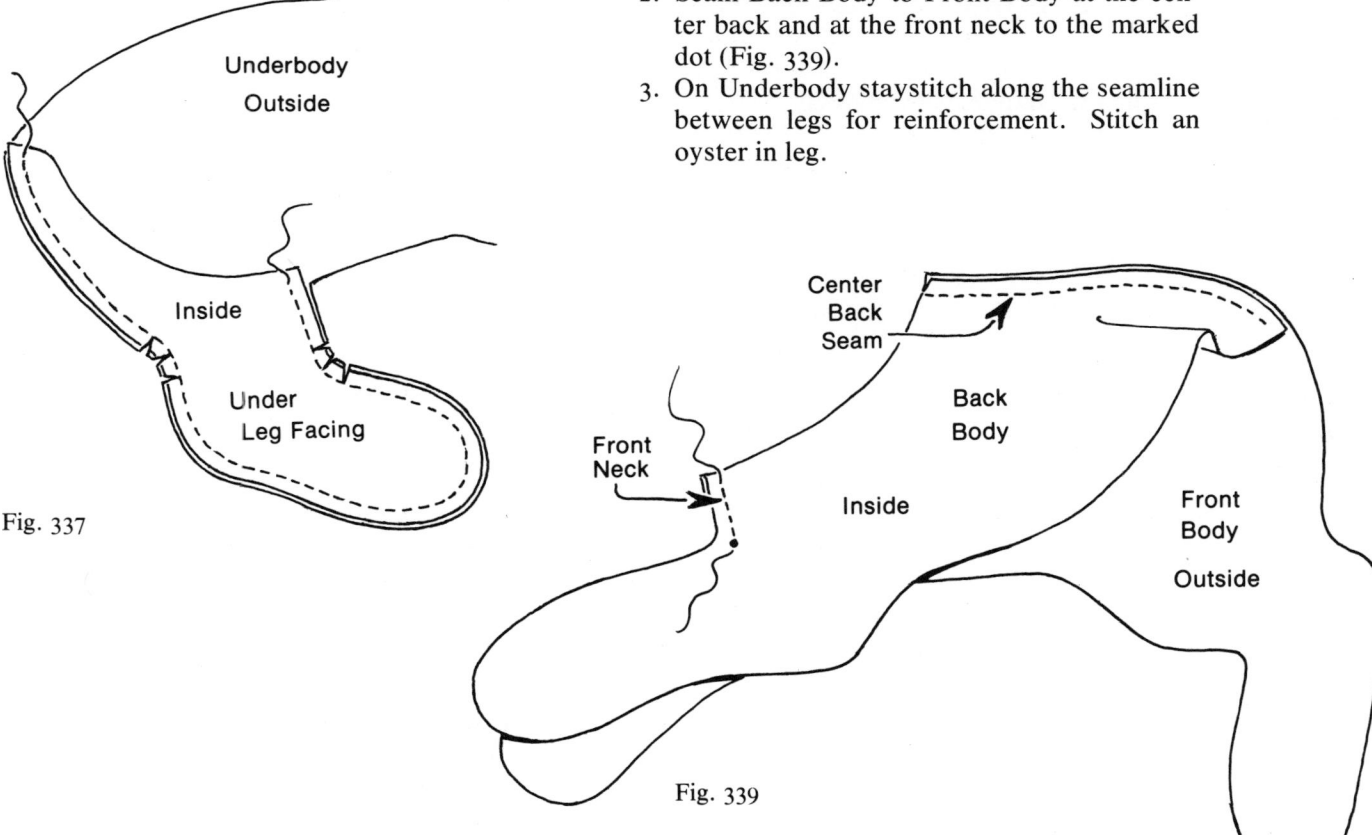

Fig. 337

Fig. 339

210 The Complete Book of Stuffedwork

4. Seam the body to Underbody, clipping to the center front dot. Clip the inside corners to but not through the stitching.
5. Seam Leg Facings together, leaving about a 3-inch opening at the top for tail (Fig. 340).

   Turn right side out. Stuff firmly except at the top of the bottom back leg where there should be less stuffing.

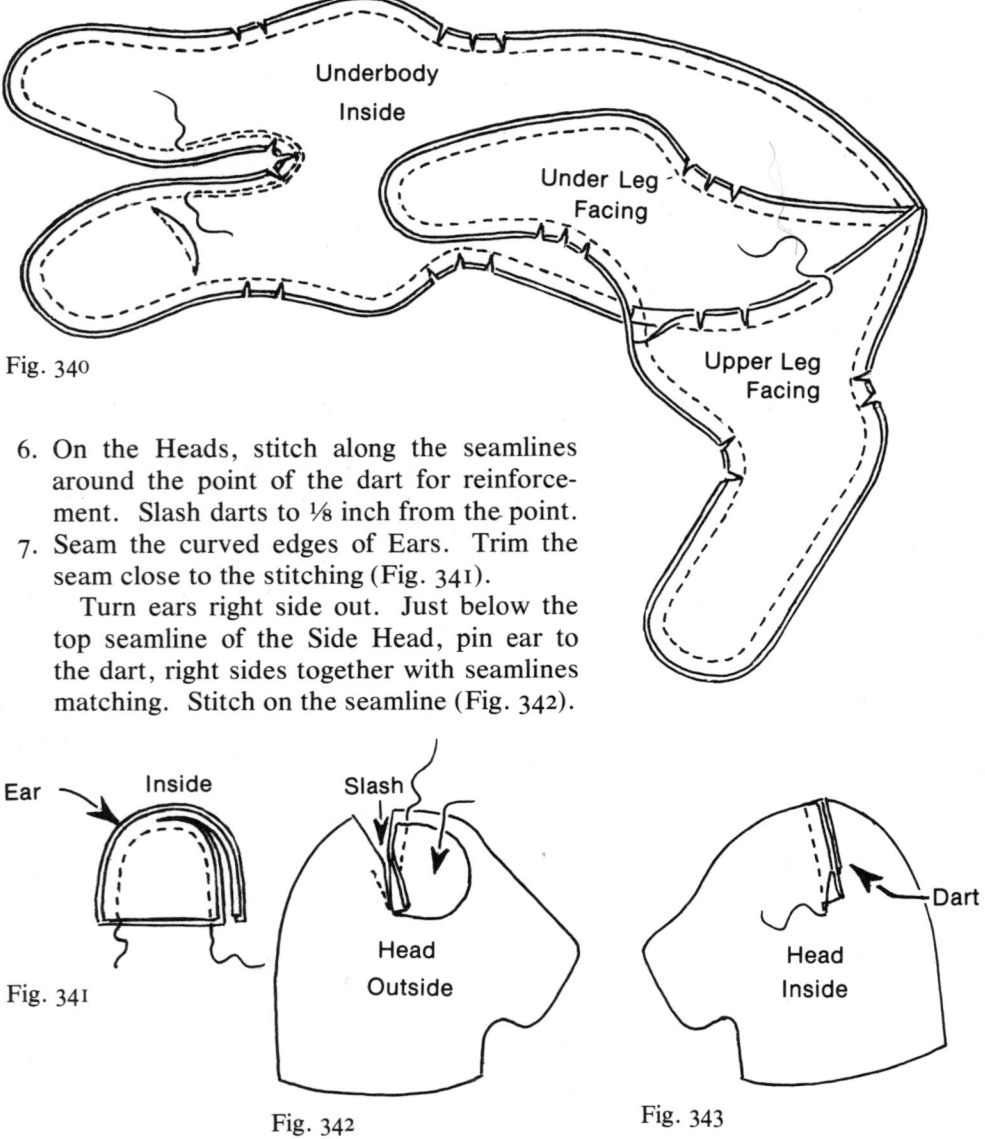

Fig. 340

6. On the Heads, stitch along the seamlines around the point of the dart for reinforcement. Slash darts to ⅛ inch from the point.
7. Seam the curved edges of Ears. Trim the seam close to the stitching (Fig. 341).

   Turn ears right side out. Just below the top seamline of the Side Head, pin ear to the dart, right sides together with seamlines matching. Stitch on the seamline (Fig. 342).

Fig. 341

Fig. 342

Fig. 343

Fold the other edge of the dart over the ear, matching seamlines. Stitch through all layers (Fig. 343).

8. With the wider end at the front, seam Head Gusset to Side Heads, clipping at inside corners (Fig. 344).

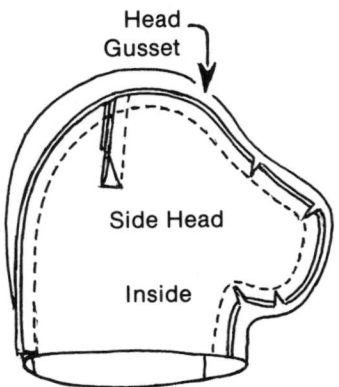

Fig. 344

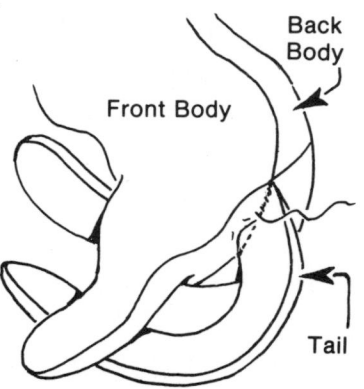

Fig. 347

9. Turn right side out. Stuff firmly. Turn under the neck seam allowance. Pin the head to the body, matching centers. Slipstitch (Fig. 345), adding stuffing as necessary.

FOX (Model in Plate 21; Pattern 14)

1. Fold Tail lengthwise, right sides in, and seam the long curved edge (Fig. 348). Turn right side out and stuff lightly. Fold so that the seam is centered. Stitch across raw ends.

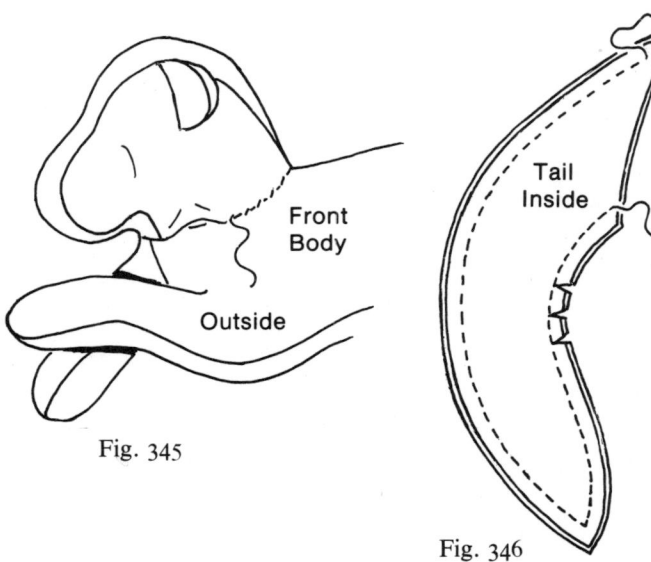

Fig. 345

Fig. 346

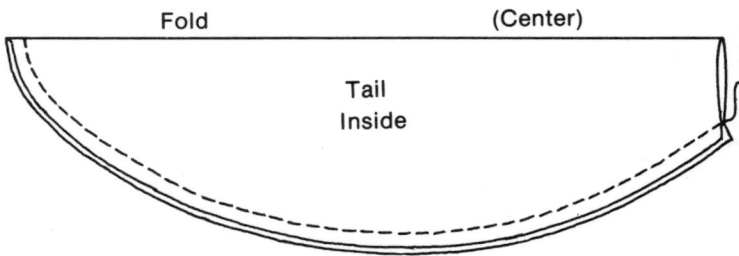

Fig. 348

10. Seam the long sides of a pair of Tails (Fig. 346). Turn tail right side out. Stuff, pushing in stuffing with a stubby instrument. Stitch to close ends. Slip tail into the back seam opening so that it slides downward between the legs. Sew tail to one edge of the opening. Slipstitch the other edge over the tail (Fig. 347).

2. Pin tail to one Side above the marked dot, right sides together and edges matching. Stitch on the seamline (Fig. 349). Seam

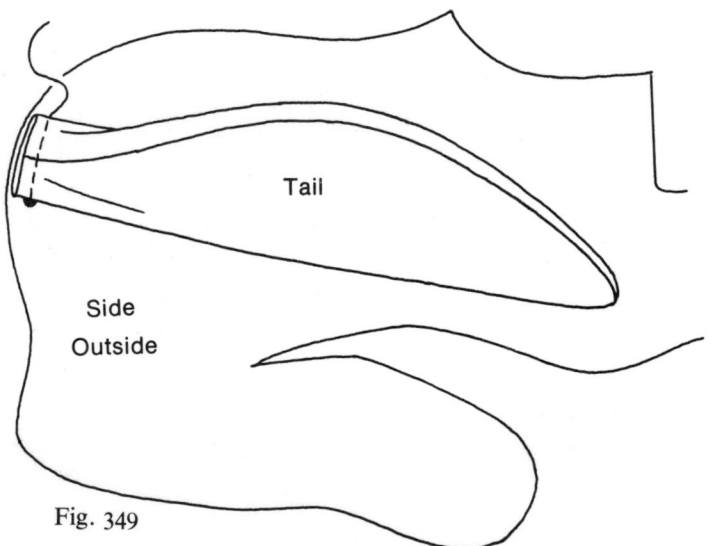

Fig. 349

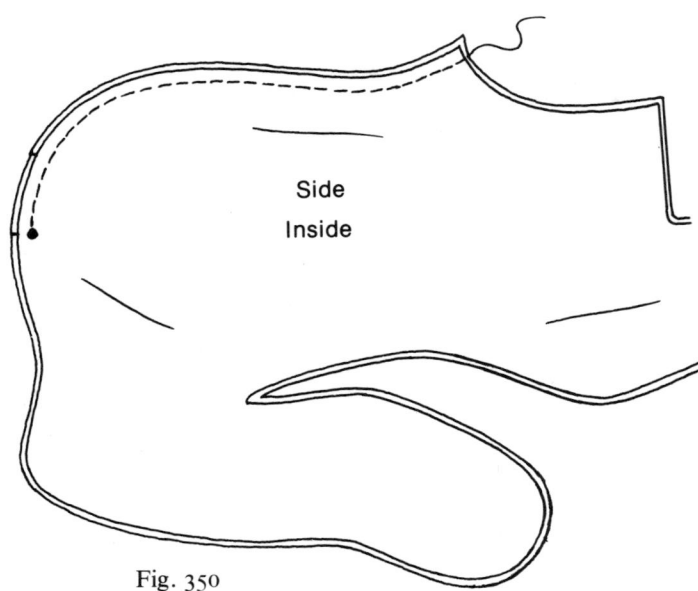

Fig. 350

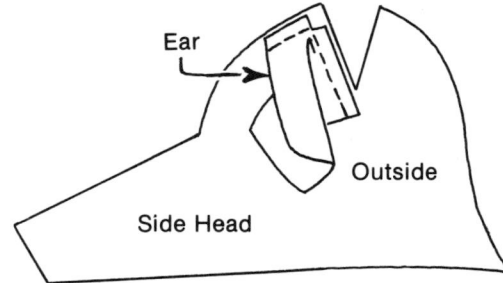

Fig. 353

Slash darts to ⅛ inch from the point. Fold the dart edge over the ear and stitch, seamlines matching (Fig. 354).

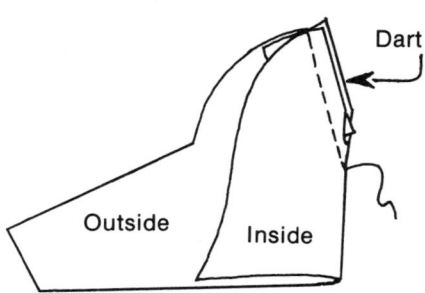

Fig. 354

5. Seam Side Heads at the front edge of the nose (Fig. 355).

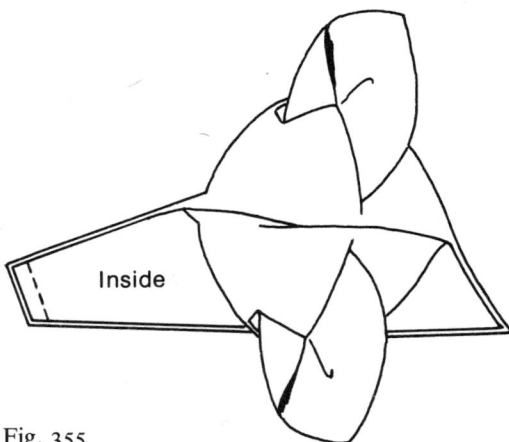

Fig. 355

Sides at the center back from the neck edge to the dot, over tail (Fig. 350).

3. Seam Ears to Ear Facings except at the bottom edge (Fig. 351). Turn right side out. Fold in half lengthwise and clip the fold to the seamline. With Ear Facing side up, fold the front edge to the clip. Stitch along the seamline (Fig. 352).

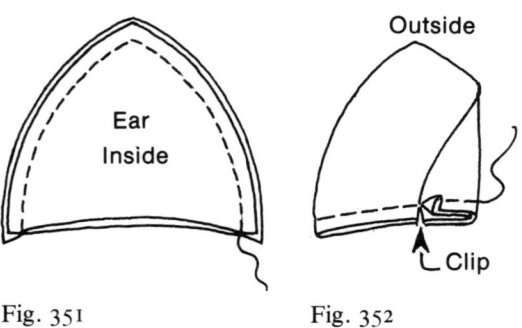

Fig. 351   Fig. 352

4. Pin each Ear to a Side Head, right sides together, the folded-under edge front and downward, with a clip at a corner of the dart.

Turn ear at the clip and pin the rest of the ear to the dart, seamlines matching. Stitch (Fig. 353).

6. Clip Side Heads at crossmarks. With the narrower end at the front, seam Top Head to Side Heads, matching centers and crossmarks (Fig. 356).

Construction 213

7. Seam the head to Sides at the back neck edge (Fig. 357).
8. Seam each Leg Facing to an Underbody, with the longer point of the facing pointing toward the back. Seam Underbodies at the center, leaving an opening between the dots for stuffing (Fig. 358).

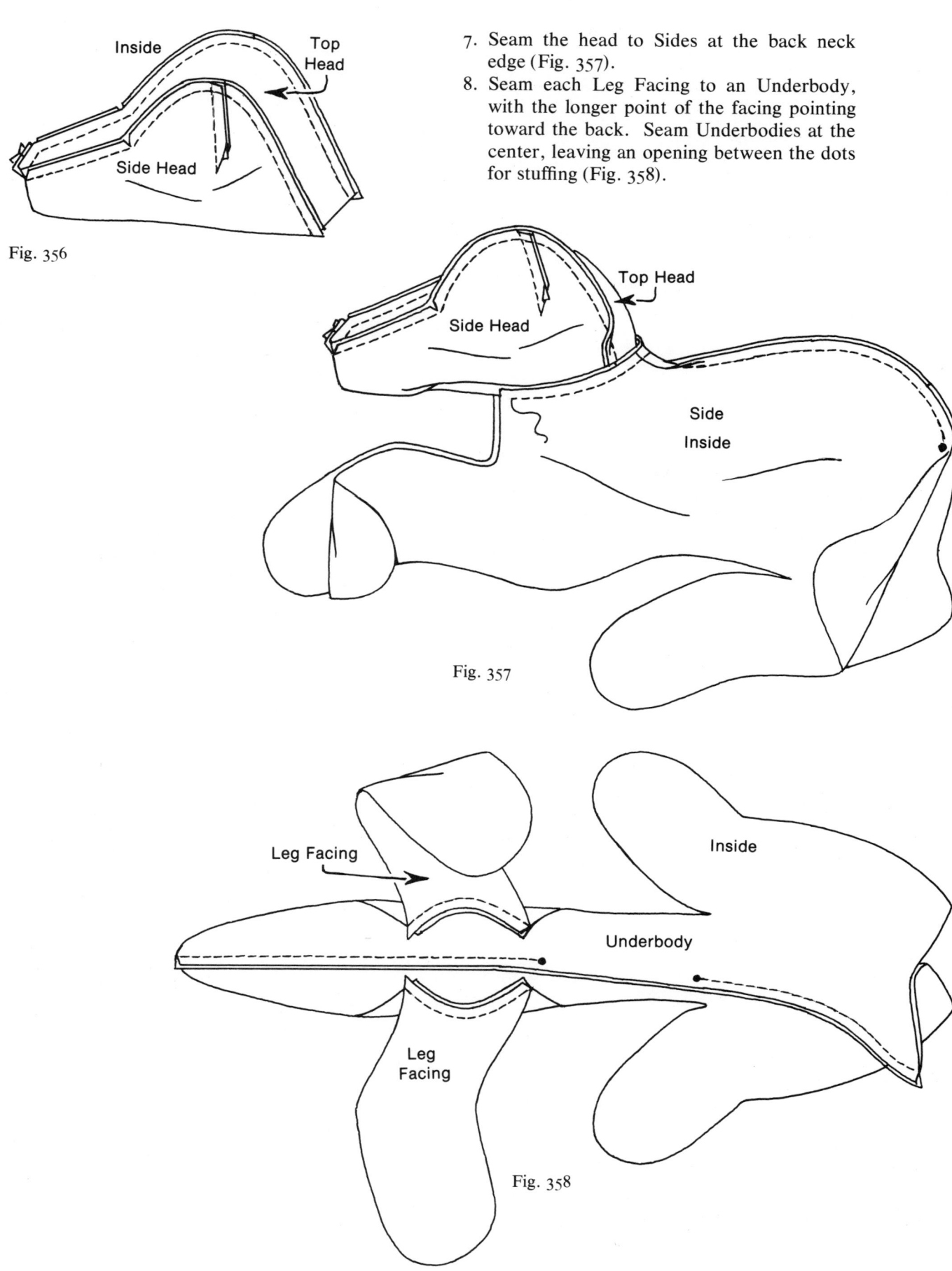

Fig. 356

Fig. 357

Fig. 358

214 The Complete Book of Stuffedwork

9. Seam Underbody to Sides and the head. Clip inside curves and corners (Fig. 359).
10. Turn right side out. Stuff firmly. Slipstitch to close (Fig. 360).
11. Push the lower part of each ear about ½ inch over Top Head and tack.

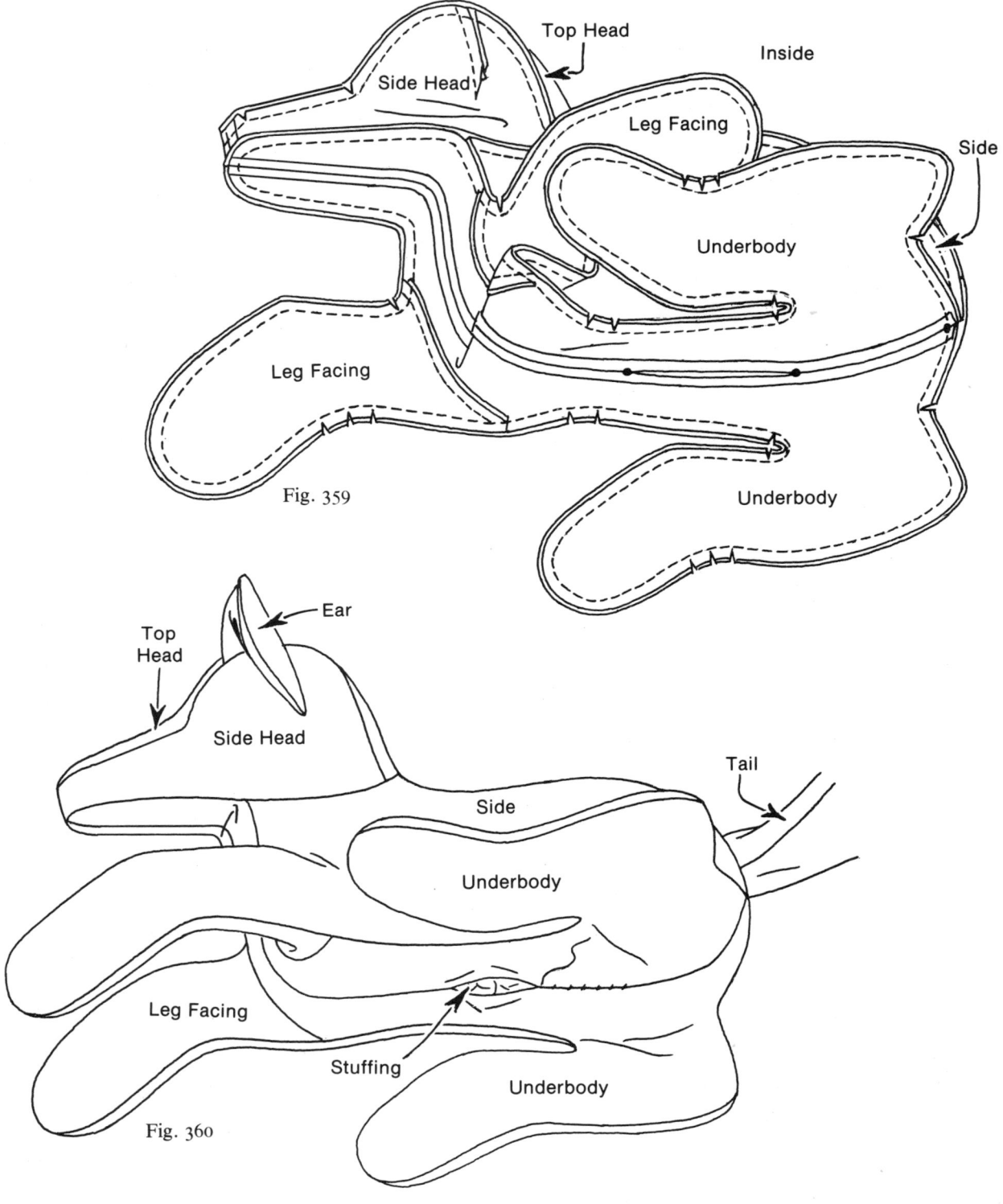

Fig. 359

Fig. 360

LOW DOG (Model in Plate 22; Pattern 15)

1. With wrong sides together, fold the short edges to match the long edge at top of each Ear. Stitch on seamline (Fig. 361).
2. Fold Ear in half lengthwise, right sides together, and stitch the side and lower edges, beginning at the marked dot (Fig. 362).

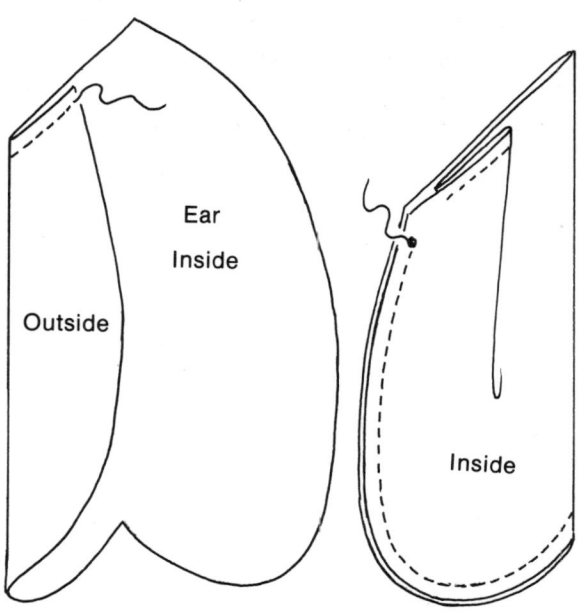

Fig. 361 Fig. 362

3. Turn right sides out. Match the top edges and stitch on the seamline. With the pleated edge up, pin the folded edge of Ear ¼ inch from the back edge of each Side Head (ear will point forward). Match and baste upper edges. Stitch on seamline (Fig. 363).

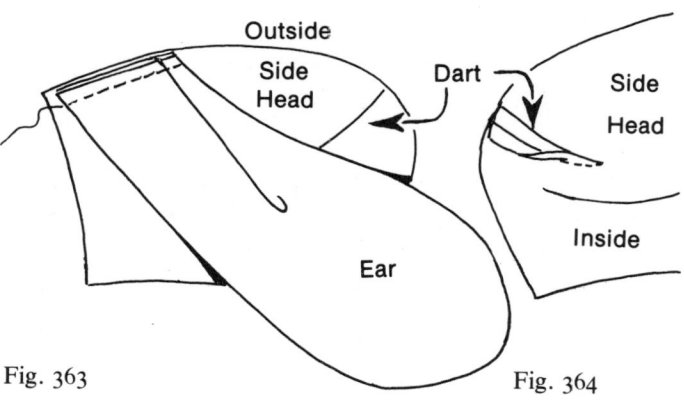

Fig. 363 Fig. 364

4. Seam the dart in each Side Head. Slash the dart and press open (Fig. 364). Seam Side Heads to Underhead (Fig. 365).

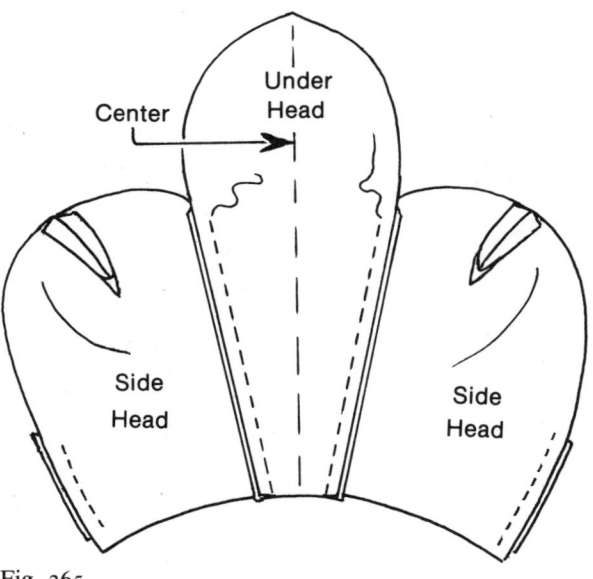

Fig. 365

5. Stitch Front Head at the center front from the dart edge to the dot (Fig. 366). Fold Front Head crosswise at the nose to bring the dart seamlines together. Stitch the dart.

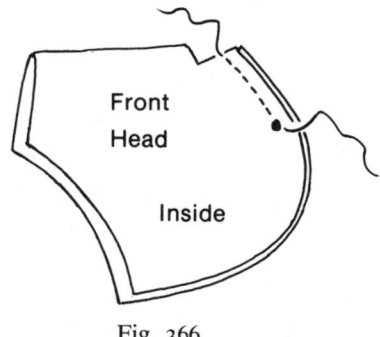

Fig. 366

6. Stitch Underhead to Front Head, matching centers (Fig. 367). Stitch this piece to Side Heads, matching the dart to the seam and clipping inside curve. Stitch this to Top Head. Stitch the dart in Top Head (Fig. 368).

7. Seam Underbodies at the center, leaving open about 6-inch space for stuffing. Seam each Leg Facing to the underbody, clipping inside curves. Staystitch inside corners at tail and legs (Fig. 369).
8. Seam Sides at the center back from the dot to the neck edge.
9. Seam Underbody to Sides, leaving open an inch each side of the center back for tail. Clip inside corners and slash between the stitching at the back legs.
10. Seam the body to the head, right sides together, matching centers (Fig. 370).

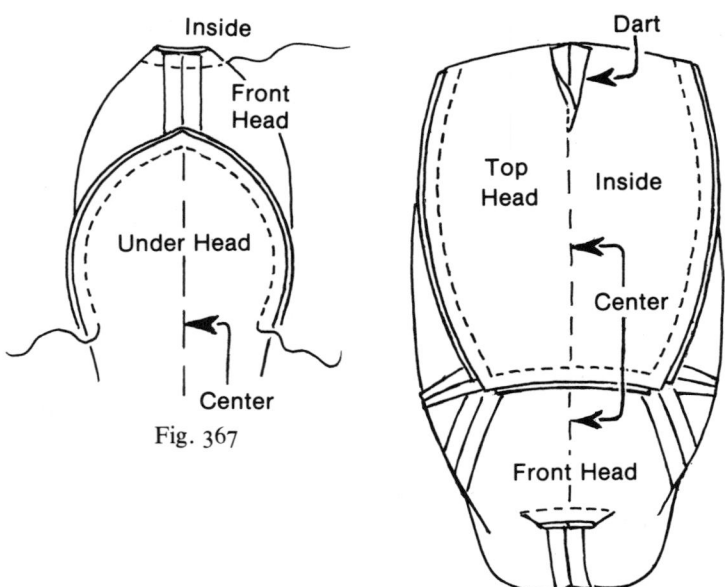

Fig. 367

Fig. 368

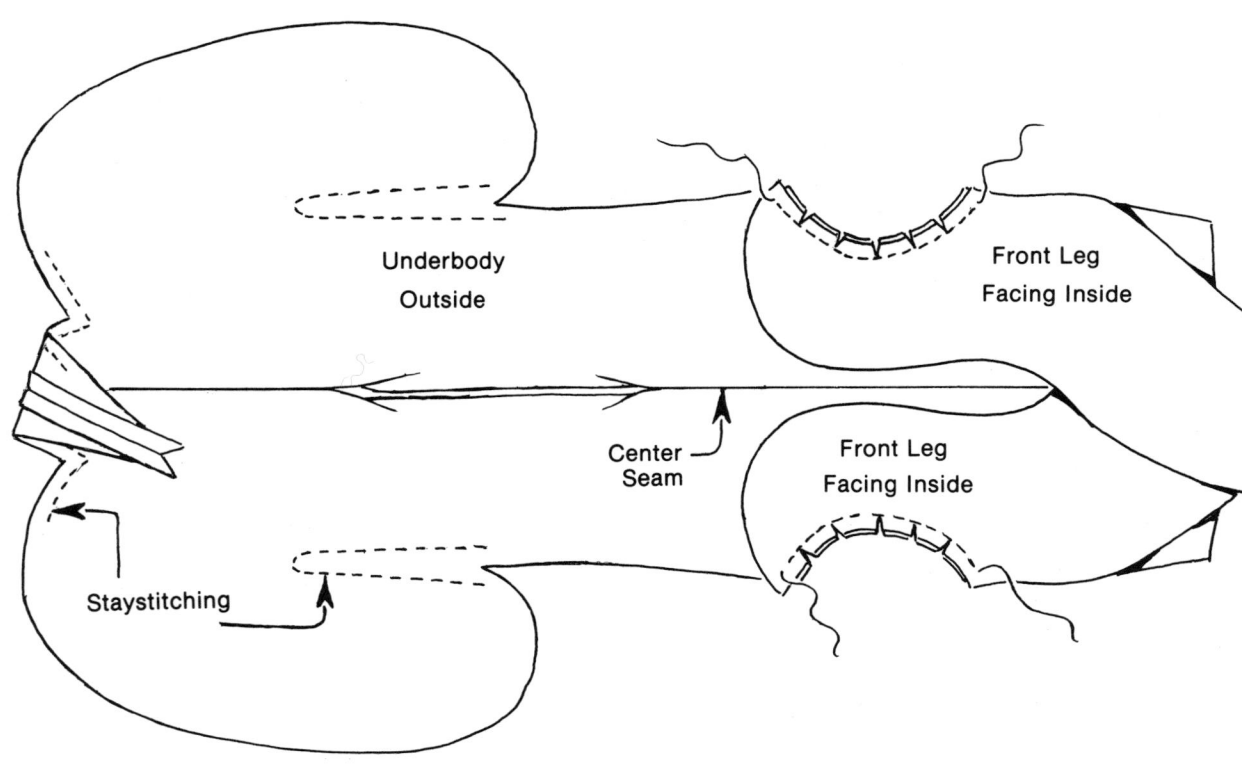

Fig. 369

Construction 217

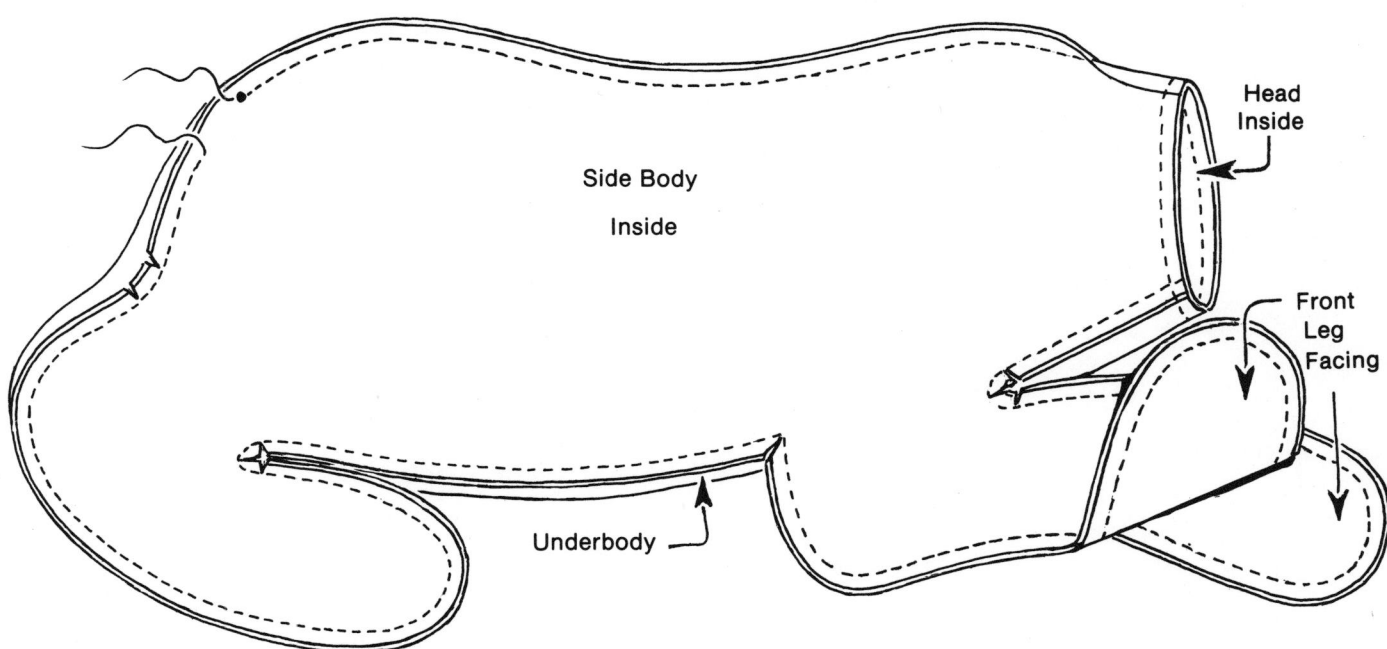

Fig. 370

11. Turn right side out. Stuff and slipstitch to close the opening.
12. Fold Tail lengthwise and seam all but the upper edges (Fig. 371). Turn right side out, stuff, and stitch the upper edges (Fig. 372).
13. Pin tail to Sides, matching centers and edges. Sew along the seamline. Turning the edges under ¼ inch, slipstitch Underbody over tail (Fig. 373).

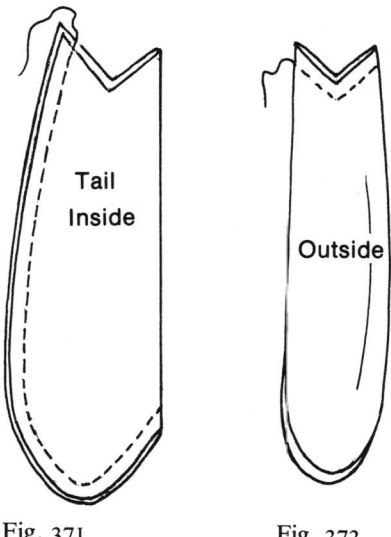

Fig. 371   Fig. 372

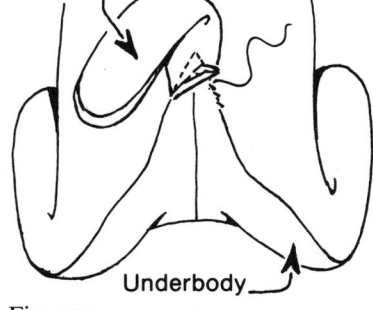

Fig. 373

218   The Complete Book of Stuffedwork

TEDDY BEAR (Model in Plate 23; Pattern 16)

1. Seam each pair of Ears, leaving the bottom edges open (Fig. 374). Turn right side out and fold in half, matching straight edges. Clip on the fold to the seamline (Fig. 375). Turn in edges at one side of the clip and overcast the two edges together (Fig. 376). On the other ear, overcast the opposite side.

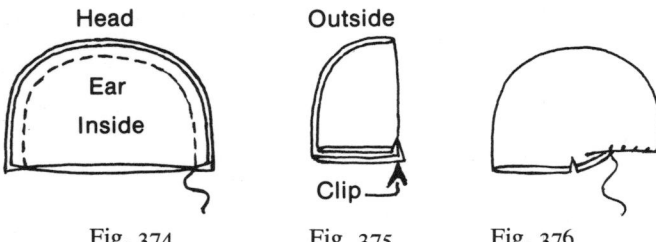

Fig. 374   Fig. 375   Fig. 376

2. Stitch along dart seamlines around the point, for reinforcement. Pin clip of ear to the corner of the dart. Continue pinning raw edges of ear to the dart matching seamlines. Stitch (Fig. 377).

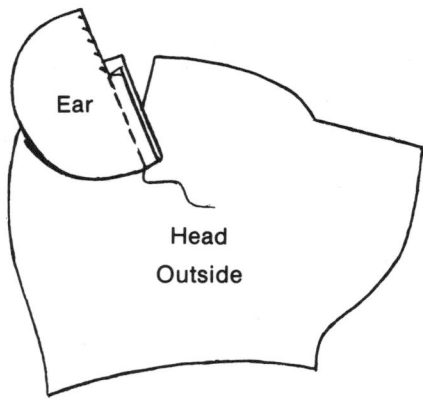

Fig. 377

3. Slash to 1/8 inch from the point of the dart. Bring the other dart edge over the ear, matching seamlines. Stitch through all layers (Fig. 378).

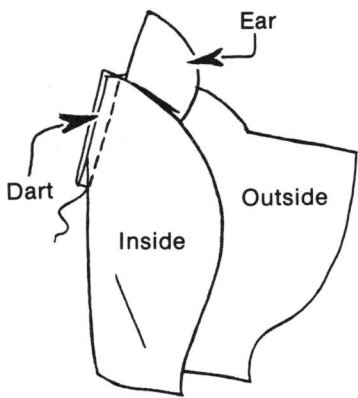

Fig. 378

4. Seam a pair of Heads from front neck to tip of nose. Clip inside curves.
5. Pin Gusset to Head, with the dot at the back and centers matching. Stitch, clipping to seam at crossmarks (Fig. 379).

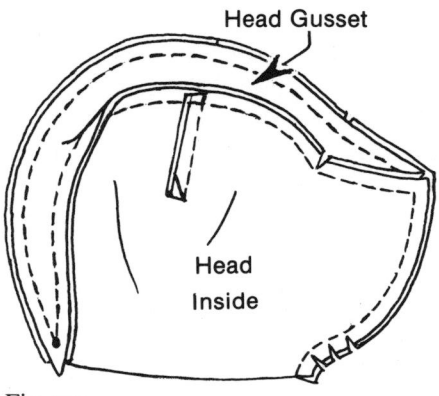

Fig. 379

6. Turn right side out and stuff. Slipstitch loose edge of ears to head along seamline (Fig. 380).

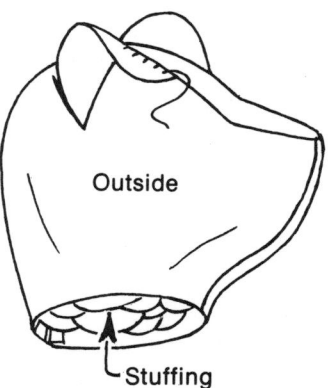

Fig. 380

Construction 219

7. Seam a pair of Fronts and a pair of Backs at the center front and the center back seams. Staystitch the neck seamline (Fig. 381). Seam at the side and bottom edges, matching centers (Fig. 382).

8. Turn right side out and stuff.
9. Turn under the head on the seamline. Pin to the body, matching centers and slipstitch, adding stuffing if necessary (Fig. 383).

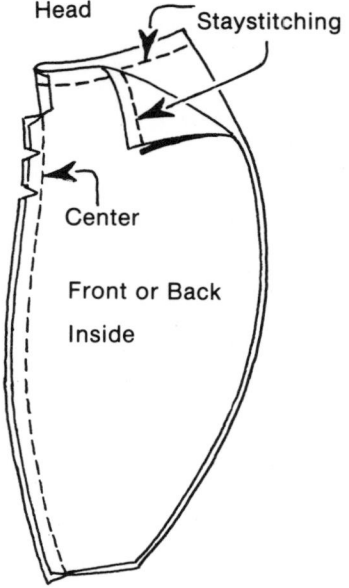

Fig. 381

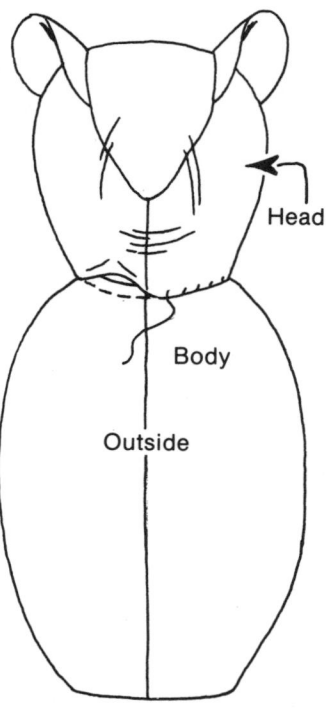

Fig. 383

10. Seam long sides of each Arm. Matching centers, seam an End to each Arm (Fig. 384).

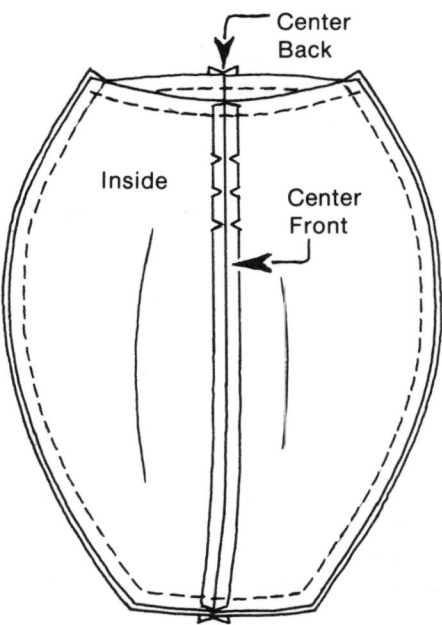

Fig. 382

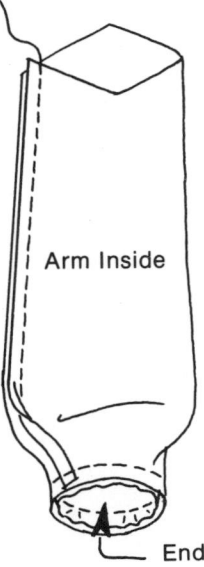

Fig. 384

220 The Complete Book of Stuffedwork

11. Turn arms right side out. Stuff to 1 inch from open end. Turn in seams at upper ends, matching seam to center. Pin and overcast (Fig. 385). Seam Legs in the same way, stuffing to 2 inches from the open end.

12. Pin ends of arms and legs to the body along side seams. Slipstitch securely (Fig. 386).

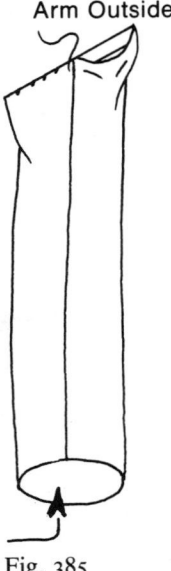

Fig. 385

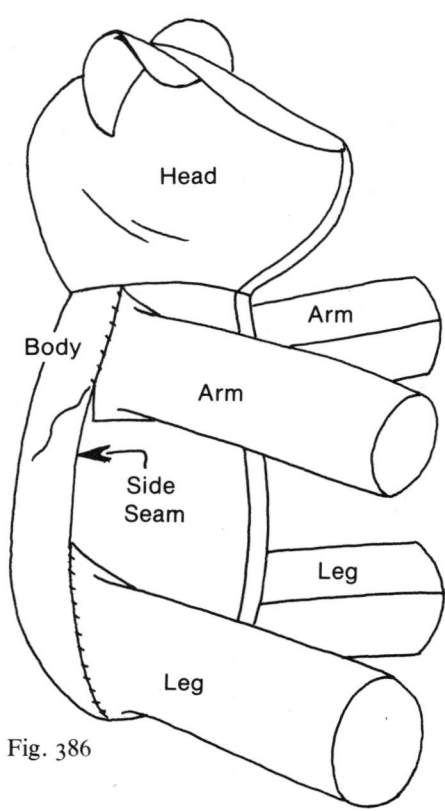

Fig. 386

Construction 221

Jo Ellen Trilling *Frog Prince* (14″ x 13″), 1976.
Velvet, nylon, silk, fur, cord, felt-tipped marker,
nylon stocking face and hands, wire armature, and
synthetic stuffing.

ST. LOUIS COMM. COL.
AT FLORISSANT VALLEY
INVENTORY 1983